IMPORTANT:

HERE IS YOUR REGISTRATION CODE TO ACCESS
YOUR PREMIUM McGRAW-HILL ONLINE RESOURCES

D1204592

For key premium online resources you need THIS CODE to gain access.
entered, you will be able to use the Web resources for the length of your course.

If your course is using **WebCT** or **Blackboard**, you'll be able to use this code to access the
McGraw-Hill content within your instructor's online course.

Access is provided if you have purchased a new book. If the registration code is
missing from this book, the registration screen on our Website, and within your WebCT
or Blackboard course, will tell you how to obtain your new code.

Registering for McGraw-Hill Online Resources

TO gain access to your McGraw-Hill web
resources simply follow the steps below:

1. USE YOUR WEB BROWSER TO GO TO: **www.mhhe.com/dewees1**
2. CLICK ON **FIRST TIME USER**.
3. ENTER THE REGISTRATION CODE* PRINTED ON THE TEAR-OFF BOOKMARK ON THE RIGHT.
4. AFTER YOU HAVE ENTERED YOUR REGISTRATION CODE, CLICK **REGISTER**.
5. FOLLOW THE INSTRUCTIONS TO SET-UP YOUR PERSONAL UserID AND PASSWORD.
6. WRITE YOUR UserID AND PASSWORD DOWN FOR FUTURE REFERENCE.
   KEEP IT IN A SAFE PLACE.

TO GAIN ACCESS to the McGraw-Hill content in your instructor's **WebCT** or **Blackboard**
course simply log in to the course with the UserID and Password provided by your instructor.
Enter the registration code exactly as it appears in the box to the right when prompted by the
system. You will only need to use the code the first time you click on McGraw-Hill content.

Thank you, and welcome
to your McGraw-Hill
online Resources!

REGISTRATION CODE

I5N8-3F06-LVK8-5SCJ-HEWS

* YOUR REGISTRATION CODE CAN BE USED ONLY ONCE TO ESTABLISH ACCESS. IT IS NOT TRANSFERABLE.

0-07-312152-5 T/A DEWEES: CONTEMPORARY SOCIAL WORK PRACTICE, 1/E

This is a much-needed series for social work education and the social work profession...one of the best I have seen in decades!

–Mildred C. Joyner, *West Chester University*

Each title is the first of its kind to offer instructors and their students a multidimensional understanding and experience of the world of social work:

- **Each book in the series is accompanied by a custom Web site, updated weekly,** that allows students to examine events in the news and to think about and discuss those events in the context of what they are reading. The Web site also links students to a wealth of carefully selected Internet resources that are constantly updated and refreshed.

- **A specially designed online reader,** *The Social Work Library,* **is also available to students,** with over 100 articles and book chapters linked to the key ideas and principles covered in each volume in the series.

- *Practicing Social Work*™, **a CD-ROM packaged with each volume in the series,** offers complex, richly populated case exercises, with multiple options in text and video for analysis and intervention. The CD gives students a real-world sense of how social workers approach cases from micro, mezzo, and macro perspectives and trains them in the use of social work tools they will likely encounter in their professional lives.

- **A free booklet on social work ethics accompanies each text** in recognition of CSWE recommendations, and is authored by Kim Strom-Gottfried, University of North Carolina, who is nationally recognized for her educational workshops on the subject.

New Directions in Social Work is a comprehensive effort by a team of accomplished social work educators to move social work education forward. We want to help you enrich and deepen your students' learning experiences. And we want to know what you think! Please e-mail us with your feedback. In the meantime, we welcome your students to a most gratifying, heartbreaking, edifying profession: social work.

Alice A. Lieberman, Series Editor
University of Kansas
e-mail: alicel@ku.edu

Marty Dewees
University of Vermont
e-mail: marty.dewees@uvm.edu

Contemporary
Social Work Practice

NEW DIRECTIONS IN SOCIAL WORK
A McGRAW-HILL SERIES

Consulting editor, Alice A. Lieberman, University of Kansas

Technical consultant, Jerry Finn, Temple University

New Directions in Social Work is an innovative series of texts, software, and custom electronic content for the *foundations* courses in the Social Work curriculum. Each title is the first of its kind to offer instructors and their students a multidimensional experience and understanding of the world of social work. Each volume in the series includes a custom Web site, online reader entitled *The Social Work Library,* and *Practicing Social Work,* a unique collection of virtual case studies.

Books in the Series

Social Work and Social Welfare: An Invitation by Marla Berg-Weger

Contemporary Social Work Practice by Marty Dewees

Human Behavior in the Social Environment by Anissa Taun Rogers

Social Policy for Effective Practice by Rosemary K. Chapin

Social Work Research by Judy L. Krysik

Also from McGraw-Hill

Social Work Practice with a Difference: Stories, Essays, Cases, and Commentaries by Alice A. Lieberman and Cheryl B. Lester

The Social Work Experience: An Introduction to Social Work and Social Welfare, Fourth Edition, by Mary Ann Suppes and Carolyn Cressy Wells

Contemporary Social Work Practice

Marty Dewees

University of Vermont

Boston   Burr Ridge, IL   Dubuque, IA   Madison, WI   New York   San Francisco   St. Louis
Bangkok   Bogotá   Caracas   Kuala Lumpur   Lisbon   London   Madrid   Mexico City
Milan   Montreal   New Delhi   Santiago   Seoul   Singapore   Sydney   Taipei   Toronto

The McGraw·Hill Companies

Published by McGraw-Hill, a business unit of The McGraw-Hill Companies, Inc., 1221 Avenue of the Americas, New York, NY 10020. Copyright © 2006 by The McGraw-Hill Companies, Inc. All rights reserved. No part of this publication may be reproduced or distributed in any form or by any means, or stored in a database or retrieval system, without the prior written consent of The McGraw-Hill Companies, Inc., including, but not limited to, any network or other electronic storage or transmission, or broadcast for distance learning.

Some ancillaries, including electronic and print components, may not be available to customers outside the United States.

This book is printed on acid-free paper.

1 2 3 4 5 6 7 8 9 0 DOC/DOC 0 9 8 7 6 5

ISBN 0-07-284598-8

Editor in Chief: *Emily Barrosse*
Publisher: *Beth Ann Mejia*
Special Projects Editor: *Rebecca Smith*
Developmental Editor: *Robert Weiss*
Editorial Coordinator: *Ann Helgerson*
Media Producer: *Sean Crowley*
Media Project Manager: *Alex Rohrs*
Production Editor: *Leslie LaDow*
Production Supervisor: *Jason Huls*
Design Manager: *Kim Menning*

Interior Designer: *Glenda King*
Cover Designer: *Marianna Kinigakis*
Art Editors: *Katherine McNab & Ayelet Arbel*
Photo Research: *Natalia Peschiera*
Composition: *9.5/13 Stone Serif by Interactive Composition Corporation*
Printing: *50# Windsor Offset Smooth by R.R. Donnelley–Crawfordsville*

Cover image: © *Photodisc*

Produced in association with NASW Press, a division of the National Association of Social Workers. NASW PRESS

Credits: The credits section for this book begins on page C–1 and is considered an extension of the copyright page.

Library of Congress Cataloging-in-Publication Data

Dewees, Marty.
    Contemporary social work practice / Marty Dewees.
        p.cm.
    Includes bibliographical references and index.
    ISBN 0-07-284598-8 (alk. paper)
        1. Social service. 2. Social service—United States. I. Title.

HV40.D534 2005
361.3'2—dc22   2004061007

The Internet addresses listed in the text were accurate at the time of publication. The inclusion of a Web site does not indicate an endorsement by the authors or McGraw-Hill, and McGraw-Hill does not guarantee the accuracy of the information presented at these sites.

www.mhhe.com

For Caroline, Will, Ricky, Delilah, and so many others
in the hopes that with more practice, we'll get it right.

ABOUT THE AUTHOR

MARTY DEWEES came to social work via the field of counseling. After receiving a master's degree in counseling in 1974, she moved on to social work and obtained another master's degree in 1985 from Adelphi University's Vermont-based program. She became a staff social worker at Vermont State Hospital in 1985 and stayed until 1988 when she became a clinical supervisor for Spectrum, Inc., a youth agency in Burlington, VT. Beginning her doctoral studies at SUNY Albany in 1990, she returned to the State Hospital to be Chief of Social Work Services for the following five years. When she completed her PhD she joined the University of Vermont faculty in the Department of Social Work, where she is now serving as an Associate Professor. Her interests remain closely related to mental health, disability practice, global human rights, and contemporary theory. At UVM she teaches generalist practice, mental health, assessment, and interdisciplinary practice. Her current research focuses on the interface of the mental health system and the domestic violence system as it relates to women in domestic violence programs.

She lives in North Ferrisburgh, Vermont, with her husband, dog, and cat, and frequently entertains her four children, their spouses, partners, and her four grandchildren.

BRIEF CONTENTS

CONTENTS

CHAPTER 3   *Applying Values and Ethics to Practice* 56

CHAPTER 6 *Intervening in Context: Initiating the Plan   144*

CHAPTER 7   *Social Work with Groups: Tapping the Power of*
Connection   *171*

CHAPTER 9   *Working in and with the Organization   231*

PREFACE

The major purpose of this book is to help translate the guiding theoretical perspectives of social justice, human rights, the strengths perspective, and critical social construction into purposeful social work practice with real people in real social contexts.

This book is about social work practice. At this point in your social work education, you probably feel quite inclined to get on with it! As an undergraduate or first-year graduate student, you want to get your feet wet. If you have already had social work practice experience, you want to get back to it and apply what you have been learning. You may already have been equipped with a solid foundation and have integrated the worlds of research, policy, and human behavior into your ideas about what social work is and what it can be. Or you may just be entering the adventure. This book is intended, then, for you as a new or returning student-worker. It will help you look at the components of your work and think about how you want to develop as a skilled practitioner.

The book begins by describing the underlying theoretical perspectives that guide the practice approach presented here. These perspectives include social justice, human rights, the strengths perspective, and critical social construction. Some or all of these may already be a part of your view of social work practice. Critical social construction may be the least familiar, and it will be addressed frequently throughout. All of these positions influence social work practice and imply the use of empowering skills, which will be discussed in detail.

You may also notice that the book is influenced by broader postmodern considerations. You will learn what that means to the contemporary practitioner, and this will equip you with some of the basic language so that postmodern approaches in the broader social work literature will be accessible to you. Specifically, the postmodern influence here will be on questioning taken-for-granted privileged positions (see Dewees, 2002); the analysis of power in varying relationships (professional and otherwise); and the recognition of "subjugated knowledge" (Hartman, 1994). *Subjugated knowledge* refers to the local, experiential knowledge of reality that is often lost in the dominant assumptions made in U.S. culture.

My goal in writing this book is to assist students in locating and working in that intersection between skills and theoretical perspectives in a way that supports the profession's values (and explores them) while recognizing the lived experience of the people served by social workers. To that end, I start with what the worker brings to the relationship in the way of assumptions, values, and commitments. Next I guide you through an exploration of what the work looks like in one-to-one practice and how it is then translated and extended into the system levels of groups, families, communities, and organizations.

HOW THIS BOOK IS ORGANIZED

This book is divided into 12 chapters. The first chapter is an introduction to the world of social work practice, some of the frameworks that have been used to understand practice, and the theoretical perspectives and ideas that shape this book in particular.

Chapter 2 addresses the questions of what the purpose of social work is and what social workers hope to accomplish. This discussion identifies tensions that exist in social work as a profession. Some of these are as old as the profession, and some are emerging as the world changes daily. Issues regarding the worker's own biases, contemporary notions of noticing what we notice, and recognizing the lenses through which we view the world resurface and are considered in this context.

Chapter 3 is devoted to a discussion of social work values and ethics as they occur in practice. Ethical concerns and issues will be infused throughout the entire book as well, particularly in practice situations, but this chapter goes deeper into various organizational position statements, the law, conflicts, dilemmas, and expected standards.

Chapters 4, 5, and 6 use the traditional practice organization of engaging, assessing, and intervening, always keeping in mind the importance of a flexible interpretation of these phases. Evaluating, the final phase, is discussed at the end of the book (Chapter 12), but alluded to periodically as part of the ongoing effort. Fluidity is stressed, and each phase will suggest contemporary approaches. Chapter 4 addresses engaging in the relationship, Chapter 5, in deepening the dialogue that constitutes collaborative assessment of the person-situation-interaction dynamic; and Chapter 6 describes the intervening process. The processes described in these chapters are applied to one-on-one work, or individual clients, and will be extended, with appropriate variations, into other levels of client groupings.

Chapters 7 through 10 extend the generalist ideas and skills of individual practice and add some new ones for working in systems with more than one person. Here there will be an emphasis on consolidation of the common ground for social work practice across service levels, as well as an identification of the dimensions that are particular to each constellation.

Chapter 7 focuses on types of small groups, group work, the indications for a group, the planning process, and the traditional phase models, as well as some examples of traditional and more contemporary groups.

Chapter 8 addresses family work and its systemic background in social work practice. Different types of families are considered, and mapping tools will be extended from their introduction in Chapter 5 to the broader constellations of family and culture. Some controversies related to families are also raised for exploration. The importance of exploring your own family is emphasized here as well.

Chapter 9 discusses organizational practice, culture, missions, and types. It looks at the social agency and considers and contrasts public, private, and social movement emphases. It also considers organizational structures and institutions that serve as hosts for social work, with their accompanying challenges. It introduces interagency alliances, partnerships, and other networks.

Chapter 10 discusses the ideas and forms of community and some of the dynamics of, and skills required for, moving into a global community. It focuses on the functions of local communities on a variety of levels and extends its concern to global interdependence and international social work, as it emphasizes our efforts to become both local and global citizens.

Chapter 11 raises the issues of troubling contexts, including those of abject oppression, involuntary clients, managed care, and situations in which the worker encounters the "unconscionable event," which may involve such an egregious act against human rights that the worker experiences a traumatic response. These span service levels to relate to individuals, smaller, and larger groups. The chapter will identify the opportunities as well as the challenges inherent in these contexts. The ideas of sustaining ethical practice and avoiding burnout are considered here as well.

Chapter 12 completes the practice sequence with coverage of ending and evaluating the work. It addresses closing the work, managing the dynamics of both expected and unexpected endings, sharing perspectives, and a few formal mechanisms for evaluation. It also focuses on the need for continuing evaluation throughout the process of work with a client. It ends with a call to critique the work by looking at who benefited and whether power arrangements are altered or not. Finally, it addresses the limitations and strengths of evaluation.

Within each chapter, you will find multiple examples, vignettes, and exercises to help you make sense of the material and experiment with how it fits for you. You will also find, most likely, that there are as many questions raised as answered about the world of practice. This should help to prepare you for a career's length of remaining open to the questions emerging from your work and your clients' experiences. This in turn can help you tolerate—and hopefully thrive in—a place in which you don't know all the answers.

Each chapter contains a section called "Straight Talk." These are intended to help you synthesize (or, perhaps, come to grips with) the major ideas in the chapter with the demands for, and requirements of, real practice in the real world of the social organization or agency. In some respects they help to bridge the transition between a thoughtful postmodern practice and some of the traditional expectations of the current professional culture. Each chapter also makes mention in the margins of readings available to you on *The Social Work Library,* the password protected Web site that accompanies this text. These readings apply, extend, and enrich the key concepts of each chapter and may be assigned to you by your instructor.

Finally, each chapter ends with three exercise sections, "Practicing Social Work," "The Social Work Library," and "Other Exercises." The first will encourage you to apply what you are learning to simulated "real" situations that are presented on the CD-ROM included with your book. The other two sets of exercises make use of the wealth of additional material available to you on the Web site that accompanies this book. These will give you a flavor of integrating the perspectives as well as the skills that are discussed in the book. Through reflection and class discussion, you will begin to shape your own distinctive social work practice.

ACKNOWLEDGMENTS

This book is an attempt to document a vision. The vision is represented in the efforts of the University of Vermont's Department of Social Work to bring alive our commitments to a set of beliefs about people and the structures we as social workers use to understand them. Our explicit focus on social and economic justice, the strengths perspective, human rights, and critical social construction provides the backdrop for this book and its approach to social work practice in the real, global community of contemporary life. In recognition of the ongoing challenge to breathe life into these ideas, I want to thank our faculty, students, and staff, who have entered into a vibrant, ongoing dialogue, and occasional struggle, over the last ten years. I thank Julie Richards, our BSW Program Coordinator for lending her creativity to the Instructor's Manual. I especially want to thank Susan Roche, who as my colleague and comrade in teaching practice, has contributed (mostly unknowingly) to my understanding and implementation of every important idea in this text. While I recognize the presence of others on every page, this rendition is my own along with whatever flaws in interpretation may abide.

This book has developed as part of a series; the long distance experience of working with and consulting three of the other authors, Marla Berg-Weger, Rosemary Chapin, and Anissa Rogers, has been invaluable in spite of the limitations of e-mail and the only occasional face-to-face gatherings. The commitment of these authors to our common social work values, strengths, and community has been important and sustaining. In addition, I want to thank people at McGraw-Hill, especially Steve Rutter, who has elsewhere been identified as an exceedingly smart and patient person, and who certainly has lived up to that wonderful, reputed combination. Becky Smith, special projects editor, Ann Helgerson, editorial assistant, and Leslie LaDow, production editor, have also delivered positive cheer in a heartening and always helpful way. Bob Weiss, developmental editor, skillfully transformed my tangled sentences into English that can actually be understood. Finally, Alice Lieberman, coordinator of the series, has been undauntingly enthusiastic and affirmative about this work. She also provides me a huge uplift in spirits with every meeting. Her ability to maintain a principled and even perspective, along with her proclivity for a good laugh and a good dinner, has been one of the best antidotes to academic fatigue I've encountered.

The book's numerous and varied reviewers have provided several intriguing and useful views of how social work practice, as a course in the curriculum of social work education, can be made real, alive, and compelling for both BSW and MSW students. This particular aspect of the writing process has affirmed for me once again that many minds are better than one and that as human beings we continuously grow only in the company of others. Ultimately, our growth is aimed to benefit the people who come to us as clients, and more basically, as human beings.

Don Dewees and our faithful dog, Jas, along with our ill-tempered cat, Moses, have put up with many delayed dinners, many pleas for "just a few more minutes" at the computer, and a lot of semi-coherent mumblings revealing half-formed ideas, responses, and "aha" moments. I remain grateful for their continued tolerance and support.

Understanding Social Work Practice

Bea stalked the hallway of the psychiatric unit in a general hospital. Wringing her hands and grimacing at the voices she was hearing in her head, she was waiting to see her social worker, who would help her find a place to stay when she was discharged. She didn't want to leave the hospital; she was frightened.

Debbie, Joan, Marcy, and Kate felt as if the whole cosmos had just opened up for them. As a group they had already shared their experiences as battered women. Their social worker had explained how they could use their stories to help educate children in schools about violence at home. Their collective power felt liberating to them.

Harry, an 11-year-old orphaned child in Southeast Asia, hung on every word the community development worker uttered. She spoke of human rights and the need for the village to provide for the safety of its children. He had never imagined such a life, with guaranteed safety.

WELCOME TO THE WORLD OF SOCIAL WORK PRACTICE. This world is sometimes exhilarating, sometimes frustrating, and sometimes heartbreaking. It is nearly always challenging, and once you have entered it, you may find it impossible to imagine doing any other kind of work!

This chapter introduces you to the practice of social work. It examines what the worker brings to her or his work and how the profession has framed its mission. It describes a number of traditional ways to think about social work practice, types of client groupings and processes, a brief account of the way the profession has dealt with theory, and the contemporary practice commitments that underlie this book. The brief vignettes you have just read describe only a few of the main characters, or clients, in social work's story. We will meet many more along the way.

WHAT SOCIAL WORK PRACTICE ENTAILS

Practitioners, as well as social work educators, define social work practice in many different ways. Generalist practice, which is taught in undergraduate programs and in the first year of graduate school, is aimed at preparing students to work with systems of all sizes, from one-to-one intervention to community development and even to global social work. The range of practice settings is mind-boggling at times. Generalist practice might mean working with someone like Bea to support her as she leaves a psychiatric hospital for a community she left long before. It might involve planning, organizing, and facilitating a support/empowerment group like the one that Debbie, Joan, Marcy, and Kate belong to, or it might require implementing human rights policies in another culture, learning another language, and traveling to another part of the world, to assist children like Harry.

Generalist practice may also require doing more than one task at a time. For example, the worker providing emotional support for Bea may also be charged with locating a living space for her in the community that she left or helping her get a government-sponsored Section 8 housing voucher that would reduce her rent. It might mean working individually with group member Marcy to find a safe place for her children while she works, or it might require developing some familiarity with global economics in preparation for development work in another country. In still other settings a social worker may help an elder find a suitable person to share an apartment, take a preschooler to a developmental testing site, or accompany a person dying of cancer to a hospice as she waits for her family to arrive. Social work practice is as encompassing as the breadth of human experience.

More specifically, social work practice is sometimes thought of as a set of activities. Often these activities are associated with particular agencies and the functions they carry out in the community. Examples of these are

- Advocating for policy change regarding an elder's right to benefits in an area agency on aging.

- Facilitating an empowerment group in a domestic violence program.

- Mentoring students in a neighborhood school.

- Developing a psychoeducational group in a mental health agency.

- Supporting families in an emergency housing shelter.

- Participating in human rights work in another country.

Social Work as Role

Another way to look at practice emphasizes the relationships between the worker and the person coming for service. These relationships usually involve the worker's taking on a role such as counselor, broker, adviser, advocate, therapist, partner, or manager. Some definitions of role relationships are driven largely by theoretical perspectives. For example, some social workers who use **narrative theory**, which emphasizes the client's story and puts it at the center of the work, have suggested that they play a role more like story editor, director, accompanist, or translator than service provider (Goldstein, 1992). Also, for every role there is a reciprocal role giving meaning to both (Davis, 1996). For example, the role of mother has significance only in its interaction with the role of child. Likewise, all worker roles are complemented by client roles, such as partner, advisee, or counselee.

Social Work as Purposeful Conversation, or Discourse

A more complex way to think of social work practice is through the idea of comprehensive, purposeful conversations, or discourse. The term **discourse** refers collectively to the language, conversation, or dialogue, as well as ideas and beliefs relating to both our most sacred values and our everyday activities. In that respect discourse involves acting and interacting with others in time and place in a recognizable manner that embodies the idea of relationship. The language of various discourses not only reflects what our ideas are, but, more importantly, it actually shapes or constitutes them. A major function of language is to frame how social relationships and activities are carried out within cultures, groups, or institutions (Gee, 1999).

Social work, as an institution, has many professional discourses that influence ideas of what practice is; for example, some workers are committed to a scientific discourse, which might mean they look for objective, factual evidence that the approach they are taking is most likely to succeed. Others see social work as an art and identify the discourse as one of expression and storytelling. In many mental health settings, the *Diagnostic and Statistical Manual of Mental Disorders IV-TR (DSM),* which is the lexicon of mental illness diagnoses, is considered a discourse central to practice (American Psychiatric Association, 2000). This is because the use of diagnosis as it is described in the *DSM* implies certain beliefs and principles that are closely related to the medical world. For example, if I visit the office used by social work interns in a mental health center, I might hear dismayed exclamations such as, "Oh, my new client is a borderline! I'm doomed!" This snippet of a much larger discourse is enormously telling to anyone in mental health practice. It communicates, among other things, one common way in which mental health or illness is understood, what the nature of the worker-client relationship is expected to be within that particular setting, and how stigma is sometimes transmitted through a system.

 Web Links

For access to the DSM and the answers to several frequently asked questions about it, go to the American Psychiatric Association Web site.

In contrast, the discourse in most child welfare work relates to risk behaviors and permanency planning for children. For example, whether a particular accusation of abuse is *substantiated* may make all the difference in a child's life in terms of how the institution responds (for example, by placing her or him in foster care). Further, the process of substantiation reflects our culture's concern about making accusations, emphasizes the ways we carry out our beliefs about due process, and helps shape our ideas about how to protect children. In work with adolescents, the discourse usually takes up definitions of freedom from parental control and questions regarding the appropriate age for independence in certain circumstances, times, and places.

These discourses, and examinations of them, are the stuff of contemporary social work. As you can see, these discourses differ from one another, each having its own relevance and context, but they also coexist and interact with one another in the larger discourse of social work. Each influences the nature of the work and the approaches to practice adopted by the profession. You will learn more about discourses and their analyses in this book.

Terms like discourse and several others that we'll consider in this book may seem difficult at first. This is partly because they may be unfamiliar and partly because they usually describe complex ideas. It is important for you to be exposed to these terms because they are increasingly used in contemporary social work literature, and you are likely to confront the ideas they describe in practice. They will assist you in considering and discussing social work perspectives and purposes of the next decade and beyond.

TRADITIONAL WAYS TO THINK ABOUT SOCIAL WORK PRACTICE

Historically, long before the term discourse appeared in social work, the profession conceived several different schematic ways to describe and shape its work. These are very much in use today and include (1) knowledge, values, and skills, (2) types of client groupings, and (3) process loops. The first—knowledge, values, and skills—describes worker attributes and dimensions, or what she or he brings to the work.

Knowledge, Values, and Skills

This trio is often considered the core of social work education and training. Together they might be thought of as what the practitioner brings to the work, as they reflect personal aspects and attributes acquired by, and some scholars think inherent to, the worker. Each is necessary for effective service delivery.

Knowledge   Here, **knowledge** refers to traditional forms such as facts and research and also to broader forms such as intuition and cultural awareness.

Knowledge that includes facts, histories, and trends about human development, policy, research, and practice are often grouped and labeled "biopsychosocial" knowledge. The assumptions here are that social workers need to be acquainted with the facts associated with these combined biopsychosocial fields in order to understand what is normal, or expected behavior, for, say, an adolescent under stress, or what the likely dynamics will be in an agency when a policy change is initiated from the top down. This arena also assumes that the knowledge required is largely agreed upon and that it is attainable through study, discussion, research experimentation, and related activities.

Another view of knowledge suggests that it is much broader than what is-considered proven, or fact, and also includes what we think about theory, ideas, and even what we've experienced as hunches or "practice wisdom." Some of this kind of knowledge may elude measurement, which has been an ongoing challenge both in the field and in social work education. For example, you may know a student who struggles with the academic course work in your program but has a knack or a sense about how to support people and help them uncover their most effective assets. Instructors in field education have long sought ways to measure and evaluate that kind of wisdom or knowledge and to reconcile it with more traditional forms of academic achievement.

Another critical kind of knowledge for contemporary practice is related to culture. We will be concerned both with the broad role of culture in general in shaping the lives of both clients and workers and specifically with cultural competence as a core dimension of social work practice. **Cultural competence** here refers to the worker's ability to navigate cultures different from her or his own. Green (1995) describes it as the capacity to deliver professional services in a way that is consistent with the cultural sensibilities of the community in which the services are offered. Because it is a major component in many social work discourses, cultural competence is integrated throughout this book, and it appears in discussions of both theory and skill development.

More recently, the notion of spirituality as another form of knowledge has been added to models of both human development and social work training. Spirituality has long been neglected in social work education, and its inclusion has greatly enriched the framework for workers and clients alike. Spirituality is integrally connected with culture and therefore gives practitioners access to important dimensions, even if sometimes less overt, of the lives of the people they work with. For example, recognizing a Navajo child's spiritual affirmation of harmony may help a worker understand the child's reluctance to engage in aggressive competition in school. We will examine various kinds of knowledge throughout this book as they impact the client and the work.

Values   Social work has always strongly identified itself as a profession of **values**, which are beliefs about what is good or right. Although there is room within the profession for a wide range of orientations, there is some agreement about values relating to (1) the general worth of people, particularly as individuals, (2) the need for honest communication, and (3) respect for cultural orientations (to name only a few of social work's values). This commonality, however, does not suggest that as a group social workers demonstrate uniformity on such issues; you will hear many a spirited discussion of difference in any social work setting. But values are held as critical, even when the particulars vary. Consideration of values and ethics will also present many challenges to you, which will often look different in complicated practice contexts from the way they do in isolation. The profession has developed a *Code of Ethics* that will play a significant role in helping you sort out complex situations in which values are at issue. Although we will explore values throughout the book as they relate to a variety of situations, we will consider the *Code* more fully in Chapter 3 and focus on values per se and their relationship to ethics, because they play such an important role in the shape of social work.

It may be useful here to make a brief distinction between values and ethics. Values, as beliefs, guide our thinking about behavior and our judgments about conduct. **Ethics** are the rules, or prescriptions, for behavior that (should) reflect those values. For example, if I believe that all human life is worthy, that is a value. From that value arises the ethical principle that I should protect human life in my work, which in most cases means I would actively try to prevent any harm that might occur to another person. You can imagine that value conflicts might arise in complicated circumstances (for example, if trying to prevent harm to one person puts another at risk). The *Code* was developed to clarify some of those phenomena. The role of values provides critical criteria for how the profession shapes itself and its rules of conduct.

Skills   Finally, the third element that the social worker brings to the work, **skills** reflect that doing is as important as knowing or valuing and that you can learn, and probably must learn, relevant skills. Most social work educators would acknowledge that some students take to the field more readily than others, or possess the kind of hard-to-measure knowledge described previously as practice wisdom. However, they also assume that all social workers can and do learn more effective skills at carrying out, or bringing to life, the knowledge, theoretical perspectives, and values they bring to their work with clients. In fact many states require that licensed social workers complete ongoing continuing education units through professional workshops or conferences that provide skills training for new situations, new populations, and new ways of thinking about the work.

The traditional skills considered important for beginning social workers entering the field include interviewing, assessing, reflecting, clarifying, supportive confronting, mediating, and many others (different terms may be used for these, also). Throughout the book, you will see how to use many of these skills as they help translate goals into the real work of practice.

Types of Client Groupings

Another organizational scheme familiar to most students is the one defined by the constellation of the service beneficiaries involved. In this scheme you might hear of individual, small group, family, organization, and community social work. In more recent times, with the expansion of global awareness and the ways in which we in the United States impact other nations and they impact us, the frames of international and global social work are entering this continuum, extending the arena in which social work practice is both relevant and critical. Social work education frequently uses this organizational scheme in the layout of its curriculum by specific course content or emphasis. We will look briefly at these here and in more detail later in the book.

- *Individual work, or casework:* This face-to-face focus may be your first association when you think of social work practice. **Individual work,** or **casework,** spans all fields of practice and populations. You might work with an adolescent struggling with sexuality issues, a mother concerned with her child's development, an elder who is facing his inability to care for himself, and a five-year-old who can't seem to pay attention in school. The nature of the work will be heavily influenced by the agency's purpose, the practice perspective, and the personal characteristics of the client as well as your own. Cultural context, social and political influences, and current community concerns will also affect this relationship.

- *Group work:* Although less common than individual practice, **group work** is a prototype social work method. Because its forum is conceptually social, it embodies the relationship emphasis of the profession. It, too, occurs in a great many practice settings and contexts, which in turn have a great influence on it. Social work with groups is one of the most distinctive practices of the profession.

- *Community organization:* The method of practice known as **community organization** usually involves a common locality, like a neighborhood, small town, or rural area. Beyond locality, however, *community* also refers to some common concern, interest, or identification. For example, you might claim membership in the community of your hometown where you were born and raised. You may also find your place in the community of gay men or Jewish women or people of Irish descent. Social work practice has always been at home in the community, however defined, and aspires toward inclusive participation of community citizens in addressing their self-defined concerns.

- *International work:* An underrecognized focus, **international social work** will certainly be a significant feature in the future of the profession. Many argue that the profession will not be able to address the most local issues intelligently without grasping a global, transnational perspective of how these same issues, such as homelessness or HIV/AIDS, occur in other cultures both near and on the other side of the world.

The organizational scheme based on client groupings contains a number of underlying assumptions. Some of these assumptions relate to skill development. For example, many social workers agree that work with groups or organizations is generally more complex than work with individuals. Another assumption is that one-to-one work is the natural place to start. As you will see later in the book, that particular assumption is well suited to our contemporary, mainstream U.S. context. It is also quite culture bound and might not be familiar in cultures in which family or community is the major organizing structure or reference point. Although the distinctions between types of groupings continue to be a useful way of thinking about social work, generalist practice emphasizes an integration of knowledge and skills across all system levels and sizes.

Process Loops

The third way to think about practice has to do with the process of the work. The schema of **process loops** suggests that the activities of the social worker and the client proceed through relatively standard phases. Although these phases are described here in a linear progression, they frequently loop back to direct the worker and client to previous phases; hence the term.

Engagement   In this context **engagement** refers to building a relationship among the worker, the client, and the client's environment. Successful engagement involves establishing a degree of trust and a sense that the work about to be taken up will be helpful to the client and professionally rewarding to the worker (not just monetarily, but with a sense of effectiveness that is satisfying).

Even in one-to-one practice, engagement is not limited to the relationship between you and the client. Rather, it also involves establishing significant and collaborative connections with the client's environment and the service systems within it that will impact your work and the client's goals. For example, let us say your client has asked for your help in negotiating the public school system in which her child with disabilities is being educated. You carefully develop a relationship with her so that you may understand what the issues are and how she experiences them. You will also need to engage with the client's network, in this case the school system, to learn what its constraints and challenges are, in order to be effective in facilitating a more productive relationship between parent and school.

Engagement will be discussed in greater depth in Chapter 4. Without a successful engagement, the work that follows may seem perfunctory or tedious. Often engagement is not completed, either because the client loses investment in a process that she or he doesn't seem to belong to in a meaningful way, or the critical network contacts in the environment do not perceive their role as appreciated or understood fully. For example, in the situation just described, if the personnel in the school system think you don't understand how difficult it is to provide extensive services with shrinking resources, they may actually become less willing to work on improving their relationship with your client.

Assessment and Planning   Generally, **assessment** has to do with recognizing the parameters of the practice situation and how they affect the participant(s). The client's goals are central to this process. Through mutual exploration of what the issues are and how the client interacts with them, the client and worker decide, for example, to address client preparation for job training, assertiveness training, or hospital discharge. Assessment then focuses on the analysis of what the major area for work is, what the environment can offer in the way of supporting a solution, what the client brings to bear on the situation, and how the client can meet her or his goals.

Assessment styles and theoretical perspectives vary considerably with the worker's interpretation of the appropriate strategy. The overall mission of the agency also plays an important role and may in fact be quite directive in defining the activity. For example, as the idea of discourses suggests, the assessments conducted in foster care agencies may vary quite a lot in tone and approach, but they are all likely to be focused on children and parenting, rather than, say, vocational development or personal growth counseling.

Planning is an integral part of assessment. Developing the plan will require you and the client to assess or evaluate the options, the resources, the barriers, the particulars of emotion, and the agreed-upon goals along with the established methods of reaching them. The plan should also include some consideration of the less-than-obvious or unexpected outcomes of reaching a goal. For example, as the worker, you may assist a couple in adopting a child for whom they provided foster care. Another child in the family might have accepted the temporary nature of the foster care arrangement but suddenly feels threatened by the permanency of its turning into an adoption. As a result, she begins to have angry outbursts or sullen periods of withdrawal that surprise even her parents. The complexity of human emotion frequently shows up in unexpected places and times in social work practice. We'll look more at assessment and planning in Chapter 5.

Intervention   The next stage in this sequence, **intervention** refers to the action—the doing of the work that will enable the client and the practitioner to accomplish the goals decided upon in the assessment. In most generalist practice situations, this means that somebody will do something like organize a tenants' union or help a family get assistance from Medicaid for an ill child. It is probably most useful to think of intervention as the joint activity of the client and the worker rather than the worker's unilateral effort. Also, in some cases, social work practice is more verbal, and the intervention may involve the worker's listening to and reflecting on the client's story and, in turn, helping the client to think about it differently or to "write" another or new life story that she or he would prefer to live.

As you can see, the intervention process is also greatly influenced by the perspective that you as the practitioner might bring to the work. In some practice models you would be very active in deciding what should happen in the client's best interests and initiating it. In other models the planning and intervention is a more shared process with the client doing some things, you other things, and both of you deciding together on the best course. As with other aspects of practice, the type, level, and focus of the intervention vary widely. We will discuss intervention more fully in Chapter 6.

Evaluation   Many agencies don't feel they have the time (when one client leaves, another takes her place!) to spend on an activity that is sometimes not seen as directly helpful to the client. Nevertheless, it is necessary to consider whether all the effort and resources put into the work are adequate and efficient. In addition, an **evaluation** of the effectiveness of the work will benefit future clients in similar situations.

Some social workers view research activities in program evaluation and individual effectiveness as an integral part of social work practice and one that should be employed throughout the delivery of services, not just at the end. This may involve evaluation tools that assess the progress of a program on one level and also, on quite a different level, may provide encouragement for a reflective approach by individual workers on the quality of their work. Others see an important link between research activities and effective client advocacy. For example, if you want to advocate for the homeless by demonstrating that existing services are inadequate or are not directed effectively at need areas, it is critical that you know who the homeless are, how many people are homeless, and what their stories are (among other things). This kind of information can be addressed in evaluation of direct services and programs as well as more general policies.

There are many kinds of evaluation: quantitative, qualitative, subjective, objective, **formative** (during the work), **summative** (at the end of the work), self-report, reflection, standardized tests, and so on. The fact that there are so many different types of evaluation complicates the scene for the worker. Overall, however, the prevailing trend within the various funding and accountability arrangements associated with social work practice is to require more evaluative activity both to demonstrate effectiveness and to justify continued or increased financial support for small practice initiatives as well as much larger policy programs. We'll address several types of evaluation in Chapter 12.

Disengagement   Ending with clients, or **disengagement**, is a long-standing area of interest for social workers. Partly because many clients have experienced abrupt, sometimes violent or completely disconcerting endings to relationships or arrangements, the profession has had a particular concern that workers "end well" with people. In general, that means reviewing the work; talking about the relationship, how it developed, and where it worked and didn't work; and planning how the client will move on, either independently or through referral to another kind of service. To many workers this is one of the most difficult as well as one of the most important aspects of the work. Those who want to focus more on the future sometimes call it "consolidation" or "graduation." Chapter 12 will address disengaging from clients.

Further Ideas about Traditional Structures for Understanding Social Work

Each of these organizational structures provides a useful way of thinking about social work practice. Each clarifies some dimension of the work that makes exploration of social work practice more manageable. Like many useful things, however, each also has its limitations.

For example, knowledge, values, and skills overlap a great deal. Separating them may fragment your growing sense of professional identity and thus confuse you. For example, if you overfocus on factual knowledge as an isolated aspect of your development, you may become a powerhouse of information but feel at a loss in knowing what to do in certain situations. Skills, likewise, run the risk of becoming somewhat manipulative techniques when they are separated from a knowledge and value base. The integration of many kinds of knowledge, values, and skills is the aim of most social work education.

Likewise, dividing the work into constituent groups of beneficiaries may suggest that the background, values, and skills necessary for each kind of practice vary significantly. In its extreme, this division also conflicts with the idea of generalist practice, which requires that the worker be proficient at all levels of client groupings and asserts that the basic knowledge and skills in social work practice apply to all system levels. Although most social work practitioners would probably agree that some particular skills are necessary for group work (for example), it is not helpful in this age of generalist practice to view these different types of work as altogether separate. Their similarities far surpass their differences; work in any of them is grounded in the practitioner's consistent set of values, theoretical perspectives, and goals. It will be helpful to think about how they are integrated as well as how each one is distinct.

Any of you who have worked with people before, either as a volunteer or a paid employee, will recognize the shortcomings of a linear phase model if it is rigidly understood. A social worker does not simply build a relationship and then become "all business" because she or he has moved on to the next phase of assessment. Like all relationships, the professional connection between worker and client must be attended to, nurtured, and encouraged to grow throughout the time of their work together, or it will wither. Likewise, assessment actually occurs throughout the course of the work, beginning with the first visit and continuing through the last. It is also mutual in the sense that the client needs to assess whether the practitioner is going to be able to help. In that way assessment is actually a component in building the relationship. If an unexpected event occurs during the intervention, the worker may loop back to revisit the assessment and/or reaffirm the engagement. It might be most useful to think of all these activities as highly connected and as going on continuously and simultaneously but with some special emphasis paid to one or the other at different times during the work. The major idea here is that such models are helpful, but they need to be used flexibly. We will use several of them in this book, and you can explore how they add to your professional identity as it develops.

THEORETICAL PERSPECTIVES FOR SOCIAL WORK PRACTICE

Not only does social work as a profession employ a number of organizational schemes, but it also has a long history of adopting, adapting, and formulating various theories to guide its work. A **theory** is an explanation of some event or phenomenon. It usually has clear principles and propositions that provide a framework for predicting what will happen and a body of empirically based evidence to support it. Theory should assist us as workers in testing ideas, anticipating outcomes of different interventions, and in applying the results to future situations. It likewise can bring order and coherence to practice situations so that activities are not capricious or arbitrary but rather are based on a logical assessment of how the case specifics fit the assertions of the theory. However, theories relating to the social world are almost never final in any absolute way—that is, theories tend to evolve and adjust in order to fit new, developing ideas or to accommodate further evidence that adds to or is contradictory to their claims. Further, theories regarding the social world are driven by values (Turner, 1996). Consequently, some theories are discarded when they are no longer acceptable to the professional community (for example, theories asserting that some races are superior over others). Other theories evolve to incorporate additional refinements or methods, such as the contemporary interpretations of Freud's 19th-century psychoanalytic theory.

A **perspective** is a view, or lens, through which to observe and interpret the world. It is generally less structured than theory but is similar in that it is often based on values and beliefs about the nature of the world or people. For example, if you believe that people are generally good, that is a perspective, which will guide your practice and through which you are likely to interpret your work with clients. In that way the ideas behind theory and perspective are quite similar. In social work, the terms theory and perspective are often used interchangeably and may also be called **theoretical perspectives.** I will use these three terms interchangeably throughout this book.

Social work has been criticized for its lack of theory, for its mislabeling of assumptions as theory, and for its eclectic adoption of inconsistent pieces of theory. Nevertheless, the use or nonuse of theory is important for social work practice. In this book we will look briefly at the implications of several theories, mostly with respect to how they shape specific practice activities differently and how they have evolved through changes in social context.

Origins of Social Work Theory

Traditionally, social work has drawn upon and taken up medical, psychosocial, cognitive, and systems theories of one kind or another (to name only a few). It has sometimes struggled with the idea of taking on the perspectives of other professions (such as psychiatry or psychology) and finding its own, more comfortable, theoretical base. Fortunately for the profession, this struggle has yielded a rich array of theoretical perspectives that have made social work practice very versatile. Because the profession is a living, breathing entity, it is continuously shaped by its context. This means, for example, that when Freudian theory swept the Western world, social work, too, incorporated many of its principles and assumptions. Likewise, when behaviorism became widely influential in the realms of psychiatry and psychology, social work, too, adopted some of its principles and interventions. In this way the origins of social work theory have reflected its sociocultural position among other professions and patterns of thought.

More recently, social work has expanded the development of its own understandings of practice to create theories. Some of these theories focus on psychosocial systems, problem solving, ecological/ecosystems, and empowerment, as they represent uniquely social work emphases on the interface between a person and her or his environment. Social work's theoretical positions have also received important contributions from sociology, anthropology, many of the humanities, and human service professions, as well as from social work itself.

The Social Work Library

For a classic model of social work theory, read Germain & Gitterman's chapter on the ecological perspective.

The Role of Theoretical Perspectives in Social Work Practice

Many students new to the profession wonder why there is so much concern with theory. If you just want to help people, what is the benefit of attaching a complicated theory to the work? Probably the most relevant answer to that question is found in the determination of what is truly helpful to people. Because theories tend to be driven by values, how social workers choose, implement, and evaluate a theory or theoretical perspective will be highly influenced by their value orientations. For example, I may "want to help" by creating an alliance with a client that results in her complete dependence on me through my adherence to a theory that supports "reparenting" as a legitimate function of social work practice. I may see that theoretical guide as helpful because I can direct the client's activities, shape her thinking, and ensure that she will do the "right thing" (or what I would do). You, on the other hand, may find that theory not at all helpful because you value autonomy and independence of spirit and respect the rights of all people to make their own choices. The role of theory in this scenario would be critical in directing the work of the practitioner.

This book will take up four practice perspectives that guide its focus and are central to its content. They are (1) the social justice perspective, (2) the human rights perspective, (3) the strengths perspective, and (4) critical social construction, a postmodern perspective. Some of these perspectives have a long history in social work education and practice (such as social justice), and others are more contemporary or even controversial (such as critical social construction). Some are also broader than others.

Social Justice Perspective

Social justice may seem to be a huge term with indistinct boundaries, but for this discussion you can think of it as the means by which societies allocate their resources, which consist of material goods and social benefits, rights, and protections. Although there are various theories of social justice regarding the criteria for distribution of wealth, the profession of social work generally takes up an egalitarian focus that is concerned with the fair distribution of both material and nonmaterial resources (Rawls, 1971) and equal access for all people (Reichert, 2003). From this perspective, developing or distributing social and natural resources based on political or social power rather than social justice or human need is unacceptable (Saleebey, 1990). This has important implications for social workers and their practice because it requires a response to much of the injustice that is status quo in our society.

Social Justice and the National Association of Social Workers   Not only must social workers in the United States address social and economic injustices, but they are also bound by the National Association of Social Workers *Code of Ethics*. The second ethical principle in the *Code* is explicit

NATIONAL ASSOCIATION OF SOCIAL WORK (NASW) *CODE OF ETHICS*

VALUE: *SOCIAL JUSTICE*

ETHICAL PRINCIPLE: *SOCIAL WORKERS CHALLENGE SOCIAL INJUSTICE.*

EXHIBIT 1.1

Theoretical Perspectives: Social Justice

Social workers pursue social change, particularly with and on behalf of vulnerable and oppressed individuals and groups of people. Social workers' social change efforts are focused primarily on issues of poverty, unemployment, discrimination, and other forms of social injustice. These activities seek to promote sensitivity to and knowledge about oppression and cultural and ethnic diversity. Social workers strive to ensure access to needed information, services, and resources; equality of opportunity; and meaningful participation in decision making for all people.

about the requirement for social workers to "challenge social injustice" (see Exhibit 1.1). This seems to be a clear statement about the profession's identity, but it has been interpreted quite broadly, and some social workers rarely put their energies directly into this kind of pursuit.

Social workers should—and most do—invest a significant amount of time and effort into championing individual and group rights, working toward more effective institutional responses, and influencing major social policy shifts. This automatically makes social work a political profession, as members look closely at and then beyond the individual client's situation to address the areas of injustice that have an impact on her or his life. For example, if a practitioner is working individually with a child with a disability and that child's family has been wrongfully denied access to services or government support programs, it is the worker's responsibility to address that injustice either directly or indirectly by making sure that someone else addresses it. This would involve more than seeking redress for that one family: The worker would try to discover whether other families are experiencing the same response. If so, the worker would focus on changing the procedures that are responsible for the injustice.

Web Links

For more on the profession's Code of Ethics and many other dimensions of social work, access the NASW Web site through the online learning center.

The Challenge of Working for Social Justice   Sometimes social work's social justice perspective is surprising and difficult for students. Most students go into the profession because they like people (the first reason for most of us!) and envision friendly, fulfilling, and satisfying relationships. However, some situations require a more energetic or aggressive approach in order to meet the client's basic human needs. In such cases social workers will advocate for clients, which often means opposing the positions of others, such as landlords or welfare officials. This conception of social justice implies that injustice is built around institutional arrangements that support an unfair distribution of resources based on relations of power. Social workers need to understand the connection between individual misery and the structures of our society (Fisher & Karger, 1997). Poverty, for example, is an enormously influential dimension of life for a disproportionate number of people of color, single women parents, elders, people of differing ethnicities, and people with disabilities. It is not an earned life status but rather is based on power relations. The advantage that comes with white skin in our larger culture is another example of the arbitrary nature of such arrangements. There is nothing inherent in white skin that supports its preference.

These are the kinds of issues social workers are concerned with in their quest to expand social justice, and this quest has a significant influence in shaping social work practice. These issues are not isolated historical, policy, or structural quirks. Rather, they are everywhere, and they interface everyday with social work practice, practitioners, and the people they serve.

Human Rights Perspective

The United Nations describes **human rights** as those rights that are

> inherent in our nature and without which we cannot live as human beings. Human rights and fundamental freedoms allow us to fully develop and use our human qualities, our intelligence, our talents and our conscience and to satisfy our spiritual and other needs. They are basic for mankind's increasing demand for a life in which the inherent dignity and worth of each human being will receive respect and protection. (*Human Rights—Questions and Answers,* 1987)

Some social workers believe that human rights form the bedrock that supports social justice. Others argue that human rights principles add a unique dimension that goes beyond the social justice notion of fairness (Ife, 2001). The principle of human rights offers a powerful and comprehensive framework for social work practice; it not only recognizes needs but addresses satisfying those needs (Reichert, 2003). The connection between social work practice theory and human rights in the United States has not been strongly made, for reasons we will explore shortly. Still, the human rights perspective provides a moral grounding for social work and reflects an ongoing commitment to the belief that all people should have basic rights and access to the broad benefits of their societies. Many social workers evaluate their practice based on its contribution to an environment in which universal human rights are honored.

The Origins of Human Rights   The idea of human rights can be traced in multiple cultural histories reaching back to antiquity (Wronka, 1998). The major treatises of Christianity, Judaism, and Islam all make references to the sanctity of human life. Many references are also made throughout ancient Greek and Roman secular literature. In a more modern and political context, both the U.S. Declaration of Independence and the French Declaration of the Rights of Man and of the Citizen reflect many of the concepts of human rights.

Of course, the sanctity of life, as a principle, represents both an exceedingly simple notion and a thoroughly complex commitment. It takes little imagination to envision a conflict in which one group, in pursuit of its human rights, infringes upon the human rights of another group. The hostilities of several contemporary international contests (for example, in the Middle East) reflect that dynamic quite clearly in disputes that result in the violation of the cultural, economic, social, political, and civil rights on both sides. Further complications arise in the conception of human rights when various types of rights are considered, as you will see as we go along.

The Universal Declaration of Human Rights   The United Nations passed the Universal Declaration of Human Rights on December 10, 1948. This 20th-century Western document reflects the conviction that human life is sacred in much the same spirit as its historical antecedents did. Largely catalyzed by the atrocities of World War II, its original 30 articles addressed five types of rights: civil, political, economic, social, and cultural.

The guidelines for human rights principles were more completely spelled out in 1966 with the International Covenant on Political and Civil Rights and the International Covenant on Economic, Social, and Cultural Rights (United Nations, 1994). These two covenants set the standard against which violations of international human rights can be judged. They include three elements: (1) the right to self-determination; (2) the principle of equality between women and men and nondiscrimination on grounds of gender, race, or religion; and (3) the principle of indivisibility, which refers to the interdependence of civil and political freedoms with economic, social, and cultural standards.

Contemporary Views of Human Rights   Some more current ideas about human rights emphasize the social understandings of our commonality rather than the rigid assertions of the UN's Universal Declaration. Accordingly, human rights can be thought of as socially constructed, reflecting differing contexts, ideas, and cultures (Gil, 1998b). Ife (2001) likewise suggests that the human rights discourse should deemphasize the focus on legalistic, Western views of entitlements in favor of a more reflective dialogue among the worlds' peoples. This dialogue would center on exploring what it means to be human and how we as humans want to recognize our interdependence, protect our futures, and safeguard our survival in the current and future global era. This focus is consistent with social work's emphasis on

Web Links

For an orientation to human rights and the Universal Declaration, access the UN Web site through the online learning center.

The Social Work Library

For more on human rights and social work practice, see Ife's work.

community, quality of relationship, and concern for the future of the world's inhabitants. It also recognizes the dynamic nature of living principles, such as those inherent in human rights, as they continuously evolve to remain meaningful to those who are committed to their realization.

Human Rights in the United States and U.S. Social Work   The indivisibility of human rights means that none of them can exist without the others. For example, the right to vote means little to a person who is starving (Noyoo, 2004). Although the United States has paid relatively close attention to the observation of civil and political rights (as represented in the Covenant on Political and Civil Rights), it has had some ambivalence in committing to the overall values of the Universal Declaration. One reason for this is that the guarantee of economic, social, and cultural rights for every citizen (as reflected in the second covenant) conflicts sharply with our political and economic tradition of free market capitalism, in which people are not guaranteed adequate resources for survival, but rather must "earn" them (c.f. Ellis, 2004). In spite of the ideal that anyone can succeed in the U.S. free enterprise system, the United States is currently experiencing a steadily deepening pattern of social polarization and a widening gap between rich and poor. Moreover, many of the poor are people of color, women, the elderly, and people with disabilities. This renders the U.S.'s full participation in the quest for human rights problematic (Dewees & Roche, 2001).

Further, the United States has been sluggish in ratifying various agreements and conventions pertaining to human rights. Perhaps the most notable example is the nation's refusal to ratify the Convention on the Rights of the Child, a 1989 United Nations declaration asserting that all children are entitled to "a healthy and safe environment, access to care, minimum standards of food, clothing, and shelter" as well as "protection from all forms of exploitation" (United Nations, 1994, p. 29). One-hundred ninety-two nations have ratified the Convention. Only two countries, Somalia and the United States, have not.

Despite the limited support of the United States for economic, social, and cultural rights, human rights have the potential to occupy a central place in social work practice and can provide a focal point in the evolution of how the world's peoples understand their place on this planet. Viewed as a set of dynamic principles that can provide a substantive contribution to guidelines on international relations as well as community-based practice, human rights constitutes a vital focus for work with people. Social work as a profession in this country can take up the lead started by many of our global colleagues in making human rights a central discourse and in exploring its relevance more thoroughly to our everyday work (see, for example, Tang, Lam & Lam, 2003; Tang, 2004).

The Strengths Perspective

An increasingly widespread approach in social work practice, the **strengths perspective** is explicit in its emphasis on affirming and working with the strengths found both in people seeking help and in the environments from which they come. Like human rights practice, this perspective emphasizes basic dignity and the resilience of people in overcoming challenging obstacles. Its most vocal proponents in social work have written prolifically on the approach and its development, application, and expansion. Contemporary advocates have established some significant breaks with social workers' historical and cultural tendency to focus their work and energies on problems and pathology. Although this comparison runs the risk of creating a polarized, either/or dynamic, it is nonetheless a useful way to emphasize the power and difference of a strengths focus. See Table 1.1 for a summary of how social work's previous emphasis on the pathological is transformed in the strengths perspective.

Pathology Perspective	Strengths Perspective
Person is defined as a "case"; symptoms add up to a diagnosis.	Person is defined as unique; traits, talents, resources add up to strengths.
Therapy is problem focused.	Therapy is possibility focused.
Personal accounts aid in the evocation of a diagnosis through reinterpretation by an expert.	Personal accounts are the essential route to knowing and appreciating the person.
Practitioner is skeptical of personal stories, rationalizations.	Practitioner knows the person from the inside out.
Childhood trauma is the precursor of adult pathology.	Childhood trauma is not predictive; it may weaken or strengthen the individual.
Centerpiece of therapeutic work is the treatment plan devised by the practitioner.	Centerpiece of work is the aspirations of family, individual, or community.
Practitioner is the expert on clients' lives.	Individuals, family, or community are the experts.
Possibilities for choice, control, commitment, and personal development are limited by pathology.	Possibilities for choice, control, commitment, and personal development are open.
Resources for work are the knowledge and skills of the professional.	Resources for work are the strengths, capacities, and adaptive skills of the individual, family, or community.
Help is centered on reducing the effect of symptoms and the negative personal and social consequences of actions, emotions, thoughts, or relationships.	Help is centered on getting on with one's life, affirming and developing values and commitments, and making and finding membership in or as a community.

Source: Saleebey, 1996

TABLE 1.1

Theoretical Perspectives: Comparison of the Pathology Perspective and the Strengths Perspective

Principles of the Strengths Perspective Saleebey (1997) has identified five principles that provide grounding for this approach:

1. Every individual, group, family, and community has strengths;

2. Trauma and abuse, illness and struggle, may be injurious, but they may also be sources of challenge and opportunity;

3. Assume that you do not know the upper limits of the capacity to grow and change, and take individual, group, and community aspirations seriously;

4. We best serve clients by collaborating with them;

5. Every environment is full of resources. (p. 12)

Challenges of the Strengths Perspective Some principles of this perspective may seem harder to follow than others. For example, social workers experienced in the problem focus of many approaches may find particular difficulty in fighting their inclination to assume that because of their experience and training they *do* know the upper limits of the capacity to grow and change. This principle asks social workers to take seriously the aspirations of people who seem to have very little history of success. Because of the educational and historical emphasis in the United States on "predicting achievement" (you yourself might have experienced this phenomenon with SATs or GREs), it can be difficult to take seriously the dreams of an 18-year-old with a measured IQ of 73 to be a physician. Fortunately, many accounts of successes illustrate the potential for beating such odds or making a rewarding peace with whatever achievement is attained. Nevertheless it may tax the social worker's creativity to shift her or his thinking in this way.

When using the strengths perspective, it is still necessary, although it can be challenging, to validate the person's suffering (physical, emotional, or existential) and not to minimize the seriousness of her or his distress. This practice approach does not deny the very real experience of pain that people may have; rather, it seeks to acknowledge clients' expertise regarding their own lives and to focus on their resilience and capacities to survive and to confront such seemingly overwhelming obstacles. This practice perspective—that all people and environments have strengths and can grow—is an integral part of social work practice.

Postmodernism and Critical Social Construction

A contemporary perspective that questions how we attain knowledge, how we value it, and how we distinguish belief from truth comes under the broad heading of **postmodernism.** Among other things, it invites examination of the cultural assumptions that underlie many of the arrangements of power and politics, and it tends to be critical of assumptions or theories that claim absolute or authoritative truth. To illustrate, the contention that "all people in the United States can get ahead if they work hard enough; therefore, all poor people are lazy" is an example of an assumption or belief that is asserted as truth. Postmodernism invites people to challenge the truth of such claims.

Social Construction   A useful postmodern perspective for understanding the social realities of the lives of the people served by social workers, **social construction** suggests that we all construct our realities based on our experiences in the social world, which occur within the context of culture, society, history, and language. This means that rather than being a product of a so-called objective external world, or the result of the individual mind, social realities are actually beliefs formed through social interchanges (usually starting with the family) that regulate how we learn to make sense of things and, often, to form judgments. For a simple example, when children experience people as good hearted and the world as a kind place throughout their youth, their adult view of reality often supports the belief that the world is a relatively decent place. This reality derives from the social experiences they encounter. On the other hand, when their social experiences tell them that the world is full of evil, hurtful people, their view of reality is often very different. This observation of how people decide what's true about their world is meaningful for social workers when they work with people who come from realities that are different from their own.

Deconstruction   Constructionist thinking opens the way to explore particular beliefs, such as the one that the world is a kind place, through a process of taking those beliefs apart to look at how they developed. This is called **deconstruction.** Through the process of deconstruction, you can explore the factors that helped these beliefs to arise and determine whose ideas had power, or dominance, and whose didn't. The following is an example of both social construction and deconstruction.

For many years in the 20th century it was a "reality" that grown people with severe disabilities were neither capable of negotiating nor entitled to engage in adult relationships, particularly sexual ones. Whether born of a protective desire to care for them as "children" (which also demonstrates how language can support a repressive idea) or an attempt to control genetic imperfections, these ideas promoted strong restrictions on such relationships. Institutions and community-based facilities went a long way toward trying to prevent relationships and sometimes even kept couples with disabilities from being together in the same room by themselves. Higher-level staff often used such terms such as *wrong* or *unnatural* in considering intimate liaisons between such couples. That particular social understanding and sense of reality contributed to the infamous practice of eugenics, which sought to eliminate the reproduction of people who were seen as genetically deficient.

As advocates for the rights of people with disabilities began to deconstruct and debunk the assumptions of the social construction that supported this callous practice, it became less acceptable. Some of the many assumptions made in this reality follow:

- People with severe disabilities are like children who shouldn't enter into adult relationships.

- People with severe disabilities are not adequate as human beings and should not have children.

- People with severe disabilities are not entitled to define their needs or desires.

- People with severe disabilities don't have the capacity for love.

This process of uncovering and questioning taken-for-granted ideas, as well as analyzing who had the influence to perpetuate them, is an example of deconstruction. In this case it points up assumptions that are not sustainable under scrutiny, and it demonstrates how such assumptions can harm a whole population of people whose entire lives were interpreted by the opinions of others. Although these assumptions are by no means extinct now, they were situated in a specific economic, historical, and cultural setting that is no longer dominant.

This concept of contextual setting, or **social location,** refers to the time, place, and prevailing ideas or discourse that influence standards, particularly about what is right or normal. The point here is not necessarily to reject the ideas that emerge within context (as, of course, all ideas do). It is rather to recognize such positions as attitudes or beliefs that arise in a certain context, rather than as absolute, moral truths for all situations and contexts (Freedman & Combs, 1996). Consider, for example, how a new social worker might have been judged and silenced if she or he had countered the so-called truth regarding people with disabilities and, based on human rights or social justice concerns, had objected to such social restrictions. Partly because most of us today have not occupied the same context in which these pejorative notions originated, we may now view such restrictive control of people with severe disabilities as both inhumane and oppressive. This current position is a long way from the "truth" reached by those who promoted the eugenics movement! You might consider which beliefs or customs are so strongly held in your own community or agency that deviance from them has significant professional or personal consequences and is interpreted morally.

For another horrendous example of social construction, in the pre–Civil War United States, when slavery was common in the South, there was a widely agreed-upon "reality" that Africans and African Americans were intellectually and socially inferior to Caucasians. This made them suitable possessions rather than peers. When this idea is questioned now on a political level (surely many had questioned it on social and moral levels), it becomes clear that it was an arrangement that benefited a certain group over other groups and empowered the dominant group—the slaveowners—to organize society to their advantage. It was not an external truth. The kind of questioning that exposes such phenomena often has the effect of freeing us from the many constraining ideas that limit the opportunities and visions, and sometimes the very lives, of the people that these ideas label as "other." Today you sometimes hear or read the term "social construction of race" as it describes slavery's legacy of hatred.

Social workers, therefore, are likely to question arrangements that bring harm to people and to be suspicious or wary of presumed expertise that denies people their own experience. For example, a social worker might advocate for an elderly person whose acute medical distress is being dismissed as insignificant by a physician. The worker, with support from a supervisor or others, may even need to challenge the adequacy of the medical care offered to the client. In this way the worker refutes the idea that any particular set of assumptions or positions is untouchable or can't be challenged. (In this case, there may be an assumption that all medical care provided through Medicaid is sufficient.) The worker operates on the idea that all beliefs, ideas, and arrangements can be respectfully questioned.

Likewise, in the contemporary climate, social workers are not likely to assume that they are experts on the experience of others, even though they may have had a lot of familiarity with a particular social issue, like poverty. They are more apt to commit themselves to the idea that there are "many ways of knowing" (Hartman, 1994) while they assume a position of "not knowing" (Anderson & Goolishian, 1992) or "cultural naiveté and respectful curiosity" (Laird, 1995) in exploring the needs and experiences of others. The poverty worker, then, does not assume she or he understands how any individual experiences poverty. Similarly, the worker with the elderly client doesn't assume she or he knows what the client's experience of physical pain is.

Critical Social Construction   The *critical* in **critical social construction** comes from a contemporary analysis of power, which recognizes that any social group can shape its beliefs to its own benefit at the expense of other groups (as, for example, white men have done for centuries in the Western world). The critical dimension then allows the examiner to question that kind of power arrangement on the grounds that many people's voices have been silenced or "subjugated" (Hartman, 1994) and that those who were able to arrange such systems as slavery had the power to **privilege**

The Social Work Library

Read Swigonski's article for a discussion on how to challenge privilege through Africentric practice.

Web Links

At the online learning center you can explore your own sense of privilege through Peggy McIntosh's "unpacking the knapsack" (1988) and you can identify those privileges that you enjoy.

themselves, while oppressing others. In this way the privileged group not only benefited from but also perpetuated the privilege by using their power to assert their beliefs, which came to be regarded as truth. One of the sad ironies of this view is that many groups today who benefit from privilege would not consciously choose such advantage, do not believe that they have any responsibility for it, and may even deny its existence (Diller, 1999; Swigonski, 1996). This is a difficult notion in social work. Although many white people would never consider themselves racist, they still benefit every day from the color of their skin (Bishop, 1994). Other groups who benefit from privilege, even though they might not seek or recognize this advantage, include people who are heterosexual, Christian, and able bodied.

One final, vivid, if also shameful, example of social construction to which we might apply our critical lens occurs within a more narrowly defined segment of the clinical practice world. For years many human service professionals in various disciplines have asserted that women who are beaten by their male partners are themselves pathological for allowing such aggression against them. In this construction of reality, battered women are seen as deficient in self-esteem or personality strength and therefore need therapy to change themselves. This "reality" was produced or created through the consensus of a very small and privileged group of people. The issues of power, aggression, and societal support for male violence were rarely even recognized and certainly not legitimized as they have been today in the field of domestic violence.

By looking critically at power relations and dominance in social work practice, you may come to understand that the "truths" developed over time may serve certain groups well but come at great cost to others. This realization has significant repercussions for social work practice, which will be addressed throughout the book.

The Social Work Library

For more on the philosophy of social work, read Weick's paper.

Complementary Aspects of the Theoretical Perspectives

Each of the four perspectives—social justice, human rights, the strengths perspective, and critical social construction—offers the student practitioner unique and sometimes complex challenges. In many respects they complement each other by putting a slightly different emphasis on the work that fits well with the other views. The strengths perspective, for example, is used in the service of bringing social justice to people who have experienced little of it. Human rights, in turn, may be seen as the moral grounding for undertaking justice-oriented work. The constructionist ideas regarding the influence of historical and cultural standpoints allow the worker to question previously unexamined ideas and approaches that marginalize people and characterize them as pathological or undeserving. Taken together these perspectives provide a comprehensive and compelling approach to social work.

STRAIGHT TALK ABOUT THE TRANSLATION OF PERSPECTIVES INTO PRACTICE

The relevance of theoretical perspectives to actual practice situations has always raised questions from students and social work educators. On the one hand, some of the frameworks and perspectives may seem abstract or far removed from, say, a homeless teenager, a destitute elder, or a politically active group of adults with psychiatric disabilities. Goldstein (1992) believes there is frequently little connection between practice and theory because theory has often reflected an ill-suited preoccupation with being scientific. On the other hand, when perspectives honor the experience of people, they can be critically important for how a social worker does her or his work. The approach that emerges must truly reflect the experiences of clients and their lives.

If you practiced the strengths perspective, for example, you would probably not criticize a resident in a psychiatric unit for his failures to remain compliant with his drug regimen. You might be more likely to ask him what went well for when he was home and what he thinks would be helpful in staying out of the hospital in the future. Such a line of questioning would affirm your assertion that he has capabilities and assets worth cultivating.

This kind of translation, though, is not generally easy to make. Even in a compatible setting of agency purpose, theoretical perspective, and style, it is often a challenge for students and workers to integrate their convictions into the work because the work is often framed by systems and structures that sometimes seem unfriendly and insurmountable. If the worker's perspective is not dominant in the setting in which the work is done—or if it is not dominant in the greater society—the task may be all the more difficult. For example, in most state psychiatric units it would generally be easier to adopt a pathology-based model grounded in an uncritical adherence to the *DSM* (that is, the *DSM* discourse) than to talk of human rights or strengths or critical social construction. Yet these ideas constitute the substance of the dialogue that active social workers need to take up, both with their clients and particularly with their colleagues (Dewees, 2002). This book will attempt wherever possible to link the perspective to practical recommendations for the work, while acknowledging this ongoing struggle of integrating theory and practice.

CONCLUSION

This chapter has presented several different ways to look at social work practice. Exploring practice as a set of activities, relationships, and discourses allows for many interpretations and emphases, some of which will be discussed in

Chapter 2. Traditional frameworks for thinking about social work practice may also be useful to you in your professional development if you employ them flexibly in contemporary contexts. By adopting some combination of the four explicit theoretical perspectives described here, you will prepare yourself to offer an empowering and liberating approach to people who have lived their lives in the margin. Although the challenge of translating these approaches into ethical, sustainable, effective work will always be present in your practice, it will also sustain your growth. Building on this frame, Chapter 2 moves on to look at social work's purposes, the tensions that have been a part of the social work discourse, and what we bring as individual practitioners and human beings to the work.

MAIN POINTS

- Social work practice is a set of activities, roles, and discourses.

- Three traditional ways to think about practice include (1) knowledge, values, and skills; (2) individual, group, family, organization, and community practice; and (3) the sequence of engaging, assessing, intervening, and disengaging/evaluating.

- Theoretical perspectives play a significant role in guiding practice activities. The four perspectives, or frames, taken up in this book are the social justice perspective, human rights perspective, strengths perspective, and critical social construction.

- The social justice perspective provides one frame for this book and addresses the manner in which resources are allocated.

- The human rights perspective is a frame that encompasses the conviction that all people have civil, political, social, economic, and cultural rights simply because they are human beings; it is associated with the UN's Universal Declaration of Human Rights.

- The strengths perspective is a practice approach that highlights and works with peoples' resilience and assets, honors their goals and dreams, and asserts that all communities possess resources.

- Critical social construction is a contemporary, postmodern frame based on the assertion that social truths are agreed-upon beliefs shaped in a common history and culture and perpetuated through assumptions, language, and stories. It also notes the power arrangements responsible for the prevalence of such truths.

* The translation of perspectives into practice is challenging and necessary for effective social work to maintain its mission, integrity, and consistency.

EXERCISES: PRACTICING SOCIAL WORK

Serving the Sanchez Family

Prepare for this exercise by exploring the Sanchez family interactive case study on the CD-ROM. Read the Introduction and familiarize yourself with how the program works by experimenting with the options and looking at the tasks of each of the four phases. Click on the Engage Tab, complete Tasks #1, 2, and 3, and imagine that the Sanchezes are people you are working with. Place yourself in the following scenario:

1. As an Immigration Service social worker you are assigned to Celia and Hector Sanchez as they receive their green cards on entering the federal amnesty program that allows them legal status. Your role is to help them understand their new rights and responsibilities.

2. What *specific* knowledge, values, and skills do you think would be particularly important for you to bring to your work with them? Identify at least one from each group. What hazards might result from emphasizing one category over the other two?

3. Considering the social justice issues involved in the family's resident alien status and how they are related to human rights, respond to the following:
   a. From your knowledge of human rights and the Sanchez family, identify two human rights that apply particularly to Hector and Celia as immigrants.
   b. From what you know of the two Covenants from 1966, which seems to be more completely honored in relationship to the Sanchez family as they live in the US?
   c. How might you expect that having a green card would impact the family?

4. Considering the consequences of different social work practice discourses,
   a. Describe how you think a social work discourse of strengths differs from a discourse of pathology when applied to the Sanchez family.
   b. Describe how you think the strengths-based worker would approach the family and what would the relationship and focus look like? Be as specific as possible.
   c. Describe how you think the discourse used in your field placement would look if applied to the Sanchez family?

EXERCISES: THE SOCIAL WORK LIBRARY

Read Swigonski's "Challenging Privilege through Africentric Practice" and think about how the phenomenon of privilege might play out in your work as an intern in your field agency. Answer the following questions:

1. Which aspects of privilege that Swigonski describes are most resonant to you?

2. Which are challenging to you?

3. Can the idea of "Africentric practice" be generalized to other groups?

4. Describe your particular standpoint and reflect on the effect it might have on your practice.

OTHER EXERCISES

Go to the interactive case study of the Sanchez family and explore the Ecolens. How does your field agency use these lenses? Is any one of them emphasized over others? If so, what implications does that have for your practice? Be prepared to discuss this in class.

Exploring the Practice Purpose

One April evening in 1914 is memorable because it brought a new and exciting sense of belonging to social work in Boston. It was Play Night . . . and the little theatre at Elizabeth Peabody House was crowded. The play was *Simple Simon and the Social Workers: A Social Diagnosis in Three Acts,* and the cast consisted of social workers and physicians, playing themselves and Mother Goose characters. I was a member of the chorus and had special reasons for being glad to be there.

Bertha Capen Reynolds, 1963, p. 13

SIMPLE SIMON, BY WAY OF REVIEW, IS THE NURSERY RHYME CHARACTER who meets up with a Pieman and tries to get a pie without paying for it. Reynolds, a classic social work practitioner and writer, recounts the action in this 1914 play:

Starting from the episode of Simon's encounter with the Pieman, the social workers assume there is something wrong with a boy who tries to get a pie for nothing. They rush him first to Massachusetts General Hospital, then the Associated Charities, the Psychopathic Hospital, a police station, and the Juvenile Court, posing the question of what they are to do with him. (p. 13)

Simon finally declares himself "a case" to Mother Goose, and the chorus enthusiastically concludes with "When hungry people beg for bread, we seldom pass them by, but human generosity is taxed to the utmost when they ask for pie" (p. 14).

As we consider further what social work practice entails and how it is understood in varying contexts, you may ask, What are social workers trying to accomplish? Is their purpose to make a case out of the Simons of this world? Is it to rid society of those who ask for free pie? This chapter looks at a number of answers that reflect both broad and narrow views of these questions. In addition, it explores some of the tensions, or pulls, that are part of social work practice. Many of these tensions are classic and have been part of the profession for many years. Others are more contemporary and have arisen out of current approaches and situations. All of them are likely to touch you as you embark on a career in social work. Finally, we will look at what you notice about your purposes, in what contexts, and with what implications.

HISTORICAL APPROACHES: BROAD AND NARROW VIEWS

As you might expect, this question of what social workers are trying to do generates a lot of different answers. The first sentence in the preamble to the National Association of Social Workers (NASW) *Code of Ethics* is quite direct in stating "the primary mission of the social work profession is to enhance human well-being and help meet the basic human needs of all people, with particular attention to the needs and empowerment of people who are vulnerable, oppressed, and living in poverty" (NASW, 1999). Social work practice is the "action to enhance and heal the social fabric" (Mattaini, 2001, p. 16). Although this wide vision is clear on one level, on another level it is open to interpretation because the purpose is stated so broadly and there are so many conceivable ways to achieve the goal.

System-Defined Roles, Methods, and End Points

Narrow views of social work's purpose include such systems-defined efforts as mental health, income maintenance, and child welfare. Unfortunately for the profession, many members of the general public may still equate the social work profession with one or more of those very particular arenas, without recognizing that they are examples of a much greater purpose. I once began a field internship at a community child welfare agency and was thoroughly chagrined at the label of "State Lady" given to me by one of the mothers I was working with. "State Lady" referred to the fact that child protection is under the auspices of the state government, and the underlying message was that such "ladies" who worked for the state had the power to take away one's children, and probably would. I had to do a fair amount of work to change that image!

Other highly specific views of purpose are related to method, such as the facilitation of a problem-solving process or the elimination of a problems focus such as occurs in the strengths perspective. Behavioral and cognitive change are other examples of specialized focal points to answer the question What are we trying to accomplish? as are such goals as adaptation or sobriety or a clean criminal record. Although these end points are real examples of social work purposes, they are embedded in the deeper and broader mission that Mattaini describes and are therefore specific examples of the larger vision.

Social Location

Another perspective on social work's purpose, which is consistent with social construction, comes from the idea of the social location, or context, of workers and theorists at any particular time. This concept was introduced in Chapter 1 as it affected ideas about people with disabilities. The same idea also applies to theorists. A look at the dates and physical locations of the authors you read may shed light on their messages. For example, a university-based, academic social work educator writing in 2004 is likely to have a very different focus, or purpose, from that of a rural, grass-roots community organizer in 1930. Likewise, workers in 2004 have different concerns from those of practitioners in 1944. Even in 1963, after the passage of nearly 50 years, Reynolds remarks that the sentiments of the chorus in the 1914 Simple Simon drama seemed "something of a shock" and "repellent" (p. 15). Because social work is a living profession that deals with people in their environments, and is itself rooted in a sociohistorical context, its purpose and mission not only change over time but also vary considerably in the same time across situations and settings.

For another example of the influence of social location on social work's purpose, this time within social work education, we can look at Perlman's work on problem solving. Introduced in 1957, her ideas represented one of the first social work theories about practice. Perlman's theory speaks to the cognitive capacity of people to meet their needs and overcome obstacles. By her own account, Perlman's work was a response made in "rebellion" (Turner & Jaco, 1996, p. 505) against the negative, deterministic views of people as dysfunctional and permanently problem ridden that emerged from the Freudian ethos popular in the early 1950s. Perlman was interested in tapping into people's strengths and what she saw as a natural capacity to address the obstacles that got in their way. Today, the theory's emphasis on problems may seem onerous, but deconstructing the evolution of the theory uncovers similarities to the contemporary focus on capacity and resilience, as in the strengths perspective.

Another example of the importance of context in theory development and purpose emerges in the history of the **Life Model**. This model, which was developed by Germain and Gitterman in the 1970s, adopts an ecological metaphor that emphasizes the person/environment fit in a reciprocal, dynamic ecosystem mediating between the individual and the various environments ("habitats" and "niches") that she or he occupies. Its original focus was on the integration of methods, which until then had largely been split into the categories of individual, group, family, organization, and community. As a unifying scheme, this model stressed adaptation, often most needed during life transitions, as an important area for work. By the authors' own account, they did not attempt to address the connection between client needs and social policy, which was an area they believed needed to be "actively pursued" (Germain & Gitterman, 1980, p. *xi*) in the future.

In spite of its groundbreaking shift toward integration of methods, the model also became the target of some avid criticism by feminist (Gould, 1987) and other theorists who faulted its emphasis on adaptation as a goal, without adequate consideration of the need for effective policies to mitigate the actual life experiences of less visible populations, such as women who are battered. Adaptation as a goal has significantly problematic implications when the issues being addressed are oppressive phenomena such as violence or poverty. Should clients adapt to being beaten? Or poor?

The later rendition of the expanded model (Germain & Gitterman, 1996) picks up the thread of the relationship between client needs and social policy that was identified in the first edition and reflects the practice context of the mid-1990s, which had changed significantly since the 1970s. The revised model deals more thoroughly with oppression and the need for more structural interventions that include organizational and legislative efforts when appropriate. In this way, then, the *critical* part of the critical social constructionist examination of who was included and who was not in theory making (in this example, battered women or the poor) uncovered the voices of those not represented adequately in the earlier perspective. In another age, neither violence against women nor poverty would have gained this sort of accountability as serious public issues. The shifting social and intellectual environment shapes ideas about what the purpose of the work is and gives it new direction.

TENSIONS IN SOCIAL WORK PRACTICE

Ideas about the purpose of social work practice are subject not only to historical and cultural variables, but also to differing program and institutional environments. The profession has struggled almost since its inception with several sets of tensions that have sometimes seemed to obscure its identity. Several of these tensions are discussed here, beginning with the apparently conflicting roles of the worker as an agent of social control and an advocate of social change.

Social Control and Social Change

In my experience, students tend to notice early in their studies of social work practice that there is an underlying tension between social work's role in many regulatory agencies and its charge to engage in social change. This is because of the placement of social work as a profession operating within, and supported by, the same society it is also asked to change. Some of the regulatory bodies in which social workers practice, such as child protection, criminal justice, and mental health, carry an authoritative sanction for **social control**. In some circumstances this control seems at odds, sometimes drastically, with social work's commitment to **social change**, a process in which social workers attempt to alter basic social structures. These two functions, control and change, are not inherently irreconcilable, but the ways in which they play out in their respective practice arenas tend to make them appear incompatible at times. Let us consider two examples here.

The Worker's Location   After graduating from college, Maria got her first job as a practitioner in a mental health program. As a case manager, she coordinated the services that her clients needed in order to become full members of the community. She was well versed in social work practice intervention theories pertaining to people with mental health challenges, and she had completed an internship at the state hospital in her community. She also had some personal experience with the mental health system because her uncle had been hospitalized with schizophrenia for several years when he was a young man. Some of his experiences inspired her to think about changing the system to be more responsive to people with mental illnesses. She had pictured herself championing the rights of people to decide for themselves whether they took medication and to advocate for changes when the system seemed hurtful to clients.

Maria eagerly entered her new job and experienced many of the joys and some of the difficulties of case management work in a mental health setting. She made sure her clients had access to the physical and mental health services they needed. She arranged for vocational rehabilitation or treatment for alcohol abuse when appropriate. She encouraged her clients to get regular exercise and to participate in recreational activities. She helped settle landlord disputes and introduced her clients to religious or spiritual groups. When she received several cases at once, she found she had little time to attend to some details she hadn't thought about before, such as whether her clients were going to the appointments that were ordered and whether their conduct in the community was acceptable. The issue regarding compliance with medication also surfaced frequently.

After several months, Maria was assigned to a young woman who stopped taking the medications prescribed for her the day she left the hospital and began using recreational drugs, in violation of the court order that she had received upon discharge. After a brief period, the woman came to the attention of townspeople and merchants because she was disorderly in public places and appeared to be hallucinating. The agency received several calls about her. Maria found herself ensnared in her role (of control) as agency social worker, who needed to abide by legal restrictions and ensure the system's view of her client's well-being. At the same time she wondered whether these authoritative rules were responsive to her client's particular needs. Her supervisor thought Maria needed to initiate the process in her state by which the court would order her client back to a hearing because she was violating her conditions; this would likely result in an order for involuntary medication.

Maria's experience with her uncle resonated in her mind: He had experienced horrible side effects from prescribed medications and refused to take them consistently as prescribed. Maria had thought she would advocate for more humane approaches regarding compliance, or make a case for being able to work much more extensively (beyond the 20 minutes she had every two weeks) with her client to strategize an alternative approach to the situation. Yet in the context of her job it was impossible for her to see a way to do that. Furthermore, she saw from another perspective the consequences of her client's not taking her medication and wondered if coercion were the only way out after all. The situation looked different to her now because she was in the middle of a difficult context in which resources were limited, the dynamics looked more complicated than she had originally thought, and she was harried in meeting the needs of a large caseload. Her original concerns for social change—in this case to work for improved institutional responses—were diverted by the pressures and realities of the working context, which tended to compromise her original standpoint.

The point here is not that Maria was prohibited from working for social change or that societal institutions are necessarily evil (neither is likely in this scenario). Rather, the issue is that it is difficult to be invested with the power of social control, to work in a stressed setting in which this power is exercised, and to remain committed to changing that very setting at the same time. This book argues that social workers need to do just that in spite of the challenges. Consider that if Maria were successful in achieving the institutional responses she was seeking (in this case, a different approach to forced treatment), she might work herself out of a job. In fact, I once had an instructor in social work school who insisted that our own unemployment should be the very aim of all our work!

The Profession's Ethics   Another brief example of the tension between social control and social change concerns the profession's ethics. In the early development of social work practice, the profession went through what is called "the morality period" (Reamer, 1998, p. 488). During this period, in the late 1800s, social work evolved from a loose organization of charities into a profession. It was also a time of large-scale European immigration to the United States, which generated many tumultuous client and societal scenarios. The profession at that time was highly concerned with the morals of its clients and much less concerned with its own morals. Poverty was widespread among the immigrant groups, and many established citizens attributed this poverty to the values and lifestyles of the immigrants themselves (another example of a social construction). Unfortunately, not all social workers were free from this kind of thinking. Consequently, judgmental responses and efforts to change people's habits, "shiftless ways" (p. 489), and sometimes even food traditions, cultural customs, and childbearing norms were common and seldom questioned by the profession itself.

Social work history often credits Jane Addams with the breakdown of this kind of thinking as social workers began to consider how they could respect people's customs and cultural traditions while still helping them gain access to the structural resources that would help them thrive. As workers' approaches shifted toward accepting clients "where they are," the profession directed some of its interest in control to its own conduct and engaged in closer scrutiny of its own ethics. The tension between examining clients' ethics and the profession's ethics is not obsolete, however. In fact, you probably have come into contact with workers who struggle with a client's morals while minimizing the importance of their own assumptions and biases. This is not always easy to avoid, as social workers become engaged in the lives of people who may carry out their daily activities in ways that seem harmful or who have differing judgments, with significant consequences, regarding what is right or acceptable.

The Social Work Library

For another perspective on the dynamic between social control and social change, read Hayne's article.

Acceptance and Change

Another related tension involves the degree to which the goal of social work is change, either in individual or environmental work, or acceptance, in some situations, of the client's status as "good enough." As you would expect, the particular circumstances and settings associated with each situation strongly influence the worker's approach to this issue. In fact, although the pull between acceptance and change occupies a place in the historical tensions of the profession, it may prove to be so contextually influenced that it will never be fully put to rest as long as individuals continue to evaluate social contexts, based on their own idiosyncrasies, in different ways. The following sections explore some views relating to this tension.

Adjustment and Challenge   Abramowitz (1998) writes about the tension between "adjusting people and programs to circumstances or challenging the *status quo*." The question of whether social work's mission is to do one or the other must be answered in context according to how the social justice factors play out. For example, many practitioners might support a female client who feels angry, distressed, and overburdened in a marital relationship and struggles with the sociological realities of contemporary families. These realities might include the expectations of partners, employers, and society at large that most mothers, even those working full time outside the home, should assume more responsibility than fathers for child care and home life. In this situation the worker would offer support in the classic sense of attempting to bolster the client's existing coping

The Social Work Library

Read Abramowitz's article for an activist's view on social work and social reform.

mechanisms rather than facilitating a change in the basic self. Support might involve helping the client to assess the relative costs, to herself and her children, of remaining in the relationship, the contributions the relationship makes to her overall satisfaction, and the benefits she and her children gain from the arrangement.

Many women clients and their social workers might see this scenario as an example of a transitional, cultural struggle occurring on the road to more equitable gender relationships within society. In short, if the client were generally managing the relationship and had little interest in disrupting it, the worker might encourage her to make the best of the situation. The worker (who could possibly see herself in the same scenario) might offer suggestions for child care respite, recreation, or self-care that would help mitigate the client's sense of injustice in the arrangement, but not address an overall change in a significant or structural way.

Other clients and practitioners would respond differently. They might not be willing to wait until parenting and homemaking become more equitable but instead might demand or at least work for substantial change, both within the marriage and in the larger society. The possible standpoints that either client or practitioners take are not polarized but can be thought of as situated on a continuum. This means that both client and practitioner may wish for large-scale social change, and both may believe that they need personally to make peace with what seems to be the current reality of an individual situation. The question is whether their respective positions are compatible enough so they can agree on the goal of the work. More than one practitioner has lost clients because of her or his zeal to change a situation that the client really wants to learn to accept (and, of course, vice versa). The critical construction–oriented worker would want to address these issues of inequity on a larger societal level in any case.

The Crossed Line   As the stakes get higher, the scenario becomes ever more complicated. As we discussed earlier, the idea of accepting and adapting to a familial situation that involves, for example, beating and degradation changes the situation dramatically for most practitioners. For some (probably most) practitioners, in situations characterized by significant physical or verbal abuses, acceptance is no longer an option. Other practitioners may suggest that the way to overcome this kind of relationship stress is through intensified efforts at working through its internal dynamics in couples counseling or other interpersonal work rather than through overt activism. The literature on intimate partner violence reflects this struggle, with many writers remaining adamant that an abused woman must separate herself from the threat of danger before working on the relationship in counseling with her partner, and others suggesting that practitioners need to respond to whatever opening is available, even if the woman cannot or will not separate from her partner. This is a controversial issue, in part because of the differences in what individuals or groups consider tolerable and the larger or political ramifications of inequitable relationships.

Clinical and Nonclinical Emphases

Yet another tension that underlies social work practice involves the question of whether practitioners should focus primarily on clinical or nonclinical work. This question has intrigued (and sometimes plagued) the profession, particularly in recent years, partly because the word *clinical* has many meanings, and also because it often seems to represent a code for a medically based private practice model that involves diagnosis, managed care, and the like. Another view associates *clinical* with cold, calculated, stiff, or impersonal interchanges that are driven by the expert and received by the patient. For some practitioners, the word simply means careful interactions in which the worker is paying particular attention to what she or he says or does.

In this book, **clinical work** means social work with individuals, groups, and/or families that is not only **direct practice**, or **direct work** (face-to-face) but also designed to change behaviors, solve problems, or resolve emotional or psychological issues (Sands, 2001). For example, working individually with a young woman to address her self-harming behavior can be thought of as clinical. Facilitating a series of groups for children who have experienced the death of a parent is another example. Assisting a family to redefine the communication patterns among its members is also clinical practice. Clinical work can extend into many practice arenas such as mental health, substance abuse, school social work, and some child welfare work. Some state social work licenses define clinical work explicitly and require a master's degree, but this varies greatly across the country. Also, in some of these practice areas, additional or different credentials (for example, an addictions certificate for substance abuse work) may be necessary.

Nonclinical work usually implies that the work addresses the environment. Johnson (1998) calls this indirect work (or practice) and affirms it as social work's "uncelebrated strength" (p. 323). She describes **indirect work** (or **indirect practice**) as the practitioner's involvement in the environments of clients and with others in collaborative service of that environment. She argues for both concrete, tangible assistance, such as clothing, toys for children, or groceries, and also for assistance that helps to modify the attitudes or behaviors of others who play a significant role in the environment.

This kind of environmental modification might also extend to include work that is more political or engaged in social reform efforts. These efforts involve such activities as working for improved institutional responses or changing or supporting laws, policies, and social structures relating to class, gender, ability, and cultural ethnicity. This kind of work is also called **policy practice**, because it focuses specifically on making policies more responsive to client needs and rights. By virtue of this emphasis on the personal or political environment, non-clinical work focuses less on the internal dynamics of an individual's experience and more on opportunity and change.

An exploration of the tension between clinical and nonclinical purposes could go in many directions. You have probably experienced the tension already in your field internship or in a practice situation. It is one of those pseudo-dichotomies that probably don't serve the profession well. Nevertheless, it is unlikely to fade from view. Perhaps the thoughtful and principled efforts made to connect the approaches are the most fortunate product of the debate. The following discussion considers some dimensions of this tension.

Developmental Socialization and Resocialization   The late Harry Specht, a social work policy educator, distinguished between what he called developmental socialization and resocialization (Specht, 1990). He defined **developmental socialization** as the attempt, through providing support, information, and opportunities, to help people enhance their environments by making the most of their roles. It also involves confronting obstacles such as abuse or oppression that get in the way of people's attempts to make the most of their roles. To Specht, developmental socialization was the natural domain of social work, and basically nonclinical. In contrast, Specht defined **resocialization** as the attempt to help people with feelings and inner perceptions that related primarily to the self. He thought that psychotherapeutic approaches associated with psychology and psychiatry, rather than social work, should deal with such issues. Significantly, Specht argued that social work had been seduced from its original mission by clinical psychotherapy, which many people characterize as a higher-status activity and with which social work has flirted since the Freudian movement began in the 1920s. As an advocate for an emphasis on the social environment, rather than inner psychological life, Specht called for social work to build its professional core in public, rather than private, services and institutions and to replace all its clinical training with adult education, community work, and group work. His last major publication, written with Mark Courtney and published in 1995, was tellingly called *Unfaithful Angels: How Social Work Has Abandoned Its Mission.*

Many social workers are heavily committed to the kind of work that Specht rejects as inappropriate. They see social work as providing useful perspectives for dealing with clinical, interactional, interpersonal, and sometimes intrapersonal issues. Many practitioners view these perspectives as appropriate tools in the realms of individual counseling, family intervention, and a host of other areas that might be called clinical, or therapeutic. This location of social work's appropriate domain has been a prevalent controversy since Mary Richmond's day. In more recent times, some workers who are committed to environmental or structural intervention have seen the movement to license social workers as a negative continuation of the move into professionalism, which in this context usually means individual psychotherapy and, often, private-pay practice.

The perceived polarity between clinical and nonclinical practice is an obstacle in contemporary social work. You have already seen that the *Code of Ethics* requires that social workers engage in work that supports socially equitable allocations of opportunity, which by definition is environmental as well as political. When clinical practice focuses entirely on individual issues and ignores or excludes the nonclinical work of advocacy and power analysis inherent in the pursuit of social justice, it comes into conflict with the *Code*. The proximity of some clinical practice settings (such as mental health and substance abuse) to the medical world and its requirements for individualized, decontextualized labels of pathology sometimes discourages or diverts workers from entering into social justice pursuits. You saw that scenario with Maria, earlier in this chapter, as she became socialized into the institution that employed her and distracted from her original values.

Integrating Approaches Fortunately, this particular debate, between an individual, clinical focus and a nonclinical, environmental focus, also has its share of reconcilers—social work educators and practitioners who believe that they can resolve this tension. For example, Haynes (1998) argues that the breadth of social work's capacity for intervention as well as its historical loyalties to both the individual and to the class advocacy pursuits of the environment actually constitute its strength and don't require an either/or resolution. She does assert, however, that social work must not abandon its commitments to environmental social action and social change or lose sight of its original mission to assist people with disadvantages, wherever that effort might lead. Let us look at some current, more specific examples of this kind of integration.

There are many contemporary and generally complementary efforts to connect clinical practice with social justice issues. We'll look at only a few here. One approach expands the definition of clinical work to include "case management, advocacy, teamwork, mediation, and prevention roles, as well as therapeutic and counseling roles" (Swenson, 1998, p. 527). The clinician also uses self-reflection to consider her or his privilege. This in turn addresses the worker's accountability to clients, clearly an important component of a social justice approach.

A more politically oriented feminist view challenges clinical social work to connect the clinical and nonclinical perspectives in the field of domestic violence (Dietz, 2000) and family services (Parker, 2003). This perspective is emphatic that in order for clinical practice with survivors of abuse or with families to be truly useful, it must deal expressly with power issues, and to do that it must be explicit in addressing the survivor's and families' situations politically

The Social Work Library

To explore the relationship between social justice and clinical practice, read the full text of Swenson's article.

through empowerment. **Empowerment** here refers to a specific approach that combines both individual growth and support with social action and political activity in the environment (Lee, 1996; Simon, 1994). The challenge to clinical work is to abandon its usual discourse in which the violence is diagnosed and attributed to an internal state of the survivor.

Another example of an interesting way to address the issue of clinical practice and nonclinical pursuit of social justice occurs in "Just Therapy," an approach developed at the Family Centre in New Zealand. Using narrative approaches in individual and family work (see Chapter 7), the Centre's founders clearly state that they must address in otherwise clinical therapy the societal injustices they encounter. The issues that individuals and families bring to the work are always put into the contextual arena of the social and power relations in the client's experience.

New Zealand has three major ethnic groups: a privileged white population from European stock who arrived in the late 18th century, called the Pakeha (Waldegrave, 1990, p. 9); the native Maori (aboriginal peoples); and relocated Samoan Islanders. A long history of racial and ethnic conflict has resulted in the separation of the Maoris from their lands, a loss of their political and personal self-determination, and constraints on their cultural practices. The organizational structure of the Family Centre includes representatives of all three cultural groups, and they are accountable to one another in their work. If, for example, a non-Maori therapist works with a Maori family, that therapist seeks consultation from the Maori members of the group. In this consideration, the work explicitly recognizes the social injustices that frequently occur in the world of the ethnically different and is, therefore, political within a clinical setting.

In addition to reconciling clinical and nonclinical approaches through expanding the definition of clinical, the profession has also developed innovative conceptions of the person in environment. For example, looking at "human actors as co-constructors of, not just interactors within, their social environments" (Kondrat, 2002, p. 435) allows for human **agency,** which is a person's ability to affect her or his own circumstances. In this view, people shape their environments, which in turn (or recursively) influence them. For example, you are a member of a community, and as such, you respond to other members of the community. However, you also take a part in creating your community, a process that goes beyond simply reacting to various individuals. Here the relationship is likened to the way a dancer participates in the ballet or a football player in the game (Kondrat, 2002, p. 439). This position is consistent with social construction, and it emphasizes the power of agency that human beings exercise in creating their social locations. By focusing on the client as co-constructor of the environment, this approach blurs the distinction between clinical work with the person and nonclinical work with the environment.

Finally, another highly integrative model bridges individual, clinical work and environmental practice concerns through the use of deconstruction (Vodde & Gallant, 2002). In this conceptualization the worker moves from helping the client conquer the internal ramifications of the problem (such as clinical depression) to helping the client connect with others who are experiencing the same kind of oppression but resist it. Georgia's story will help demonstrate many of these points.

Georgia is a 25-year-old woman from the southern United States. She has come to a large city in the Midwest to see a different world and another part of the country. Very early in her stay, she met and fell in love with Tom, a native midwesterner. Georgia and Tom developed a serious relationship, and Georgia moved into his apartment when she discovered that she was pregnant. Things didn't go well for Georgia from that time on. Tom began to resent her interest in the coming baby, and at times he was verbally abusive, insulting her southern background and degrading every personal aspect he could find wrong with her. He then started to be rough with her when they had any difference of opinion. Eventually he began to shove her into the wall, slap her, and kick at her belly. Georgia was disillusioned and frightened both for her own safety and her baby's. She could not understand how she had failed Tom so badly, or what she had done to become so disgusting to him, or how she had become so hard for him to be around.

When Georgia finally believed she could no longer manage this situation, she contacted a local women's shelter. She was devastated. By this time she believed herself to be entirely worthless and thoroughly unlovable. Tom had made it clear to her how ugly and stupid she was. Georgia was at a very low point and was fearful for her future.

Georgia's worker, over time and with a lot of patient skills, helped her to see that Tom's battering was not a function of her personality or unworthiness but rather of his own impulses. Therefore, Tom, and not Georgia, was responsible for Tom's abusive behavior. With support, Georgia began to regain her sense of worth and resilience and to feel stronger about her own capacities. Gradually she felt less in need of intense work on her esteem. She began to explore how our society supports violence. She met with other women at the shelter and joined in their resistance to societal violence through advocating for education in the schools and providing personal testimonies to groups of women who requested them.

This work empowered Georgia by enabling her to take control of her own emotions while addressing an environmental issue in a meaningful manner. It demonstrates the kind of integrated approaches described earlier that address both clinical issues and social justice concerns. The approach spans the inner psychological turmoil that Georgia experienced as it began to become more political. Finally, it fostered Georgia's role as co-constructor of her environment. In this way the work has gone from an individual clinical focus to a nonclinical, integrated political focus without sacrificing either as each supports the other.

Experts and Shared Power

The relationship between the ideas of expertise and shared power creates a particularly contemporary tension within the social work profession. The history and development of both the educational and professional systems in U.S. culture have revolved around the idea of expertise, or **expert knowledge.** We get ourselves educated in professional programs with the idea that we will become respected members of a profession in which there are others with the same or similar expertise. In fact, when we do not sense the authority of that expertise, we may find ourselves doubtful or uncomfortable.

In contrast, the idea of shared power is relatively recent in professional culture and challenges the claims of expert-power. In **shared power,** the individual is the expert on her or his life, culture, dreams, experience, and goals. This creates a mandate in the work for practitioners to assume power only over limited activities in which they are trained while the client retains the power to direct the work. For example, if you were working in a college setting as an advocate for an African American student who experienced discrimination in housing options on campus, you might claim expertise on the process of advocacy, but your client would retain control regarding which issues required your focus and what goals might be met through the advocacy. In this way, the power is shared. Let us explore the dynamics of this tension more fully.

Like several of the sets of tensions discussed here, this one could expand to many levels and many books! Furthermore, shifting our views of our expertise is not easy; we are socialized to value expertise, and therefore, we may interpret our own value and contributions through its lens. Given the competition that sometimes develops between complex specialization on the one hand and client empowerment on the other, this tension is likely to persist.

The Metaphor of Professional Expertise   Consider how you would feel if you discovered that the dentist about to do a root canal procedure in your mouth was not really expert in the procedure but thought she would share the power of the experience with you. Our world is so highly complex that we believe that by necessity we must specialize. Having done that, we come to trust the expertise of specialists, both others' and our own. The resulting "faith" that is required sometimes obliterates our sense of participation in the service. For another example, many of us blindly agree to any treatment for, say, a migraine headache, that our physician might recommend because we assume that migraine headaches are too complicated for us to understand. As we trust the expertise of the physician, we abdicate any role in decisions about the treatment.

In these examples, you probably see that we, as professionals, value expertise. The examples relate to physiological, medical processes (the root canal and the migraine) and not to primarily social processes. We feel excluded from the advances in technology associated with dentistry and medicine and so defer to the expertise of the professionals who presumably possess the requisite knowledge. Expertise, then, is usually limited to narrow, highly specialized processes that often involve the skilled manipulations of technology.

Social work is, by its very nature, much more generally about people, their relationships, and the human condition. Yet it is tempting to believe that social workers are experts on *particular* people and relationships. Workers may even find that some people coming to them for help *want* them to be expert on the totality of their lives in the way that we want the dentist to be an expert on our mouths or the physician on our heads. Like much of our culture, the profession has been caught up in the status and seeming legitimacy of being scientific and thus tends to take on the same metaphors of expertise. Social workers have spent decades trying to "prove" the effectiveness of their interventions, and have fought for professional prestige through this "expert" label. Root canals are not the stuff of social work, however, and workers have come to recognize that the expertise on the experience of any particular relationship, oppression, or phenomenological event belongs to the person who has lived it.

Quiet Voices Made Audible   In the contemporary world, many strong client voices in the realm of human service interchanges, situations, and relationships have made it known that adopting the role of expert is not necessarily helpful, particularly when it obscures their own ownership or participation in the work. Social workers recognize the disillusionment and, sometimes, anger in the voices of people—for example, people with disabilities, women, and people of color—who have experienced service systems that rely on expertise as humiliating, insulting, or patronizing. The development of many contemporary social work perspectives reflects this reality in their deliberate attempt to reduce the centrality of expertise and to substitute an enhanced commitment to partnership, or shared power.

Minimization of Distance   Such theoretical perspectives as the strengths perspective, nearly all feminist approaches, and empowerment approaches make a conscious effort to minimize the rigid boundaries of expertise between worker and client. The client is seen as the expert on her or his life, whereas the worker is seen as skilled in various arenas that will help the client get to a client-defined destination. This shift is played out in practice approaches that involve visiting clients' homes or meeting in community facilities like coffee shops and public parks. These approaches emphasize client comfort in familiar surroundings, in contrast to the 50-minute clinical hour in the agency office, which tends to send a message of worker authority and increased distance between worker and client. Freud used to stand behind his patients, who would lie on a couch and therefore couldn't even see his face. A lot has changed in our views on expertise!

This trend toward more fluid relationships is not a casual manifestation of 21st-century culture. It represents a deliberate shift in thinking and a transformation of values. For some theoreticians it signals a new way to respect the experiences and views of people who previously had never been closely listened to. For others it is a critical response to a power analysis that results in the elimination of abusive or oppressive authority relationships. In broader terms, this shift to a more egalitarian relationship affirms that many people have not experienced professionally assumed expertise about their own lives as very helpful.

These approaches do not suggest that social work has or should have no power. Rather, they affirm the right of the client to enter into a relationship of shared power in which the assets of both the client and the worker are recognized, valued, and taken into account. Accordingly, in this conception, one person does not have power over the other; rather, a collective power is facilitated through sharing.

One of many Native American views of shared power has much to offer contemporary practitioners (Lowery & Mattaini, 2001). This approach conceptualizes shared power as shared responsibility allocated according to the particular strengths of each participant. It does not mean equality of responsibility, but recognizes that skill levels differ and emphasizes the worth of all contributions. Social workers are responsible for maintaining professional ethics, and clients are responsible for making changes in their lives. For example, in a situation of client substance abuse, social workers would ask questions like, "How does your drinking affect your children?" rather than making a statement such as, "You need to quit your drinking" (p. 116). The relationship created by this approach discourages hierarchies in the client-worker relationship and encourages a sense of joint investment in both the process and the results.

Global Citizenship and the Local Community

The final tension that we will consider—the pull between local and global investments of effort—is probably more relevant for social work practitioners today than it has ever been. Traditionally, U.S. social workers have carried out most of their activities in local or neighborhood contexts and have regarded global developments as remote, if not irrelevant. The social and cultural history, geography, and resource wealth of the United States have all contributed to national and professional insularity. Some believe that the tendency of people in the United States to evaluate their own experience as the most important has added to the "elusiveness" of a global perspective (Ramanathan & Link, 1999, p. 222). The tendency to judge U.S. culture as preferable is shaped by and reflected in such devaluing language as "third world" or "underdeveloped" that is almost exclusively based on the U.S.-defined dimensions of economy in any given culture. For example, as Ramanathan and Link point out, gross national product as a single indicator of development disregards quality-of-life indicators, such as death from handguns or domestic violence, as well as the contributions of millions of women who work without getting paid. Traditional Western markers are primarily limited to economic assets that are important for all people but are not the totality of life for any person. The visual perspective on the world demonstrated in the map in Exhibit 2.1 and your own response to it might surprise you.

Globalization is a complex of economic, social, and technological processes that have resulted in the formation of a single world community in which we are all citizens. Concern with globalization among students and others interested in international politics has been building for several years. The events of and since September 11, 2001, have probably confirmed that response among many citizens of the United States. We have begun to sense that the world has become very small and that the distinctions between a nearby community and a village in Afghanistan are at least partially artificial. At the least we are now more aware that events occurring across the world affect our own lives. Many of us have seen, directly or indirectly, how the political or social actions of one country influence people in other countries. We have also observed that

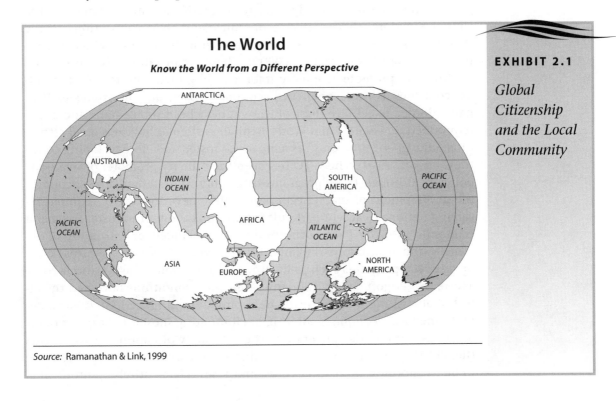

The World

Know the World from a Different Perspective

ANTARCTICA

AUSTRALIA

INDIAN OCEAN

SOUTH AMERICA

PACIFIC OCEAN

PACIFIC OCEAN

AFRICA

ATLANTIC OCEAN

ASIA

EUROPE

NORTH AMERICA

EXHIBIT 2.1

Global Citizenship and the Local Community

Source: Ramanathan & Link, 1999

international occurrences, such as refugee movements, have a direct and compelling influence on the environment and practice of social work at home and require workers to develop new skills and devise new perspectives (Asamoah, Healy & Mayadas, 1997). Finally, we have seen that social problems like AIDS, homelessness, neglect and exploitation of children, poverty, violence, and epidemic infections are worldwide issues that know no national borders.

Our growing awareness of globalization also leads us to recognize an economic process that has been under way a long time, most dramatically since World War II. You may have traveled yourself or heard of others who have traveled outside the United States and marveled at the Coca-Cola signs in Bangkok or Pizza Huts in Manila. These are not just amusing indicators that everyone loves U.S. junk food. Rather, they are signals of U.S. dominance of many world markets. Further, the **outsourcing** of many U.S. jobs to countries in which much cheaper labor can be located has resulted in high rates of unemployment at home as well as exploitation abroad. Yet many U.S.- and other Western-based companies are thriving. These dimensions of globalization are part of the reality of expanding international trade in the **Global South** (Link & Ramanathan, 1999, p. 1), which is a more accurate and respectful term for the nations of the southern hemisphere that have also been called third world or developing countries.

The United States as Everywhere   Since the end of World War II, economic globalization has been closely intertwined with the United States and the United Kingdom, their market economies, and their connections to the World Bank, the International Monetary Fund (IMF), and—since 1995—the World Trade Organization (WTO). These organizations were originally instituted to promote economic stability and growth and to help individual countries as they experience economic crises, but the strategies they have adopted to achieve these objectives have been problematic and counterproductive. The IMF and World Bank in particular have designed "structural adjustment programs" as a means to foster trade in developing countries (Prigoff, 1999). The WTO has been the primary promoter of free trade policies. Although these programs ostensibly were designed to encourage the development of market economies, they have frequently required receiving nations to accept particular conditions thought to foster trade and economic growth. These conditions have included privatization of resources and restrictions on imports and exports, as well as cutbacks in many social programs such as health, education, and housing and income assistance (Prigoff, 1999). In many cases these conditions have had the effect of abolishing welfare entitlement programs and social safety nets, debilitating local economies, altering or eliminating substantial aspects of indigenous ways of life, and eroding the autonomy of national governments (Ife, 2001). In their place, large multinational corporations have been free to build enormous industries whose purposes relate entirely to profit. It is estimated that 85 percent of the world's income is controlled by the wealthiest 20 percent of the population (Crosby & Van Soest, 1997), with women and children bearing the largest share of the inequality.

Globalization policies have been associated with a substantial increase in worldwide poverty, misery, violence, HIV/AIDS cases, drug addiction, and economic stratification (to name a few), as well as the exploitation of the land and other important environmental resources. You will recognize these concerns as common to the United States as well. In such a context, social work as a profession needs to develop models of understanding that go beyond the narrow periphery of a privileged vision and consider its general way of doing business. For example, social workers must prepare "to work with the diverse populations in this country and to understand the culture, the needs, and the experiences of new immigrants and refugees" (Hartman, 1994, p. 69). Further, a strong case can be made for U.S. social workers to learn from global experience that the historical and persistent interest in remedial works (individual treatment) for curative purposes is simply not an affordable strategy, either financially or socially, especially in countries whose major goals are social and economic development (Midgley, 1999). Midgley calls for social work to incorporate the social development perspective as "a process of planned social change designed to promote the well-being of the population as a whole in conjunction with the process of economic development" (Midgley, 1995, p. 25). We will explore the tension between the global society and local development issues in greater detail in Chapter 10.

The Legacy and the Challenge   A commitment to reciprocity, interdependence, and human rights practice requires more than a passing interest in the developments we read about every morning in the newspaper. The implications for social work practice are immense across the world. They are likely to become greater and more critical in your practice lifetimes and also to influence the way U.S. social work does business (Finn & Jacobson, 2003). Ironically, increased localization has been one of the important responses to globalization (Ife, 2001) as people seek alternatives that are more appropriate for their particular circumstances. This requires social work to focus on both global and local perspectives and to make the meaningful connections between global inequities and domestic social justice issues that will discourage any artificial local/global polarity (Polack, 2004) and further, through educational initiatives and collective political action, offer up hope for the world of the future.

The Social Work Library

For more on the connection between globalization and disempowerment of the poor, read Polack's article.

Web Links

You can access more information on overseas opportunities and resources through the Web links on the online learning center.

NOTICING OUR NOTICING

As social work students, you may have noticed that you are asked to contemplate many dimensions of your own behavior, the state of the profession, and even the state of the world, that you may not have considered before. Perhaps you never thought about the historical purposes of social work, or of the idea of expertise, or of U.S.-based fast-food restaurants all over the world. Or perhaps you have come to realize that noticing what you haven't noticed before opens up a whole new set of ideas and views of the world. Noticing is both a political and a pragmatic act. If, for instance, you notice that as a woman of color you are excluded from various everyday activities relating to student governance that are dominated by white men, then you are taking up the powerful and sometimes painful discourse of gender and race relations and politics (Smith, 1987).

Here you probably see that what you don't notice is as important as what you do notice. For example, if you don't notice your exclusion from the activities that are critical to full-fledged participation (such as decision-making, management, and leadership roles in government or organizations), you are likely to live in a world in which you have very little say, or representation. This is another way to say you will have no power. Both noticing, then, and not noticing can have significant repercussions in your life and in the lives of your clients. This kind of noticing is critical for developing and sustaining a meaningful purpose in your practice.

Noticing Our Practice

In the more relational practice world, if social workers fail to notice that their tone of voice is patronizing when they work with clients, they are not likely to make successful connections because they will be perceived as having power over the clients. If they fail to notice how poverty restricts a person's ability to get to an appointment on time, they are likely to call a client "unreliable" when she or he does not keep the appointment. (Workers may exert and extend their power through bestowing such labels on others.) Similarly, if you are traveling and you enjoy the benefits of finding a familiar clothing store in Nairobi and fail to notice the impact that such an enterprise has on the local population, you are missing some important information, in exchange for your own comforts, about how the world is working. Noticing what you don't notice is also important for practice; your purposes will be confounded if you are not aware of your blind spots.

Context influences what you notice, and what you tend to notice is influenced by who you are. For example, in the summer I tend to notice the state of every little flowerpot I have around my house. If the tomatoes are wilting, I notice them quickly. I notice each new blossom that signals another tomato-to-be. In late August, though, when school has started again, I stop noticing tomatoes and shift to noticing students and committees and class schedules. I am still the same person literally, but I have shifted from careful gardener to scheduled academic, and so my context of reference and attention has also shifted. As the tomatoes wilt, I respond with only a passing bit of regret and the assertion that I don't have time to notice such things now.

It is critical for clients that workers notice them and their contexts faithfully, and clients should be able to tell workers what they are not noticing. This is more challenging because the arrangement of client and worker may make it difficult for a client to raise such matters (Witkin, 1999). For example, if your client notices that you are always just a little late for your appointments, it will be important for you to allow that information into your reflection about your own work. You will need to notice, for example, if your client's report to you offends your sense of appropriate communication between client and worker, or if you are irritated at being called on your tardiness, or if you develop countless excuses for why you are late.

Noticing Multiple Realities

Noticing your own social location in this way is consistent with postmodernism and social construction (discussed in Chapter 1). Recognizing that a person's reality is based on her or his perceptions and experiences in the social world, you can see that there are multiple realities, as each of us perceives the world differently and has different experiences. This highlights the need to approach clients from their realities, rather than yours. This is often difficult to do. For example, when you can't understand why your clients seem to have no ambition to support themselves or to participate in civic life, you will need to understand the realities of, say, African American ghetto life in Los Angeles, or Latino life in New York, or Asian life in Cleveland. Institutionalized racism is just one of the social phenomena that may leave clients bitter and nonparticipatory, with little vision of what their life might be.

Recognition of this postmodern principle of multiple realities has an impact on social work practice, especially when your purpose is to advocate for or take up the causes of people who have little power. Expanding your capacity to notice is an ongoing challenge. It requires that you acknowledge the boundaries of your own world and allow yourself to enter someone else's. It also requires continuous vigilance. It is not a technique but rather an overall approach that has the potential to enrich your practice of social work far beyond what you may notice now.

STRAIGHT TALK ABOUT QUESTIONING YOUR OWN BIASES

In the midst of noticing the nuances of social work's purpose, it seems clear that social workers need to know themselves. Probably no other overall message about doing this work is more important. Knowing yourself is not enough, however: You also need to examine how that knowledge influences the way you carry out the work.

Biases at Home

If you notice that you respond differently to very poor people from the way you do to middle-class people, for example, you will want to explore where that difference comes from. As a younger person did you get a sense that poor people were somehow less worthy than affluent people? This is common in our culture. Are people living in poverty not as hardworking? Does your family or the wider culture support that view? How might this view clash with another view that sees poor people as hugely resilient in the face of debilitating exploitation through no shortcomings of their own? How does your view play out in your work? Are you less empathic, energetic, or invested when you work with poor people? Are you less likely to advocate or seek out resources? Have you noticed your own pattern about such issues? Do you have an opinion about a client that is a "truth" in your mind, or do you treat it as one interpretation out of many possible interpretations? The questions go on.

Our decisions are shaped by ourselves—that is, our experience, motivations, and attitudes influence our work (Mattison, 2000). Further, some of these patterns unknowingly influence the way we make choices. This means that you need to understand how you prioritize your values and what patterns you develop in integrating your attitudes into daily life. This exploration may include recognizing your own idiosyncratic approaches, quick responses, and patterns of reaction. Are you patient and likely to stand by your client, even when things don't go so well? Are you quick to assume someone is judging you or wants to do you harm? Are you likely to blow off steam when you are rebuffed? Are you more inclined at times to lick your wounds by yourself in a corner? Do you assume you are competent to deal with any crisis? Are you inclined to address an interpersonal problem privately and quietly? Are you more likely to "sound off" in a meeting? All of us have idiosyncratic ways of dealing with relationships, stresses, and other types of social interactions. Bound by a few parameters, these behaviors are not usually associated with good or bad responses, but rather with personality variations. The important idea here is to recognize your own patterns, to know how they impact your work, and to identify those responses you want to change or temper, as well as those you can trust to carry you through.

Biases of Culture

On another level, you might consider how your own culture has influenced what you think about an individual's role in the family, the degree of autonomy you think is appropriate for a young person, or even what style in professional or social conversations is optimal. For example, do you consider that an adolescent's choice of vocation should take precedence over the family's ideas about what is most suitable? Do you believe that in social relationships the participants should consider themselves equal and speak out honestly about what bothers them? As in the discussion of social construction in Chapter 1, the idea here is not that you should change any such beliefs; in fact, the two examples cited are part of mainstream U.S. culture. Rather, you need to recognize them as cultural variants that are not necessarily shared by all people and therefore do not represent a universal truth about what is best. The emphasis on individual drive and ambition as well as equality and forthrightness are peculiarly Western and particularly United States oriented, and they might seem self-centered and crass to other groups. For example, your Asian client, who is 20 years older than you, seems formal and appears reluctant to share many details about her family life, even though she's been referred for parent support. In this scenario you might consider that she may have a different mindfulness about the style and content of what you are asking her about. Rather than labeling her "resistant" or "closed," you will want to recognize your own perspective about such relationships and style and evaluate how well it fits with hers.

As you have probably noticed, this emphasis on our own biases and assumptions is closely related to values and how these values influence our ideas of ethical practices. These constructs are critical to social work practice. The next chapter will deal more explicitly with the ideas and contexts relating to values and ethical frameworks and the emphases placed on them in practice.

CONCLUSION

In considering varying purposes and historical approaches that social work practice has undertaken, you have acquired a more thorough understanding of where the profession has been and where you might fit in. Regardless of whether you now think, for example, that your own focus will emphasize clinical or nonclinical components, or an integration of both, you can consider the profession in its ongoing concerns and have a sense of reference and context. The discussion of the changes that occur over time and place also allows you to speculate on what you think the challenges for the future will be.

Being aware of what you notice and what you fail to notice enables important examination of your own assumptions, both individual and cultural, as they make an impact upon practice. This has significance both generally and more specifically in your sense of what values and ethics should drive the profession. Chapter 3 will go into much greater detail regarding the role these values and ethics play in social work.

MAIN POINTS

- The purpose of social work practice has been viewed through several perspectives throughout its history, from the very broad one of enhancing human well-being to the narrow ones of method and social location.

- Tensions that persist in contemporary practice include those between social control and social change, acceptance and change, clinical and nonclinical perspectives, experts and shared power, and global citizenship and the local community.

- Noticing what you notice and what you do not notice is consistent with postmodernism and opens a set of ideas and views of the world that are significant for practice relationships.

- Noticing is contextual and allows you to recognize and acknowledge multiple realities.

- Effective practice requires questioning your own assumptions, understanding the impact they have on your work, and framing your methods.

EXERCISES: PRACTICING SOCIAL WORK

Prepare for this exercise by reviewing Emilia's case file (including her history, concerns, and goals). Explore Emilia's relationship with others by looking at the family genogram, the ecomap, and her interaction matrix. Answer her Critical Thinking Questions and then place yourself in the following case study:

Looking Back at Emilia

Consider the very brief "historical" vignette below and respond to the questions:

Going back in time, you, as a hospital social worker, are assigned to Emilia Sanchez. Emilia is 24 years old and has just given birth to Joey. She has also been involved with crack-cocaine and Joey has just tested positive for the drug. You have had conversations with the child protection team and believe Joey will be taken into state's custody and probably placed with Celia and Hector who have indicated their willingness to take him into their household. As Emilia's social worker, your specific job is to work with her on a plan to deal with her addiction and to adjust to the placement of Joey in foster care. You've been told she has just had an angry outburst and is now quietly sullen. You are heading to her hospital room.

1. What do you think the tensions might be in this situation between social control and social change?

2. What do you notice about your own visceral responses to Emilia? How will they influence your work?

3. What do you think your position regarding "experts" and "shared power" might be?

4. What are you thinking as you walk to her room to meet with her? (What are you bringing into the room with you?)

EXERCISES: THE SOCIAL WORK LIBRARY

Read the Haynes article, "The One-Hundred Year Debate: Social Reform versus Individual Treatment." Focus on the question of what David, in the following scenario, needs. Is it social work "treatment" (as distinct from medical treatment) or to experience some change in the social environment in which he lives, or what?

Where Do I Start?

David, a 25-year-old gay member of the Hispanic community, has been admitted to the local hospital where you work as a medical social worker. He has developed acute symptoms of AIDS over a very brief period of time. He is miserably sick and overwhelmed with his situation. After he finished high school, he left the area and had been living with a partner in a predominantly gay community in a much bigger city in the Midwest. He had many friends, Hispanic and not, of both sexes and considered himself reasonably well "adjusted."

When his employer found out about his illness, David was fired. Because he needed help from them, he was forced to reveal his homosexuality to his parents, which resulted in his being unsure whether they still accepted him as their son. He was fully aware that his sexual orientation was very difficult for his traditional parents to understand. His loneliness is evident whenever he talks of them.

His situation is further complicated by a lack of health insurance and a lack of any backlog of savings on which to live. He has coped well with obstacles in the past, but he is currently overpowered with anxiety and grief.

Given that you would collaborate with David regarding the most pressing aspects of his situation (all of which seem overwhelming to him), how might you begin to prioritize and shape your first intervention?

1. Support David individually = individual emotional intervention and support.

2. Contact David's landlord = individual/structural advocacy.

3. Contact hospital resource person about insurance and income programs = structural resource building.

4. Meet with family = individual resource building and pursuit of familial and cultural reconciliation.

Compare with responses of other students and be prepared to discuss your rationale for starting point. Suggest alternative approaches that might integrate these approaches. Where will your choice lead you?

OTHER EXERCISES

Julie's Story

You're a social worker in the local Community Mental Health Center. Your usual role is case manager, which seems to mean "do a little of everything." Your assignment is to the psychiatric follow-up team, which means your clients have usually just been discharged from the "psych unit" of the general hospital or the state hospital. For the most part your work involves supporting clients in "problems of living." That can mean taking them to the laundromat, discouraging them from buying devil dogs and root beer for dinner, helping to negotiate leases with the landlord, driving to the podiatrist, or acting as the primary comfort for their unspeakable loneliness.

Julie, one of your favorite clients, has just been released from the hospital. You had some concerns about her readiness, but you know also that she desperately wanted out, since she experienced the hospital as a terrible prison. You help her get settled back into her apartment and leave for home. Later on that night as you return from a movie you see her, wandering near the theater, apparently with little purpose. The theater is in an unsafe area and she is not dressed very warmly for January. She is also breaking a city curfew. You stop and try to offer her assistance, but she rejects all of your suggestions; you're not absolutely sure she knows you. When you can get to a phone you check with the crisis people and the respite programs in your agency. There are no empty beds.

Your client has done nothing (apparently) to harm herself; she doesn't look oriented; it's cold. You believe she might accept an overnight stay with some of her recent street cronies, but you know they use a lot of drugs and you're concerned about her ability to manage that scene. You can identify no other options. You have the capacity to recommend her for screening for involuntary treatment, which would mean she'd go back to the hospital.

Identify the ways in which you might operate from a model of social change if you were Julie's social worker. How might you exert social control? What do you think is the appropriate role of the profession here? Develop a rationale to compare with your classmates.

Worker's Lament Or Know Thyself

You have suddenly been notified by your field instructor that the agency in which you are doing your internship will be closed for a period of two weeks while it undergoes some building renovations that are necessary for safety. This means that you will need to double your hours for the next two weeks in order to meet the required number of field instruction hours for your school's program. You predict you will be exhausted with the increase in hours, you think your other school work will suffer, and you will have to cancel plans for a long weekend jaunt you've been counting on.

1. What would be your likely *initial* response?
   - I can't do it
   - I shouldn't have to do it
   - I *can* do it; it'll give me a chance to get to know my clients better
   - No big deal, this is just another school hurdle
   - Take a deep breath
   - Social work is too hard
   - Organize a practicum students' union
   - Other

2. How would you mostly likely behave?
   - Picket the dean's office
   - Send an angry e-mail to field coordinator of my program
   - Drop out of school
   - Burst into tears
   - Stay in bed
   - Start reorganizing my calendar
   - Other

3. Why? What do you think most likely accounts for your response?
   - Life is usually unfair
   - Social workers need to think of their clients first
   - My field instructor is counting on me
   - I usually burst into tears when I'm disappointed
   - Students have to protect themselves
   - Social workers always rally when there's a need
   - Other

4. Compare your answers with those of other students.

5. What do your answers mean about your assumptions? Patterns under pressure? Personal idiosyncrasies? How you make sense of obstacles? How you see the demands of the profession?

CHAPTER 3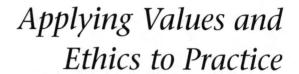

Applying Values and Ethics to Practice

A S YOU READ THE FOLLOWING LIST OF STATEMENTS, decide which ones you agree with and which ones you disagree with.

- People who choose to smoke cigarettes are responsible for resolving their own health problems when they contract lung cancer.

- There are times when it is acceptable for parents to discipline their children physically.

- There are situations in which suicide is an acceptable strategy.

- If people who experience alcoholism refuse to get help, that is their own choice.

- Children who are sexually abused should never be returned to the residence of the person who perpetrated the abuse.

- Workers who agree to the terms of agency employment do not have the right to criticize agency practices.

- Most homeless people want to live out in the open.

- All world citizens, regardless of what they have done, deserve to be free from hunger.

- People who test HIV-positive should be tattooed on the heel so that potential sexual partners can take safety precautions.

Although you will probably find a lot of disagreement among your peers on the value positions presented here, perhaps one of the most agreed-upon ideas about the vision and mission of social work practice is the value it puts on values. This is not to say that social workers agree on all values; rather, that the idea of values itself is central to conceptions of why social workers do what they do.

Chapter 1 defined *values* as beliefs, and *ethics* as the rules of conduct that embody those beliefs. This chapter focuses particularly on the professional ethics that are informed by values. It explores ethical codes and their application to practice in various contexts. It also considers the relationship between ethics and the law and, finally, how social workers manage challenging ethical conflicts and dilemmas.

A BRIEF HISTORY OF SOCIAL WORK ETHICS

You learned in Chapter 2 that social work once had more concerns about the morals of clients than about its own conduct (Reamer, 1998). There were two major periods in the history of U.S. social work when the profession especially noticed and began to expand its concern with its own ethics (Reamer, 2001a). In the first, in the late 1940s and early 1950s, social workers made a variety of attempts to develop an official, written code, or document, that articulated the current, collective thinking of the profession. In 1947 the American Association of Social Workers (a predecessor of the current National Association of Social Workers) adopted the profession's first formal code that established guidelines and standards for its ethical conduct (Reamer, 1999).

The Social Work Library

Read Reamer's paper for the history of the development of social work ethics.

The second period occurred in the late 1970s and early 1980s. Advances in biotechnology (relating to such phenomena as organ and bone marrow transplants as well as genetic manipulation) launched the introduction of bioethics in medical settings. This was especially influential in sensitizing social workers (and other human service workers) to the importance of their own values and the relationship between their values and the decisions they or others near them needed to make. This included how the decisions themselves are made (for example, who makes them), as well as how to decide questions such as who receives a liver transplant, or who should have access to genetic information, or who has the right to choose death and under what circumstances. Other societal phenomena such as developments in computer technology, globalized eco-politics, and the surge of interest in human rights have also shaped and intensified the concern for values in ethical practice.

Web Links

The National Institutes of Health deal with bioethics and provide many resources and documents as well as educational opportunities and funding resources.

In response, the social work profession has attempted to develop standards to guide workers, prioritize principles, affirm its values, and distinguish which parameters define the profession's responsibilities. For example, social work's code reflects its differentiated views on how social workers should conduct themselves with clients, with one another, and with respect to organizations, the profession itself, and society at large.

Web Links

Get more perspectives on the promotion of global ethics through research, public discourse, and practice at the Institute for Global Ethics' Web site.

PROFESSIONAL CODES OF ETHICS

One result of the process of ethical development has been the emergence of a comprehensive code of ethical standards and guidelines. The **NASW** *Code of Ethics* (1999) serves a dual function of (1) affirming social work as a legitimate profession, covering a multitude of practice circumstances in which social workers may find themselves, and (2) explicating the standards through which the public may hold the profession accountable. Practitioners generally see this development as a positive and sometimes even comforting phenomenon because they are consciously reminded of the complexities of engaging in and sustaining ethical practice in today's world.

Social work has several other codes of ethics directed at the promotion of ethical practice. Some of these include

- National Association for Black Social Workers (www.nabsw.org)

- Clinical Social Work Federation (www.cswf.org)

- International Federation of Social Workers (IFSW) (www.ifsw.org)

- Radical Code of Ethics (Galper, 1980)

The NASW *Code* is probably the best known of these and is certainly the most widely cited. In this chapter I will discuss the NASW *Code of Ethics* and—because of its global significance—the most recent IFSW statement as two examples of codified documents concerning ethics.

NASW *Code of Ethics*

Web Links

You will find a more thorough review of this section of the Code, at the NASW Web site.

By now, you may have considered the NASW *Code of Ethics* at some length in earlier courses, and you probably have been asked to read it thoroughly in relation to your field practicum. I will briefly summarize the main points here.

The *Code* is built around six core values from the preamble, which match six broad ethical principles, as shown in Table 3.1. The core values represent a mix of the worker's activities, skills, principles, character, and attitudes, and they relate integrally to the *Code* in its specifics. The heart of the *Code*, the ethical standards, follow the six principles. These cover and are organized according to the following six relationship categories or standards:

1. Social workers' ethical responsibilities to clients.

2. Social workers' ethical responsibilities to colleagues.

3. Social workers' ethical responsibilities in practice settings.

4. Social workers' ethical responsibilities as professionals.

5. Social workers' ethical responsibilities to the social work profession.

6. Social workers' ethical responsibilities to the broader society.

Core Values	Ethical Principles	
Service	Social workers' primary goal is to help people in need and to address social problems.	**TABLE 3.1**
Social justice	Social workers challenge social injustice.	*The Foundation of the Social Work Perspective*
Dignity and worth of the person	Social workers respect the inherent dignity and worth of the person.	
Importance of human relationships	Social workers recognize the central importance of human relationships.	
Integrity	Social workers behave in a trustworthy manner.	
Competence	Social workers practice within their areas of competence and develop and enhance their professional expertise.	

Within each of these categories the *Code* contains from 4 (category 6) to 16 standards (category 1), along with varying subcategories, to total 155 in all. These standards are both "aspirational and enforceable" and delineate "opportunities for errors of omission as well as commission" (Strom-Gottfried, 2003). In that respect they address both the rules and the hopes of the profession, and Standards 2.09 (a) and (b) make an explicit assertion that social workers can behave unethically by simply doing nothing in certain circumstances.

Although the *Code*'s language does not specifically include the discourse of human rights, Reichert (2003) argues that human rights principles can and should be applied especially to Standard 6, the broader society. As discussed in Chapter 1, the United States has been ambivalent regarding its adoption of human rights principles, and so it is not surprising that the NASW *Code* does not use explicit language to incorporate them.

IFSW Ethical Statement

The International Federation of Social Workers (IFSW), a worldwide professional organization of social work organizations and individuals, also documents its position on ethical practice in a statement that reflects concerns that are quite similar but not identical to the NASW *Code*. The IFSW draft document, *Ethics in Social Work: Statement of Principles* (IFSW, 2002), was created at its general meeting in Geneva, Switzerland, in July 2002, revised in Copenhagen in June 2003, and finalized in 2004. This document contains a more explicit and pervasive emphasis on human rights than the NASW's *Code* does, as reflected in the following language:

The Social Work Library

Read Reichert's chapter for more on human rights and typical case scenarios in social work practice.

Definition of Social Work: The social work profession promotes social change, problem solving in human relationships, and the empowerment and liberation of people to enhance well being. Utilising theories of human behaviour and social systems, social work intervenes at the points where people interact with their environments. Principles of human rights and social justice are fundamental to social work. (www.ifsw.org)

The next section highlights seven international conventions that form "common standards of achievement and recognise rights that are accepted by the global community" (www.ifsw.org). These include the Universal Declaration of Human Rights (1948), the International Covenant on Civil and Political Rights (1965), and the International Covenant on Economic, Social, and Cultural Rights (1965), as well as some conventions that the United States has not yet ratified.

The final two sections in the IFSW statement, on human rights and social justice, are the equivalent of the first two principles in the *Code.* These equate human rights with human dignity and address social work's commitment to them. The full text of the Principles is shown in Box 3.1. The broad value base reflected in these statements probably seems familiar to you and is quite similar to that of the NASW *Code.* However, if you review the Universal Declaration of Human Rights, which is central to the IFSW statement, you will notice some additional emphases that the United States does not take up fully. These relate particularly to a global (rather than national) perspective and the importance of economic, social, and cultural rights for all people. As a federation, IFSW assumes that member organizations adhere to its standards. NASW is a member.

Web Links

See the full IFSW statement and other links to publications, position statements, conferences, and resources in the Web links section of the online learning center.

Further Thoughts about Ethical Codes

Although the NASW *Code* can be helpful to practitioners wrestling with difficult ethical situations in practice, it presents the worker with the conundrum that all such codes do: The codes tend to be general, they may be difficult to interpret, and they may be unrealistic given the specifics of the worker's practice (Strom-Gottfried, 2000). The critique I present here takes up the issues of context, risk taking and creativity, and diversity.

The Role of Context   Ethical decisions are not made in isolation or in the abstract. They are made within a practice context, which may shape the decision-making process in ways that are not entirely visible. As discussed in Chapter 2, if social workers do not notice that they are attributing negative qualities to a client because, for example, she or he does not keep appointments

Human rights and human dignity: Social work is based on respect for the inherent worth and dignity of all people, and the rights that follow from this. Social workers should uphold and defend each person's physical, psychological, emotional and spiritual integrity and well being. This means:

1. Respecting the right to self-determination—social workers should respect people's rights to make their own choices and decisions, irrespective of their values and life choices, providing this does not threaten the rights and interests of others.

2. Promoting the right to participation—social workers should promote the full involvement and participation of people using their services in ways that enable them to be empowered in all aspects of decisions and actions affecting their lives.

3. Treating each person as a whole—social workers should be concerned with the whole person, within the family and the community, and should seek to recognise all aspects of a person's life.

4. Identifying and developing strengths—social workers should focus on the strengths of all individuals, groups and communities and thus promote their empowerment.

Social justice: Social workers have a responsibility to promote social justice, in relation to society generally, and in relation to the people with whom they work. This means:

1. Challenging negative discrimination—social workers have a responsibility to challenge negative discrimination on the basis of irrelevant characteristics such as ability, age, culture, gender or sex, marital status, political opinions, skin colour or other physical characteristics, sexual orientation, or spiritual beliefs.

2. Recognising diversity—social workers should recognise and respect the racial and cultural diversity of societies in which they practice, taking account of individual, family, group and community differences.

3. Distributing resources equitably—social workers should ensure that resources at their disposal are distributed fairly, according to need.

4. Challenging unjust policies and practices—social workers have a duty to bring to the attention of policy makers, politicians and the general public situations where resources are inadequate or where policies and practices are unfair or harmful.

5. Working in solidarity—social workers have an obligation to challenge social conditions that contribute to social exclusion, stigmatisation or subjugation, and to work towards an inclusive society.

Source: IFSW, 2002

BOX 3.1

Final Proposal for New IFSW Ethical Document, 2004

consistently, they may believe the client is not able to take full advantage of very scarce resources. A worker may even decide the client is not deserving of such resources. If the worker is in a position to choose who will (and will not) have access to a limited service, she or he may disqualify the client without further reflection. On the one hand, this could be seen as good judgment because it seeks to maximize the influence of the scarce service. On the other hand, the dynamics reflect an interpretation that is not openly visible and is perhaps not accurate. If the client had reliable transportation to appointments, for example, the scenario might appear vastly different. Such judgments may not only be inaccurate but also present an ethical question relating to the professional discretion and impartial judgment that the *Code* requires.

The point here is that even though a code provides guidance, a great deal of discretion and individualized perspectives are also at work (Mattison, 2000). You cannot rely totally on relatively decontextualized, concrete rules to provide a simple answer at the expense of much more critical self-reflection. Thoughtful social workers frequently come to the nonconclusion of "it depends" (Strom-Gottfried, 2003) when ethical questions confront them. This does not reflect their inability to be decisive but rather their recognition of the importance of the surrounding circumstances, social location, and current pressures. It also suggests the value of a "dialogic process" (Strom-Gottfried, 2003), which engages all the parties (or positions) involved in an ethical question in an in-depth conversation regarding their thinking, the implications of varying choices, and an analysis of their values.

Risk Taking and Creativity   Another concern regarding the rigid interpretation of ethical rules relates to the potential for oversimplification. If the worker jumps too quickly to standardized, rote responses, based on her or his view of the meaning of the *Code,* she or he may not respond creatively. Participating thoughtfully is a valuable component of social work practice and sometimes requires some risk taking. Witkin (2000) suggests that hypercautious adherence to a formal authority can discourage creative, responsive relationships on the part of the practitioner and can also lead a practitioner to overlook (or not notice) alternative responses to a situation.

Here's an illustration of this idea: A school social worker named Cora, in strict adherence to the ethical principle of practicing only within her area of competency (Code Standard 4.01a), at first declined to see a young student who clearly was struggling with the abuse of a variety of substances. Cora felt thoroughly competent in working with adolescents regarding developmental issues, but she was not trained in dealing with substance abuse, so she decided it would be unethical to work with the student. The student, however, was in great need, was ready to work on the problem, and had no other obvious or realistic options in the small, rural community. Furthermore, the substance use was intertwined with other variables that seemed related to growing up in difficult circumstances, so it overlapped with several developmental issues. In discussing this dilemma with her colleague (through a dialogue), Cora was reminded that she had many skills and much experience that would directly benefit the student. She was knowledgeable regarding adolescent development, had good relationship skills with young people, and was committed to a hopeful, resilience-based perspective regarding people in general. In addition, Cora's colleague advised that she might find a resource in her former supervisor, who had become certified in the area of alcohol and drug use. Cora contacted the former supervisor, who was interested in the scenario and recommended available training for Cora, as well as a nearby clinician who could be contacted for ongoing supervision.

Because substance abuse in school populations is so common and potentially so deadly (and because Cora had good self-advocacy skills), Cora successfully negotiated for time and reimbursement to obtain the training that would allow her to better serve her clients—in this case the school. Although everyone involved might have preferred that Cora already have advanced certification, many agreed that this solution made sense, given the context. Cora was creative and willing to explore options in response to important needs, and her client(s) were likely to receive competent services from an experienced worker who sought both training and supervision in an area related to her overall skills and education. There is some risk in Cora's assumption of this role, but it seemed more in keeping with the profession's values than denying the student help.

Furthermore, strict and nonreflective adherence to a standard code can help preserve the current social order, which may be in direct conflict with the profession's commitment to confront social injustice and oppression (Witkin, 2000). If the student's family in the example was limited financially and belonged to an ethnic population that was frequently discriminated against, the student would not be likely to get needed services otherwise. This would have constituted one more situation in which the family's access to key resources was constricted and injustice was fostered. Cora's commitment to responding differently to the student's need can be seen as serving social work's obligation to confront such situations.

Keep in mind that this is one example, and Cora's solution is only one of many possibilities. It may not even be the best choice. Not everyone reading this account of Cora's context will agree that her solution was acceptable. Advocates for diversity empowerment might look at Cora's effort as just another example in which ethnically diverse people get substandard services through noncredentialed workers. Also, the *Code,* in Cora's context, did not itself preclude her from using her creativity to address the student's needs. A too-narrow interpretation was the would-be villain here. The resolution of issues like this is seldom easy and frequently overlooks some worthwhile concerns, but the dialogic process offers a rich and full exploration of the issues and contributes to the ongoing dynamics of the profession's overall ethical stance.

Diversity   The final area I raise here in critique of universal codes of ethics segues from the preceding one and involves a concern for a postmodern recognition of diversity and multiple realities. The charge here is that universal codes meant to apply to everyone in all situations often lag behind the experiential contexts of both workers and clients and fail to recognize differences among people and cultures. Briskman and Noble (1999) argue that an all-encompassing code of ethics that emphasizes "universality, inclusiveness, and conventional conceptualizations of community" (p. 58) impedes the diverse interests of modern pluralistic societies. For example, **confidentiality**, which refers to the social worker's obligation to keep the private lives, facts, or events of their clients from becoming public in any way, is often regarded as absolutely critical in maintaining an ethical relationship. But a universal application of confidentiality as an ethical mandate may turn into an obstacle in cultures in which the community is both the reference point and the source of solution. In such communities, maintaining confidentiality can be experienced as secretive, alienating, divisive, and harmful.

Briskman and Noble are convinced that it is in the interests of diversity to develop an ethical model that is more affirming of difference. To that end they suggest the possibility of several approaches to the development of multiple codes. One approach is grounded in client-based and service delivery schemes. For example, the authors cite a center against sexual assault in Melbourne, Australia, that shapes its code based on the perspective that sexual assault is a violation of human rights (p. 64). This is an example of a specific code tailored to the organization's commitments to a particular client population. Another way to recognize difference is to develop constituency-based codes based on specific concerns, such as tolerance for sexual orientation in the schools. In this case norms would be developed with specific reference to the issues (in contrast to population) raised by gay, lesbian, bisexual, transgendered, and questioning groups. The development of specialized codes for different groups departs from the universal application of the U.S. and Canadian codes.

In some cases a **bicultural code of practice** may be desirable. For example, the New Zealand Association of Social Work currently uses a Bicultural Code that reflects an effort to deal justly with its native Maori people through recognition of the independence guaranteed to them in a treaty negotiated in 1840. The historical emphasis on the Maori people's independence has led New Zealander social workers to recognize the contemporary demands that this principle places on their work with Maori people. The code is based on the IFSW code and explicitly requires a bicultural focus for all of New Zealand's social workers. See Exhibit 3.1 for an excerpt from the code, and then take a moment to consider its implications.

In New Zealand, the Treaty of Waitangi, negotiated in 1840 between the occupying British and the native Maori chiefs, recognized the native Maori people as Tangata Whanua and guaranteed their right to independence. This treaty is an integral part of contemporary ethics in New Zealand social work, and it reflects an active commitment for the promotion of indigenous identity. The following is an excerpt from Section C, the Bicultural Code of the Code of Ethics of the New Zealand Association of Social Work.

EXHIBIT 3.1

Sample Bicultural Code of Practice

Independence

Social work organisations and agencies and individual social workers should acknowledge and support the whanau [here, Maori clients] as the primary source of care and nurturing of its members.

1.2 Social workers are expected to work in ways that recognise the independence of the whanau and its members, by empowering the whanau and its members to handle their own lives and living conditions, and by enabling them to take care of themselves and to develop autonomously and collectively.

1.3 NZASW [New Zealand Association of Social Workers] recognises the right of Maori clients to have a Maori worker. Social work agencies and organisations should ensure that Maori clients have access to Maori workers at all levels, and social workers are expected to open up access to Maori workers. If no Maori worker is available, appropriate referral may be made if the client requests that. During their social work education Maori social workers should receive appropriate training in Maori models and methods.

Liberation through Solidarity

2.1 Social workers should work with agencies and organisations whose policies, procedures and practices are based on the Treaty of Waitangi, and actively and constructively promote change in those agencies and organisations that operate from a monocultural base.

Cultural solidarity: Maori address health issues.

Non Discrimination

3.1 All social workers are expected to participate in Treaty of Waitangi education as part of their entry into social work and on an ongoing basis. This should include a knowledge and understanding of their own ethnicity and the actual history of Aotearoa New Zealand.

The discussion here on the merits of codes of ethics is not meant to suggest that the existing NASW *Code* should be abandoned. Articulating expectations and providing overall guidance about conduct is worthwhile, so that workers know what is generally expected and can identify points of departure. Moreover, the *Code* is value based and is consistent with many common (if mainstream), traditional commitments. It cannot, of course, cover everyone and everything. This discussion is aimed at uncovering some of the limitations and is framed in consideration of experiences out of the mainstream. As such, it addresses growing concerns for recognition and affirmation of diverse peoples, both in the United States and particularly as we think more and more of the whole world. This critique is also meant to encourage your interest and enthusiasm in challenging what may too often go unquestioned. It supports the notion that "we must expect such codes to be constantly disputed and evolving for a profession to be robust, relevant, and living" (Briskman & Noble, 1999, p. 60). Let us in the spirit of open inquiry keep our profession robust!

ETHICS AND THE LAW

Overall, the law has a significant impact on social work, and its constant changes create a complex, sometimes bewildering climate in which to practice (Dickson, 1998). Because violations are so often the focus of the ethics literature (Strom-Gottfried, 2000), and because there is often a connection between ethical codes and state or federal laws, students and practitioners sometimes tend to consider ethics and the law the same thing. They are not. Although there is a lot of overlap, and certainly many illegal behaviors are also unethical, certain distinctions are important to note. Here we will look at some parallels and conflicts between social work ethics and the law, as well as the potential for, and benefit of, collaboration between the two professions.

Parallels between Ethics and the Law

Many parallels exist between social work ethics and the laws that affect practitioners, and they are best illustrated by an example. If I frequently make pejorative comments to my colleagues about clients who are living in poverty, I may be accused of violating the *Code* (Section 1.12). Moreover, I am violating the spirit of the profession in the sense that I harbor oppressive attitudes that I am not examining.

To add some complexity here, technically, in most states, if I am licensed and I make derogatory comments about a particular group of clients, one of them could initiate a complaint with the state's licensing regulators, charging violation of the *Code*. Further, if the client's culture differed from my own, then violation of *Code* Section 1.05b (which requires the worker to understand the function of culture and recognize the strengths of all cultures) might be added to Section 1.12. Assuming that compliance with the *Code* is part of the licensing agreement, I could also lose my license as a legal repercussion of my unethical conduct. As a member of NASW, I may also be sanctioned by the local chapter through a review by their Committee on Inquiry. This is not a legal process but a professional exploration, which may lead to publication of my name as one who has violated the *Code* and was required to make restitution.

The point is that ethics are developed and often defined legally by the profession from which they derive. Values are carefully translated into codes to reflect approved conduct that affirms the profession's commitments and mission. The law is then likely to adopt the profession's criteria for professional conduct. Likewise, in social work, there may be ethical concerns about behaviors that are not violations but may look like stepping-stones that need to be addressed (for example, my reluctance to notice my disdain for people in poverty).

Conflicts between Ethics and the Law

Unfortunately, social work ethics aren't always consistent with legal regulations. There are many situations in which social workers experience an overt conflict between what they consider ethical practice and the law. These situations can be agonizing to workers. We will consider two legal duties here, the duty to report and the duty to protect. Both of these legal mandates support ethical practice in many situations, but each also presents social workers with conflicts in particular contexts.

Duty to Report: Child Protection Social workers operating in the arena of child protection frequently find themselves in a contentious environment. Like many professionals, they are required by law to report to child protection authorities or the police when they suspect a child is being mistreated. This is the **duty to report.** A common sequence of events leading to a report of suspected child abuse begins with a child telling a teacher, school nurse, or another adult that she or he has been abused. The charges are then investigated by a child protection worker, who often interviews the parents as well as the child. Frequently this process takes a day or two, depending on the worker's caseload and the seriousness of the charges. The person making the referral (often a school social worker or medical social worker) may be convinced that the child is being abused, but she or he may also suspect that the abuse is going to be difficult to substantiate. In such a case, reporting the abuse might place the child at much greater risk, as a frightened, angry parent learns that her or his child made the accusation. Where there is no obvious way to protect the child, the referring worker may be tempted not to obey the reporting law.

A similar situation may occur when the worker is cynical about the adequacy or timeliness of the response of the child protection agencies. For example, if the worker reports a case of suspected child abuse to a department known to be so overloaded that reports go for weeks without being investigated, rendering substantiation nearly impossible, then that worker may be reluctant to enter that kind of situation again. As you might imagine, this kind of scenario is much more problematic and painful to deal with when it involves a child whom the worker knows and cares about.

Another scenario might involve the worker's judgment that the law is not really relevant and that compliance will create more harm than help. For example, a 15-year-old is pregnant, and the social worker's task is to help her work through her options for how she will respond to the pregnancy. In the conversation with the client, the worker discovers that the father of the baby is known and is terribly frightened of what his family's reaction will be. Because the client is technically a child, her pregnancy (which by her own account occurred in a consensual way) becomes a matter of child sexual abuse and, according to the law, must be reported. However, the worker sees this as nonproductive: It will not assist the client; it will possibly alienate the baby's father, who might otherwise participate in the decision-making process; and it could even put the baby's father at risk of a violent reaction from his family.

The legally imposed duty to report applies to elders as well as children and is only one of the seemingly countless regulations that have sometimes helped and sometimes hindered—but have certainly changed—the concept of privacy and confidentiality in the social work relationship.

Duty to Protect: Threats of Violence   A real-life example will help illustrate the duty to protect. In 1969, Tatiana Tarasoff, a young student at the University of California at Berkeley, had a casual dating relationship with a graduate student from India. He apparently didn't know much about dating customs in the United States and consequently was despondent over Tatiana's seeing other men at the same time she was going out with him. Depressed, he went to a psychologist at the University Health Services and told the psychologist that he intended to kill Tatiana with a gun. The psychologist wrote a letter to the campus police and asked that the graduate student be detained in a psychiatric hospital. The police interviewed the young man but did not feel there was evidence to prove him dangerous. They required him to promise that he'd stay away from Tatiana. When Tatiana returned from a summer visit abroad, the man observed and stalked her, then finally stabbed her to death.

Tatiana's family sued the campus police, the University Health Services, and the Regents of the University of California for failing to warn them that their daughter's life was in danger. The trial court dismissed the case because although there was precedence for notifying the victim, there was no precedence for warning a third party (Tatiana's parents). The appeals court supported the dismissal, and an appeal was taken to the California Supreme Court, which overturned the dismissal, citing the therapist's responsibility to warn people threatened in this way. This was *Tarasoff I* of 1974 and is often thought of as the **Duty to Warn** decision.

 Web Links

Explore the Web links on the online learning center for a full description of the court process leading to the Tarasoff *decision.*

This ruling opened the way for the family to sue the police and the therapist. Massive outcry from members of both police and treatment-related groups led to the California Supreme Court's hearing the case again. *Tarasoff II*, in 1976, stressed that when a therapist has determined that her or his client presents serious danger of violence to another, the therapist must "use reasonable care to protect the intended victim against such danger." The court's position was that the therapist might have to take any of several steps to ensure the safety of the person threatened by the client, and the emphasis was on the **Duty to Protect** rather than the warning emphasized in *Tarasoff I*. Although the Tarasoff decisions were based on the work of a clinical psychologist, social workers, as well as other human service professionals, are subject in most states to the same legal precedents.

As a social worker in a state hospital about 10 years after *Tarasoff II*, I can attest to the influence it had on my practice life. It heightened my own and my hospital's alertness to several issues. For example, I had to reconsider how to respond when a client who had a history of violence threatened to "belt" his girlfriend just as soon as he was discharged. My colleagues and I had to assess the seriousness of his threats (a difficult task in a psychiatric hospital) as well as how to protect ourselves against legal charges, which was a new concern in those times. In many respects, these questions reflect the nature of our world more than the ethics of social work practice. Although this kind of situation can clearly result in a nightmare for all parties involved, the complication in *Tarasoff* arose because the court, and not the ethics board of the therapist's profession, defined the parameters of responsibility. The ethics committee of NASW, for example, may have made a different interpretation depending upon its assessment of the case specifics.

Not every interface between the courts and practice is this problematic, but in an increasingly litigious society, quandaries related to the law may occur in policy practice, research, and community practice, as well as in direct practice. For example, a worker may be directed by a policy to disclose information in a way that she or he considers unethical and oppressive. To illustrate, a new adoption law might require adoption workers to provide the "adoption triad" (birth parents, adoptive parents, and adopted children) with access to all the information regarding the adoption. If a birth mother had been guaranteed confidentiality at the time of the adoption, she, along with her social worker, may be distraught by this sudden breach of what she considered a binding legal agreement. Similarly, a worker might be required by law to keep the name of a research participant confidential when that person has requested identification as an empowering phenomenon in "owning" the experience. Another example is a worker who is faced with maintaining a city zoning ordinance against the establishment of a group home that she or he believes is critically needed in that locality. Insofar as the worker values practicing within the constraints of the law, these situations can be defined as problematic.

Collaboration between Ethics and the Law

In the best scenarios the law and social work professions can work together to empower people whose legal and social rights are frequently violated. There are many examples of this kind of collaboration in joint law and social work degree programs, in legal clinics for refugee and immigrant peoples, and in family law and social work partnerships, to name only a few. In U.S. society the law drives much of the complex social welfare system, as well as the private structures for shaping income and benefits distribution. A joint effort between the professions of social work and the law, based on common goals, can benefit a great number of people, with each profession enhancing and enriching the work of the other.

The Social Work Library

For another view of how the law may affect social workers, see the Marty & Chapin article.

The law also serves as an external pressure on all the helping professions to maintain their own agreed-upon agendas. It can protect the general public from internal networks that may attempt to cover for, or obscure, the unethical conduct of their own. Although the incidence of covering up unethical behavior is relatively low, all professions are sometimes lax in self-regulation, and there is an obvious temptation from within to minimize the seriousness of any offense raised. Often the victims of such transgressions are women (Bohmer, 2000) or children. Recent child abuse scandals in the Catholic Church are sad reminders of how our most vulnerable citizens can become victims of unethical behavior by people in helping professions.

DILEMMAS AND CRITICAL PROCESSES

As you have probably discovered in prior courses, values and ethics can reside in very murky waters. The complex context of real client situations often highlights competition between values and makes ethical intervention difficult to identify. Some situations involve conflicts in values, and others create dilemmas. We'll look briefly at the distinction between ethical conflicts and dilemmas, the idea of an ethical screen, various models for resolving dilemmas, and some examples of common dilemmas in social work practice.

The Distinction between Conflicts and Dilemmas

Value conflicts occur when one person's values clash with those of another person or system. Although such conflicts are frequently distressful (think about your last argument with a friend over contrasting values), they generally are simple disagreements between two opposing viewpoints. An **ethical dilemma** occurs when an individual holds two or more values that compete with each other. This creates a more complicated situation.

For example, assume that I am a devotee of Henry David Thoreau and consequently believe in the right of any citizen to engage in civil disobedience. If I ignore the restrictions against demonstrating at the site of a WTO meeting and decide to picket it because I believe the organization is responsible for great global and social harm, I will face a conflict. This will be difficult for me, and I must be prepared to face the consequences of my choice, such as fines, tear gas, and accommodation in the local jail. It is not a dilemma, because I am not torn between two mutually exclusive ideas I want to uphold.

In contrast, suppose my friend has always valued strict obedience to the most minute details of all legal demands. My friend is in a different situation. He may be just as committed to challenging the role of the WTO as I am, but he is also acutely uncomfortable with the idea of breaking the law. In this scenario, the two values—demonstrating beliefs in a particular way and upholding the law—are in competition with each other. This is an ethical dilemma.

The Ethical Principles Screen

You already know that social work practice is the source of many dilemmas. You have probably already experienced or at least witnessed some in your fieldwork. There are many kinds of dilemmas: between personal and professional values, between two professional values, between professional and cultural values, or any combination of these.

An example of a dilemma arising out of the conflict between personal values and professional values is whether counseling on abortion is ethically allowable if I am committed to the right-to-life perspective. A dilemma arising from two or more professional social work values might be between protecting my client from harm and maximizing her autonomy. A useful tool in considering ethical priorities is the **ethical principle screen** (Loewenberg, Dolgoff, & Harrington, 2000). This screen can help highlight the relative significance of values and the likely results of your decisions. The elements in the screen, listed in Box 3.2, are all reflected and prioritized in professional social work values. Principle 1 has the highest priority and Principle 7 the lowest. The ordering of the principles in itself is thought provoking because it constitutes a socially constructed priority with which not everyone would agree.

The following scenario demonstrates a simple use of this screen: As a social worker in a family service organization, I am involved in a case in which

- **Principle 1: Protection of Life** This refers literally to guarding against death, starvation, violence, neglect, and any other event or phenomenon that puts a person's life at risk.

- **Principle 2: Equality and Inequality** This reflects a commitment to equal and fair access to services and basic treatment.

- **Principle 3: Autonomy and Freedom** This affirms the notion of self-determination and supports people's right to make free choices regarding their lives.

- **Principle 4: Least Harm** This supports the idea of protecting people from harm; when harm seems likely in any event, it asserts that people have the right to experience the least amount possible.

- **Principle 5: Quality of Life** This confirms that people, families, and communities all have the right to define and pursue the quality of life they desire.

- **Principle 6: Privacy and Confidentiality** This supports the right of people to be protected from having their private stories made public. This usually means the worker must not share client circumstances, struggles, or decisions without the client's explicit (generally written and signed) permission. Information revealing any identifying characteristics (such as name, physical description) is also included in this principle.

- **Principle 7: Truthfulness and Full Disclosure** This implies that workers should tell their clients the truth and help them understand it, and that any information they give to clients should be accurate. It also suggests that workers relate fully any information that is relevant to the client and her or his circumstances.

Source: Loewenberg, Dolgoff & Harrington, 2000

I believe a child's life is at risk because his father regularly beats him. This case clearly reflects Principle 1. At the same time, I am concerned about violating confidentiality: I want the child to continue to trust me with the secrets he's revealed. Thus, this case also involves Principle 6. To resolve my dilemma, I isolate the ethical questions involved (protection of life versus confidentiality), prioritize them by applying the screen, and then shape my response accordingly. Here, the child's life provides a more urgent and compelling principle to guide my actions than does my desire to maintain silence so that the child will continue to trust me. This is the rationale for the child abuse reporting laws.

Not all workers would agree with the prioritizations of the screen in this situation, and so even this dilemma may not be as simple as it seems. As you can see, the principles address very broad concepts that are subject to interpretation, and their relative evaluation in the real practice world often invites some hard thinking.

Models for Resolution of Dilemmas

Several generalized schemes for evaluating and resolving specific ethical dilemmas have been proposed. Some use the ethical principles screen; all are based on professional social work values. I will briefly describe two of these strategies.

Reamer (2001a) suggests that social workers follow four steps to enhance the quality of their decision making:

1. Identify the ethical issues, including the social work values and duties that conflict.

2. Identify the individuals, groups, and organizations that are likely to be affected by the ethical decision.

3. Tentatively identify all possible courses of action and the participants involved in each, along with the possible benefits and risks for each.

4. Thoroughly examine the reasons in favor of and opposed to each possible course of action. (p. 107)

Strom-Gottfried (2003) adds several options for addressing ethical dilemmas, including researching the literature, consulting formally with established committees, obtaining supervision, and consulting peers (employing the dialogic approach mentioned earlier). She also suggests the following strategies for solving dilemmas: (1) consider the "worst case scenario" of each option; (2) consider the principles of least harm, justice, fairness, and the level of publicity that will result; (3) consider clinical and ethical implications; (4) consider the process; and (5) consider barriers to acting on the principal identified power relationships.

Each of these approaches is helpful in thinking through the issues involved in any particular dilemma. Reamer's model is more methodical than Strom-Gottfried's because it prescribes a specific sequence of analysis. In contrast, Strom-Gottfried's allows for a creative strategy that can accommodate some of the specifics of the client situation. Like codes of ethics, neither can provide an infallible result. Therefore, you should be flexible in applying these models, or any others like them, to the specifics of the individual context.

Representative Examples of Practice Dilemmas

Of the many potential dilemmas among the ethical principles that social work has committed itself to, three types that commonly present in the practice context can be categorized as dual relationships, professional versus private tensions, and struggles between paternalism and client self-determination. Let us look at a few representative examples of these types of dilemmas.

Dual Relationships   Relationships between social workers and clients that exist in addition to and are distinct from their professional contacts create **dual relationships**. Such relationships are often written about (or reported on) only in extreme circumstances, such as when the worker has a sexual relationship with the client. Many reports concerning dual relationships are about such conduct, although few reputable individuals or professional groups (none, to my knowledge) actually advocate sexual dual relationships. In that sense, sexual relationships, although an egregious affront to the profession, are easier to resolve in that they are almost always seen as intolerable.

Nonsexual dual relationships pose another set of questions that are raised across many kinds of situations. Consider, for instance, that you just got the job of your dreams in a local community health center. You are working with young people who have been identified as delinquent by legal authorities, and your job is to support their integration into the work-study program that the center sponsors in the community. You find your work both interesting and rewarding. You particularly enjoy working with one client, Joe, and he seems to be making good strides in the program.

When you visit your nearby family one weekend, you're pleased to hear your 20-year-old sister expound enthusiastically about her new boyfriend. She tells you all the details about what he looks like and what he does in his training for work. The description begins to sound familiar. It becomes clear to you after some further conversation that your sister's new boyfriend is Joe.

The dilemma created by this dual relationship is between your personal values and your professional responsibilities. You love your job and you particularly value your work with Joe. You don't want to resign, and no other worker is assigned to this program. You also want to participate in the summer picnics and other festivities that your family celebrates, which are likely to include your sister's new boyfriend. Your professional code, however, tells you it is not ethical for you to continue to work with this client if you are going to see him in this social context. Further, you are not free to share with your family that Joe is your client, nor can you reveal anything about his situation.

Section 1.06c of the *Code* stresses that social workers should not engage in dual relationships with clients or former clients in which there is a risk of exploitation or potential harm to the client. Reamer (2003) classifies dual relationships as unethical when they

- Interfere with the social worker's exercise of professional discretion.
- Interfere with the social worker's exercise of impartial judgment.

- Exploit clients, colleagues, or third parties to further the social worker's personal interests.
- Harm clients, colleagues, or third parties. (p. 129)

It is easy to see in this scenario that your dual relationship with Joe has the potential to affect your professional discretion and your impartial judgment. For example, if you discover personal information about Joe that suggests he might not be a good candidate for marriage to your sister, you would probably find yourself feeling neither professional nor impartial. This is why social workers should avoid such dual relationships.

Nevertheless, as Vodde and Giddings (1997) point out, in isolated rural areas particularly, it might be all but impossible not to have some relationship with your clients other than a professional one. They may have worked for a member of your family, go to the same synagogue as you do, or show up in the same checkout line at the local grocery store. Further, in a world characterized by expanding notions of community and multicultural experiences, social workers may find that they are asked to maintain relationships in several domains with others and to perform multiple roles. For example, in some cultures it would be insulting to a family if the child's social worker refused an invitation to a family dinner party. Not everyone sees rigid boundaries as necessary or even desirable in social work practice.

The human services literature contains many strategies for evaluating and managing dual relationships. Counseling, community mental health, and psychology have all addressed the issue, often citing questions of power and roles, as well as exploitation. For an example from the social work literature, Vodde and Giddings (1997) call for a revision in the way social workers think about dual relationships. They maintain that some aspects of dual relationships—such as greater connectedness and an increase in the client's self-determination—can actually benefit rather than harm the client. They discuss a specific framework to break down the idea of exploitation into more manageable components and to determine whether a certain aspect is potentially beneficial or hurtful in any particular relationship. The continuum, which appears in Exhibit 3.2, allows the worker to explore the areas and degrees to which a specific relationship dimension (for example, the worker has a social relationship with a client) might benefit or harm a client.

Think about which of these variables would apply to you as Joe's worker. For example, you might evaluate the risk of exploiting Joe rather than empowering him if you continue to work with him. Or you might consider the likelihood of increasing Joe's vulnerability through your knowledge of his past struggles. Some variables, such as control of resources, might not be applicable; unless, of course, you tended to favor Joe as a potential brother-in-law by allocating more than his share of resources, such as work allowances. Almost

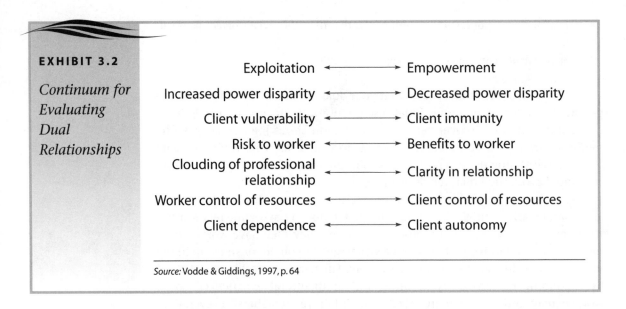

EXHIBIT 3.2

Continuum for Evaluating Dual Relationships

Exploitation ←——————→ Empowerment

Increased power disparity ←——————→ Decreased power disparity

Client vulnerability ←——————→ Client immunity

Risk to worker ←——————→ Benefits to worker

Clouding of professional relationship ←——————→ Clarity in relationship

Worker control of resources ←——————→ Client control of resources

Client dependence ←——————→ Client autonomy

Source: Vodde & Giddings, 1997, p. 64

certainly, you would be at high risk for clouding the professional relationship by working with him while he is seeing your sister. Is the level of risk too great to continue working with him?

Another framework proposed by Vodde and Giddings (1997) allows the worker to decide whether the dual relationship occurs naturally (with no intention of the social worker) or is contrived (arranged by the social worker for her or his own purposes). It also looks at whether the relationship is exploitive (for the worker's benefit), essential (for survival in the community), or enhancing (beneficial to the client). Looking back again at your own situation as Joe's social worker, you might consider how these apply. Although your relationship with Joe is naturally occurring (you didn't make it happen), it is neither essential for the community's well-being, nor does it empower Joe. Further, it has the potential to be exploitive. This kind of analysis can be helpful in situations in which dual relationships are impossible to avoid. It also uses the specific content of the case rather than applying a one-size-fits-all model that simply prohibits all dual relationships.

Responsibility to the Larger Society and Client Well-Being   As you no doubt have noticed in your social work training, relationships that seem to be private in one way have become highlighted in the public view. For example, child abuse and domestic violence were once considered private, family issues outside the jurisdiction of the law or of any public sector interest. The question of whether a particular event is simply a private matter to be resolved by the individuals involved or a public issue that impacts society leads to the territory of ethical inquiry. Because of their close connections to individual clients, social workers often tend to value the private experience—they want to recognize and acknowledge clients' experiences and how they make sense of them. However, because social workers must also deal with the environment that clients (and they) have to negotiate every day, workers are likewise concerned with public issues that reflect the quality of all of our lives. The dilemma in this kind of situation arises when the worker values both the client's right to privacy and the potential benefit to the community of making the issues public.

For example, what is the obligation of the social worker to encourage a survivor of rape to report the incident to the police when she wants nothing more than to be left alone (Dombo, 2005)? The worker knows that women who have experienced rape are often treated poorly by authorities and also has observed that a very small percentage of rape cases are prosecuted effectively. Because rape is often thought of as a silent crime—it is underreported and the public is ambivalent about supporting a more aggressive response to it—many social workers feel that it is critical to make reports that document its frequency, associated consequences, and general significance for our society. One way to do that is to make sure that every single example gets reported. But what of the woman who has been raped? She may want only to heal and to work on beginning her life again. She may fear her parents' response or rejection by her peers. Furthermore, the grilling she can expect by authorities could retraumatize her by making her feel like the guilty party. In this scenario any attempt to take the issue beyond the individual may exact a great price from that person and jeopardize her well-being. These are serious issues for both the client and the worker.

This type of dilemma raises some broad questions that do not have easy answers: What is a public issue, and what do social workers have the right to be silent about? Is rape simply an individual event occurring between two people, or is it a violation of a larger social order as well? Does it affect the community in which we live? Does a zealous social worker have the right to raise a public issue that could exploit the client's pain? This dilemma is profound in our increasingly violent society. On the one hand, workers want to honor clients' wishes for privacy. On the other hand, there will be more and more clients like her as long as the issue remains private and silent.

Paternalism and Client Self-Determination   Long a cornerstone of the social work profession, **self-determination** is an individual's right to make choices and control her or his own life. You may notice that in the *Code*, self-determination is listed in Section 1.02, second only to a general commitment to clients. In contrast, **paternalism** refers to a process of interfering with clients' self-determination because the worker believes she or he knows better what is in the clients' best interests. Reamer (1999) identifies three different forms of paternalism: (1) withholding information (for example, not communicating a medical prognosis or the extent of injury in an accident); (2) deliberately lying to clients, which is more overt than withholding information (for example, assuring a distraught family member that a dying client will get better); and (3) intervening to prevent clients' behavior by controlling their physical placement (for example, facilitating involuntary hospitalizations). Many social workers would agree, however, that the definition of paternalism is often broader than these three types. For example, it is easy to see that withholding information, lying, or physically controlling a person can be paternalistic in certain situations. It isn't as easy to determine whether the assistance or advice provided is too much or too controlling, reflecting a paternalistic approach.

Questions about what rights and responsibilities social workers have to interfere in client situations have been debated since the profession began. In some situations the law dictates a resolution. For example, it is fairly clear that social workers must intervene (legally at least) when a client tells them of an intent to harm someone (either another person or her- or himself). Most workers would agree that the extremity of such a situation warrants professional interference. There are many murkier areas, though. Sometimes you may be called upon to intervene simply because someone is disorderly or embarrasses someone's sense of propriety, an issue often raised in the mental health sector. For example, questions might arise about whether someone should be forced to conform to mainstream standards of cleanliness, or whether you should facilitate the involuntary hospitalization of a person with a mental illness who is not adequate in her or his self-care. In such a case, it is not clear who determines what is "adequate." For another example, by some standards it is a danger to someone's life to eat Twinkies six times a week rather than spinach and whole wheat bread. But does it call for intervention? Perhaps if the client has diabetes?

You will notice that these practice questions relate to the issues of social control and social change discussed in Chapter 2. They may seem like frivolous or unlikely exaggerations, but such questions of conformity routinely appear in evaluations of people with mental illnesses, and their relative seriousness is often difficult to determine. They raise broader issues, such as to what degree our society tolerates (or does not tolerate) eccentricities or even mere differences.

In contrast, many social workers would find it negligent or perhaps in violation of acting in the client's best interests if they did not intervene in a client's inclination to avoid bathing or to eat Twinkies several times a day or to stop taking psychiatric medications as prescribed. They might cite the responsibility of social workers to "promote the well-being of clients" (Section 1.01 of the *Code*). The clash here is between the classic social work values of caretaking and self-determination. The problem is in the determination of what is responsible caretaking and what is excessive interference with a client's choice.

A more subtle variation of this dilemma occurs when the social worker pushes clients to engage in some activity that the worker values. Reamer (1983) has called this "pseudopaternalism" because the paternalistic interference does not arise out of professional values but from personal self-interest. However, sorting out what is professional here and what is personal is not an easy task. For example, most social workers would agree that it is consistent with the profession's values to encourage a young person to achieve the highest level of education possible. At the same time, however, most social workers also value education personally. If you are working with an adolescent who you think has great potential to go beyond what her or his family envisions in terms of education and you push that student to achieve—even if she or he is less enthused than you are—are you being paternalistic? Are you imposing your own dreams and goals on the client? In contrast, if you simply accept what seems to be the adolescent's limited view of life, are you upholding the social worker's commitment to promote an individual's well-being?

You may notice that this discussion is not moving toward a definitive answer. In my experience, the issue of self-determination versus paternalism is one that pops up frequently in social work practice. Perhaps the most useful way to think about it is that you will always need to think about it. A simple formula is probably not going to be helpful in resolving these more subtle manifestations.

STRAIGHT TALK ABOUT EXPECTATIONS AND STANDARDS IN A LITIGIOUS WORLD

You have seen in this chapter that many issues concerning ethics and values are complicated by context and are quite fuzzy when they are embedded in real practice situations. As a careful, ethical social worker, you will want to consider such issues thoughtfully throughout your practice career. The following sections consider what it means to practice ethical social work in both the postmodern and litigious worlds. These worlds view the idea of ethical practice through very different lenses, and it will be necessary for you to negotiate both of them skillfully.

Thoughtful Practice in a Postmodern World

Practitioners often discover that just when they think they have a complex issue figured out, another viewpoint confounds their confidence. Both clients and colleagues have a way of demonstrating the principle of multiple realities by introducing other experiences and possibilities that will challenge your thinking and your certainty that you know what's right. You can expect to be challenged on a regular basis.

The current substance of professional ethical inquiry, although broadening, is at the same time somewhat restricted in content. As Witkin (2000) notes, much of what is written about U.S. ethics is more concerned with their viola-tion than their strengths, more concerned "with individualized conduct than collective responsibility" (p. 199), more concerned with morality than with power excesses, and more concerned with the poor than the rich. These are re-flections of our current culture. Also, there are more complaints about sexual vi-olations than about racism, and more complaints about fee regulations than about poverty (Strom-Gottfried, 2000; Witkin, 2000).

We could explore many other dimensions as alternative ethical concerns, however. For example, Walz and Ritchie (2000) suggest that Gandhian principles (based on the work of Mahatma Gandhi, an Indian pacifist) could make a valu-able contribution to Western thinking about ethical issues in social work prac-tice. These principles include service, social justice, nonviolence, priority to the disadvantaged, and the notion of the heart as unifier of all things. You might ask, for example, in your ethical monitoring, to what degree your work is consistent with nonviolence, or maintaining material simplicity, or prioritizing the needs of the disadvantaged. This kind of inquiry, although only one of many possible alternatives and decidedly not of mainstream U.S. culture, would substantially change and enrich the ethics discourse in social work practice.

Ethical questions rarely get settled permanently, and new workers are not the only ones to experience them. Ethics will be an integral part of your ongo-ing practice. I believe that it is your ethical responsibility to challenge solutions or assumptions, even those consistent with the *Code,* that you see as harmful or nonresponsive to real people in real situations. This means to question, dia-logue, explore, and work for the changes you think are important.

Risk Management in a Litigious World

Although you have an ethical responsibility to challenge accepted solutions that you find problematic, you probably sense that some situations will demand that you be very concrete and decisive about your position. We live in a highly litigious society, particularly with regard to the activities of professionals work-ing with people. If you become licensed, you will be expected by a regulating body both to know and uphold the *Code of Ethics*. You may also have questions about certain aspects of the *Code,* and you may actively challenge them to en-courage change. But you will be at risk for serious trouble if you disregard them casually. Social workers face certain risks of censure and lawsuits charging mal-practice or negligence that you should be aware of. Strom-Gottfried (2000), in an examination of 781 ethics violations, discovered that boundary violations (with sexual relationships as the most numerous) composed the greatest num-ber (at 254). "Poor practice" (160) was second, and "Competence" (86) was third, with "Record keeping," "Honesty," "Breach of confidentiality," "In-formed consent," "Collegial violations," "Billing," and "Conflicts of interest" accounting for the remainder.

Reamer (2001a) calls the area of professional and legal accountability "ethics risk management" and asserts that students need to be acquainted with these kinds of repercussions of violating the *Code*. If, for example, you decide after careful analysis that you will choose a route of practice that conflicts with the *Code* (such as bartering for your services with a client who lives in poverty, which is highly discouraged in Section 1.13b), you will want to do a lot of homework and be prepared.

Probably the most basic caveat for evaluating and counteracting ethical violations is to take advantage of the knowledge and experiences of other competent and concerned social workers through supervision. Strategic thinking and planning with another person, particularly one with more experience in recognizing various angles, can be invaluable in troubling ethical contexts. As a professional social worker, you will be expected to be familiar with many basic, but sometimes confusing, legal mandates (duty to report, duty to protect, duty to provide a reasonable standard of care, duty to respect privacy, and duty to maintain confidentiality) as well as with principles specific to social work. It is enormously helpful to talk with your supervisors and peers when questions concerning these concepts come up. Further, if you have been supervised throughout the course of your client-worker relationships, the likelihood that you will inadvertently commit an ethical violation will be reduced simply as a result of your supervisor's ongoing input.

The curious contrast here between (1) soul-searching, reflective, contextual practice in which values are explored and rules about them are challenged and (2) the straight-backed, litigious, and absolute world of the rights and wrongs of ethical violations points to a puzzling dimension in contemporary social work. This is part of the transition process of moving back and forth from a postmodern frame to one in which your legal and professional obligations are set out before you in stark black and white. This world requires that you be "bilingual" in the sense that you are aware of the expectations of the law and the profession as well as your own obligation to think and question.

CONCLUSION

This chapter has encouraged you to question (but not necessarily reject), respectfully, some of the moral and value rules by which the profession governs itself. Consistent with the postmodern ideas of challenging taken-for-granted precepts, you are invited, as an active participant, to explore the implications of the profession's values and ethics.

The representative areas in which dilemmas frequently occur should help you begin to strategize approaches for resolving other complex ethical dilemmas. Although the chapter has encouraged your active participation in questioning various aspects of the profession, it has also emphasized the nature of the relationship between social work practice and contemporary concerns with violations, and the need for an understanding of societal expectations.

MAIN POINTS

- Ethical codes are useful in providing standards of professional conduct, but may also restrict creativity when dealing with different contexts and multiple realities.

- Social workers have an ethical responsibility to contemplate, challenge, and work to change the profession's ethical awareness.

- Social work ethics and the law are not the same thing, although they have parallels and potential for collaboration. They also conflict when legal duties, such as the duty to report, come into question in certain contexts.

- Ethical dilemmas arise out of competing values—for example, dilemmas involving dual relationships, privacy versus public issues, and paternalism versus self-determination.

- Social workers need to develop sophistication in risk management practices that protect them from ethical violations by learning from others' experiences and familiarizing themselves with basic legal mandates.

EXERCISES: PRACTICING SOCIAL WORK

Review the case files for Gloria Sanchez Quintanilla and the social arrangements under which Gloria and her husband, Leo, live. Also review the Values Inventory. Then consider the following practice scenario:

Ethical Issues in Relationship: Gloria and Leo

You have been working with Gloria Sanchez Quintanilla and her husband Leo, at their request, to try to help them manage their household budget more effectively. Even though Leo has a good income, there never seemed to be enough money to run the household and Gloria was beginning to resent the lack of what she considered simple necessities.

In the course of your work together, they have told you of a previous period in their marriage in which Leo hit Gloria with some frequency. Each of them assures you that Leo has worked on this issue, that he is no longer battering, and that they want to stay together for the sake of their family. They feel, however, they must improve the quality of their relationship, which is especially strained, when they argue about money. In such situations, Leo tends to stay out late with his co-workers and Gloria is home alone and angry. They have agreed that direct, open, and honest communication is their relationship goal and indicate that sexual fidelity is an essential dimension of that goal. Between the fifth and sixth meetings, you receive a telephone call from Leo who says, "I think it would help you to know that I am involved romantically with another person. Gloria does not know and I know that you will not reveal this information. I want you to know because I respect your expertise. You are doing a wonderful job."

1. What do you notice about your own response to this scene?

2. What do you notice about your ideas of expertise and professionalism?

3. How do you think you would go about responding to this request?

4. Identify the components of the *Code* that assist you in thinking about your obligations in this situation.

5. What do you find in the *Code* that might help you avoid this kind of scenario?

6. What impact does Leo's prior battering of Gloria make on you? Where might it fit in the Values Inventory?

EXERCISES: THE SOCIAL WORK LIBRARY

Read Reichert's chapter on applying human rights to social work practice. Review the five very brief case vignettes and the questions she applies to them. Then generate at least two similar case scenarios of your own (either from your internship, volunteer work, or other coursework) and identify:

1. What human rights issues are relevant to the case.

2. What ethical issues are involved.

3. The link between the ethical issues and human rights issues.

OTHER EXERCISES

Peggy, Annie, and the Code of Ethics

The young woman, Peggy, answering the hotline at the rape crisis center felt anxious. It was one thing to read about sexual violence and another to respond to people experiencing it—one thing to commit yourself to ending it and another to realize what the process of ending it would require.

Annie was on the other end of the phone, weeping. She just wanted to die, she said. She felt filthy and her life was now torn apart. Annie agreed to meet with Peggy at the emergency room at the hospital. There she was able to listen to Annie and hear the story of her experience. A nurse and then a doctor examined Annie. She was asked if she wanted to report the incident to the police. She said she wasn't sure, it was so awful she didn't feel like much like talking about it, but she'd think it over. She asked Peggy what she thought about it. Peggy knew something about the process and how the protocols of the police, the hospital, and the courts worked. She knew the treatment Annie might received and she knew how long it might take and the effect that those processes had on women sometimes. Peggy struggled with her answer. Meanwhile, Annie had begun crying again, saying she just wanted to be left alone.

1. What are the ethical issues here?

2. What is the dilemma?

3. Does the *Code of Ethics* inform Peggy here? Can you trace and relate this scenario to specific sections of the *Code?*

4. How would you respond to Annie?

IFSW

The International Federation of Social Workers lists the following International conventions as guides for social work practice.

• Universal Declaration of Human Rights

• The International Covenant on Civil and Political Rights

• The International Covenant on Economic, Social and Cultural Rights

• The Convention on the Elimination of All Forms of Racial Discrimination

• The Convention on the Elimination of All Forms of Discrimination against Women

• The Convention on the Rights of the Child

• Indigenous and Tribal People Convention

Choose any two of the last four in the list and research their status on the United Nations Web site (www.un.org). What can you discern about the U.S.'s role in ratifying (or not) these agreements? Confer with your classmates and develop a group statement regarding their status and the implications.

Case Scenario: What about Bea?

You are a social worker in a psychiatric hospital setting. Because there is so much pressure from insurance companies and hospital administrators to discharge patients as soon as possible, you are used to planning discharges beginning at admission. Bea, whom you met in the first chapter, was admitted for long-term psychiatric reasons and is terrified to leave the hospital after a stay of over thirty years. You find her tearfully pleading, quite desperate, and she really doesn't seem ready to go.

You feel caught between the demands of your agency and the requirements of your client, as you see them. How will you go about resolving this situation? What three primary values are represented in your thinking? In what section of the *Code* would you look for guidance? Choose one of the two strategies for resolving ethical dilemmas in the chapter and apply it to Bea. Compare your response with other students; do differing strategies lead to different resolutions?

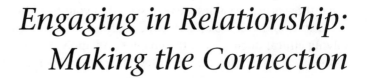

CHAPTER 4

Engaging in Relationship: Making the Connection

She is like a big sister. She is there checking on me. She says, "So, you behavin' yourself?" I say, "Yeah." She says, "I haven't heard from you. Are you okay?" That helps that she calls and checks on me like that. I got to keep my nose clean.

> Richard Rapp, in Saleebey, 2002, p. 139

What do I need out of relationship? What can I give in a relationship? I am no different than any of you out there today. I have the same heart, I have the same feelings, I have the same aches and pains and the same hope and dreams that you do. I have suffered disappointment in relationships, as have you. I have been hurt too, but through all of this I have grown . . .

> Resa Hayes, disability activist, in Mackelprang & Salsgiver, 1999, p. 161

RELATIONSHIP IS AT THE VERY HEART OF SOCIAL WORK. It is probably what first appealed to you about the profession and will likely be an abiding component that sustains your commitment. From social work educator Helen Perlman's *Relationship: The Heart of Helping People* (1983) to Judith Lee's *The Empowerment Approach to Social Work Practice* (2001), social work scholars and practitioners have recognized relationship as a critical part of the profession's work.

When you think of relationship, you may first think of the close, careful, one-to-one partnership that characterizes much of direct practice. These relationships, however, rarely stand alone and are usually enhanced and facilitated by effective connections with other players who are significant to the client. These players include teachers, landlords, therapists, case managers, clergy, friends, and family, as well as other participants in community services and institutions who help the client to reach her or his goals.

Relationship is also as critical in group, family, organization, and community development work as it is in interventions with individuals. As suggested earlier in the book, relationship between cultures may become the single most important dimension of our global well-being in the future. Relationship shapes the connection between the worker and client and stimulates the investment in the work they set out to do together.

This chapter explores several aspects of engagement, the process of building relationships across (largely) direct practice settings, and its importance to the overall success of social work practice. The first section examines the importance of hearing the client's story and suggests a number of specific beginning and interviewing skills and approaches that help the worker both elicit the story and enlist the assistance of others. This section also includes some skill combinations that are helpful in establishing the connection and setting the stage for a productive effort. Later sections in the chapter view this continuous engagement process through the lenses of strengths-based, social justice, and human rights practice as the perspectives that ground the work.

HEARING THE STORY

Probably the most important few moments of a social work relationship occur at the very beginning. No matter what the focus of your agency is or what theoretical perspective you may be using, you first want to hear the client's story. The story may be a long and detailed account, or it may be brief. If your agency's protocol gives you only 50 minutes to establish a plan for intervention, eliciting the client's entire story will be a challenge. Further, some agencies will expect you to gather a comprehensive psychosocial history that details the client's whole life, which may seem much more focused on the past than on the present.

Despite these obstacles, you will want to prepare for your work with the client by hearing the story first, to whatever degree possible. As you listen, you might ask yourself the following questions:

- How do clients describe their situations, and what meaning do these have for them?
- What will life look like when the situation is better?
- How do they spend their time?
- What talents do they have?
- What do they want to happen in their work with you?

Although these may seem like general considerations, they are helpful in establishing the respect and affiliation in the first connections that lead to successful work together.

Opening Skills and Approaches

The social work literature identifies many compilations of skills that are directed to establishing a successful engagement with clients. A particularly useful one, proposed by Middleman and Wood (1990), begins with a group of four "perception skills" (p. 19). These consist of

- Looking with planned emptiness
- Looking at the old as if new
- Jigsaw puzzling
- Looking from diverse angles

These skills represent what the social worker takes into the meeting room before ever seeing the client. In that sense they address the worker's openness (or lack of it) and have more to do with attitude than with technique. Each of these skills is discussed in the following section.

Looking with Planned Emptiness   The skill of **looking with planned emptiness** suggests a purposeful effort on your part to remain open and sincerely curious. This skill involves curtailing your impulses to jump to interpretations or conclusions regarding the client or the client's situation. It requires you to maintain a genuinely empty spot into which you can receive a new experience, view, or idea and not place it into an existing category.

In the practice context, looking with planned emptiness might mean accepting that you don't understand why, for example, your five-year-old client is so angry, or why the particular community you work in seems so apathetic, or why your agency is so poorly received by its clients. It requires that in any of these situations, you explore, listen, and avoid making premature interpretations to fit what theoretical or personal perspectives you already hold.

Looking at the Old as if New   This skill requires viewing the familiar as something new. **Looking at the old as if new** asks you to take on a childlike openness, which can help reduce or eliminate the cynicism that sometimes infects social workers. It keeps you from the pessimistic "I've seen one, I've seen them all" stance that not only is likely to be erroneous but also stifles creativity. This skill gives each client, no matter how she or he is classified by the agency or the world, a fresh chance as the beneficiary of your optimism, hopefulness, and creative efforts.

Jigsaw Puzzling   As the client's story unfolds, certain pieces may seem contradictory, or don't follow, or are hard to make sense of. Usually those kinds of holes are purposeful—that is, the client is not ready to share them or isn't sure how much she or he wants to divulge about them. To satisfy your own need for a coherent story, you might immediately address the inconsistency or lack of detail. Adopting this approach, however, could be a mistake. Instead, respectfully waiting until those pieces "fall into place," or **jigsaw puzzling**, is an important, if subtle, expression of validating the client's judgments about what to include and what to fill in later. This skill involves restraining your curiosity, which can be a difficult task to learn.

Looking from Diverse Angles   Recognizing perspectives other than your own, or **looking from diverse angles,** is another strategy to remain open and avoid looking only from your own viewpoint. The ability to understand a situation from the client's (or the family's or the group's) point of view is a crucial skill in social work, particularly when you are working with people who are different from yourself.

The Four Perception Skills   Together these skills lead to a position of genuine curiosity, which means you will ask questions that you really don't know the answers to and that you really want to know about. This helps keep the conversation fresh and honest, as you are less likely to ask questions designed to confirm what you already think. You may yourself have experienced some frustration with people who have assumed they understood your thoughts or situation because they knew a lot about others' thoughts and situations in the same realm. It's hard to be open to and hear the story of the person before you if you are waiting for another story that's in your textbook or in your mind.

I emphasize these skills here because they play such a vital role in social work practice and because they relate so strongly to social workers' attitudes. The skills are not necessarily innate, but rather are a product of thought and will. You can cultivate, work on, and improve your use of these skills. They carry great potential for helping you to hear the client's story as she or he has experienced it and for being open to the experience of difference. I also want to note here that these skills are not techniques the worker pulls out just to work with clients. Rather, they constitute a genuine approach to working with people in general, and as such are just as meaningful for interactions with the people who are significant to clients as they are with clients themselves.

For example, you may have made a skillful connection with a client in that you have heard the story, conveyed both a professional and warm acceptance, generated confidence and hope, and clarified the tasks you and your client have agreed upon. If one of those tasks is to help the client locate and secure housing that better suits her needs, you may want or need to work with a reluctant landlord. In such a situation you might perceive the scenario only in the client's terms—that is, you might be inclined to criticize a landlord who resists renting to your client. For this reason, in your beginning contacts with the landlord, you use the same perceptual skills that you used with your client. That is, you try to enter the conversation with "planned emptiness," and you avoid jumping to conclusions about slumlords or accusations of evildoing when you really haven't had a dialogue. You will also want to "look from diverse angles" to understand the particular difficulties the landlord has in maintaining rental properties. You may further consider "looking at the old as if new" to avoid stereotyping the landlord or deciding you know all about the rental business because you worked with a difficult landlord in another client situation.

Because social workers are frequently so invested in the rights of clients (as they should be), they are sometimes tempted to leap to conclusions regarding perceived adversaries that are based more on eagerness than on the person's actual responses. For example, if you enter into the dialogue with the assumption that the landlord will be prejudicial or will violate the client's rights, you are not likely to hear the landlord's story. In my experience, in more than one case, I've found that the very person I felt most inclined to judge negatively turned out to be the most helpful. In some cases, that person may be the only person or the key person who can assist the client. Therefore, it would be a great disservice to make anything less than a full effort at engaging in an effective relationship.

It is, of course, possible that despite every skill you can muster, the landlord will not behave equitably or perhaps even legally with regard to your client's right to obtain reasonable housing. In this case you might need to work through other avenues, such as a city fair housing board or a rental commission. In those scenarios, in which contentions run high, you will find that you need your skills more than ever. You will need to be fair, articulate, and open with all the concerned parties. You will need to recognize your own biases and understand the client population you're working with. In the next section we will explore some of the specific skills for going beyond the initial interchange and establishing a productive dialogue.

Specific Skills for the Dialogue

Because we communicate in complex ways, using several different skills, students frequently find that it is helpful to isolate some of these skills so they can study and practice them more directly. Here, we will examine some specific approaches and skills that are useful in the process of interviewing, or initiating a purposeful conversation. We will also look at some attitudinal skills and components of body language such as eye contact and positioning. Consistent with the strengths approach, we will "focus more on conversational skills than interviewing skills" (Kisthardt, 2002, p. 172). The following discussion emphasizes the quality of the dialogue rather than the interrogation that interviewing suggests.

Intent vs. Impact   As we begin this discussion, it might be helpful to remember that intention is different from impact. You've probably known this fact much of your life, but it has particular significance when you're trying to enter a relationship with people whose orientations, cultures, and personal situations are different from yours. Simple things like how close you sit to your client or whether there is a desk between you and the client communicate much about you and your purpose and can also make an impact you might never have envisioned and certainly not wished. For example, if you appear "fortified" by heavy furniture, you may seem distant or pretentious. Similarly, if you sit too close, with too steady eye contact, the client might perceive you as intrusive or brash. Part of your preparation will be to consider elements of culture or style—both yours and your client's—to which you need to attend. Supervision, peer consultation, and a general assessment of the particular culture in which you are carrying out your work will be helpful here.

By the same token, you will want to weigh whether your dress, posture, and language are appropriate to the person you're working with and the setting in which that work takes place. For example, in most practice contexts you will not want to wear jeans to a courtroom appearance or use dorm room slang to the judge. Conversely, you might dress informally and feel relaxed in making an outreach home visit to a toddler and his family. The biggest general concern about clothing, appearance, and behavior of this kind is that you communicate respect for your client and for the nature of the event in which you are accompanying her or him. Such behavior will also be translated differently in different localities, based on such factors as urban versus rural setting, ethnic customs, part of the country, and the like. People are individuals and can't be pigeonholed easily. This is one of the reasons why social work doesn't fall easily within a scientific frame of reference and why categorical lists of dos and don'ts don't apply in all contexts.

Discovery-Oriented Questions   In general, you will want to hear your client's story in the way she or he wants to tell it. **Discovery-oriented questions** are designed to invite your client to communicate her or his purposes in coming to see you and to express goals for the relationship. They assist you in getting to know the client, and they can put the client at ease. This process may mean waiting a minute after you make welcoming introductions to allow your client an opportunity to begin. If she or he doesn't take up that cue, you can invite her or him with such phrases as, "Where would you like to begin?" or, "Can you tell me what brings you here?" Some clients may be prepared for a much more directive stance on your part, so you may need gently to encourage their ownership of the dialogue.

There are many lists of specific interviewing skills in the literature that can help you initiate and encourage helpful conversations. Middleman & Wood (1990), as discussed earlier, is a good example. Another list, based on the empowerment approach to social work, presents a continuum of nine response skills that range from least to most directive. Exhibit 4.1 examines these skills in some detail.

EXHIBIT 4.1

*Response Skills
for Social
Workers*

- *Making space:* You will want to permit moments of silence that allow the client to gather thoughts and feelings, as well as to think about how to explain a situation to you. Silence may also provide a little time to regroup and refocus, which is especially helpful when the client is explaining a painful situation. Try not to fill the space, as many of us verbal and social folks tend to do. Becoming comfortable with silence can be immensely helpful to the client and you alike.

- *Responding nonverbally:* A wide range of behaviors, from how close you sit to your client to how much eye contact you make, come under the heading of nonverbal response. In most cases you will want to sit relatively close to the client. In situations in which the client is not upright (for example, the client is in a hospital bed), the worker will usually want to minimize the height differential by sitting on a low chair at an angle. By assuming this posture, you empower your client to control the amount of eye contact and full face contact in a way that is comfortable. As with all of these guidelines, however, you need to judge whether your client is responding positively to your position or whether you need to alter it. A facet of the interchange that can be both highly variable and powerful is the degree of eye contact that you maintain with your client. In most cases you will make intermittent contact to indicate interest and connection. For clients of almost any culture, eye contact that is too constant and intense may be acutely uncomfortable; to some clients, even minimal amounts may seem intrusive. These are areas you need to consider and rethink if the client appears to be uncomfortable.

- *Responding with minimal verbalization:* Simple one- or two-word expressions are usually encouraging to the person telling the story, for example, "Go on," or, "Can you tell me more?" In this early phase of the meeting, in most scenarios, you want to provide only enough response to inspire the client to continue speaking. To respond fully with your own experience or reaction may interrupt the client's direction and distract the unfolding of the story. Even if your client appears to require redirection or support for going ahead, you still will want to provide only the minimum needed.

- *Paraphrasing:* Repeating part or all of a client's statement in your own words provides a useful (and underestimated in my view) opportunity for assessing whether the meaning you derive from that statement is accurate. In addition, if it is not, the client is invited to correct you. This communicates both that you care enough about the story to get it right and that you recognize that you are not infallible in understanding the specific issues at hand.

- *Clarifying:* The role of clarifying is closely related to paraphrasing, but the worker is more directly asking for client feedback. For example, the worker might say, "What I understand you to be saying is …" Clarification contributes to understanding the uniqueness of the client's message rather than generalizing or framing it in a way that matches your own perceptions. Consequently, like restatement, it increases the accuracy of your assessment while communicating a respect for the complexity of the person before you.

EXHIBIT 4.1

continued

- *Summarizing:* A summary can provide closure and consensus either after a segment of the session is complete or at the conclusion of the whole session. It can also help to establish organization for the entirety of the work as well as frame the particular session. In situations in which the issues evoke significant client emotion, or in which the work is directed at some complex task, summing up the session can demonstrate manageability and hopefulness. In addition, summing up can provide both you and your client with a snapshot of where you've been, which usually helps to point the way ahead.

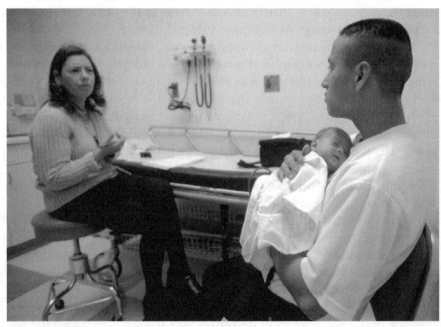

Social workers respond.

Direct, Closed Questions   Having asserted that the goal is almost always to expand the story, we will now focus on the exceptions. Certain situations seem to demand much greater precision at the moment than a comprehensive story is likely to provide. Usually these situations involve dangerous conduct or some imminent threat of harm that must be dealt with directly in order to ensure safety. **Closed questions** get at specific and concrete answers, often involving yes or no.

Often these situations involve a client who is expressing an intention of hurting her- or himself or someone else. You need to know if the client has a real plan to engage in the dangerous behavior (for example, suicide) and the means to carry out the plan. Although views differ on the usefulness of formal client agreements to refrain from self-injurious behavior, you need to know as clearly as possible what the client intends.

Engagement Skills in Combination: Radical Listening

For the most part, when communicating, we apply disparate yet integrated skills, attitudes, approaches, and values in such a way that it is difficult to sort them out. That's why learning a list of skills as simple entities that stand alone isn't usually as helpful as we might like in real work with real people. It is possible, however, to deconstruct a full approach by analyzing the specific skills it contains. One approach that combines several of the skills just discussed is called "radical listening" (Weingarten, 1995).

Web Links

Go to the Advanced Leadership Group site to do an online assessment of your listening skills.

One way to increase your openness to hearing the story and appreciating its meaning is to employ a combination of processes and skills defined as a form of **radical listening.** The term was introduced to emphasize the importance of validating clients through a process that recognizes their expertise on their life experiences (Weingarten, 1995). Subsequently, Weingarten's term was defined to include four specific processes that require specialized skills: (1) listening with planned emptiness, (2) attentive listening, (3) deconstructive listening, and (4) listening to bear witness (Wood & Roche, 2001b).

You have already learned the importance of listening with planned emptiness in the engagement process. According to Wood and Roche, this activity can lead to **attentive listening.** This skill requires the social worker to listen for and hear the client's story, not for symptoms or insight, but rather for the experience and what it has meant to the client. Here the worker uses simple words of encouragement or restatement and other communication cues, such as nodding, to establish a connection with the client.

After the worker has understood the client's story and established a connection, she or he then engages in **deconstructive listening,** in which the worker helps the client consider alternatives to her or his understanding of the story and the explanation for it. For example, a worker might help a young man with a spinal cord injury to deconstruct his understanding that the disability renders him incapable of full employment or participation in the community. This process might involve exploring how the client came to that understanding and recognizing that this construction is only one of many that could be made of the experience. The hope is that this process leads to another interpretation (or at least recognition of the possibility of another interpretation) of the client's situation that more fully integrates his strengths and assets as well as his liabilities.

Further, through a process of "perspectival" (Roche & Wood, 2001b, p. 586), or circular, clarifying questions, the worker can uncover other views that might apply to a client situation. **Perspectival questions** (or **circular questions**) ask about the client's perception of another person's perspective. This helps the client recognize that there are additional ways to view the situation. For example, such questions might include, "How might your mother have seen your great success in school?" or, "Who in your family most admires your musical skills?" or, "What do you think your last employer meant when he wrote that you are smart and well motivated?"

The final process is **listening to bear witness**, which suggests that you join with the client, aligning with her or him in recording and taking a stand on the experience of hardship, discrimination, or violence (for example) that she or he has endured. Although this is more a values position and process than a technical skill, it reflects the genuine, empathic dimension of the social work relationship, and it consolidates the engagement connection. This particular example of how skills can be combined in an effective approach is especially applicable in the context of abusive situations (for example, intimate partner violence), but it also applies to any client experience in which validation is a critical component of the relationship.

ARTICULATING PURPOSE: WORKER ROLE AND AGENDA

Now that you have learned various strategies for understanding the client's story from her or his perspective, we will examine the skills that help social workers articulate the purpose of their intervention to the client. **Transparency** refers to the worker's communication about what she or he is trying to do. More specifically, transparency can be defined as the worker's openness in discussing such issues as "why s/he asked a particular question, why s/he pursued one particular direction or 'line' of questioning" (Morgan, 2000, p. 126). This kind of openness can help the client understand the connections that the worker is making in the client's story. Transparency helps to remove the mystery from the work and flatten whatever hierarchy may exist between the worker and client. It also invites workers to "locate" themselves; for example, you acknowledge that you are a student who will leave at the end of the year, or you are young, or have no children, or you are not a person of color. That kind of candor can also directly address possible obstacles in the working relationship. Although not the same as self-disclosure, transparency reduces the distance between worker and client and provides the client with insight into the worker's thinking. We will explore other aspects of narrative theory (the theory associated with client stories) more fully in Chapters 5 through 8.

This is often the place in your articulation of purpose for a clear, concrete description of roles or job responsibilities. For example, if you are a court advocate for a family violence shelter, you will want to be clear with your clients that counseling their children is not what you do. Similarly, if you work as a case manager in a community mental health center and your role is to identify and coordinate the services your clients need, it will be helpful if you describe your coordinating role. You might also clarify what you do (help link to services) and what you don't do (adjust medications).

When you consider the bewildering array of services and professions in today's world, you can see how easy it might be for clients to confuse roles and purposes. Your clients in the family violence shelter, for instance, may also be seeking supportive psychotherapy, in which case they deserve to know that this isn't your realm. It can be exceedingly confusing and disempowering for any of us to discover our erroneous expectations of others. For this reason, workers owe it to clients to be as straightforward as possible about what the clients can expect.

On a more subtle level, the overall purpose of the work should also be transparent and explicit. If you and your client agree to work on, for example, the client's troubling relationship with school authorities regarding her child, that is and should be the real purpose of the work. It is sometimes tempting to engage the client in work on one issue and attempt, somewhat surreptitiously, to work on other issues you may think are more worthy. For example, in the school authorities situation, you may think the client really needs to examine previously unquestioned negative relationships with men (vis-à-vis the troubling relationship with school authorities). This is dangerous business. To maintain a genuine and honest relationship with clients requires that you are open about the jointly agreed-upon direction of the work, the methods you are employing, and the goal of your intervention.

If you believe that another construction of the issue is more relevant or that the goals should be different, you should raise this issue early as a tentative point of negotiation about the nature and scope of the work. You would then take your cue from the client's response. (Chapter 5 will deal with this issue in more detail.) Secret agendas have no place in ethical practice. The genuineness of the initial engagement will make a great deal of difference to the client's sense of being valued and accepted for what she or he is bringing to the relationship.

This respectful stance regarding the client is one way to demonstrate a strengths-based approach. The following section will elaborate on the strengths approach in the engagement process.

MOVING FROM SPOTTING DEFICIENCY TO RECOGNIZING STRENGTHS

You already know that the strengths perspective is central to this book's approach to social work practice. Here we will look at its explicit role in engagement, along with its assumptions of client resilience and personal agency. Because so much of social work practice has focused on what's wrong, or identifying the problem, initiating and sustaining this emphasis on strengths might be more challenging than you imagine.

As you saw in Chapter 3, social work as a profession developed during a period in the late 1800s in which moral conversion was a focal point. Poverty was often seen as a reflection of moral deficiency or laziness rather than as a structural failing that places and maintains people in adversity. As professional fields of helping (including psychology and psychoanalysis) developed more sophisticated and complicated assessment schemes (including the *DSM*, first published in 1958), the focus on pathology became more pervasive.

Although social workers have a long history of recognizing their clients' strengths, this emphasis on pathology, problems, or dysfunction is deeply embedded in the culture and the traditions of the helping professions. It also persists in the current service delivery system. You will probably recognize that agencies are often created around specific types of problems (for example, substance abuse or major mental illnesses), and these problems in turn define the focus of the agency. It seems almost instinctive to ask, "What's the problem?" when you meet a new client.

Nevertheless, when there is support for, and commitment to, a departure from illness-based models, social workers can implement strategies based on client strengths rather than deficiencies. For example, an increasingly visible body of literature reflects a different perspective from the various models of deficit, damage, or blame. Much of this literature focuses on **resilience**, the belief that many people—some say most people—raised or living in the most daunting of circumstances, not only survive, but thrive. Resilience theory asserts that adversity can generate strengths and coping capacities even in some of the most oppressive and compromising scenarios.

Skills and Methods

Charles Rapp (1998), who has written substantially on mental health issues from a strengths perspective, identifies a series of methods for building a strengths-based relationship between mental health clients and case managers, which can also contribute significantly to generalist social work. These methods are (1) core conditions, (2) mirroring, (3) contextualizing, (4) self-disclosure, (5) accompaniment, and (6) reinforcement and celebration.

 Web Links

The Empathy site is dedicated to the study of interpersonal communication, small group dynamics, and the phenomenon of empathy. You can participate in a moderated e-mail list if you wish.

Core Conditions   Rapp defines the foundation of the relationship in terms of the **core conditions** "empathy, genuineness, and unconditional positive regard" (p. 64). This idea arose from the counseling literature of the late 1970s and is still seen as critical. In general, the core conditions suggest an open, honest, caring relationship between worker and client in which the worker does not have exaggerated notions of her or his professionalism or expertise.

Web Links

For a look at the use of empathy in schools and families, the Roots of Empathy site features curricula and publications.

Mirroring   This metaphor is employed to counter the negative reflections many clients have of their own value and worth. Because all mirrors distort to some degree, the social worker uses one that is more positively focused in building the relationship (and throughout the work). **Mirroring** reflects the client's talents and capacities in such a way that the client can see herself or himself from a perspective other than deficiencies and problems. The worker then focuses on these strengths, emphasizing their presence in the client's daily life and stressing their importance.

Contextualizing   Social workers use **contextualizing** to put clients' issues into the wider context in order to discourage them from blaming themselves for their problems. For example, when landlords discriminate against clients of the mental health system simply because they don't want "those people" to live in their building, some clients blame themselves for somehow being undesirable. In such a situation, the worker might explore with the clients the effects of stigma in an intolerant society or provide evidence that they are acceptable to other, more positive landlords. Significantly, Rapp warns against transforming self-blame into "environmental blame" (p. 67) (that is, blaming the environment) and emphasizes that environments are also composed of opportunities and resources, as well as constraints.

Self-Disclosure   The extent to which social workers should reveal their feelings, background, and life story to their clients remains a controversial issue in social work practice and is called **self-disclosure.** Rapp points to the inequities of expecting clients to disclose the most personal and profound aspects of their hearts and souls, while professionals sit back and artificially remain closed and mysterious. Because a strengths-based approach is based on normalizing the relationship in genuine ways, it calls for some degree of worker self-disclosure insofar as this disclosure helps to establish trust, validate the quality of the relationship, and model effective ways of managing emotions for the benefit of the client. Unfortunately, there are no accepted standards governing the amount, nature, and purpose of the disclosure, because appropriateness is so highly influenced by context.

In general Rapp suggests that workers be explicit about their messages rather than developing a relationship in which their verbal cues differ significantly from their behavioral ones. For example, if you describe yourself to a client as committed to strengths-based work, open communication, and a caring relationship, you will need to "live" that message. Not following through, for example, by not communicating about your life, refusing to accept a gesture of affection, or adhering to strict formality, you will send mixed messages at best, and be seen as hypocritical and untrustworthy at worst. Even clients struggling with the most horrific issues can recognize the difference between the "talk" and the "walk."

Accompaniment Rapp advocates for accompanying a client in the performance of a task. This can be **accompaniment** in the literal sense of going with a client to court or to a landlord's office, but also in a metaphorical sense, as in joining the client in her or his journey of change. He also acknowledges the concern for dependence that sometimes comes up in such situations. The need or desirability for accompaniment should be assessed critically according to the specifics of the situation. Nevertheless, we are all interdependent, and this is an area in which social workers should be careful not to frame their clients in terms of *their* cultural or personal sense of the optimal level of independence, especially when the client either does not share or cannot attain their ideal. When literal accompaniment is not appropriate, the metaphor of accompaniment can resonate with the client long after the work is over.

Reinforcement and Celebration To carry out a strengths-based approach successfully, the worker needs to know the client well and to understand the meanings the client attaches to such behaviors as praise or recognition of particular events or accomplishments. Some expressions of support, for example, can affirm one person and embarrass another. By the same token, indiscriminate praise can be insulting, whereas purposeful, immediate, and specific positive feedback may be highly valued and strengthening. Although nearly everyone wants to feel appreciated, the worker needs to anticipate client responses in a particular context.

Additional Strengths-Based Methods Walter Kisthardt (2002), also a strengths-focused writer and practitioner, draws from several "targeted populations" to generate strategies for effective engagement. As mentioned earlier, Kisthardt focuses on conversational skills rather than interviewing skills. He has this to add:

- Send a clear message that you are not there to make negative judgments or to try to change them, but rather to affirm their own aspirations and work together toward making those dreams a reality;
- Engage in activities you both enjoy;
- Be sensitive to cultural factors; honor diversity and seek to assist people in involvements that hold meaning for them;
- Seek to incorporate humor, joy, and laughter into the helping process. (pp. 172–175)

Web Links

The Veterans Administration site for Alternate Dispute Resolution emphasizes communication skills, including "Practicing Listening Skills," "Listening to Paraphrase," and "Listening to Clarify."

These solid, basic strengths-based approaches will serve you well in a great variety of practice settings.

Logistics and Activities

Many strengths-based practitioners assert that location and arrangements for the first contact convey an important message about the nature of the ongoing work and the assumptions made about the partnership. Accordingly, these workers will give the client the choice of where and when to meet. Consistent with traditional arrangements, clients will frequently assume that workers expect them to travel to the worker's office (and many workers do). When given a choice, however, clients often prefer a community location. Some clients may request that the meeting be held at their home, either because they have small children, they lack transportation, or they are simply more comfortable in this setting. As is true of much of social work, the client's choice of location depends on the nature of the context, concerns regarding confidentiality, and the agency purpose.

The incorporation of activities can also help the client to engage and feel comfortable. Social workers often forget that they may be a lot more verbally oriented than some clients. To many people, talk is of limited value and serves primarily as a way to communicate about doing. For this reason, playing basketball with an adolescent or walking in the woods with a mental health client can create an environment that is much less intense (and therefore more tolerable for some clients) than an interview-type meeting in a clinical office.

An interesting variation on this theme is a strategy known as "talking in the idiom of the other" (Middleman & Wood, 1990, p. 66). This approach assumes that some clients will use metaphors in their verbal communications as a way to communicate without exposing the specific details of their own lives until they are ready. Middleman and Wood use this example:

> After a staff meeting in which the psychologist's plan for a new service was turned down, she asked me if I ever thought about how long it takes a spider to spin a web and how fast it can be wiped out of the corner with a dust rag. I said it sounded very demoralizing. She looked at me with a sad expression on her face and nodded. I said that spider webs were very vulnerable, and she said that spiders were very vulnerable, too. I nodded. Then I said that sometimes people were vulnerable, giving her a chance to be more direct if she were ready to be. And apparently she was ready, because she said she should never have allowed herself to get so invested in that project. (p. 67)

As you can see, in these cases the worker responds by using the same metaphors and then being sensitive to the other's readiness to be more direct. The purpose of talking in the idiom is to respect the client's communications rather than seeing them as a form of resistance. The worker can then use the information conveyed by the client to support the client's efforts to communicate the depth of her or his experience. This strategy honors the client's meaning and validates her or his approach to engagement in the work.

RECOGNIZING AND ARTICULATING POWER

Even practitioners who embrace a strengths perspective acknowledge that social work practice almost always involves issues related to power. The idea that power enters into the work is one that many students would rather avoid. If you came to social work because you genuinely want to engage with people in their struggles and help them achieve their goals, you may not immediately see the relevance of power. Yet in most instances the obstacles clients face have much to do with power, and the effective management of power can benefit the client. Power is a component in a variety of social work relationships, from political advocacy to one-to-one counseling.

Sources of Power

There are four sources of power with which social workers engage: agency resources, expert knowledge, interpersonal power, and legitimate power (Hartman, 1994).

The Social Work Library

For a classic article on power in social work, read Hasenfeld's paper.

Agency Resources   Social service agencies have access to and control over a number of resources. These include **tangible resources**, such as clothing or money for emergency housing, and **intangible resources**, such as individual counseling and education groups. Traditionally, workers and especially administrators have allocated these resources to client groups or individuals depending upon their evaluation of the fit with agency purposes. The concepts of power sharing and client-consumer advocacy threaten the conviction that workers and administrators should continue to control the disposition of agency resources. Not surprisingly, then, most agencies have been reluctant to give up their authority in this arena.

In contrast, however, some contemporary organizations, and even some federal programs, have experimented with arrangements that empower clients to determine and control the resources they receive. For example, an agency that serves children with disabilities might encourage the child's family members to identify the services they need, both within and outside the agency, rather than undergoing an agency-driven assessment in which a professional tells them what they need. By the same token, some Medicaid provisions include a waiver that permits a family member (usually a parent) to act as case manager, thereby coordinating services for the child and eliminating the costs of professional case management. Such services, which the family chooses and then obtains with assistance, are called **client-directed resources.**

Expert Knowledge   Chapter 2 discussed the idea of expertise and the tensions associated with it. Many social workers find that some clients see them as prestigious experts simply because they have credentials and they are in a helping profession. Workers can counter that assumption in part by using the strengths perspective because it helps to validate and empower clients. By articulating clearly that clients are the experts on their own lives, workers can develop a partnership with clients that focuses on reaching client-defined goals.

Interpersonal Power   The personal attribute characterized by the ability to build strong relationships, develop rapport, and persuade people is known as **interpersonal power.** It's a personal power in the sense that either clients or workers might have it, and it's similar to charisma. Although the worker's interpersonal power can benefit clients when the worker uses it to attain resources or access to services, it can also perpetuate the power imbalance between client and worker by diminishing the client's efforts to reclaim power. If the social work profession truly means to empower clients, workers must strive to reduce their interpersonal power by establishing more egalitarian relations and genuine collaboration with clients (Hartman, 1994).

Legitimate Power   The term **legitimate power** refers to legal power to perform actions of social control (see Chapter 2). Social workers need to be very careful about this power. They must acknowledge the responsibility to protect clients and others (as in cases of child abuse), but they should also recognize that legitimate power must have limits. Therefore, they must be careful not to simply replicate the power abuses of the past by exercising legitimate power beyond what is necessary. Although workers may choose to retain their various powers to use for client benefit, they may alternatively try to work on the more structural level of policy and organizations in order to empower clients. Although the first objective can be important, Hartman asserts that "to take the second option commits one to radical change in service delivery systems and in our practice" (p. 176).

Power in Client Lives: Jasmine Johnson

There are many other ways to think about power with clients. One approach focuses on whatever power relationships the client is struggling with that are external to the worker relationship, either in interpersonal terms or larger cultural terms. The second involves power issues experienced directly between the worker and the client. We will look at these types of power in a case vignette about Jasmine Johnson.

Jasmine's Situation   You work in a family support agency. Your client, Jasmine Johnson, is an African American who comes to you with a concern about parenting. Her young son is difficult to manage behaviorally both at home and, increasingly, at school, and Jasmine isn't sure how to deal with him. He doesn't seem to respect her authority, and he ignores her attempts to discipline him. He is "sassy," talks back, and is occasionally quite rude to her. He ignores the limits she sets, and he doesn't obey school-night curfews or help with any household chores. Jasmine is also struggling financially to support him with only sporadic help from his father. Her job pays poorly, carries little status in the work world, and doesn't provide extra money for either her or her son to enjoy any recreational activities. Overall, Jasmine doesn't feel very good about herself.

Jasmine and Power Relationships   At first glance the issues appear to be personal ones for Jasmine. She knows she doesn't feel good about herself or her situation, and she assumes she needs to be better at something than she is currently. You might assume that she needs to work on her self-esteem, or you might even conclude that she's depressed and needs medical attention. Yet, from another vantage point, it is likely that power, or lack of it, plays an important role in her experience. She is both a woman who performs interpersonal roles (ex-wife, single mother, daughter, worker, friend, neighbor) and a member of a cultural group that has experienced pervasive and persistent oppression for more than three hundred years in our culture.

The Social Work Library

Visit the Social Work Library *to read Gutierrez's work on empowering women of color.*

These are areas that can be deconstructed and examined (Krumer-Nevo, 2005). Although Jasmine may have interpreted her experiences as signs of her own deficiencies, she has also exhibited remarkable resilience in dealing with disadvantage and oppression. She has managed to survive in trying circumstances that have had a far-reaching political repercussion in her life. If she is to be empowered, she will need to recognize those political events in which her life is embedded. You can bring these events to her consciousness through purposeful (and skillful) articulation.

This does not mean that Jasmine's own sense of her problem is erroneous and that the real problems are racism and sexism. Rather, as a social worker you want to validate her experience and recognize the meaning she makes of it. However, it does mean that Jasmine has genuine feelings of inadequacy, and she has experienced the negative side of the power differential. That realization can open many doors. For example, Jasmine may begin to separate her feelings of inadequacy from her sense of identity and start to look at her experiences as a function of her social location. In turn, this new perspective might inspire her to engage in some action, such as forming an informal support group for single, African American mothers. This group might share stories and experiences, provide day care arrangements for one another, or coordinate grocery shopping. Adopting a different outlook also might encourage Jasmine to become a spokesperson for more stringent requirements regarding child support payments or increased benefits for working women with children. The possibilities are endless, and they may affirm Jasmine's experience even as they are instrumental in changing the quality of it.

Jasmine and the Social Worker   There are nearly always noticeable differences between workers and clients. As long as the profession sustains the concept of the social worker as the expert, there will be a felt power differential between the worker and the client based solely on their roles in the relationship. There are also likely to be additional differences related to gender, age, race, status, and so on. These differences, if perceived as problems, can complicate the engagement process.

For example, Jasmine might find it challenging to think of social work students or younger workers in general as a genuine source of help to her. They may come from a different ethnic background, and they may be too young to have families of their own. They may also seem to her to be so privileged by their race and education that she can't see them as connected with anything she experiences in her life. Yet, they are supposed to be experts, and as such they have some level of power she may resent or admire or barely recognize. In most cases, these differences related to worker and client roles or attributes are about power. It is necessary, then, to discuss these differences openly when they get in the way of the work. Simply raising them can open up the whole relationship.

Jasmine Johnson: Conclusions   Situations that involve power differentials are sometimes awkward or even embarrassing to confront, particularly for you as a student or an otherwise humble person. You may understand that the client sees you as having power simply because of your role as a helping person, an employee, or a student. At the same time, you might secretly wonder yourself how much you can offer to an exasperated parent who might be of a different race and remote social class. You might feel some hesitation at working with an oppressed client when you have enjoyed so much privilege. Thus, the concept of power in the relationship can become quite complex and problematic.

When these situations arise, you might hope that the concern will pass or that clients will just trust that you know what you're doing in spite of these differences. Unfortunately, however, once these issues are perceived as problematic, they will not simply go away. Therefore, you and your client should confront them directly through open acknowledgment and exploration. Exhibit 4.2 provides a case example from the literature that demonstrates this approach. In this excerpt, consider the ways in which the worker addresses the issue at hand. What impact do you think this approach will have on the future of the relationship?

This case study in Exhibit 4.2 conveys an extended message. First, it addresses the immediate obstacle, namely, the worker is both much younger than

EXHIBIT 4.2

Recognizing and Articulating Power

"Look, Mr. Cook, I know you think I'm a nice kid and that you like me," I said.

"I do like you," he confirmed.

"But you know I'm too young to have experienced what you go through every day!" I said.

Silence.

"And you may even figure that a kid like me can't help you."

Silence.

"Right?" I continued.

A nod.

Raising differences

"But you want to get out of this depression real bad, don't you." I said.

"I sure do," he said. Then he sighed and added, "I'm probably being foolish. You youngsters are right out of school with the latest techniques. I guess I'd just be more comfortable talking to someone closer to my own age. But here I am already talking to you, aren't I? So I guess I already decided to try it out with you."

I nodded. "How about if anytime you feel uncomfortable, you say so and every time I think you may be a little uncomfortable I'll say so?" I suggested.

"It's a deal," he said.

Source: Middleman and Wood, 1990, p. 163

the client and comparatively inexperienced. Then it paves the way for ongoing honesty in the relationship that involves addressing the obstacle openly and directly. It also illustrates a relatively complex scenario in which both participants seem to feel an initial lack of power that is subsequently alleviated by open acknowledgment. Ultimately, the case suggests that there is a broader context for the work than the one-on-one issues that emerge between worker and client, leading to recognition of social justice and human rights issues in client stories.

VIEWING THE STORY FROM SOCIAL JUSTICE AND HUMAN RIGHTS PERSPECTIVES

Most social workers respond on a gut level to the stories they hear. There is something very powerful about sitting in the same room with a person and hearing the story that is brought to you. This experience almost always creates a personal connection of some kind that seems quite intimate in the sense that it is between you two people in a particular time and place. When the story is one of oppression or extreme hardship, this sensibility can build. In such circumstances the larger perspectives of social justice and human rights may seem like remote, intellectual concepts in the face of the personal pain that your client is experiencing. Nevertheless, these perspectives provide the rationale for your practice, and they help to connect one story to another. They thus provide an organizing frame for your work so that your practice transcends the parameters of individual emotional response or simple sympathy and becomes a carefully planned and cohesive activity in response to clear, principled commitments.

Although you will always want to recognize personal pain and respond on a human level, you will also want to go beyond the intensity of the direct relationship and see your client's experiences as social justice and human rights issues as well.

Full Participation in Culture

 Web Links

Visit the United Nations Web site to read the Universal Declaration of Human Rights. Article 27 defines participation in the cultural life of the community and access to its benefits as a human right.

As discussed in Chapters 1 and 3, work toward social justice is a cornerstone of social work practice and is mandated in the NASW *Code of Ethics* (1999). A number of isms—racism, elitism, sexism, heterosexism, ageism, and the like—that you have probably already studied reflect the degree of social injustice that is prevalent in our culture. Although these prejudicial attitudes toward the "other" are generated by our society and suggest a discriminatory standpoint that most social workers find profoundly distasteful, they also carry concrete repercussions for individuals and groups who live under their shadow. Most of these repercussions assume the form of exclusion from, and limited mobility within, society. The term "exclusion from society" refers to the process through which people are unable to participate in the benefits of public and cultural resources. This inability can be felt quite literally (for example, when there is no access ramp to the public library for people with disabilities) or more indirectly (for example, when poverty limits public investment in decent schools). Clearly, exclusion of this type is an injustice because it represents arbitrary allocation of access to public benefits, and it violates the principles of human rights. Such exclusion tends to be pervasive and on all levels—individual, organizational, and structural. Box 4.1 examines these three levels of social and cultural exclusion.

Maintaining sight of the story on all three levels is necessary if the practitioner's work is to have an impact on larger systems. Although many practitioners see their labors in terms of individual, one-by-one achievements, it is the collective achievements that make a difference in the larger environment. Engaging with clients is not a matter of choosing which level to engage on; rather, you need to respond on a personal, one-to-one level while acknowledging that social injustices and human rights violations exist on a variety of levels that can and must be addressed.

Individual exclusion

While telling you her or his story, your client may make an explicit reference to the way exclusion has influenced the development of the narrative. Individual exclusion refers to the perception of being left out or barred from participation in interpersonal situations. This often seems to be an intuitive level on which to connect, and it could include, for example, that your client was a victim of racist harassment by peers in school or was dismissed by teachers as having no future because of her or his ethnicity or ability status. Other clients may not give voice to any strong or concrete sense of their own exclusion or the violation of their human rights but rather describe it as "fate" or the "way things are."

Organizational exclusion

Like individual exclusion, organizational exclusion, which refers to the phenomenon of being prevented from participation by an organization, can be obvious to clients (and others), although sometimes it occurs in such a way as to be somewhat obscure. For example, even hiring practices that appear to be fair may actually favor some groups over others through their written or unwritten rules, regulations regarding promotions, or subtle differences in work assignments. In fact, many battles over such efforts as affirmative action arise from a concern for the organizational structures in which unjust practices and advantages have taken hold. For example, given that there is no equality in access to this country's top-rated educational institutions, the organization that automatically hires the candidate with the most prestigious degree—even when the requirements of the job don't mandate it—is engaging in preferential practices that are rooted in injustice.

Just as Jasmine Johnson interpreted her difficulties as individual failings, your clients may not be sensitized to the role that discrimination plays in their place of work. It is important in connecting and engaging with clients to recognize manifestations of organizational exclusion and work with clients regarding the meanings they attach to these life events. In some situations, this alone can be a liberating activity.

Structural exclusion

Institutionalized arrangements such as poverty tend to maintain and perpetuate themselves. Structural exclusion refers to the role of institutions and societal forces in preventing participation or limiting access. Hence there are connections among poverty, poor schools, limited achievement, limited employment options, restricted housing, poor health care, and shortened life expectancy. Recognizing poverty as a structural problem can be difficult because it conflicts directly with presumptions about equal opportunity and the myth that anyone can get ahead.

BOX 4.1

Levels of Social and Cultural Exclusion

Strategies and Skills for Promoting Social Justice and Human Rights

Social justice and human rights issues call for well-organized strategies and skill sets that usually fall within the realm of policy practice. The following strategies are particularly applicable in such situations.

The Social Work Library

For more on the relationship between policy and practice, read Schorr's article.

- Understanding the repercussions on clients of social injustices.

- Helping clients gain access to their legal entitlements through social advocacy.

- Convincing legislative bodies to adopt, amend, or repeal laws when such changes would benefit clients.

- Educating the community regarding certain populations, for example, giving a talk on the needs of refugee children or families with disabilities.

- Developing resources (this involves identifying and procuring resources that are needed but do not exist currently).

- Facilitating the redistribution of resources.

- Testifying in court hearings regarding issues that affect clients.

These strategies are discussed more thoroughly in Chapters 5 and 6. This list is by no means exhaustive, but it suggests the flavor of work focused on systems larger than the individual. These strategies do not negate the importance of individual connections with human beings on a personal level. Just the opposite, they enrich the engagement and the worker's understanding in a way that is consistent with the complexities of people in the contemporary world.

STRAIGHT TALK ABOUT THE RELATIONSHIP: INTERPERSONAL PERSPECTIVES

Being transparent, or explicit about your work, means being clear about the restrictions you encounter as a practitioner. Because one of the goals of the work is to establish a meaningful and trusting relationship with the client, the tasks of discussing constraints or inviting critical evaluation may not seem very appealing. In fact, the worker may tend to postpone or avoid them altogether. Nevertheless, attending to these issues early on can avoid a lot of grief later. The two major constrictions discussed in this section—confidentiality and privacy—along with the task of continuous evaluation, all involve maintaining a respectful sensitivity to the meanings that clients attach to the various dimensions of your work.

Confidentiality

As you know, social workers, among many human service professionals, are legally required to report cases of child abuse or neglect. In most states this requirement extends to the elderly and adults with disabilities as well. Legal ramifications regarding this requirement for reporting child abuse may also vary somewhat by state or locality, but basically the mandate means that you must report incidents that are witnessed by or described to you. Depending on the setting of the work, this mandate may seem to be a huge obstacle to establishing a relationship of trust. In fact, I have had students tell me they don't think any client will tell them anything if they proceed to announce that they will be calling the authorities right after the first session. This concern, of course, may be an exaggeration. Still, to represent yourself fairly, you must communicate your responsibility in that area very early in the work.

Further, you may find that informing clients of the limits of your confidentiality affects the relationship in ways you wouldn't expect. For example, I once worked with a woman who struggled with substance abuse and had a difficult time keeping track of her five children, for whom she was the single, caretaking parent. During our sixth meeting, she told me that she felt sure she was grossly neglecting the younger children and that she often struck the oldest child "hard" when he "mouthed off" to her. After discussing how we would handle this situation, she informed me that she had finally confided in me *because* I was a mandated reporter and she knew she would get help.

Admittedly, in this case the mandated reporter role produced an unusually fortunate outcome. Nevertheless, the lessons are clear: You owe the client your honesty, and you need not assume that an adversarial relationship will evolve simply because you have mandated reporter obligations. Most clients who struggle with taking care of their children want to be good parents. Further, even if the client is guarded about what she or he tells you (which you might expect), you still have significant opportunities to build a relationship while you are jigsaw puzzling. You can address the obstacles to the client's successful parenting (or caretaking for the elderly), model a genuine relationship in which you support the client's parenting competence rather than search to discover sins, and build the foundation for further work. Adopting this approach does not suggest that a child's imminent safety should be compromised. Rather, it is a strategy of beginning to work in those countless scenarios in which there is concern but no clear mandate for legal intervention.

Privacy

The concept of client privacy is sometimes tricky: Actions that some people consider invasive can seem caring to others. When negotiating with clients about the nature and parameters of the work during engagement, you and your client should address the issues of privacy and invasiveness. For example, a client who perceives your care and enthusiasm for the work may get the impression that you want to know everything about her or his life and become an active participant in it. If this is not your intention, you should make the client aware of this. Similarly, you might plan to hold frequent meetings; whereas your client might feel that approach is unnecessary and would deprive her or him of the opportunity to take responsibility for what she or he brings to the work. Clearly, if you aren't straightforward about your involvement, the client will feel disappointed and perhaps even betrayed.

At the same time, if your position is one of monitoring and you have established a mutual, client-driven relationship, you will likely be the initiator in situations that the client didn't expect. For instance, if you have suggested that the client call you when she wants to meet again, but you then drop in unannounced "just to see how she's doing" (or to see how the children seem or if they have eaten that day), she may rightly perceive your visit as an invasion.

On a deeper level, as a practitioner in your particular role and setting, you might consider how much privacy you believe clients are entitled to. What is important to know? If your work involves a social control function, do your clients then deserve less privacy? How does your agency's purpose affect the degree of privacy granted? These questions all relate to the importance of knowing yourself and what you bring, and noticing how you (and/or your agency) may or may not be influenced by predominant social norms about the rights (or lack thereof) of clients.

Ongoing Evaluation

All through the engagement process, you have invested your energy and skills in establishing a solid initial connection with your client that will grow as your work together progresses. Another task you must undertake in this early stage, and throughout the work, is evaluation of the effectiveness of your efforts. Relationships can be easily misunderstood. You may be concerned that your client is hesitant to be as open as you would like, or that she or he seems uneasy in some way. Conversely, you may feel wonderful about what you think is a productive beginning. In either case, it is important to find out how your client feels about your relationship and to make changes in your approach if they are indicated by your client's feedback. Although you are not likely to use formalized tools at this point, you will want to ask your client about how it's going. For example: Is he comfortable talking about the issues you've discussed? How does it work for him that you're a Hispanic woman and he's a black man? Is the process of meeting with you similar to, or different from, what he thought it would be? If it's different, how does he feel about it? What can you do to be more supportive or clearer or helpful?

The process of continuously monitoring your work also applies to your engagement with the people who are significant in your client's life. You will want to validate your understanding of their role in helping to achieve your client's goals and to check for any misunderstandings. This strategy will be particularly important in situations that involve contentious feelings, such as the reluctant landlord considered earlier in this chapter. Because landlords might assume that you will take sides with your client, you will want to take care not to alienate them from your client's goals.

CONCLUSION

Now that you have explored the importance and various aspects of engagement, or building the relationship in social work practice, you are well prepared to support your connection with your client as you enter into the assessment arena of the work. Although you are not likely to have addressed all the issues presented here in the first sessions, you have the framework to go beyond the initial connections and respond to an ongoing, dynamic association. Because you have taken care to anticipate the meaning for the client of your particular work together, you will find that this dimension grows and is shaped by the nature of your shared activities and experiences.

One further caveat about skills: At first you may feel that thinking about and trying to use them interferes with your spontaneity and sometimes even your responsiveness. This is a common student complaint (I remember feeling that way, as well). However, as you develop your practice style, you will become much more relaxed about how you make the skills your own and how they fit with your own style. In short, ease in using the skills will come. As you know, the engagement is never over. You will continue to notice its dynamics, your own growth as a worker in establishing it, and how it assists your client as the work continues into the assessment, planning, and doing of the work.

MAIN POINTS

- The social worker's first and probably most important activity in the engagement process is hearing the client's story. This activity requires the worker to initiate a skilled, purposeful dialogue that nurtures the relationship.

- Negotiating the purpose and direction of the work enhances the trust between the practitioner and client. For this process to be successful, the agenda must be open and must not contain any hidden aspects.

- Respecting the strengths, resilience, and personal agency of the client has an enormous impact on the work. It is critical in establishing the relationship, and it is pervasive throughout the relationship.

- Power and its relationship to social work practice present both obstacles and potential. The various sources of worker power, the power in client lives, and the power between the worker and the client are all part of the relationship. These sources should be recognized and articulated as explicitly as possible.

- Although client stories may appear to be private and are certainly unique, they can always be seen from the perspective of social justice and human rights. This perspective gives the entirety of the work meaning and frames your commitments.

- The worker and client should discuss the issues of confidentiality and privacy openly and directly, even if these topics make them uncomfortable. The client may not welcome some of these constraints on practice, but the worker owes it to her or him to be respectful and clear about them from the beginning.

- Evaluation of the work, including the relationship, should occur at all stages, beginning with engagement.

EXERCISES: PRACTICING SOCIAL WORK

1. As a preliminary exercise, review the Engagement phase on the interactive case study of the Sanchez family and the tasks of that phase. Discuss the needs of the Sanchez family and record what you've learned in your notebook.

2. Within the case study, focus on Alejandro by looking at his file. Then review the neighborhood to locate the Center, review Alejandro's Critical Thinking Questions, and explore his Interactional Matrix. Consider the following scenario:

Life Is No Picnic

You are a social worker who has been seeing Alejandro Sanchez, 19-year-old son of Hector and Celia. He presents himself as somewhat melancholy although pleasant and respectful. He says he is "unhappy" and seems to carry with him an existential sort of sadness that relates to his family. He notes on the first interview that his father Hector was also 19 when he came to this country as an undocumented worker.

With a classmate assuming the role of Alejandro, practice your first session in which you want to help Alejandro tell his story. Alejandro should prepare by reviewing his concerns and goals, as well as his strengths. Other classmates should act as an observation and consultation team. All students can prepare for this exercise by paying particular notice to the questions and directions below:

1. Which perception skills (described earlier in the chapter) would you want to employ and why?

2. Use a radical listening approach. What is most challenging to you about this?

3. While validating his feelings of unhappiness, identify and share with Alejandro what you see as his greatest strengths.

After about 10 to 15 minutes of role play, consult with your classmates who have been observing and may have ideas about what has transpired. Debrief by discussing issues that might have arisen (for example, how it might work to emphasize someone's strengths when he or she is not receptive to hearing that).

4. Ask the student who played the role of Alejandro how the session seemed to him or her.

The whole class might then discuss:

5. How Alejandro's very personal story can be seen through the perspectives of social justice and human rights.

EXERCISES: THE SOCIAL WORK LIBRARY

Read the Gutierrez paper "Working with Women of Color: An Empowerment Perspective." Return to Jasmine Johnson in the text and focus especially on the four significant client changes that Gutierrez identifies as empowering women of color. Brainstorm in small groups how you might facilitate each of those client changes. Then select the one way you think is most probable for each change and prepare to report to the rest of your class.

OTHER EXERCISES

Review the engagement skills in Exhibit 4.1. Then role-play the following:

My Life Is a Mess

You are a social worker in a neighborhood community mental health center. You are awaiting the arrival of a new client assigned to you. She is Jasmine Johnson from the text and she lives near the center. After you introduce yourself and allow some space for her to begin, she says "My life is a mess; nothing I ever do is right; sometimes I think I can't go on."

Engaging your relationship building skills and keeping Gutierrez' work in mind, indicate how you might respond by giving a very brief verbal (one sentence or less if possible) or behavioral example if you were:

1. Making space

2. Responding nonverbally

3. Responding with minimal verbalization

4. Paraphrasing

5. Clarifying (assume a statement from the client)

6. Summarizing (assume what was covered)

What other skills do you think are important here?

Talking in the Idiom of the Other
                    or
How Does Your Garden Grow?

I had heard my client's son had been involved in an armed robbery and taken into police custody that afternoon. We had an appointment and I received a message that she was at the jail trying to see him. I knew she was horrified that this could happen to anyone in her family, although she had expressed worry about him before. I wanted to offer her some support. She was a simple, straightforward woman of 65. She took pride in caring for her house and raising several children in spite of her physical disability. She loved to garden.

I found her in the reception room at the jail and noticed she was holding a single red tulip, apparently a gift for her son, as she wept quietly. I sat down next to her, without saying anything. After a few moments she asked me if I'd ever been a gardener and did I understand how the weeds grew in some gardens while others grew beautiful, strong flowers. I told her I understood from my grandmother who had gardened that all the care and attention a person could give was sometimes not enough to keep a plant healthy. She said she never thought she'd see a son of hers in jail and wondered how the weeds got into her yard.

Underline the sections that reflect use of the idiom of another. Compare to your classmates. What is the potential effect on the work?

CHAPTER 5

Assessing and Planning: Deepening the Dialogue

Three umpires are sitting around over a beer, and one says, "There's balls and there's strikes, and I call 'em the way they are." Another says, "There's balls and there's strikes, and I call 'em the way I see 'em." The third says, "There's balls and there's strikes, and they ain't *nothin'* until I call 'em."

Walter Truett Anderson, in Freedman & Combs, p. 19

Barbara is a sixteen-year-old mother of a baby, is on public assistance, and lives alone in one room. She dropped out of school when she became pregnant, her family and the father of the baby have abandoned her, and her only social contact is a neighbor who works during the day.

One afternoon the young mother, lonesome and depressed, went out for an hour and left the baby alone. The baby fell off the bed and cut his head on an object, seriously injuring himself. When Barbara returned home she took him to the hospital, where the doctor in the emergency room, suspecting child abuse, referred her to the child welfare agency.

Carol Meyer, 1993, p. 22

I N *ASSESSMENT IN SOCIAL WORK PRACTICE,* Meyer (1993) notes that the way social workers think about such situations as Barbara's, or the conceptual boundaries they apply to them, includes many dimensions. Consider your conceptual boundaries, as you read about Barbara: What first comes to mind? Do you see her as an unfit mother? As a lonely young woman? What are the major issues you see? What do you want to know more about? Where would an assessment begin?

This chapter considers assessment, the process that looks for the meaning in client situations, orders and prioritizes the relevant factors, and leads to appropriate action. We will look briefly at the history of assessment, the importance of the client's goals, and then at approaches and skills through the lenses of theory, diversity, and graphics. Later on in the chapter we explore the assessment of resources, as well as approaches when resources are inadequate. Finally, we review the planning process and address two challenges to it.

Returning now to Barbara, let us look at several basic questions about her situation that Meyer (1993) poses: Is hers a "case of a mother and child, a teenager without any family, a teenager subject to the rules of social institutions? would one focus on child abuse? child neglect? adolescent acting-out? the lonesomeness of a single teenage parent? loss of family and social supports? poverty?" (p. 22). The risk here is in taking too narrow a focus so as to make Barbara a case on one dimension rather than another. The task then becomes how to acknowledge the complexity of the situation and at the same time focus with enough specificity to intervene in a helpful way. The assessment process, therefore, attempts to make sense of the particulars within a larger understanding of the client's context. At the same time, the worker will want to discover Barbara's goals and keep them central to the process.

When you, as the worker, begin a relationship with Barbara (or someone like her) through the engagement process, you probably also consider many of the preceding questions. Highly interconnected with engagement, the assessment and planning process has already begun as you've taken the time to hear Barbara's story and consider its meaning to her as the person who has lived it. Putting her story into the context of the values of social justice and human rights frames your understanding. As part of your careful listening, you will most likely by now have some initial idea about how she sees her life, where she wants to go, and how you might help her get there. Perhaps you will also have some reservations about the obstacles that seem to be in the way of Barbara's goals and your agency's, or even the law's, priorities. Thinking through these issues, including Barbara's dreams and strengths, constitutes the assessment process.

A BRIEF HISTORY OF ASSESSMENT

Assessment is one of those words that some social workers see as "loaded" at this point in the history of the profession. Traditionally, it has been considered a critical component of social work ever since Mary Richmond published her pioneer work, *Social Diagnosis,* in 1917. Many contemporary social workers still consider assessment to be absolutely central to practice in that it guides the worker's focus and directs the intervention.

Some practitioners have a problem with the language used in assessment and with the implications it may carry regarding the worker's expertise. The idea of assessment seems to suggest that the worker has the power to define the client's situation and to impose that definition. A look at how the profession arrived at the word *assessment* may provide some perspective on this debate.

Since Mary Richmond introduced the term into social work practice, *diagnosis* has been a part of the profession's history. However, diagnosis now firmly connotes a medicalized understanding of disease, dysfunction, symptoms, and the authority associated with the declaration that there is illness. Social workers rarely use the term in any but mental health settings (which, however, constitute a very large part of social work practice). When they do employ it, they usually refer to a psychiatric, not specifically social, status.

Contemporary social workers have adopted the term assessment as representing a more complete understanding of the client's context, one that focuses on strengths and resources as well as problem areas. These resources include the geography, history, culture, and traditions embedded in the client's life experience. Treating assessment as an act of discovery shifts the focus from professional expertise and analysis toward client definitions of the parameters for work. This process is a source of empowerment for clients.

This approach seems more consistent with the profession's emphasis on the interface between the client and the environment as it occurs in the client context. Furthermore, it invites social workers to examine the whole person, whose many dimensions are never recognized in psychiatric diagnosis. For this reason, the title of this chapter stresses the importance of **dialogue** as a way of looking fully at client situations, considering their significance, hearing what goals clients have, and understanding how clients believe they can achieve these goals. It recognizes this larger view of assessment and assumes that it is primarily the client rather than the worker who directs the resulting decisions about the substance of the work.

The Social Work Library

Read Karl, Mattaini, and Wandne's article on PIE for a comprehensive, contemporary assessment scheme in social work.

WHERE DOES THE CLIENT WANT TO GO?

Having established the importance of dialogue between worker and client in the process of gaining a holistic picture of the client's situation, how social workers go about initiating it is the next step. Many assessment schemes begin with long, detailed social histories. These histories have their advantages and disadvantages. On the positive side, asking clients to talk about their life events can reveal important issues, such as their great resilience in the face of childhood abuse, that might not emerge right away but that are important to fully understanding the client's situation. On the negative side, long accounts sometimes seem intrusive, irrelevant, or even judgmental to clients. They may seem to cover all sorts of very personal aspects of a client's life when, for example, a single parent came only to talk about a child care allowance so she can attend a class. Such histories may also seem to emphasize previous difficulties or situations that the client would prefer to leave in the past. Finally, they might appear to be driven by the worker or agency or even the profession itself, because they seem disconnected and remote from whatever sense of urgency the client brings to the first session.

For example, in Barbara's story at the beginning of this chapter, it is easy to see how she might find an extensive history-taking process invasive and beside the point, when she finds herself in trouble with child protection and may be interested only in getting her baby back. At the same time, however, it is possible to imagine that such a process might reveal aspects of Barbara's life that could assist you in helping her to reach some kind of peace with her situation through more or better-placed supports. The major requirement here, as you might imagine, is that you, as the worker, have good communication and relationship skills in order to make the client feel comfortable and respected, no matter how long or involved the initial period of information gathering is.

Regardless of whether you take a little or a lot of history, it is critical that the work center around where your client wants to go. The most detailed, painstaking social history will be of little use if the history, and not your client's goals, becomes the driving force of the work. This observation also applies to rapid assessment tools or surveys, such as screens for alcohol abuse or depression inventories. These tools may be excellent sources of helpful data, but they don't always reflect the way the client sees her or his situation.

IMPLICATIONS OF THEORETICAL PERSPECTIVES

Assessments are not neutral gatherings of the facts, despite efforts to minimize prejudices and personal biases about the client's situation. The nature of the facts that you gather and questions that you ask suggests, at the least, your theoretical biases. For every story line you pursue, there are others you do not. For example, if you focus on Barbara's relationship with her baby because you see her as "case of mother and child," and you don't consider her experience as child herself, you are choosing not to explore an area that could influence the work you do with her. Likewise, if you stress her history of delinquency but not of sexual abuse, you are adopting an approach that will affect the nature of your work with her.

In both of these scenarios, you take a specific approach that is a result of your judgment about what is both relevant and important. This judgment is usually influenced by many personal attributes (for example, who you are, what you believe about the nature of people, and where you work) and by what type of information you believe helps to make a story understandable. The theoretical perspective and its assumptions will also influence what you consider useful here, as will the context and function of the agency. All of these components shape the kinds of questions you ask and therefore the information you receive. Framed as it is by your perspectives, their assumptions, and your own way of making sense of a situation, the assessment process is never unbiased.

Classic Theories

As you have seen, the theoretical perspective that the worker adopts strongly influences the assessment, the client-worker relationship, and the subsequent work. The following sections present simplified and very brief accounts of three classic theories that have influenced assessments: psychoanalytic theory, attachment theory, and cognitive theory. The discussion then shifts to an examination of strengths-based assessments and narrative approaches as contemporary alternatives.

Psychoanalytic Theory   Based primarily on the writings of the Austrian physician Sigmund Freud, **psychoanalytic theory** maintains that the unconscious is at the root of human behavior. Freud identified three structures that interact to determine human behavior: the id, ego, and superego. Each structure has a distinct function. The id is the repository of unconscious drives such as sex and aggression. In contrast, the ego is the managerial, rational part of the personality, which mediates between drives and perceived obligations. Finally, the superego serves as judge and conscience.

A social worker who believes that inner, unconscious motives and explanations determine the client's choices would orient an assessment toward interpreting the client's unconscious wishes. This psychic determinism usually involves an assumption that chronic complaints are the unconscious wishes of the complainer (Strean, 1996). For example, if Barbara repeatedly describes herself as a "loser," the worker's assessment would likely be directed toward discovering the rewards and gratification she receives from perpetual failure. These rewards might include more concern from previously disinterested parents or protection from the high expectations of others.

Attachment Theory   Looking through another lens, the worker might first want to address Barbara as both a person who was parented and is now parenting. The assessment might take up a perspective influenced by attachment theory, which is currently the subject of some interest, especially in child protection work. **Attachment theory**, originally proposed by U.S. psychologist John Bowlby (1969), holds that very early bonding occurs between a mother and infant and subsequently plays a critical role in the child's future capacity to provide and sustain opportunities for her or his own children to attach. Most of this bonding activity occurs within the first two years of life, and it creates the foundation for the health of all future relationships.

A social worker who uses attachment theory would focus on Barbara's relationships with her early caregivers and how these relationships may have contributed to her current struggles. An assessment of the attachment between Barbara and her child might include experimental observation in a laboratory to see what behavior patterns both child and mother demonstrate when a stranger is introduced into the scene. In stressing these relationships of parental bonding, the worker would deemphasize Barbara's other relationships in the environment.

Cognitive Theory   In contrast to psychoanalytic and attachment theories, if the theory guiding the work emphasizes the importance of **cognitions**, or thoughts, then the worker will see things differently. This approach is consistent with **cognitive theory**, which asserts that our thoughts largely shape our moods and behaviors. In this approach the focus in assessment is more likely to be on what Barbara thinks about herself, what she subsequently says to herself ("self-talk"), and how her thoughts and feelings influence her behavior (Beck, 1995). The cognitive approach assumes that people are thinking beings and that if they change their thinking, their emotions will also change. Further, people's feelings influence both specific behaviors and general approaches to life. For example, because Barbara felt depressed and lonely, because she felt abandoned or hopeless, she used poor judgment in leaving her baby. The work with her might involve helping her to appreciate her assets more fully, which in turn would help her feel better about herself and lead her to make caretaking choices that would be safer for her baby.

You may find the assumptions in cognitive theory more similar to your own than those of the psychoanalytic perspective or more hopeful than those concerning attachment. Nevertheless, they are still predicated on assumptions that make a huge difference in how the worker perceives, relates to, and works with the client. The point is not to reject every theory: We are all guided by theories, formal or not. Rather, the point is to recognize that none of them is "truth" and that none is untouchable or unquestionable.

Contemporary Theories

The three classic theories illustrate how theory can influence social work. The following sections describe the implications for assessment approaches and skills of two contemporary approaches, the strengths perspective and narrative theory. Contemporary theoretical approaches, like classic theories, influence the assessment in that their focus is shaped by the worldview inherent in the perspective.

The Strengths Perspective   One of the four major perspectives of this book, the strengths perspective is widely discussed in the literature on assessment. Strengths practitioners are likely to explore (sometimes *uncover* is a better word for people not used to thinking of their own strengths) what clients do well, what they want, and what their dreams are. This approach also examines the potential of the environment to nurture and support the strengths of individuals. The assessment does not focus on a history of failures but on successes, resources, and goals for the future. The strengths perspective was developed for working with mental health clients but has since been used with many populations, including youth, elders, and people who have substance abuse issues. Saleebey (2002, p. 90) has identified two broad principles for strengths-based assessments that are useful with all populations:

- *The worker should acknowledge the pain:* Saleebey emphasizes that many people have real struggles. There can be a fine line between supporting the positive dimension of a client's personality, skills, or accomplishments and denying what the client experiences as lasting grief, terror, sorrow, or discouragement. For this reason, it is critical to the relationship that you validate the pain that clients feel.

- *The worker should stimulate the discourse and narratives of resilience and strength:* Saleebey suggests that a narrative approach is sometimes helpful. With supportive questioning—for example, you might ask, "How have you managed with the demands of all those kids"—you can return the focus to client strengths. Even in the face of repeated, entrenched stories of trouble and pain, you can help clients to recognize their inner capacities for survival and learn the language of strengths in order to uncover a small seed of hope.

Another specific approach for assessing strengths incorporates a series of guidelines for the worker that focus on understanding the client's perceptions regarding the problem situation (Cowger & Snively, 2002). See Exhibit 5.1 to consider these guidelines. In this approach, the assessment itself includes a two-component model in which the worker first explores a series of questions with the client to define the problem situation (Component 1), and then together they identify the relevant strengths and obstacles that the client brings to bear. These strengths and obstacles can be charted on the grid in Component 2 to provide visual representation of the assessment results. See Exhibit 5.2 for the two-component model.

This assessment process helps clients identify their own strengths, use the resources in their environment, and tell their story about the problem. The approach is also explicitly political in that it recognizes and articulates the power relationships that clients experience and/or in which they participate. In addition, the strengths approach encourages a complex view of the environment as a source of both resources and obstacles. Although this approach seeks to identify obstacles, they are not the primary focus of the assessment.

Narrative Theory   Recall from Chapter 1 that narrative theory focuses on the client's story as the central component in the work. Therefore, narrative workers rarely use the term assessment. Their primary interest is in discovering the stories of the people who consult them and in helping them to "re-author" those stories if they wish to. A story is defined as consisting

Web Links

For a slightly different type of strengths-based behavioral health training in Power Point form, go to the Arizona Department of Health Services site.

Web Links

The Pennsylvania Department of Public Welfare site contains an essay on strengths-based work with children; also describes strengths-based staff practices.

EXHIBIT 5.1

The Strengths Perspective in Assessment

Cowger and Snively have suggested some guidelines for a strengths-based assessment:

- Give preeminence to the client's understanding of the facts.
- Believe the client.
- Discover what the client wants.
- Move the assessment toward client and environmental strengths.
- Make assessment of strengths multidimensional.
- Use the assessment to discover uniqueness.
- Use the client's words.
- Make assessment a joint activity between worker and client.
- Reach a mutual agreement on the assessment.
- Avoid blame and blaming.
- Avoid cause-and-effect thinking.
- Assess; do not diagnose. (pp. 106–123)

Some of these guidelines may be more challenging for workers than others. For example, the simple directive to "believe the client" may in some contexts tax a worker's ability to refrain from making judgments. It asserts that the client's understanding of reality is just as worthy as the worker's.

Source: Cowger & Snively, 2002

of "(1) events; (2) linked in sequence; (3) across time; (4) according to a plot" (Morgan, 2000, p. 5).

Narrative practitioners are interested in helping the consulting person (note that they are rarely "clients" in narrative work) to broaden or "thicken" her or his story. For example, recall Georgia from Chapter 2, a woman who experienced intimate partner violence. Georgia developed a negative self-story response to a pattern of abuse that was perpetrated by her partner. Whereas her story originally was that of a strong and competent young woman, it slowly began to erode, reflecting increasing doubt and finally wholesale dejection as she adopted the persona of an unworthy human being. It became a thin story in that it lacked complexity, reflecting only her self-rejection.

In addition to seeking a thickened story, the worker recognizes the importance of the broader social context of storytellers' lives. In one sense this is a story just about Georgia and her partner. In a broader sense, however, it is also about a pervasive social phenomenon in this culture that kills thousands of women every year. The work with Georgia is to help her rewrite that very thin story of worthlessness to one that more accurately reflects her talents, attractiveness, and competence. The goal of assessment is to discover what alternative story the consulting person wishes to author.

In Cowger and Snively's two-component model for assessing client strengths, Component 1 is a process by which the worker and client define the problem situation and clarify how the client wants the worker to help. Component 2 is a graphic representation of the analysis of the problem defined in Component 1. It invites the worker and client together to chart strengths and obstacles in each of the four quadrants. Quadrant 2 is highlighted and may contain subcategories relating to cognition, emotion, motivation, coping, and interpersonal.

EXHIBIT 5.2

Two-Component Model for Assessing Client Strengths

COMPONENT 1

Defining the Problem Situation: Getting at Why the Client Seeks Assistance

- *Brief summary of the identified problem situation.* This should be in simple language, straightforward, and mutually agreed upon between worker and client.
- *Who* (persons, groups, organization) is involved, including the client(s) seeking assistance?
- *How* or in what way are participants involved? What happens between the participants before, during, and immediately following activity related to the problem situation?
- What meaning does the client ascribe to the problem situation?
- What does the client want with regard to the problem situation?
- What does the client want/expect by seeking assistance?
- What would client's life be like if problem was resolved?

COMPONENT 2

Strengths

Quadrant 1	Quadrant 2
Social and political strengths	Psychological strengths - Cognition - Emotion - Motivation - Coping - Interpersonal Physical and physiological strengths
Environmental factors ←	→ Client factors
Quadrant 3	**Quadrant 4**
Social and political obstacles	Psychological obstacles

Obstacles

Source: Cowger & Snively, 2002, pp. 115–121

In Barbara's situation, the narrative worker would first want to hear her story. How does she fill the day? What is it like to be mother to this baby? When are the best times? When did her loneliness first interfere with her life? When is she able to conquer it? Who would say she's a good mother?

These are a few of the most basic ideas of narrative theory and how it is used to assess the work to be done. As you can see, it is quite different from many of the more classic theoretical perspectives, but in some ways it is familiar in that it emphasizes the story. It is largely driven by the person seeking assistance, although you, as the worker, would contribute your ideas as well. It also fits well with the strengths perspective because it assumes that people are the experts on their lives and that they have multiple talents, values, beliefs, and skills for improving their lives. We'll look at narrative approaches in more detail in Chapters 6–8.

Theory Matters   The contrast between the traditional theories and the newer models provides just one example of how theoretical orientations help to shape and define the assessment processes and skills as well as the roles of the participants. Again, the idea here is not that one theory is better than another, but rather that theory matters in assessment and should be consistent with the worker's basic assumptions and beliefs concerning people. Although this book clearly endorses strengths-based work and the narrative approach, these perspectives should be subjected to the same types of questioning as the other theoretical perspectives.

IMPLICATIONS OF DIVERSITY

Although theoretical perspectives play a major role in assessment, other lenses are also crucial to recognize. The impact of diversity on assessment can hardly be exaggerated in contemporary social work. We will look next at the implications of keeping diversity central and the approaches and skills this focus implies.

Social work as a profession is an institution of culture; it is affected by the same pressures and forces that influence other aspects of culture. Because of the shifting patterns of diverse populations in U.S. society, social work must develop appropriate approaches that are responsive to different cultures. The theoretical perspectives of the strengths-based worker, as well as the narrative worker, call upon her or him to develop an approach that affirms individuals' strengths and honors their culture. This point has important repercussions for assessment. Here we will look at (1) cultural competence, (2) ethnographic interviewing, and (3) connecting with the spiritual.

Cultural Humility

The social worker's ability to provide services in a way that is consistent with the values and expectations that are standard in a given community is a measure of her or his **cultural competence** (Green, 1999) or "cultural humility" (Clowes, 2005). It requires that workers are aware of their limitations and have respect for the unique culturally defined needs of others. As you have learned, assessment involves discovering what is important to the client, which cultural influences shape her or his values, how they have affected the client's experience, and how the client's perspectives differ from the worker's.

Clearly, the worker's ability to approach another culture in this way is predicated upon her or his thorough self-knowledge and knowledge of her or his culture (Schultz, 2004). That is, workers must examine the influences of their own culture on their work and understand the role culture plays in all of our lives.

The assessment process is contingent on the development of cultural competence so that you, as the worker, don't simply assess the degree to which your client differs from you. Your understanding of the issues that the client brings and how they are shaped by culture impacts the way you will perceive the presenting "problem." For example, when your client describes communicating with the spirit of his deceased father, you might wonder if he is demonstrating psychosis or hearing voices, unless you have a clear understanding that this kind of spiritual communication is part of his culture and represents a strong, loving relationship.

Ethnographic Interviewing

Developing the skills necessary to conduct a culturally competent assessment can take time and significant effort. Here, we will consider one primary method for working with people who are culturally different from the worker—ethnographic interviewing. In **ethnographic interviewing**, the social worker acts as a "stranger" and the client as "cultural guide" (Leigh, 1998; Ungan, Manuel, Mealy, Thomas & Campbell, 2004). It requires that the worker takes the stance of "not knowing" (as discussed in Chapter 1).

Workers who adopt this model begin the helping relationship by initiating friendly yet purposeful conversations. Rather than focusing on long social histories, the worker may consider some aspect of the client's cultural frame that is puzzling or particularly interesting and ask about it through a "global question." For example, if your client is a single mother of Middle Eastern descent with three children, dresses with her face veiled, and works as a bartender, you probably will have several questions for her. For example, you might ask if she knows anyone else with her cultural background who works in a bar, how her family reacts to her occupation, or how she makes arrangements for child care at night. As the client/cultural guide answers these questions, you remain highly attuned to the language she uses and inquire about **cover terms**, which are expressions and phrases that seem to carry more meaning than the literal meaning the words would suggest. For instance, our bartender might respond to the question about what her family thinks with a comment like, "I don't care what those old biddies think about me; I will never be a welfare mother!" In this case the cover terms are "old biddies" and "welfare mother," because they seem to have a cultural relevance to how the woman understands her social location.

Although this kind of extensive cultural interviewing may seem somewhat removed from assessing the particular issue that is pressuring the client, attending to and understanding the impact of the client's culture influences the overall effectiveness of the work, especially in those areas that will become barriers if they are ignored. For example, given what you have discovered about the bartender, you will likely make a big mistake if you begin work by suggesting that she enroll in a welfare program.

Connecting with the Spiritual

The Social Work Library

For more on spirituality and religious diversity in social work, see Canda's article.

In recent years the profession has placed greater emphasis on the value of helping people define what gives their life purpose and meaning (see, for example, Hodge, 2005a). Insofar as this effort might be seen as a spiritual quest, it can encourage people to find the most sustaining areas of their lives. Such areas of meaning may be found in religious practices, outdoor activities focusing on nature, and in social connections like volunteering in a hospice, to name only a few. They can also be incorporated into both the assessment and action stages of the work in meaningful ways. For example, you might identify your client's volunteer work as evidence of her or his value to the community, which in turn might reduce her or his sense of isolation. Facilitating a client's connection with her or his spiritual side is likely to be a lasting and significant contribution of your work.

SKILLS FOR DEVELOPING A SHARED VISION

At this point in the process of assessment, the worker will begin to form a view of the future that includes the client's vision and her or his own sensibility about how they might engage in its fulfillment. This is the sense of a shared vision between client and worker. In developing this vision, workers will want to help clients articulate the kinds of changes they want to make. The questions that workers ask will affirm that change is possible and that it can be shaped in a way that makes the client's life better.

Preferred Realities

The term **preferred reality** refers to the client's goal for a changed reality. It reflects a postmodern and narrative assumption that there are different realities. Long before postmodernism became a common theme in social work theory, however, the profession engaged in efforts to make things different—that is, to work toward a different or preferred reality.

The discussion of the assessment process has emphasized that the worker's role is to engage in a dialogue with the client about her or his goals and dreams. This process requires the practitioner to work with the client to develop a picture of what could be. Sometimes this process is quite difficult for clients, who may feel overwhelmed by the obstacles they face and thus find it quite challenging to be hopeful. Even more challenging, clients may be accustomed to seeing their dreams defeated through their long experience in living at the margins of society. In these cases the worker has an important job in helping the client see that things can be different, that there are other realities, and that the client can work toward one that she or he prefers.

This process of being genuinely hopeful and translating that hopefulness to the client can be challenging to social workers as well. Sometimes when you hear very painful stories you feel swallowed up in them. For example, you might have to struggle to be hopeful after hearing about generations of violence or oppression. However, one attraction of the idea of preferred realities is that it benefits the worker as well as the client. More specifically, the conviction that the client's reality can be different helps to protect the worker from the contagion of despair.

Remember that working toward a preferred reality does not necessarily require a grand sweeping vision of riches where there was poverty, or complete harmony where there was vicious violence. As much as anyone might wish for these long-range dreams, they will appear elusive and unrealistic in many contexts if they are not shared by the client. Workers need to start with the client's vision of how things should be different. Clients will often frame this vision in clear, small-scale terms when workers are drawn toward a more grandiose transformation.

Support for the Client's Dream

As an illustration of the process of moving toward a preferred reality, consider once again the case of Jasmine Johnson, the single mother whom you met in Chapter 4. Recall that Jasmine is concerned because she has sometimes hit her son "hard" when he talked disrespectfully to her. Jasmine may verbalize a request to you, as a family support worker, for help in developing another way to respond to him. Although this might be seen as a relatively concrete goal for behavior change, it might also be thought of as developing a preferred reality because it suggests creating a different mother-son relationship, which could have many positive ramifications. Right now Jasmine is asking for help with a behavioral response. Her goal might be simply to avoid child protection charges or to reduce the likelihood that her son will respond violently back to her. Therefore, your work with her might involve exploring what she envisions as a long-term goal. For example, Jasmine might want to establish a more satisfying emotional connection with the most important person in her life. She may not have allowed that kind of emphasis on feelings to enter into her interpersonal experiences, or she may never have had the time to think that way. It's even possible that she's never known anyone who articulated that kind of goal, or she may simply not be inclined to consider relationships that way. In this scenario, it is important to start with Jasmine's meaning of the situation and then explore it further without imposing your own meanings.

The shared vision in this case will be that Jasmine learns other ways to respond to her son because she has articulated that vision as her concern and because you have agreed that is an appropriate area for work and that you can contribute to it. As you work together toward achieving this vision, other, more encompassing dreams about the possibilities for her relationship with her son might evolve. Your role in this kind of assessment strategy is to support her dream, always affirming its potential for fulfillment. In order to help Jasmine's dream become reality, you will need to engage in a process of specifying both her goals and how you and she will work together. We'll look at both of these.

Setting Goals   The reason for **setting goals** is to emphasize the usefulness of clarity of purpose and the utility for clients of recognizing the difference between central, current, behavioral concerns and the longer view of the dream. Referring back to the previous scenario, Jasmine Johnson wants to respond differently to her son when he is disrespectful to her. This goal can be measured in a variety of ways. For example, does Jasmine want to "feel better" about their conversations? Does she want to reduce by half the number of times she is tempted to respond physically to him? Does she want to eliminate those episodes altogether? Does she want him to report that things are better? Clearly, the selection of an appropriate measure should reflect Jasmine's priorities. Setting priorities will also help Jasmine and the worker sort through expectations to determine which outcomes are more critical within a particular time frame. For example, what if Jasmine's son is very sweet two times and then rude once, which provokes her inclination to hit him? Does his sweetness matter in terms of the goal? Is the goal to change Jasmine's behavior or her son's behavior? As you can see, establishing goals and measuring progress toward achieving them can become complicated. Nevertheless, it is worth the effort to clarify how each party defines the goal of the work and how each one will know when the goal is achieved. Unless you are clear about agreement on an end point, Jasmine may believe you will be there to work on her particular situation until she feels it is "fixed." To avoid misunderstandings, you will want to make sure you have a mutual agreement regarding this issue.

Probably the most useful clinical dimension of setting goals is that it helps both the client and the worker evaluate the degree to which they are communicating clearly and have similar expectation, and are making progress. It is also true, of course, that agencies and organizations need to understand what the work is and where it is going, often in concrete, measurable terms. This topic is discussed more thoroughly in Chapter 12 as a function of formal evaluation.

Contracting   The process of **contracting** is one in which the client and worker reach an agreement about what is to happen, who will do what and when, and what the priorities are. Contracts vary greatly depending on practice setting, and they can be formal or informal. A formal contract generally takes the shape of a written document signed by both parties. In contrast, an informal contract can consist simply of a verbal agreement. If a formal contract is used, it should spell out the details about how often client and worker meet, what the goals are, who is responsible for what, how a change in the plan can be brought about, how progress will be checked, and to what degree each goal needs to be met.

Honest Responding

Up to this point you have learned how workers and clients can identify and work toward a preferred reality. This discussion has emphasized the importance of establishing a shared vision that reflects the client's goals and dreams. However, as a social worker you might find yourself in a situation in which you are inclined to challenge your client's priorities after hearing the story. For example, if your client's overall goal is to avoid getting caught again selling illegal drugs, you might want to contest that goal as a purpose for work. To you, a more healthful goal might be for the client to abstain from using and selling drugs, or to separate from a drug-using peer group. Conflicts over goals raise many difficult questions for social workers. For example, do you have the right to disagree about the client's priorities? Are you inappropriately pushing your values? At the same time, how can you engage enthusiastically to achieve a goal you really don't approve of? I don't think I've ever met a social worker who didn't struggle with these questions on occasion.

You can ask yourself some helpful questions that might serve as guidelines here:

- What is your stake in the assessment that you prefer?

- Does it reflect your priorities, values, or cultural practices?

- What are your legal and professional commitments in this situation?

- Will you violate an ethical principle by not addressing the issue, even if the client would rather not deal with it?

- Do you think the client's goals are either unrealistic or not extensive enough?

Although there are no easy solutions in this kind of scenario, you can respond honestly if you "own" your own biases, which might include more belief in the client's potential than the client seems to possess.

When Confrontation Is Necessary   You have probably concluded from the preceding discussion that in some situations in which the goal conflict is particularly acute, the worker has to confront the client directly. To examine how this process can be conducted, let's return to the Jasmine Johnson case for a moment. Jasmine has requested your help to change the way she responds when her son talks back. However, you have discovered through reliable sources that she is actually beating him regularly. How will this revelation affect the assessment? You may be convinced that a temporary separation between Jasmine and her son is in order (for many reasons, such as her son's safety, for your protection as a worker) before you can begin to work with her on a different way of relating to him. In this case you are establishing a new, short-term goal and postponing work toward Jasmine's long-term goal. The assessment then moves to an intermediate plateau in which there is a dangerous, or potentially dangerous, situation that requires a more immediate (and ethical) response. You will need to be honest with Jasmine about your understanding of the situation and what you see as your ethical obligations. This process will likely involve some confrontation. In this situation, Jasmine needs to hear that there is an immediate need that must temporarily derail her long-range goals.

You may have noticed in this scenario that any decision to separate Jasmine temporarily from her son does not necessarily negate her preferred reality of getting along better with him. In fact a temporary separation might help her achieve this reality. It will be critical in your work with Jasmine to find the common ground and support her dream, even though you must initiate another intervention at the moment. Ideally this respite will improve her chances of working on her original goal after the crisis is past. Your honest dialogue with her will then reassure her that you share her vision and you want to help her work toward it.

When Alternatives Are Necessary   In most cases, people who come to social workers for assistance are realistic about their goals and dreams. Many clients are keenly aware of the level of change that would be required to realize their vision of a more satisfying life. In other cases, workers must help people expand their vision of what is possible because they have been discouraged, oppressed, or otherwise have had their vision restricted. In such cases the task is to affirm the client's potential and power in changing her or his life.

Occasionally, however, clients will need assistance in clarifying and articulating their goals and their understanding of the situation. Their goals might seem unrealistic or even grandiose to you. These situations are tricky, particularly for strengths-based social workers. One strategy for responding in this type of situation is to help clients lower their aspirations, that is, to become more realistic. The argument for establishing realistic goals is that to endorse goals that clients cannot achieve is to set them up for failure, which represents a major disservice to them. Many social workers appreciate the sentiment in this position.

At the same time, there is likely to be a small voice in the back of the strengths-based worker's mind that calls out "assume that you do not know the upper limits of the capacity to grow and change" and "take individual, group, and community aspirations seriously" (Saleebey, 2002, p. 15). These principles at least suggest that you are not really in the position to know what is realistic or what those upper limits are. Therefore, you should not simply disregard a person's dream as unrealistic. Moreover, many strengths-based workers insist that clients have the right to fail in the pursuit of their dreams, just like the rest of us. The issue then seems difficult to resolve and will undoubtedly take on a different look in different contexts.

One way you can approach such a situation is to help clients see exactly what their goals entail. For example, if you are the high school social worker and your client states that she wants to be a nuclear physicist, you and she can consider together what level of education she would require, what it might cost, and how long it would take. You should not use this kind of step-by-step discussion to discourage her, but rather to provide information that she may not have considered. You might then help her consider alternatives that could serve as stepping-stones. Breaking down goals into workable subgoals, or procedural goals, can help people get a clear idea of the practical side of the dream and how far they want to take it. This may or may not alter their enthusiasm, but it is an honest response to a sometimes troubling scenario.

Using Mapping Skills to Enhance the Dialogue

As you have seen, assessment on any level is influenced by your interpretation of the client's story. This interpretation is shaped by both your own and the client's culture, ethnicity, class, gender, sexual orientation, and age, as well as your theoretical perspectives. Human stories often have many layers, however, and can be difficult to grasp in their complexity. Frequently, a visual picture can make the information more accessible. **Mapping** is a technique that represents complex phenomena visually so that they can be taken in perceptually rather than linguistically. Two fundamental types of mapping—genograms and ecomaps—are discussed next.

The Social Work Library

Read Meyer's chapter on graphics to see other forms of social mapping and to read about its conceptualization.

Genograms   Technically a family tree—geneticists call it a pedigree—the **genogram** usually represents three generations and indicates various aspects of the relationships of the individuals included. Exhibit 5.3 presents some of the conventions for indicating these relationships. When used flexibly a genogram can portray an extremely broad range of issues and family patterns, such as early deaths or exceptionally stable marital relationships. By adding labels to the map that indicate such dimensions as vocational accomplishment or alcohol use, you can also use genograms in a more focused way to address a single issue.

EXHIBIT 5.3

Genogram Symbols

People in a genogram are represented by the following symbols:

- Males = ☐ (occasionally represented by the medical symbol of ♂)
- Females = ○ (occasionally represented by the medical symbol of ♀)
- Unborn or aborted children are triangles (△)
- X through a person symbol indicates death (usually accompanied by age or year of death)

Relationships are represented by the following symbols:

- Strong, solid black line = strong, positive relationship ──────
- Dotted line = tenuous relationship ----------
- Railroad track line = contentious or strained ⟋⟋⟋⟋⟋⟋
- Slanting vertical lines = separation or divorce (on marriage line) //
- Circle enclosing people indicates household
- Arrows along connecting lines indicate the flow of energy, reciprocity ⟷

Genograms should be introduced carefully with vulnerable clients. Their visual nature can evoke more intense emotions (for example, a sense of loss or regret) than mere words can. For example, I had a particularly unhappy experience as an intern when I decided to do a genogram with a couple who became so distraught at the memory of a relative who died by suicide that each abruptly and separately left the meeting.

Additional cautions concerning the use of genograms are that they are frozen in time (that is, they represent relationships at the moment of the map's creation), they are sometimes subject to privileged interpretation (making it important to remember that the map represents one person's perception), and, probably most important, they may seem deterministic, especially when they exhibit family patterns. For example, if a multigenerational exploration reveals that all or nearly all young male members on one side of a family have had major substance use problems, it may be tempting to see such a pattern as inevitable. One of the greatest gifts you can give clients is hope and the assurance that they can change. Therefore, family pattern exploration should never suggest that people are doomed by their history. Rather, a family history provides context and can help you locate your most effective intervention points.

Ecomaps   A diagrammatic representation of the client's world that illustrates the client's levels of connection to such institutions as schools, religious centers or spiritual practices, the workplace, extended family, friends, and recreation is known as an **ecomap.** It helps clients to make sense of their experience by showing them how their day-to-day world looks. Ecomaps can also focus on a particular aspect of the client's life. For example, a worker who is involved with children with special health needs can use an ecomap of medical and social supports relating to the child's health status to help shape the intervention. Some ecomaps include a miniature genogram.

Like all mapping techniques, the ecomap enables your client to explore patterns of everyday living that may or may not be initially accessible in verbal form. For example, your client may complain about being lonely and estranged from his community. An ecomap could reveal that he has very few supports in the community—no satisfying work life, only one friend, no spiritual connections, and no outlet for recreation. Such a diagram would suggest that you expand your dialogue with him into these areas. Here, as always, it is important not to interpret and make conclusions directly from the map without exploring the meaning of the indicators with the client.

Social workers occasionally use a sequence of ecomaps to evaluate the effectiveness of the work. For example, if your lonely client wanted to expand his social world but felt fearful of that prospect, your work with him might be to develop safe connections, which could be indicated on subsequent ecomaps.

Variations in Mapping   Many other mapping techniques can prove helpful in social work. Among them are the **culturagram** representing a family's experiences in relocating to a new culture (Congress, 2004) **social network maps,** which represent the types and nature of social connections of the client (Tracy & Whittaker, 1990) and Cultural Genograms (McCullough-Chavis & Waites, 2005). Maps are limited only by imagination. Among the elements they represent are multiple dimensions, the passing of time, interacting components, interpersonal interactions and patterns, levels of intimacy, specific types of connection (such as material or emotional support), and spirituality (Hodge, 2005b).

Some more literal maps of physical arrangements such as floor plans in housing situations illustrate concretely the challenges in daily living or the disparities in economic circumstances. For example, a map that shows five children's cots in a tiny bedroom or an elder on the couch demonstrates a person-in-environment reality that may be difficult to comprehend fully through verbal means (Meyer, 1993). A legend on the map that describes the meaning of all symbols, and a general heading to orient the reader can be used and are especially helpful in any creative or unconventional mapping.

 Web Links

Visit the Integrated Approaches to Participatory Development Web site for a broader cultural view of social mapping in the Philippines; includes several links.

SKILLS FOR ASSESSING RESOURCES

By developing individual skills, such as creating a shared vision, becoming culturally competent, and mapping, social workers can work toward an effective assessment. Nevertheless, even the most skilled workers can rarely provide all the assistance that a client needs. Workers should also familiarize themselves with resources that are available in the larger environment. There are several dimensions to assessing resources that are useful in reaching client goals, from their type and source to their availability.

Formal and Informal Resources

External, structured opportunities for assistance, which usually take the form of services, are **formal resources.** Training in parent education, financial assistance, and support groups for children in schools are all examples of the hundreds of services you might be able to name that are helpful to clients.

Not all resources are formal, however. Because our culture is so specialized, you may tend to lose sight of the informal, internal, or community-based assets that could be used in the service of clients. **Informal resources** may be people, your own creativity, or naturally occurring social networks, like church groups or families. Don't overlook these resources that individuals and communities bring to the practice context. For example, many children benefit from regular contact with an older child who befriends them, understands their troubles, or is just supportive of their abilities. It is not necessary in all such situations to hire someone or obtain a service. Some of the most meaningful relationships emerge from informal contexts of community life.

Assessment When Resources Are Available or Unavailable

Your familiarity with both formal and informal resources is an enormous benefit to your client. It is not enough simply to locate them. Rather you also need to know enough about the client and the resources to estimate the fit and likelihood of a successful interaction between them. For example, your client asks you, as a family support worker, for help in managing an ill infant, and you concur that some supports would help her become more like the effective parent she wants to be. In particular, you might recommend some regular time away from the demands of the child and also some assistance in managing the child's challenging behaviors. You would probably then explore the availability of both formal and informal resources that could stabilize the situation. For example, you could investigate formal parent support programs, focusing on how collaborative the trainers are, as well as concrete issues such as cost and schedule.

Unfortunately, even the more careful social workers cannot locate necessary resources in all situations. In fact, most have had the experience of looking for a particular way to help a client and finding that it doesn't exist. Even in these situations, however, you are not powerless. You have at least two options when adequate resources are not available: You can advocate for a change in formal resources, policies, or programs that are not responding adequately (for example, an uncooperative welfare office), or you can create resources where none have been developed. For example, you might assist single parents in a housing complex to organize a network of child care where none existed.

These points suggest that workers do not simply accept, for example, that the welfare office doesn't respond appropriately to their client, or this housing project has no child care facilities. Workers need to remain hopeful and energetic in identifying and developing resources but must also be realistic and careful not to promise more than they can reasonably deliver. In a client's world, where many promises may have been broken, workers need to maintain trust through an honest approach regarding what is possible.

Social Action When Resources Are Inadequate

Many of the cases in which the resources you think necessary are either inadequate, nonexistent, or discriminatory are clearly political situations that call for policy practice approaches. Action on behalf of clients is one possible response to an unjust situation. **Social action** is a policy practice method in which the worker generally aims to shift power structures in order to change an institutional response. The efforts come in many forms and may involve varying degrees of confrontation. For example, helping your client file a formal written complaint to the welfare agency and organizing a welfare rights demonstration at the agency's headquarters are both forms of social action. However, the latter is clearly more confrontational than the former. In situations where this kind of action is contemplated, the assessment will take on an additional dimension in that it will require an analysis of what actually should or will happen, who will do it, and what the consequences will be. In addition, the assessment must address the client's interest in, and capacity to engage in, the action indicated. It also requires the worker's complete honesty and sensitivity to the possible consequences of political action for the client or the client's family. In many ways this last requirement can be considered a dimension of ethics. Read how this might play out in the tenants' story in Box 5.1.

Web Links

For an interesting look at social action/social witness internships at a Quaker Center for Study in Pennsylvania, go to the Pendle Hill Web site.

Despite whatever risks may be involved, when an understanding is truly reached in partnership, few experiences are more positive or powerful than a successful social action based in client-worker advocacy. Even if the results are somewhat less than hoped for, the process itself can be remarkably empowering for both worker and client.

Although this scenario expands into the phase of intervention, it points up the importance of assessment throughout the client relationship. Because the assessment drives the action stage of the work, it must also address the very action inherent in it.

BOX 5.1

*Social Action:
The Tenants'
Story*

In a privately run, not-for-profit housing project in a midsize city, there are several families with young children and some with elderly grandparents. In the past the housing was kept in marginally acceptable repair, but the residents stayed there because the rent is fixed and relatively low. However, a change in ownership leads to a distinct deterioration in maintenance, adequate and timely repairs, and the amount of heat allotted to each apartment. Toilets are clogged, rats are visible in the basement, and lead-based paint is beginning to crumble from the walls. The residents are unsure how they can respond to this deteriorating situation so they request that you, as a social worker from the city's housing authority, advocate for them. After discussing the situation with client spokespeople and then asking each client for approval, you sponsor a meeting for residents with the landlord's representatives. Although you have been careful to hear the landlord's side and have used your best engagement skills, the meeting results in a deadlock, and no progress is made.

Convinced that you have exhausted all of the available approaches, you consult with peers who affirm your position. At that point you consider the possibility of organizing your tenants to withhold their rent. You feel for many reasons that this is an appropriate and effective strategy to elicit a more satisfactory response from the landlord. At the same time, however, you know from prior experience that this particular landlord has a history of retaliation against complaining tenants.

You fully recognize the need to collaborate with tenants about the potential plan of withholding their rent. There is some hesitation among them because they too are concerned with the likely consequences of riling a powerful landlord who could throw them out. Some of the residents are people of color, and they are especially concerned with the availability and accessibility of other housing.

Let's consider the following ways the story might play out:

- *Plotline A:* You are so convincing that this is the way to deal with the problem that you are able to engage the tenants in a full-blown movement to withhold their rent. Your clients nervously await the landlord's response. And then you go home to your warm, middle-class apartment.

- *Plotline B:* You hear those who have specific concerns and play out alternative responses. You locate other sources of housing, and you identify legal advocates for those interested in pursuing new housing. You arrange for press coverage and obtain the full support of your agency and supervisor in taking this action.

Social action: The moral of the story

I'll let you fill in the ending of this story. It could be empowering or disastrous or a lot of things in between. The point is that when others live the results of your advocacy attempts, they need to have all the available information about possible consequences, the likelihood of certain outcomes, and the opportunity to choose which path they want to take. You, as the social worker, need to be very clear about who will pay the price of any repercussions. Because the "who" is often the client, the client should enter into such an agreement only when she or he clearly understands the risks and is motivated to follow through with the action consequences. Can you identify an alternative Plotline C?

PLANNING: SUMMARY AND CHALLENGES

When you and your client have developed a shared vision and specified the goals, means, and end points you envision for the work, you will have addressed the components of a solid, detailed plan. In this section we will revisit these briefly and then consider the potential impact of two insidious influences—oppression and the emotional impact of change—on the planning process in particular and on the assessment in general.

The key components that we have addressed that influence the concrete plan for work include

- Setting and prioritizing goals

- Identifying methods of reaching goals

- Developing a clear understanding of who does what

- Setting time frames

- Recognizing when an alternative plan is necessary

- Identifying resources

- Identifying an end point for the work

Incorporating these elements into a plan can enhance the client's understanding of what will happen and how she or he will experience the process. Because these components have been negotiated as an ongoing feature of your work together, they should not present any surprises, but rather constitute the mutually developed plan.

Although the ideal is that workers and clients collaborate to plan the process, even the most careful approaches cannot account for all of the potential obstacles that might arise. Many clients face very real disabilities. They may have emotional, cognitive, or physical challenges that make it almost impossible for them to participate in planning. Although workers should never minimize these obstacles, they need to work directly with the client to the greatest extent possible. As they do so, they should keep in mind that many clients who have experienced lifelong challenges have never been considered as adequate participants in service provision planning. Consequently, clients may be hesitant or even afraid to participate, even though they have the ability to make substantial contributions. Many others who have experienced racial or ethnic oppression will find it difficult to trust the process of mutual assessment and planning.

The transgression of excluding clients from this process has generated two negative consequences. First, service providers have often lost, dismissed, or ignored helpful information that only the person experiencing the context could provide. Second, many of these clients have internalized this kind of oppression and actually have come to believe that they have no right or capacity to participate. **Internalized oppression**—the process by which individuals accept prejudicial opinion against themselves and make it their own reality—is one of the most sinister aspects in the oppression and domination dynamic (Phetersen, 1990) and clearly undermines the spirit of human rights.

Another component of assessment and planning that workers need to keep in mind relates to the impact of emotions. In their zeal to develop a plan, address the issues, mobilize the resources, and engage the contract, workers may sometimes forget that certain elements of the work are not as visible or as easy to categorize as others. By the time workers have listened to the story and established a preferred reality, they will probably have heard and felt a lot of the emotional content that is related to the client's experience. They may not as easily, however, recognize the power that complicated feelings about change can generate.

For example, the literature on substance abuse has suggested that whole families are sometimes organized around one member's addiction to alcohol. Everyone knows how to respond, for example, if Dad is drunk and has passed out on the couch. John, the eldest son, may be the one to carry him to bed; everyone else might ignore Dad, step around him, and pretend his drinking doesn't happen. Mom takes this opportunity to make decisions about the family finances that Dad has always made. The specific patterns may not be as important as the idea of changing them. Although, let's say, Mom has come to your agency to get help with Dad's addiction problem because it is obviously destroying his health, their marriage, and their family life, the worker still needs to remember that there is some cost to change. Mom may feel uniquely competent, for instance, when she is so clearly needed to make major decisions, or John may take great pride in being able to manage the chaos. Again, the patterns are not as important as the disruption of them. If Dad successfully withdraws from alcohol, Mom may actually have some regrets because she will have to develop a new role when her husband is more present. John may lose his place as competent caretaker, and all members of the family will need to relate to Dad and each other differently. This need for renegotiating family roles can have some disturbing emotional consequences.

Although there is a risk of overinterpreting here, remember that any change that you are eagerly planning and that the client is genuinely seeking is embedded in a social context and therefore can generate a powerful emotional response. This response may take the form of reluctance to engage in ongoing collaboration or hesitation when making progress on specific goals. In such cases it will be helpful to explore what the change itself will mean on levels beyond those related to the technical or mechanical processes of goal setting and contracting.

STRAIGHT TALK ABOUT THE RELATIONSHIP: ADDITIONAL AGENCY PERSPECTIVES

You have seen that several general agency constrictions that influence your work with clients, such as methods, schedules, length of the work, and agency resources, all need to be recognized and discussed openly. Other agency requirements are less generic and may not apply everywhere; nevertheless, you will want to be clear about these perspectives as well. For example, it may be the custom of your agency to present new cases at an agencywide meeting each week. Sometimes when workers talk about confidentiality, they don't consider that using peers for supervisory purposes may not seem very confidential to the client, especially if she or he has had other contacts within the organization. Workers can become so used to their own practices (such as supervision) that they may not anticipate clients' responses to them. They need, then, to describe such processes from the beginning of the engagement.

Other formalities you will want to inform the client about relate to bureaucratic arenas or financial coverage. For example, if you are required to submit monthly reports to the court, you should discuss this stipulation with your client. Even when clients aren't happy with such an idea, they are likely to respect your communicating that fact up front. For another example, if your client will have to file a Medicaid application in order to continue working with you, you should explain that as early as possible. As you might expect, for many people making that kind of application has serious, negative implications, such as admitting defeat, disability, or helplessness. Even if you see such requirements as these as simple mechanisms that make your work possible, it is obviously important that you understand what they mean to clients.

Another mandate that is becoming increasingly problematic in community agencies is the requirement for diagnosis. As discussed earlier, many institutions now demand a *DSM* diagnosis for insurance purposes. This mandate can provide some very uncomfortable moments for social workers who believe strongly in helping clients to identify and use their strengths. The attempt to sort out a psychiatric diagnosis requires a lot of focus on deficiencies and can create a great deal of stigma. For example, a school social worker who is providing support to a five-year-old whose parents are addicted to heroin might find it problematic to diagnose the child with an "adjustment disorder," which will then appear in school records, label the child for years to come, and may be transmitted to other institutions. Regardless of the circumstances, many social workers who don't support this kind of labeling consider the very act of making a diagnosis to be "selling out."

Obviously, if your agency requires its workers to make diagnoses, then you need to consider your feelings on this issue before you accept a position. Interns are not likely to formulate diagnoses, but some may object to working in a setting that does. Others may find the process tolerable as long as it facilitates service provision. I believe that ethical conduct obliges all workers to inform their clients when a diagnosis is required to access services. The client can then decide whether she or he wants to participate in that exchange. For some clients and workers the diagnostic process may seem a small price to pay for getting services, whereas for others it is too high.

CONCLUSION

We've explored a range of issues related to assessment (including the very idea of assessment). Clearly, the process of assessment involves a major combination of efforts. At the same time, with the exception of mapping and the strengths grid, we have not looked at particular instruments for assessment. The reason for this omission is that there are literally hundreds of instruments that social workers can use depending on the practice setting, type of client served, and the range of issues. Your agency will probably use a few selected instruments that it has found useful.

Assessment should be seen as an integrated activity that arises out of an effective engagement with the client and progresses into the action-oriented phase of the work. Its tone and focus should be consistent with the practice process as a whole. Finally, to emphasize a point made in Chapter 1, assessment goes on throughout the practice process, sometimes shifting the work slightly and sometimes significantly. It is a fluid activity that fits into an ever-evolving integrated whole.

MAIN POINTS

- Assessment involves dialogue to discover where the client wants to go.

- The theoretical perspective used by the worker has significant implications for the assessment and the intervention. Five theories discussed in this chapter are psychoanalytic, attachment, cognitive, strengths based, and narrative.

- The worker will want to develop a shared vision with the client by respecting the client's preferred reality and responding honestly to it.

- Mapping is a useful addition to verbal assessment. Two types of maps that are widely used within the profession are genograms and ecomaps.

- Assessment also evaluates the types of resources, both formal and informal, that the client and the client's environment can bring to bear.

- When resources are not present or adequate, workers need to respond appropriately, possibly with social action.

- The assessment and planning moves from a shared vision to specific details regarding the intervention. Internalized oppression and the emotional impact of change can influence the entire assessment process and the client's capacity for participation in planning.

- Workers need to be clear and honest with clients about specific agency constraints and requirements that will influence the client's experience of the work.

EXERCISES: PRACTICING SOCIAL WORK

Review Emilia's case file on the CD. Then study the genogram and ecomap of the family for both its content and form. Click on the Assess tab and view the tasks you will need to complete.

Emilia's Map

Using Emilia as the anchor family member, develop two genograms. The first should reflect what her relationships looked prior to age 14 and the second should be an "update" to her current age of 28. Include as much information as you can while keeping the drawing informative and clear. Between the two genograms, develop an ecomap that represents how you think the systems and networks supporting Emilia's "change" (her involvement in the drug world) might have operated in the estrangement of her family. (See "Create a genogram" on the CD and/or Exhibit 5.3 for some brief notes about conventional symbols.)

Partner with another student and exchange the three drawings. Are they similar? In what respects do they differ? What information is particularly helpful? What facets of Emilia's life are the most effectively represented in a social mapping format? Which ones are the most challenging?

Propose and develop an original mapping device that you think would communicate Emilia's story effectively and creatively (use pictures or symbols or other devices).

EXERCISES: THE SOCIAL WORK LIBRARY

Read the Meyer chapter on graphics in assessment and then consider the following questions:

a. In what specific ways does your use of graphics in an assessment (as opposed to a linear or verbal account) help you to understand your client? (Apply this question to a client for whom you may have drawn a genogram or to Emilia Sanchez.)

b. Choose one of the other graphic models that Meyer presents and apply it to your client, making her or him the central character. What do you discover?

OTHER EXERCISES

To prepare for this exercise, review "Focus on Strengths" in the Values Inventory on the CD.

Finding Emilia's Strengths

Emilia Sanchez has finally come to you for help because she has decided she must conquer her drug addiction. Because of her long history and her family's outrage regarding her son and the following abortion of another child, Emilia feels very discouraged about her ability to make a place for herself in the family again and to make the changes she wants to make. Chose a member to play Emilia. Using the guidelines from Component 1 of Cowger and Snively's strengths perspective assessment scheme, you, as the worker, should look to identify and assess Emilia's strengths. When you and Emilia have completed Component 1, you and she can fill out the grid from Component 2. Swap positions.

Write out or prepare to discuss your answers to the following questions.

1. What was the most challenging aspect of identifying the strengths of someone who has had so many difficulties?

2. How do you as the worker encourage Emilia to recognize her strengths?

3. What does Emilia experience in such an assessment?

Hector's Assessment

Go to the Sanchez family case study and play the streaming video of social worker Lynn Notestine's opening meeting with Hector Sanchez. Play the video all the way through once. Then return to it and note as many specific strengths-based reflections on the part of the social worker as you can. Discuss how this approach shapes both the work with Hector and his response to it.

Mr. Tightwad

When the student residents of an apartment house returned from Christmas break, they discovered that the landlord, Mr. Tightwad, had begun to remodel their apartments without informing them of his intentions. Tightwad, hoping to increase his income, was combining an entry hall with portions of the original apartments to create another two apartments. His plan called for shaving three feet off the rooms on either side of the hallway and adding them to the hallway space.

The new apartments affect all the residents, who will each lose three feet from the end of their apartments. They will also lose the second exit since all apartments had two exits, one to the hallway and one to the outside. To make matters worse, he has turned off the water in the building since he says he has to do this to work on the new apartments. As a consequence, residents now have no water, cannot use the bathrooms, and must listen to the pounding as work on the apartments continues. They have complained to Mr. Tightwad who has told them them to stop complaining as he has no intention of halting work on the project.

As the ombudsperson for the student housing office, you have often heard complaints about Mr. Tightwad. Now the tenants have come to you for help. You must decide what you can do to assist them.

First consider:

1. How would you like to frame your role here?

2. What information about the tenants would you like to have before attempting to assess the situation?

3. What alliances might be available to you or would you want to develop? How would you assess them?

4. What social network issues would you want to explore?

5. What issues of power do you think are operant here?

6. What information about Mr. Tightwad would help you assess his willingness to respond to your advocacy efforts?

CHAPTER 6

Intervening in Context: Initiating the Plan

Help thy brother's boat across, and lo! Thine own has reached the shore.

Hindu Proverb

Where after all, do human rights begin? In small places, close to home—so close and so small that they cannot be seen on any map of the world. Yet, they're the world of individual persons: the neighborhood he lives in; the school or college he attends; the factory, farm, or office where he works.

Eleanor Roosevelt (1958)

THROUGHOUT THIS BOOK I EMPHASIZE CONTEXT AS IT SHAPES THE meaning of experience for clients and for social workers. In this chapter you will see how this idea of context is integrated into the work you actually do—how, where, and with whom you do it. Context both shapes what you do and likewise is shaped by what you do. Whether you are rowing a boat, engaging in social transformation, or pondering human rights, you interact with the choices and capacities of individuals, the systems in which people are embedded, and the accessibility of existing and potential resources. All of these dimensions contribute to the totality of the social work practice context.

Accordingly, there are multiple ways to intervene in any issue or problematic situation. Viewed through a critical constructionist lens, a useful, direct intervention for one person will not necessarily meet the needs of another person in a similar situation. For example, a single woman with a six-month-old baby may identify job training and finding suitable day care as the objective of the intervention. In contrast, another woman in seemingly the same circumstances may need assistance with locating housing, handling roller-coaster emotions, and keeping a safe environment for her infant. Yet another single mother will need intensive advocacy efforts in order to deal with discriminatory practices in her employment. Social workers often encounter difference like this, and they frequently have to argue against the one-size-fits-all interventions that are sometimes imposed by social service organizations or public policy.

In recognition of the client's unique story, you will locate the starting point of your work in her or his most pressing issue. This location should reflect the priorities for action that are agreed upon in the assessment and planning phase. Because the client is the chief negotiator of the journey, the work will first assume and then reflect her or his strengths and capacities to be successful in that journey.

From this starting point, the chapter examines the generalist practice activities and skills of supporting client strengths and client environments. Within these areas we will consider and deconstruct a variety of social work roles and methods that support client-worker relationships. Finally, a case example illustrates a unifying theoretical perspective that bridges the work with clients' strengths and environments from the perspectives of social justice, human rights, strengths, and critical social construction.

The Social Work Library

Read Goldstein's article to explore the importance of context more fully.

SUPPORTING CLIENTS' STRENGTHS

Through its theoretical lens, the strengths perspective offers a focused, committed effort for identifying, expanding, and sustaining the resilience and assets that clients bring to their interface with the world. Using a strengths-based method suggests that the worker will not only seek out and identify client strengths in the assessment (see Chapter 5) but will also support and maximize them throughout the working relationship. For many practitioners this effort will be the major focus of the work.

Clearly, then, the strengths approach views supporting clients as central to the worker's action. Workers often need to remind themselves of this because in our culture even the most strengths-oriented practitioners occasionally are seduced into focusing all their energies on "what needs fixing." Strengths, like all human dimensions, need recognition, validation, and nourishment to remain vital.

Principles for Strengths-Based Intervention

Let us consider two more broad principles of the strengths-based approach as they apply to the practice context and the action of intervention. Saleebey (2002) identifies these as follows:

- The worker should act in context: education, action, advocacy, and linkage.
- The worker should move toward normalizing and capitalizing on the client's strengths. (pp. 90–91)

Acting in Context   Here the worker's activity centers on helping the client actually use the strengths she or he is beginning to recognize, as well as those already discovered, and to link them with her or his goals and dreams. That kind of effort might lead, for example, to worker support for more independence or more assertiveness than a client has previously been comfortable in demonstrating.

Consider the situation of the client who has experienced trouble in dealing with landlords and now feels that she cannot negotiate a lease arrangement. The worker can help her think through the advantages of establishing a positive rental history as they work together to identify appropriate options. The worker can also encourage her to recognize her capacity to understand the business-focused details of renting and to negotiate for certain options. This endeavor involves some risk taking on the client's part as she stretches beyond what is comfortable for her to initiate, but it also offers her an unusual opportunity to decide and act on her own. When the venture is successful—for example, the client negotiates a lease and bargains for some rental rebate in exchange for her painting the living room walls—the client experiences the benefit of adding another competency to her growing list. Conversely, when the effort doesn't go as planned, she becomes more aware of the specific areas in which she wants to direct her energies in order to make changes.

Capitalizing on Strengths   This is the consolidation step in which the worker and client together recognize the successes they've had in establishing and stabilizing the client's competencies. Using the same example, let's assume that the client has managed to find an apartment she likes at a rate she can afford. The worker would then affirm the skills she demonstrated, encourage her to generalize those particular skills into other arenas, and support her ability to generate new skills. The worker would also want to help the client recognize that she is building useful relationships in the community. For example, when she has established a record of reliability in paying her rent on time and keeping up her apartment, her landlord is likely to become a resource if she needs a reference for a job or wants to find a larger apartment across town. The worker's efforts at education, advocacy, and support for the client's developing this kind of network that links her accomplishments to her goals is critical for the consolidation of her growth. By normalizing the task, in this case, of securing housing, the worker not only demonstrates the client's capacities, but also reinforces the availability of community resources, and establishes that disengagement, or ending the work, is appropriate. The ultimate normalization is the client's continued development and the recognition that she or he can successfully manage the everyday tasks of living.

Strengths-Oriented Processes and Skills

When used effectively, many classic social work processes or skills can affirm client strengths and support their underlying position in the work. For example, the familiar "reflection of empathy" has remained a time-honored skill because it mirrors the respect and regard for human beings that is inherent in social work. The processes discussed in the following sections have also earned their place in social work practice history as consistent with the profession's commitments.

Dealing with Feelings   A useful grouping of several related skills that help people feel heard and respected, termed "**dealing with feelings**," includes the skills "reaching for feelings" and "waiting out feelings" (Middleman & Wood, 1990, pp. 59–72). The action of **reaching for feelings** simply invites the client to express her or his feelings more explicitly or forcefully when they aren't clear to you, as the worker. When the client is not expressing any emotions in a situation in which you would expect her or him to do so, is expressing emotions that don't seem to fit with her or his body language or the situation, or is expressing feelings nonverbally, you reach for more. In certain situations—for instance, when feelings are too painful to express—this process will not yield clear results. Nevertheless, when you make this invitation without demand, you communicate your respect and value for your client's feelings.

In contrast, **waiting out feelings** involves silence. When you sit with a person who is experiencing powerful emotions and simply wait until that person is ready to speak, you are waiting out feelings. In a profession characterized by verbal purposefulness, respecting your client's silence can be a challenge. Clients generally experience this process as nonpressuring, accepting, and highly respectful. You have seen that maintaining this kind of silence in the early phases of assessment can be helpful; however, it is just as important in the action phase. It can also be one of those dimensions of relationship that clients notice, remember, and value long after the work is completed.

Checking Out Meaning   Previous discussions of engagement and assessment emphasized the need to be certain that you have understood the client correctly. In fact, this process is critical in all phases of social work practice. Sometimes, **checking out meaning**, or **clarification**, is needed at the most unexpected times, especially as you and your client grow to know each other better and may begin to make assumptions regarding each others' intent, interpretations, and meanings. For example, as mentioned earlier, sometimes a client may experience feelings when a goal has been reached that are contrary to what you would expect from someone who has just been successful. If your client who has just negotiated a lease independently for the first time in her life demonstrates tearfulness or giddiness or another sign of intense emotions, you might assume the emotion is joyful. However, it might also arise from regret or loss or confusion. Because there are so many opportunities to misread any person's communication, checking out the meaning is always an important component of the work, particularly as the relationship deepens and the work becomes more complex. The continuing use of this kind of clarification assures the client that her or his meaning is worth understanding clearly. In that way it also supports both burgeoning and well-established strengths.

Supporting Diversity   As discussed in Chapter 5, a client's cultural background should be seen as a potential source of strengths rather than an obstacle. Therefore, you want to use the traditions or aspects of your client's culture that nourish and give meaning to life. For example, many cultures demonstrate far greater respect for authority or the wisdom of age than U.S. culture does. When you work with clients from such a culture, you will want to learn what kinds of actions on your part will support those values, because they are assets. Although you should always confer with your clients regarding your actions, you need to remain especially sensitized to the fit of your approach with your client's culturally influenced sense of propriety. You would probably not encourage the client from such a culture to participate in a rent strike aimed at a prominent elder statesman, especially when such an action would likely become highly adversarial.

SUPPORTING CLIENTS' ENVIRONMENTS

Having confirmed the importance of recognizing and supporting client strengths in the intervention process, let us now focus on identifying and intensifying the strengths of the environments in which clients live. This dual focus on person and environment is consistent with social work's tradition. Accordingly, social workers often direct their efforts toward making the environments in which their clients live more responsive to client needs. This approach looks to the institutions and policies outside of the client rather than viewing the client's difficulties as a symptom of inner pathology. In maintaining this focus on improving environmental response, the work reflects an underlying commitment to a social justice framework. In the process, it assumes that clients possess the capacity both to identify their difficulties and to participate in the work necessary to alleviate them.

Principles for Taking Environments into Account

In a classic application of this kind of intervention, Wood and Middleman identify six major principles (1989, pp. 35–67). Because these principles strongly emphasize a social justice orientation, we will review them in some detail.

The Worker Should Be Accountable to the Client   This principle requires the worker to respond to the client's perception of the problem. If, for example, the client is having substantial difficulty in accessing certain welfare benefits because he does not speak English fluently, you will direct your energies to addressing that need. You might arrange for an interpreter, request a welfare department worker who is fluent in the client's native language, or simply accompany the client to discourage intimidating behavior on the part of anyone in the welfare department.

The Worker Should Follow the Demands of the Client Task   Wood and Middleman created a "Frame of Reference" that is illustrated through a quadrant diagram covering the parameters of social work's tasks (see Table 6.1). This scheme suggests that practitioners may (1) work with clients on their own behalf, (2) work with clients on behalf of the clients and others like them, (3) work with others on behalf of clients, and (4) work with others on behalf of a category of clients. The principle of following the demands of the client stresses that the worker should always look beyond the individual client in order to see if there are others in the same situation. If so, the worker needs to adapt by moving from one quadrant to another or functioning in multiple quadrants.

To see how the Frame of Reference works, consider the case of a practitioner who is working with the mother of a child with disabilities who has no viable transportation to school. The worker, with the mother's agreement, might locate a driver, or a person to accompany the child on the regular school bus, or request extended school hours so that the mother can pick up the child after work (working with a client on behalf of the client, Quadrant A). However, if the worker discovers that there are four other children with disabilities in the school who lack adequate transportation, she or he, still working with the mother, might organize and coordinate a team of drivers for all five children in the school (working with the client on behalf of the client and others like her, Quadrant B). If the worker's efforts were directed at enlisting the aid of a community group to help locate and fund, say, a small van that could hold six

 Web Links

Visit the Childrens Disabilities site for information on parenting children with special needs, tips on advocating for them, articles on specific issues (ADHD, feeding, etc.), and resources useful to parents of children with disabilities.

 Web Links

The Social Security site advises parents and caregivers about benefits for children with disabilities in the U.S. It provides links to other government sites for benefits.

FOCUS OF INTERVENTION	INTENDED BENEFICIARY	
	SINGLE	MULTIPLE
Clients	Work with clients on their own behalf **Quadrant A**	Work with clients on behalf of themselves and others like them **Quadrant B**
Others	Work with others, such as nonsufferers, on behalf of clients **Quadrant D**	Work with others, such as nonsufferers, on behalf of a category of sufferers **Quadrant C**

TABLE 6.1

Frame of Reference for Structural Approach to Social Work Tasks

Source: Adapted from Wood & Middleman, 1989

Web Links

The site for the National Association of Protection and Advocacy Systems addresses efforts in disability rights, as well as other areas, and provides state policies and links to a variety of other sources.

children, the work would fall in a different quadrant (working with others out of concern for specific clients, Quadrant D). Finally, if the worker proposes statewide transportation funding to the legislature on behalf of a category of clients—in this case, children with disabilities—the work falls into Quadrant C, working with others on behalf of a category of clients. Although the worker's efforts may vary, move from one quadrant to another, and operate simultaneously, the work is always performed on the behalf of clients.

The Worker Should Maximize the Potential Supports in the Client's Environment   This is a generic principle and requires the worker to identify, access, and, where necessary, modify or even create the supports that a client needs. These supports might include such resources as temporary housing for a homeless family, hospice services for a family dealing with an elder's imminent death, and child care services for a young mother who has to work outside her home. Chapter 5 discussed this aspect of resource development; it remains a central focus for the work phase as well.

The Worker Should Proceed from the Assumption of "Least Contest"   This tenet holds that the worker should use the minimal amount of pressure that is required to meet a client's need. For example, a worker should explore the availability of affordable child care for a client before pressuring the mayor to initiate a city-sponsored day care system. If these early attempts fail—that is, it truly appears that there is no adequate, affordable child care—then the worker can "up the ante."

In a different situation, the "least contest" approach might encourage the practitioner to contact another service before engaging in advocacy. For example, a practitioner working with a young woman who was not accepted into a local parent support group might make a referral to a different group. If a series of appropriate referrals doesn't yield results, the worker will consider other approaches of greater contest, such as advocating with the person who organized the original group.

The Worker Should Identify, Reinforce, and/or Increase the Client's Repertoire of Strategic Behavior for Minimizing Pain and Maximizing Positive Outcomes and Satisfaction   This principle cautions the worker against holding the client responsible for a lack of community responsiveness in the development of resources or support. It recognizes, however, that the client may need assistance in developing behaviors that are likely to elicit cooperation from the community. For example, some clients who have been excluded from the community on various levels might present as eager to the point of aggressiveness. They can probably improve their chances of being accepted if they curb their enthusiasm a bit, by speaking in a softer voice, for example.

In applying this principle, workers need to keep in mind that our culture has led many people to blame themselves for various acts of violence or oppression that they've experienced at the hands of others. Therefore, it's important that they don't attribute their difficulties in accessing resources to their own failures. Workers whose clients have adopted this perspective can employ consciousness-raising techniques to challenge these beliefs and transform personal issues such as child abuse and violence against women into political issues.

Workers Should Apply Principles 1–5 to Themselves   This final principle asserts that the worker can consistently sustain effective practice through the principles that she or he uses in work with clients. Accordingly, it suggests that workers make clear, accountable contracts and explore common practice issues with other workers. It also encourages workers to apply the principles to their work in agency settings.

Environment-Sensitive Processes and Skills

The three processes or groups of skills discussed earlier—dealing with feelings, checking out meaning, and supporting diversity—can also be applied to the environment. Here, we will explore some other processes that are also relevant to supporting clients' effective use of environmental supports. Keep in mind that none of these processes is limited to this type of practice situation. Some of them require a little more caution in their use, both because they may take longer to master and because their use can be misunderstood.

Providing Information   Clients often want, need, and ask for information about the environment, which may be their most valuable resource. This tendency may concern some of you who are uneasy that you will overinfluence decisions or be too directive or create dependency. These concerns are sometimes legitimate, but they also can be managed. When you consider that information in our society is clearly linked to power, you may become less reluctant to provide it to clients. The problem with information seems to arise when it is confused with advice or is strongly one-sided. Because none of us knows all sides of all issues, this concern is probably more difficult to mitigate. Still, you can offer what you know as a simple proposition, always framed by the limits of your knowledge.

You also need to be clear that you don't hold any expectations about what clients do with the information. It is not yours to be given away only with certain restrictions. For example, if you are a child welfare worker helping a young couple to learn more effective methods to care for their three-year-old who has recently been diagnosed with autism, you may want to generate a compilation of resources you think would be helpful to the parents. You may believe that they would benefit from respite services because you suspect it will be helpful for the mother to develop some trust in a caretaker outside of the family. Therefore, you provide her with the names of several agencies that provide respite services. When she doesn't follow up on this information, you may become frustrated or even irritated. In this case it is clear that your "information" is actually "advice," and the mother isn't ready to take it. This simple example illustrates how problematic an investment in giving information might be at times. Fortunately, you can almost always process this kind of situation with the client so that your agenda becomes transparent and the client is free to accept or reject it.

Refocusing   A time may come in the work when you require **refocusing**, or bringing the client back to the original focus of the work. It spans several possible directions, including two discussed here: referring back to purpose and confronting clients' behavior. Workers frequently use these processes in assisting clients to take advantage of the potential in their environments.

When clients seem to be wandering off into arenas other than the agreed-upon focus area of your work, a simple reference to the original agreements about what would happen during the action phase of the work is sometimes all that's necessary. This is referring to purpose. Occasionally the client (or the worker!) will simply become sidetracked by other compelling issues. Although this type of diversion is understandable, you are responsible for using your time with the client productively.

In other situations, the client may not carry out the plan as agreed. This may be because the plan was not truly embraced by the client as a priority or because it is proving uncomfortable. For example, your client Jane established a plan to seek counseling because she had been sexually abused and was experiencing many painful memories. However, initiating that kind of contact involved breaking the culturally and family imposed rule of conduct that she should never discuss anything so personal with an outsider. She finds the effort to initiate this counseling more difficult than she had imagined. You need to confront her very gently, even though she may simply need more informal support and acknowledgment from you to manage the unanticipated struggle. This development might also signal that the plan isn't working for Jane and isn't likely to lead to the outcome previously anticipated. In situations like these you need to return to the goals, review the client's experience, and make changes as necessary.

Significantly, clients often perceive gentle confrontation of their behavior as not only helpful but supportive. If the worker carefully contrasts what a client said she would do with what she actually did, the client might experience this activity as respectful because it affirms her capacity to meet her commitments. This process must be carried out sensitively, of course, or else the client might experience the confrontation as hostile and argumentative. It is certainly not the first approach to use in working with people in such situations; rather, referring to purpose should be tried first. When it is used selectively and sensitively, however, gentle confrontation can convey hope and respect.

Interpreting Client Behavior   The last process we will look at is **interpreting**, which refers to the worker's making sense of the client's behavior in ways the client probably doesn't perceive or at least acknowledge. The goal is to inspire a new or different way of thinking about a situation. From a constructionist view, interpreting is probably the most difficult and problematic of the process skills discussed.

What a client's behavior suggests to you may be very different from what it suggests to the client. Still, there may be a place for interpreting when you are very careful to test it out with clients and when you acknowledge that the meaning you take from the situation is only one possibility. Returning to the earlier example of Jane, you might, in helping her to use her environmental supports, say something like, "It seems as if you don't feel ready to take on the kind of work that this type of counseling is likely to be."

Although many of us have encountered situations in which someone else's thoughts about what we were doing were helpful, another person's interpretation of what we experience can also be frustrating and alienating, particularly when it seems judgmental or "expert" (as if someone else possesses the secret of understanding our behavior). Interpreting is a widely applicable process but one that should be used tentatively and with ongoing supervision.

DECONSTRUCTING TRADITIONAL SOCIAL WORK ROLES

As you were reading the preceding descriptions of social work activities, you may have thought about the specific roles that workers assume in order to support client strengths and environments. As another way of demonstrating the actual work that social workers do, some of the specific role formulations that are commonly discussed in the social work literature and used in practice settings can be isolated, highlighted, and deconstructed. We will look at the assumptions that underlie these roles and the ways they are taken up in the context of the work. Specifically, these roles are

- Broker
- Mediator
- Case manager
- Advocate
- Educator

Together they represent much of social work's activity across the dimensions of supporting both client strengths and client environments.

These five roles are not mutually exclusive. Rather, there is considerable overlap in some of them—for example, educating the legislature regarding the needs of foster children may also, on another level, pave the way for a future effort at advocacy for this group. This kind of mix is common in social work practice, which is rarely tidy. Sometimes it will be difficult to make a distinction between roles, and the label probably isn't as important as understanding the underlying assumptions of each position as you take it up. If you were to assume a collaborative position as an educator in presenting useful and relatively unbiased information about, say, adults who have experienced psychiatric hospitalization, you would not want to confuse your immediate purpose by aggressively advocating for a particularly controversial aspect of their treatment.

Broker

Social workers typically act as **brokers** when they link their clients to the services that provide what they need. "What they need" may range from instrumental assistance (food, clothing, and children's toys) to intangible services like counseling, support groups, and advocacy. Let us consider the functions and context of brokering, the process of building the necessary networks, and making the match of client to service.

Brokering Functions and Context   Five social work functions of brokering are

- Assessing client needs.
- Assessing available resources.
- Matching and initiating referrals to appropriate services.
- Linking services or networking.
- Sharing information.

Some practitioners make the case that the brokering role also includes modifying, inventing, or otherwise creating new resources where none exist. All of these activities can serve to strengthen the client's environment, or context, as well as to support her or his strengths. These activities also overlap, and they reflect much of what was discussed in Chapter 5 regarding assessment of clients, resources, and the fit between them.

Brokering is probably the oldest social work role. Nevertheless, it might have less status today than it once had because of the profession's increased interest in psychological and therapeutic roles. Brokering may also seem fairly simple at times. For example, if your client requests assistance with locating used children's furniture, you simply "refer" her or him to the appropriate agency. It is probably somewhat misleading, though, to think of the brokering role as simple, because it requires the worker both to be familiar with the resources and to nurture and maintain a network of such resources. In the complex world of contemporary, urban social services, the ability to know one service or resource from the next can itself be a feat. In rural areas, where the service system may be much less comprehensive, with fewer choices, knowing and maintaining effective relationships with the available resources is even more important.

Building Networks for Brokering   Developing a network will include such activities as making initial and subsequent contacts with appropriate workers in other agencies, discovering who will help your client most, and becoming familiar with eligibility criteria. It also involves establishing stable working relationships with people who will help your clients.

To build a network successfully, you must acquire some knowledge of the informal aspects of the resource as well as the formal ones. For example, it will be helpful to you to understand the mission statement of a particular community hospice program—what its goals are and how it sees itself delivering services. In addition, it will be helpful for you to know that the program has just received a large grant for an additional building, that the local university is about to place a field unit there for student training, or that the board has approved funding for a development director. Although you will not have access to all informal developments in the services you use, your attention to, and continuous connections with, both formal and informal aspects of the network you maintain will enrich your understanding of your community's resource environment.

Making the Match in Brokering   As discussed in Chapter 5, you need the skills and knowledge to estimate the match between clients and services as you maintain an ongoing and continually growing network of contacts. It is also worth noting here that developing and maintaining a resource network (or "service system linkage") nearly always requires you to use the very skills you first learned about in Chapter 4 in connection with clients—that is, looking with planned emptiness and others. When you understand what the service is trying to accomplish, under what kinds of constraints, and with what assets, your ability to use it well will increase.

You will want to follow up on your referrals, both to see that the client is participating in and benefiting from the service and to get a sense of the provider's response to your referral. Remember that the match between clients and services is important from the service's point of view as well as from the client's. When you have taken the time and care to learn what makes a "good referral" to a particular service, you will gain the trust of other providers who will respect your competence and skills. Further, when you develop a genuine understanding of, and appreciation for, the work that others do, you are likely to find your own work more enjoyable, and perhaps more to the point, you will find "the system" more responsive to your client.

Mediator

Mediation has both a formal and informal dimension in human services. Mediation as a professional practice has its own identity and is often associated more with the law and public policy than it is with social work. At the same time, however, many social workers enter mediation training programs in which they become specialists, and most social workers engage in some aspects of mediation fairly frequently, if on a less formal basis. **Mediators,** as outsiders, try to establish common ground between disputing parties, try to help them understand each other's point of view, and try to establish that each party has an interest in the relationship's stability past the current area of difference.

Finding Common Ground   Locating the points of agreement in the midst of a dispute is a common activity in social work practice. For a direct practice example, assume you are working in a youth agency and have just seen Josh, a 15-year-old who has recently run away from home for the first time. After some conversation with him, you understand his story to be about the relationship between his mother and her new live-in boyfriend. He is now upset and scared and isn't quite sure of the ramifications of being on his own like this. He dislikes his mother's boyfriend and objects to the curfew and other house rules he imposes. Josh also says he misses his mother's companionship the way it was before "he" entered the scene. When you are satisfied that Josh is safe at home (that he is not being abused in any way), you ask him if it's all right if you set up a meeting with him, his mother, and her boyfriend to explore the issues among them. He somewhat reluctantly agrees.

When his mother enters the youth center, she seems exasperated with her son, but she is also relieved to see him. She begins to cry and hugs him. Her boyfriend remains quiet, but when he catches Josh's eye, he smiles at the boy just slightly.

Walking through It   Let us explore the process for one possible avenue of mediation in Josh's family. You might do the following:

- Attempt to establish common ground. In this case Josh's present well-being would be the immediate point of common interest. This is what you discover: Josh is 15 years old and is not prepared to support himself physically, financially, or emotionally (or legally in most places). He is scared and concerned about his future. At the same time, however, he is vocal about his freedom and doesn't want to be bound by all those rules. His mother cares for him and wants him to be safe. Her boyfriend wants a peaceful household and likes Josh well enough, although he has no strong connection with him. He cares deeply for Josh's mother, however.

- Represent yourself genuinely as one who wants to help resolve this issue, trusts the process of working it through, and doesn't favor any one side.

- Help Josh, his mother, and her boyfriend understand and appreciate one another's points of view. Insofar as Josh's mother and her boyfriend represent one side of the dispute but may differ between them, acknowledge all points of view. Facilitate their direct dialogue with one another. (Use all your social work skills here; planned emptiness and looking from diverse angles will be very beneficial.)

- Establish with Josh, his mother, and her boyfriend that it is in the interests of all of them to work together, here and now, so that they can come to a resolution regarding Josh's living arrangements and his general safety.

- Help all parties recognize that each will benefit from an ongoing positive relationship in which they can settle differences that go beyond this one dispute. The quality of Josh's future may depend on their ability to work together, as well as the quality of the relationship between Josh's mother and her boyfriend. These are the abiding points of common interest.

This scenario represents just one way in which this situation might play out. You might make other arguments to reach the same goals of finding common ground and identifying solutions. You'll notice that no *particular* solution is implied in this process. Josh, his mother, and her boyfriend might agree that Josh should return home, live with a relative for a while, try to survive on his own on a trial basis, or any number of other possibilities. The major point here is that the relationship between Josh and his mother (and boyfriend) is collaborative and that each has a stake in working out a solution that affirms their mutual benefit.

Case Manager

A classic view of **case management** defines it as a "boundary-spanning approach" meant to assist particularly vulnerable clients, usually with multiple needs, in gaining access to services, across professional fields of interest, in different spheres (Rubin, 1992). This would mean, for example, that if your client has a serious mental health issue as well as a back injury; a need for both medication and a referral to vocational rehabilitation; and a housing issue, she or he might be a good candidate for case management. **Case managers** not only coordinate these services but are also responsible for monitoring the responsiveness of services to clients by holding providers accountable and for ensuring client participation.

Varying interpretations of the parameters of case management, particularly in different settings, have unfortunately confused its meaning. Although social workers often serve as case managers, the profession does not necessarily embrace case management as its own. This is in part because of social work's interest in direct, clinical work and partly because of the tensions underlying some of the values of case management, as a distinct field from social work.

Common Components of Case Management   In spite of the fact that there are many case management models, five typical functions are included in almost all of them: (1) needs assessment, (2) service or treatment planning, (3) linking or referring, (4) monitoring, (5) advocacy (Rose, 1992). In some models, the case manager also serves as an informal, personal support/contact person or even therapist. In contrast to brokers, who may match a client to a single service, case managers take responsibility for assessing and monitoring the coordination of all services required by a client.

The term case management has been used to describe this overall coordinating function for about 30 years, although many scholars believe that modern generalist practice is really a form of case management. In more recent times, the component of cost containment has become crucial to case management. Accordingly, contemporary versions of case management have two primary—and often conflicting—purposes: to improve the quality of care through coordination of services, and to control the costs of care.

Archetype 1   Looking at the tension between care and cost in a slightly different way, Moxley (1997) identifies "two archetypes" of case management. The first is related to the management of rationed societal resources that will assist individuals in increasing their quality of life or health. Efficient management of these resources is the primary goal and is prioritized. In this scheme the worker is a technician of sorts, who is always looking for the most efficient way to resolve the problems of the people she or he serves, within the cost constraints imposed. In this way, the worker mediates between the client and the society by meeting client needs while safeguarding precious resources. There is no particular attention to challenging the restrictions placed on the level of investment made.

For example, within this first archetype, if you are a case manager in a community mental health center, you may be called upon to offer an opinion about (or determine) whether one your clients should be evaluated for psychiatric hospitalization. You may believe the client's condition warrants hospitalization but also find that within your agency 10 other clients are currently receiving inpatient services. Your agency's limit is 10 beds a day. Although your agency won't necessarily refuse to hospitalize your client, it will emphasize that it currently is over budget and might pressure you to reprioritize your client's needs (or those of another client who is already hospitalized). Here your job is to be savvy about resources and efficient about their expenditure. You act as "trustee [who] assures that the person in need is worthy of societal beneficence, that the problem is technically and diagnostically defined, and that the solution appears (at least on face) to be an efficient one" (Moxley, 1997, p. 5). Therefore, your job is not to address shortages in the mental health budget with the governor or to lobby the state legislature. It is to operate as effectively as possible within the bounds set out for you.

Archetype 2   The second archetype grows out of the consumer movements in the mid-1970s and emphasizes the values of rights over trusteeship and equity over efficiency. These consumer movements engaged people with serious mental illnesses, developmental disabilities, and physical disabilities. They shared an underlying theme that these populations had been hurt by the prevailing systems of the past (which included lack of access and discrimination) and were *entitled* to more responsive services as a kind of ongoing restitution.

As you can see, Archetype 2 addresses issues related to social justice more fully than does Archetype 1, and it implies that your role as the worker will shift to "steward" (p. 6) by taking into account the concern for structural, systemic factors. Advocacy and empowerment are integral to this construction of case management.

Conflicts and Incompatibilities   Some of the confusion about case management rests in the lack of clarity regarding what or who is being managed. Some find the language of the term pejorative: What is a "case," and what does it mean to "manage" it? Is the client (and presumably her or his behavior) being managed? Or is the worker managing the system? These are not just semantic questions; the answer affects the approach that the worker adopts. There is an overall contradiction between the two archetypes that also creates an ethical dilemma between the competing values of client self-determination and resource efficiency, among others (Kane, 1997). Moxley envisions the case management of the future as a blending of the archetypes that is likely to look very different in different settings and will be shaped by financial constraints, the relationship between state and federal revenues, developments in managed care, and consumer activism. Insofar as these are likely to shape the well-being of clients in your practice, they will be critical components to the future of social work practice.

The Social Work Library

For another perspective on the state of social work advocacy, read Lens & Gibelman's paper.

Advocate

Advocacy in social work practice is aimed at securing the rights and well-being of vulnerable clients. The **advocate** may obtain resources, modify existing policies or practices, and promote new policies that will benefit clients. Regardless of the specific activities involved, however, this kind of policy practice almost always represents a struggle over power, and by definition it seeks to obtain and ensure clients' access to resources. This role of defending, championing, or otherwise speaking out for clients is one of the original cornerstones of the profession's commitment, although its intensity has varied somewhat according to the political climate (Haynes & Mickelson, 2000). Although advocacy often focuses on the political or civil rights of clients, as a worker, you will also frequently advocate in informal, everyday situations when a client is treated disrespectfully or inefficiently. Advocacy assumes an active role that is not always comfortable or popular with others.

Many workers distinguish between **case (or client) advocacy,** defined as advocacy on behalf on an individual client or a single group of clients, and **cause (or class) advocacy,** which is initiated on behalf of a category of clients. **Legislative advocacy** may be thought of as a specialized version of cause advocacy in which some aspect of the law is addressed. We'll take a brief look at each type.

Web Links

Go to the Social Justice site found on the online learning center for more about advocacy issues and the disparity between the rich and poor in North America.

Case Advocacy   Social workers usually practice case advocacy on an agency or organizational level. For example, if your client has been denied food stamps to which she or he is entitled, you may want to advocate with the welfare organization that houses the food stamp service. To be an effective advocate, you will need to know a number of variables, such as eligibility requirements, agency appeal policies, regulations, and power structures, as well as contextual variables like how the food stamp program fits into the overall welfare organization. You will also want to recognize the situation as one of potential conflict and to enter at the point of least contest so that you do not inspire more resistance than necessary. This means that you will first take up the situation with the worker who originally denied the food stamps before you call the media or organize a protest.

Cause Advocacy   More political than case advocacy, cause advocacy involves both larger numbers of people and, by definition, a cause that affects them all, either by imposing obstacles to attaining resources or by directly depriving people of these resources. Cause advocacy is sometimes seen as problematic in that it involves speaking for large numbers of people you will never meet and who are not likely to be empowered to participate directly in forming either the goals or the preferred methods related to the cause.

Nevertheless, cause advocacy can be effective when you can partner with other concerned organizations. It is also helpful when the issue is very clear and doesn't impose any solution on people who don't choose it. For example, if your community has no adequate facilities for child care after school, there may be agencies, churches, or other institutions that are concerned and want to develop an optional facility for people who need it. Assuming that you will require funding from the city, your coalition of interested partners (well rehearsed and well organized) will be in a position to advocate for adequate child care. As in case advocacy, you will need to be skillful and to have done your homework regarding the number of children to be served, their needs, the estimated costs of providing the service, the likelihood of participation, the process of getting the issue on the city's agenda, and the benefits to all stakeholders.

Legislative Advocacy   This type of cause advocacy is devoted specifically to adding, amending, changing, or eliminating legislation in order to benefit a large group of clients. For example, when a social worker advocates to lower the legal alcohol limit for driving an automobile from .10 blood alcohol content (BAC) to .08, that is a case of legislative advocacy designed to benefit a huge category—drivers and passengers.

You can probably imagine many other kinds of scenarios in which a large group of people would benefit from some change in legislation, because nearly all entitlement policies have limitations that may present obstacles to your clients. Controversial resources such as family planning and abortion clinics are likely to have more access constraints (such as age limits or pregnancy duration) than do other less disputed services like food shelves.

It takes a considerable amount of savvy and organization to change a law. It is, however, well within the arena of social work practice to initiate or collaborate in such activity and is quite doable with careful preparation and hard work in appropriate situations. Legislative advocacy usually requires intensive, cooperative work with one or several organizations.

Thoughts about Power and Advocacy   Because social work advocacy is so frequently related to the social justice dimension of resource allocation, it is helpful to recall some general assumptions about power. In general, advocates recognize that power is not easily given up, it is not equally distributed, it involves conflict, and it is necessary in order to make substantial change. These points may seem a little harsh to you if you haven't thought in these terms before. They will help prepare you to enter a more political arena and are beneficial in understanding the social locations of those who have been oppressed and have had very little power to exercise in our culture.

Advocacy can be a highly rewarding undertaking (Abramowitz, 2005). It can also be tricky, and when not well done, it can be costly to clients, as you'll recall from the tenants' story in Chapter 5. See Box 6.1 for a list of cautions and strategies regarding advocacy.

 Web Links

The Advocacy Guru site offers a number of free services and links to workshops, seminars, and writing projects.

- Always enter any situation in which you want to advocate at the point of least contest (Wood & Middleman, 1989).
- Whenever clients are directly involved, make sure they genuinely support your efforts and understand the possible repercussions of them.
- Prepare yourself fully with the knowledge that is relevant to the situation—for example, eligibility requirements, entitlement limitations, number of people in a given category.
- Be absolutely clear and specific about what you want to happen; a complaint about a policy means little if there is no solution presented.
- Begin with simple efforts at persuasion; to assume that all others are deliberately sinister in withholding benefits, for example, may be as naive as assuming that no one is. In a complex and bureaucratic world, it is probably most reasonable to assume first that there has been a mistake or an oversight.
- Be clear when persuasion is not working and you must enter a new level.
- Assess that new level: Can you be successful? Are your clients still supportive? Do collaborative partners agree on the next step?
- Use your most carefully cultivated social work skills in any advocacy effort. Clarity and firmness do not preclude listening and empathy.
- Use the discourse of collaboration and common ground.
- Seek supervision and consultation along the way. You are as vulnerable to "not seeing" in thinking about legislation as you might be in the most intense interpersonal work.
- When entering into formal processes, such as legislative advocacy, become knowledgeable about the technicalities of the legislative process.

Educator

There are many ways in which most of you as social workers will function as educators. Practice settings are likely to influence the nature and level of this activity, but educating is common to most of them. On an interpersonal and concrete level, as an **educator**, you will often teach clients about services, new programs, how to fill out an application form, or which bus will get them uptown before noon. You may assure an adolescent client that she is indeed normal when she worries that her moodiness indicates she is not, or you might suggest that rent should not exceed a certain percentage of your client's income. Much of the direct service aspect of acting as educator relates to helping clients to access resources and also to make the behavioral changes they want to make.

Developing Client Skills   On a direct level, you, as the worker, might assist clients in developing the skills they actively seek in particular situations in which they want to change their own participation. The motivation for this kind of change needs to generate from the client's vision for how things might be different, rather than from your opinions about how she or he should improve. You can assist clients in understanding what they need to do to accomplish that change. For example, if your client, Ramon, feels pushed around on his job and wants to increase his assertiveness in the workplace, you might help by demonstrating a more assertive (but respectful) stance in a relevant interchange in which he could then practice or role-play.

In other settings, you can help elderly clients learn to organize their medications so they aren't so confusing. You can teach parents how to support their children through positive feedback. You can model clear communication and gradually assist your client in participating more effectively in problem situations. For example, you're working with an adolescent who is frequently expelled from school for short periods because of her angry outbursts at teachers. After working with her on how she can express herself more effectively without alienating adults, you might accompany her to her first meeting with the school principal on her return to classes. You could help her describe her situation and support a more focused, direct, and respectful level of discussion, according to her goals. Outside of the meeting you can help her process the session, evaluate what went well and what didn't, and support her ability to negotiate these relationships with some further practice. You might then role-play the next meeting rather than attend yourself.

In all of these situations the ultimate goal is a more positive sense of strength and agency—a change in clients' thinking about themselves and a greater integration of self and skills into the wider world of the environment. Remember too that every skill you use with a client is there for her or him to learn and use in relationship to others. In that sense modeling is unavoidable and should be respected.

Working with the Public   Some of you as social workers will frequently (more in some settings than others) be called upon to educate larger groups about issues that affect your clients. In some instances, these efforts take on aspects of primary prevention in that they are designed to prevent the development of a problem. For example, you might teach a parenting class or how to support racial tolerance in the classroom to a preschool group.

Other education efforts might involve providing testimony in a legislative hearing regarding the cultural needs of a group of refugee children in the local school or speaking to a community group in response to their concerns about a new group home for discharged clients with psychiatric histories that is to be established in their neighborhood.

Although the activities are very different in nature, all of these scenarios involve working in an educator's role. Finally, as you know, social work practitioners have a long history of acting as educators when they take on the position of field instructor for students in an academic program leading to a social work degree.

PUTTING IT ALL TOGETHER: THE EMPOWERMENT PERSPECTIVE

So far, this chapter has deconstructed various aspects of social work practice in action. Specifically, we have looked at supporting clients' strengths and their environments as well as various actions by workers. In order to see how the ideas here might integrate, let us take a look at empowerment practice as a model.

Empowerment Practice

Social work as a profession has been committed to empowering clients for much of its history. Although the literature discusses the source of empowerment extensively, in its purest sense, empowerment cannot be given to someone else because empowerment is not ours to give (Simon, 1990). Empowerment resides within the individual and can only be encouraged or perhaps released, but not given, by others.

Empowerment theory identifies three dimensions (Lee, 1996):

- Development of a more positive and potent self.

- Knowledge and capacity for a more critical understanding of the social and political reality of the person's environment.

- Cultivation of resources and strategies for attainment of personal and collective social goals, or liberation.

These three points make a clear theoretical connection among individual client strengths and their environment and their capacity to act in a way both to empower themselves and liberate others. This connection in turn supports intervention in multiple and highly interconnected settings as well as recognizes the importance of unleashing or strengthening the client's sense of self and agency. The case example in Box 6. 2 illustrates an appropriate and sensitive empowerment approach.

STRAIGHT TALK ABOUT THE REAL WORK: UNEXPECTED EVENTS AND ONGOING EVALUATION

As we explore the various ways to look at what social workers do, you may tend to consider the intervention process to be orderly. If you do your part in sensitive engagement, careful assessment of both the players and the environment,

BOX 6.2

Thomas's Story

The story takes place in a small New England city in the 1970s. Thomas was born with the neurological disorder of cerebral palsy. His family had little idea of how to deal with his severe physical limitations and had three other children to raise as well. His parents cared about him and did what they could to learn ways to support him and his abilities, as well as cope with his disability. He received the standard medical care of the time and was sent to school along with his age group.

Early on it was evident that Thomas's tortured body did not reflect his aptitude for schoolwork. He was, in fact, very bright and did exceedingly well in the subjects in which teachers supported him. His family did not understand, however, how Thomas's socialization was affected by his physical impairments or how he experienced his life. Although he had only a few friends, he attempted, for several years, to maintain a positive outlook, even developing an excellent sense of humor. Nevertheless, he continued to feel excluded by peers and adults alike.

COLLIDING WITH THE WORLD

Over time he became hostile with teachers because he had to prove himself over and over again, every time he entered a new grade or school. Teachers and school administrators first assumed that he was unable to do grade-level work. One teacher questioned his very presence in the regular classroom. His pastor at church advised that he seek supported employment through the welfare office. Everyone seemed to assume he was unable to do anything or know anything or even feel anything. His medical treatment included the excruciating requirement to walk in physical therapy that was promoted in those days. No one noted Thomas's pain or responded to it.

By the time Thomas was an adolescent, his parents sent him to a psychotherapist to find out why he was so angry. To him this was just another insult to someone who had already suffered so many. His therapist told him he needed to "get the chip off his shoulder" and tend to his schoolwork. There would be no money for college—he would have to earn scholarships if he wanted to do more than sit in the living room until he could be matched to a job he didn't want.

MEETING MAURA

Finally, Thomas was in need of a new wheelchair. He therefore was directed to a social worker for assistance when his parents couldn't pay the required deductible. The worker, Maura, who worked in the primary care office of Thomas's physician, first spent some time getting to know him and hearing what he had to say about the wheelchair. She assisted him in getting the funding for it and continued to ask about his overall experience. He began to talk about his needs to sort out some of his options regarding school, his family, his anger, and his growing sense of estrangement from the world.

Maura helped Thomas by hearing with an openness and reflexivity that assumed he was the expert on his experience. She heard his story, took him seriously, and helped him look at what his disability meant to him by asking him to talk not only about the physical pain but also about the exclusion that he experienced. She helped him look at his great resilience in the face of all he had been through. She did not try to challenge his perception

BOX 6.2

continued

of his experience but was completely respectful of it. She asked how he wanted his life to be different in view of his strong capacities. She encouraged him to reflect on his own position and how he might address it. As some time went on, she helped Thomas secure vocational rehabilitation funding for college and validated his by then strong commitment to working in human services on disability issues. She also met with Thomas's family to help them understand his choices and the impact these choices would have on the family.

CHANGING DIRECTION

Today, Thomas is studying for a master's degree in disabilities and is preparing for a career in which he can advocate for others with disabilities as well as himself. He is a full participant in school and in the surrounding context of his family, friends, and culture. He is still angry sometimes, but he is not fearful or alone.

Reading this (almost all) true story, you can see how Maura implemented the empowerment focus identified in the chapter: She assists in liberating Thomas's "potent self" and encourages his interpersonal connections. She supports his understanding of his environment and she helps connect him to a direction in which he can address the more political aspects of his experience. Now, let us explore the fit of his story with the perspectives emphasized in this book.

- *Social justice:* Maura works diligently to expand Thomas's access to the benefits of his society by helping him to find funding for education he could not otherwise attain. She does not accept the status quo arrangement in which those with private resources are privileged and those without are not. To complete this role, Maura would work toward reallocation of educational funding for all people, not just Thomas.

- *Human rights:* Thomas's status as a person with disability is not accepted as a rationale for discrimination in education, nor does his disability preclude the "full development of the personality" (Article 26, United Nations, 1948) through education. Maura recognizes him as a person who has both needs and abilities and the right to fulfill his life as he chooses.

- *Strengths perspective:* Maura recognizes Thomas's considerable strengths, validates them, and encourages linking their full expression to his goals. She sees him as a whole human being, with many talents to offer, not as a "victim of cerebral palsy."

- *Critical social construction:* Maura sees Thomas's disability as a social construction that results from the prevailing collective meaning given to it by our culture. She questions the limitations imposed by that construction, and she believes Thomas can do what he sets out to do. Further, Maura accepts that there are multiple realities and so honors his experience of exclusion and oppression. Because his experience has developed within the context of his social location, on which he is the expert, she makes no attempt to "correct" his understanding. Her effort goes into changing his future experience in order to make it more consistent with how he wants his life arranged.

and planning consistent methods of taking action on behalf of your clients, you might be seduced into thinking that the work will always go smoothly. That would be a huge error!

In the real world, not everything goes as planned in spite of the most diligent efforts. Because social work is completely immersed in people's lives, workers have only limited control over their work with clients and need to develop an acceptance (or at least tolerance) of that fact. People get sick. They get into accidents, they change their minds, they get fired, they become disheartened, they leave town, their kids get into trouble, and they experience violence. They also get promoted, find their strengths, find their voices, fall in love, get jobs, read an inspiring book, discover a new friend, and develop insight. All of these factors and many more have the potential to interrupt, postpone, redirect, or even terminate your work together.

In some cases—for example, if the client becomes discouraged or seems simply to lose interest—you will want to inquire what role you might have played in contributing to these developments. In many cases your responsibility will be to honor, acknowledge, and explore what the new situation means to the client, and reconfigure your work when indicated. It will generally be helpful for you to *expect the unexpected.* This is work with people, and flexibility is one of the most critical of social work attributes.

Just as you have been consistent in evaluating the progress of your work with your client and others involved, throughout the engagement and assessment processes, you will want to evaluate the direction of the intervention periodically as well, particularly if there have been substantial changes or unexpected events in the client's life. You may easily get carried away in the plan that you so carefully put together, even when it may no longer fit very well. Checking in and rechecking in will serve you well during the whole process of taking action. In that way you can stay connected to your client throughout and sustain a greater likelihood of providing relevant service.

CONCLUSION

This chapter has looked into several dimensions of the action that social workers take. The practice setting, theoretical perspectives, and perception of roles influence the ways in which you work to support clients' strengths and to support their environments. The overall fit of what you do with what you believe creates a sound backdrop for expanding your work into other system levels. The following chapters will integrate and extend these same processes to groups, families, organizations, and communities. This will serve both to consolidate the principles and skills in this first part of the book and to take them beyond, across system levels.

MAIN POINTS

- The most pressing client issue is the starting point for the intervention. This issue is defined by the context of the client's unique story and by the actions agreed upon in the assessment and planning phase.

- To support clients' strengths, workers should act in context and move toward normalizing and capitalizing on those strengths. Workers also engage in dealing with feelings, waiting out feelings, checking out meaning, and supporting diversity.

- To support clients' environments, workers should be accountable to the client; they should follow the demands of the client task; maximize the potential supports in the client's environments; identify, reinforce, and/or increase the client's repertoire of strategic behavior; and they should apply these principles to themselves.

- Deconstruction of traditional social work roles and their assumptions provides another view of what social workers actually do. The five traditional roles are broker, mediator, case manager, advocate, and educator.

- Exploring a case situation through the lens of empowerment perspectives demonstrates the work in context and how it fits with the perspectives emphasized in this book.

EXERCISES: PRACTICING SOCIAL WORK

Review the case file on Vicki and answer her Critical Thinking Questions. Click on the Intervene Tab to consider what will be needed for your work with Vicki and her family.

Time Warp

Imagine you are in a time capsule and could place yourself in the Sanchez's community fourteen years ago when Vicki, then 11, was first noted by workers to exhibit signs of autism. Imagine that you work in the schools and are assigned as child support worker to Vicki. School authorities recognize her autism and her family describes her as "touched." Consider the following questions:

1. How would you go about supporting Vicki's strengths? In what specific ways would you begin your work with her?

2. How would you go about supporting Vicki's environment? How would you work with the family? How can being "touched" be seen as a strength?

3. What social work role(s) would be most appropriate here? What assumptions does each make?

4. Working with another student playing the role of Vicki, develop a hypothetical work plan. What skills will you use to engage Vicki and encourage her participation?

5. Evaluate how well each of your plans for action fits with the theoretical perspectives of social justice, human rights, the strengths perspective, and critical social construction.

EXERCISES: THE SOCIAL WORK LIBRARY

Read the Lens and Gibelman paper on advocacy and then consider the following case situation.

Just Call Me "Crazy Maureen"

Maureen O'Rourke is sitting before you in the mental health clinic where you work as a case manager. She is distraught, looks as if she threw on whatever clothes she could find. To tell the truth, she looks a little out of control, as if she may be experiencing a recurrence of her mental health problems. As her case manager, you've worked hard with Maureen for nearly a year now, since she got out of the psychiatric hospital. When she came into the clinic she seemed pretty scared. She'd really done well, though, over the year. You helped her find a part-time job, which she likes, she got some surgery she needed taken care of, and she came to her appointments, hardly ever missing. Sometimes you met with her at her house. Seeing her like this today is quite sad and you feel disappointed.

Even though Maureen is in some disarray, she seems basically coherent, if upset. "He's started up again," she finally tells you. "Started up again?" You're not sure what she means at first. After talking for another half hour or so, you understand clearly that Ron, Maureen's husband from whom she had been separated, has returned home and has started to "slap her around a little" and call her "crazy." When you ask more, you discover that he beat her quite badly two nights ago and it's still difficult for her to walk. She says she thought about going to the shelter again but they told her it was full—she's sure she didn't get in because she seemed "crazy." She sighs and summarizes her plight—"just call me crazy Maureen"—and puts her head down.

1. Indicate which system you think is *most* relevant here:
   a. Mental health
   b. Family violence
   c. Welfare

2. How can you carry out the advocacy role here?

3. Who would you call first and why? (What is your first priority here?)

4. What assumptions are you making in the way you're carrying out your role?

Compare your answers with your classmates and consider their choices if different from your own. Be ready to discuss.

OTHER EXERCISES

What's in a Name? A Worker's Story

"Several years ago, when I worked at a state hospital, the admissions unit issued a daily report to all staff on a single sheet of paper that summarized all the patient admissions, discharges, visits, legal proceedings, etc., for the preceding 24-hour period. This was meant to convey useful information for all workers and it was especially helpful to social workers who needed to keep track of their clients' comings and goings. One of the categories on the form was titled 'body count' and was a tally of the number of patient/residents actually in the hospital at midnight. A colleague from a local community mental health agency (a case manager) was visiting her client who was in the hospital and she heard reference to this sheet. She was horrified at the language of 'body count,' to which I was by then accustomed. She made rather an issue of it!"

1. What do you think is the issue here? Why does it matter? Be as specific as you can.

2. In what way would you want to address it? Would such an activity be consistent with your view of a social worker's role?

3. Develop a plan, starting with least contest, of at least three steps you might take (a third one in case the first and second don't work).

Compare with other students and be prepared to discuss in class or write brief responses to each question to hand in.

CHAPTER 7

Social Work with Groups: Tapping the Power of Connection

If you need help, help others.
To help others best, let them help you.
Mental health can't be taught—it has to be learned together.
You alone can do it, but you can't do it alone.

From GROW's *Blue Book*, Rappaport, Reischel & Zimmerman, 1992

I found myself slipping into that self trashing thing, man, you know, putting myself down, thinking and saying I'm a dumb broad, ugly and worthless, just like J. used to tell me. But they got on me, those awesome women! They told me I was breaking the friggin' rules! Me! Breaking the rules, and then I remembered what they meant. We're not doing that stuff in this group. The end. Not okay. They are really the most awesome! What would I be without them?

Marcy, of the Debbie, Joan, Marcy & Kate Battered Women's Group

NONE OF US LIVES WITHOUT SOCIAL CONNECTIONS. Many of us spend much of our lives negotiating how close we want to be to family, neighbors, friends, associates, and colleagues. In whatever way the connection is experienced, we all have some relationship to small collectives of other people or groups. By *group* here I mean natural or planned associations that evolve through some common interest (such as supporting the local Little League), state of being (such as having a child with a disability), or task (such as getting through the workday at the local Wal-Mart). The degree to which we are connected to groups of others is contingent not only on our individual needs for affiliation but also on cultural norms, social arrangements, and our social location.

This chapter addresses the nature of groups, briefly reviews the history of group work in social work practice, and explores a variety of dimensions related to types, purposes, theories, structures, and skills of contemporary social work practice in groups. You will get a taste of what group work is like, how it fits in with the rest of the profession, and how you might approach various aspects of it.

THE SOURCE OF COMMUNITY

The social dimension of social work implies that people need and want to relate to others. Yet we aren't always sure how to meet this need. In contemporary U.S. culture there is a pervasive emphasis on independence, mobility, and pursuit of success. Employment opportunities far away, upward mobility, and pressures to do better influence all of us. These are not necessarily negative, but they can take a heavy toll on our sense of connection and our links to stable, consistent groups on which we can depend over time.

A quick look in the advertisement section of any major newspaper seems to support this need for connection. The number of announcements for therapy groups, support groups, community groups, and the like suggests that as a culture we are looking for something. What do artificially created group experiences (that is, those developed as a service) offer to people? Such groups provide a sense of belonging, a chance for reality testing, a source of mutual aid, and a means of empowerment (Reid, 1997, p. 4). By implication these dimensions of social group work seem to afford people the means to participate in significant experiences that may be lacking in the natural contexts of their everyday lives.

Group as a Natural Orientation

Beyond individual idiosyncrasy, the influence of culture has an important impact on the amount and type of connections people seek. "People relations" (Diller, 2004, p. 65) is one of the cultural paradigms that distinguish one cultural group from another. European Americans are more apt to be individual in their social relationships as contrasted with the collateral focus of many cultures whose members are people of color. The degree to which a culture embraces individualism over collective demands varies greatly. Group decisions in some cultures will preclude an individual's choice, and "most persons are not aware of this cultural imperative" (Leigh, 1998, p. 7).

Implications of Group Orientation for the Profession   In earlier chapters you have seen that the National Association of Social Workers (NASW) tends to focus more on national than international concerns and self-determination more than cooperation. This is a natural reflection of our cultural emphases and should be noticed, and perhaps questioned at times, but not necessarily rejected. You can commit yourself to self-determination (a hallmark of U.S. social work) and still know that it is not understood the same way in all cultural groups. The postmodern, reflective thinker will notice when these concepts are empowering and when they are oppressive.

An increasingly global perspective on social work practice adds support for increasing sensitivity in this area. The 1996 NASW *Code* added an international perspective in the statement "social workers should promote conditions that encourage respect for cultural and social diversity within the United States and globally" (Standard 6.04©), which indicates an increasing global consciousness.

Many mainstream U.S.-oriented social workers need to recognize the degree to which their own orientation to achievement, independence, and competition as cultural variants is not compatible with the cooperation and collaboration that clients from other cultures may value more highly. No matter what your own cultural heritage is, take care not to privilege your position as normal just because you take it! It may serve you well in some instances and impede your effectiveness in others.

Implications of Group Orientation for Practice   If social workers who have been socialized in the dominant individualistic, competitive manner assume this position is right, they can negatively impact the people with whom they work because they are likely to misinterpret them. Independence as an ideal can create obstacles in working cross-culturally with clients who don't share an enthusiasm for it. For example, if you encounter a child, Joey, in a school setting, who seems lacking in eager, competitive spirit, who seldom raises his hand when a teacher asks a question, and who always defers to others, you may attribute a deficit of one kind or another to him. You may find him slow, too shy, or lethargic, and you may see him as dependent, or even as depressed or developmentally delayed. Joey may simply be reflecting the cultural imperative to cooperate, to prioritize the communications of others, and to behave demurely in the company of people who are older and who have authority.

The nature of "groupness" is complex and variable according to social location. We all need and seek social connections, but this phenomenon is also tempered and shaped by cultural expectations having to do with family and community, customs, propriety, loyalty, authority, individualism, and how they all fit together. Although Western values of competitiveness and individualism have been responsible for a great deal of what U.S. culture has accomplished and how much power it has attained, these values have also created disconnection, isolation, and detachment as well as a fertile environment for the design of constructed groups, particularly in the human services. Social work has responded to this need throughout a long history of group practice.

Historical and Contemporary Contexts for Group Work

The early roots of group work, like other legacies in social work, derive from England and the Industrial Revolution. The political and economic context of this time period resulted in disrupted lives and broken social connections of countless children and families. The time was ripe for the development of group social work. A brief history (informed by Kurland & Salmon, 1998, pp. 13–21) provides a glimpse at the role of groups in social work practice.

Group work developed in the United States in the 19th century in the midst of professional and political tensions. As the concept of the charity organizations became influential in what has become social work practice, a prominent concern of many workers related to the morality of individuals and their need for change. In contrast, another group of human service workers of the time looked more to social reform with a humanitarian impulse (Reid, 1997) than to personal transformation and believed that social change was the critical ingredient in making a positive difference in people's lives. These reformers were more likely to see the group (rather than the individual) as the medium for that kind of work. You will notice here some reverberations from the social control/social change tension discussed in Chapter 2. In addition, group work was not yet firmly a part of social work. Group workers often were partisan Socialists, concerned with political action and identified with several types of social services, among which social work was only one.

By the end of the 19th century, the Progressive Era added fuel to group work's growth. Settlement houses, community organizations, and self-help groups sprang up everywhere in response to the influx of immigrants and the dramatic needs of the teeming urban environment. These organizations stressed group methods (language classes, cooking groups, recreation, the arts, youth services) and were aimed at the social justice issues of inclusion. They were designed to maximize the ability of newly arrived residents to make a good life through access to society's assets. Still, group work was not clearly identified with social work.

Throughout the 1930s, group work continued to have less status than social casework in the minds of many professionals. This is partly because most of the recently developed curricula in schools of social work were aimed at individual casework and because Freud's influence was pervasive. Also, group work had by then a strong association with recreational activities, such as sponsoring dances or creating arts and crafts with children—activities that were not held in as great esteem as the more clinically focused casework. Even when group work had developed a greater affinity to social work, practitioners proposed their own association, which emphatically declared itself a part of social work, but as a discrete unit, using distinctive methods within it.

In the 1950s, group work expanded its venue from the community into hospitals and psychiatric institutes and introduced **therapeutic group work**, or **treatment groups**, which are groups designed to heal or change people. This altered the nature of the formerly community-based model by adopting a more professional stance. Through the process, group work began to tread on the turf of casework, and the distinctions between the two blurred somewhat.

The **Council on Social Work Education (CSWE)**, the accrediting body for social work education in the United States, required in the early 1970s that all schools of social work adopt a generalist focus throughout undergraduate programs and for the first half of master's programs. The generalist focus is aimed at integrating all the practice methods across levels. This requirement served to deemphasize the distinctive role of group work as a method and, many believe, to forsake its very soul. Most school curricula already emphasized casework, and with the CSWE mandate, there was little incentive to develop more group work courses. The result has been that many social work students never take any courses that focus specifically and comprehensively on social group work. Nevertheless, a strong core of social workers committed to the power of social work with groups is vital, and the Association for the Advancement of Social Group Work (AASWG) was founded in 1979.

Web Links

Visit the AASWG site for more about the international professional organization for group work. It includes links to other group work sources and to ethnic organizations, such as the Latino social work organization.

The climate of social work practice today offers practitioners a unique opportunity to work with groups in a way that will help to meet some of the needs people have for genuine connection and social action in our challenging culture. In that respect, the value of social work with groups will be on sticking to a focus that emphasizes the group as a whole. This is one of the characteristics that distinguishes social group work from psychology or mental health counseling groups. True social work with groups is not an inexpensive way to conduct psychotherapy with many individuals at the same time, a notion which many human service administrators still seem to favor. Group work that misses the group's unique potential and exists only as a cost-cutting effort has been referred to as "group-oblivious work" (Middleman & Wood, 1990, p. 91). In genuine group work, the worker's effort is on the development of the group, and while individual well-being is one goal, it is achieved through the interactions and structures of the group.

DIMENSIONS OF SOCIAL WORK WITH GROUPS

For the purposes of this discussion, a social work group refers to a small, face-to-face gathering of people who come together for a particular purpose. Its major dimension is the interdependence among person, group, and social environment. Like many aspects of social work practice, the concept of group work can be broken out in several ways to represent distinctions. Here we will consider types, forms and functions of groups, group work logistics, process perspectives, and worker perspectives. Later on in the chapter we will look at theoretical perspectives, models, skills, and social justice, diversity, and human rights issues. Finally, we will explore several specific types of social work groups as exemplars of both traditional and innovative practices.

The Social Work Library

For a rich overview of group practice in social work, read Schopler & Galinsky's entry.

Types, Forms, and Functions of Groups

The major division at the most basic level in social work groups is between formed, or constructed, groups and natural groups. **Natural groups** occur in the context of socialization and are not organized from the outside. These may be based on spontaneous friendships, common interests, or common social location, such as living in the sophomore wing of a college dormitory. Families are the original natural group. Natural groups usually do not have formal sponsorship or agency affiliation, but social workers may have occasion to work with them (particularly families). In general, however, social workers are more likely to facilitate **formed groups**, which are organized by an institution, such as a school or hospital, agency, or community center.

Formed groups are sometimes divided between **task groups**, designed to accomplish a specific purpose, and treatment groups, geared toward change. These two categories can be further broken down as follows: Task groups include task forces, committees and commissions, legislative bodies, staff meetings, multidisciplinary teams, case conferences and staffing, and social action groups. Treatment groups may be aimed at education, growth, therapy, socialization, empowerment, and remediation. In whatever way these are carved out, the group's major purpose and form is usually emphasized in its title. However, most groups have more than one purpose, and the types are not mutually exclusive since there is a great deal of potential overlap. We will see this overlap in the section "Common Social Work Groups," later in the chapter.

Groups may also be distinguished by the role of the worker. In treatment or psychotherapy groups, the worker may tend to use methods consistent with counseling and interpretation, while in educational groups the focus may be on teaching and processing. Task groups are likely to support the worker's focus on facilitation, as she or he assists the group in taking action to address an undertaking.

Group Work Logistics

Social work groups may occur in community agencies, schools, community mental health centers, medical practices, welfare offices, job training centers, or any other setting in which participants come together. The physical location may be a setting that group members already use (such as a school), or it may be a local community facility that makes itself available to such activities (a community hospital housing a grief and loss group, for example). Many residential settings such as prisons or psychiatric hospitals also host social work groups, and these may be restricted to residents, their significant others, or may include a mix, such as a group for about-to-be-released prisoners and their partners.

Social work groups may differ on other variables such as how many times they meet or how they are organized. Any particular group may meet for a fixed number of sessions, or it may be more or less ongoing, with changing membership over time. Some groups are structured as **closed groups**, which means the membership is fixed along with the number of sessions. Many others are **open groups**, which allow new people to join at any time (or occasionally only at fixed times, such as after the third and sixth sessions). Whether the group is closed or open can have a significant impact on how quickly the group develops a sense of connectedness or unity.

Another important distinction rests in whether membership in a group is voluntary or mandated by legal or coercive pressures on members. In mandated situations, the worker may have different expectations (not always realized!) of member investment, and the influence of the mandating institution (such as the court) is likely to be greater relative to voluntary groups. Mandated groups are discussed further in Chapter 11.

Process Perspectives: Planning

Although you might think of group work and group formations as entirely natural phenomena in the social life of all of us, it doesn't follow that a successful social work group will just happen. There are many considerations that you, as the worker, should take up before engaging in the process of constructing a group in social work practice. It is also likely that the planning and preparation will take a good deal of time, as well as thoughtfulness, and so recognizing the effort involved will help you develop your approach thoroughly.

As the practitioner, you need to consider eight specific areas before organizing a group. I also want to stress here that you will need to consider these in the context of the agency, your supervision, and the larger social environment. These eight areas (from Kurland & Salmon, 1998, p. 24) provide a useful guide:

- Need
- Purpose
- Composition
- Structure
- Content
- Pregroup contact
- Agency context
- Social context

Keep in mind that these areas of consideration are interrelated, and decisions in one category may influence decisions in another. There is also room for a great variety of approaches in group work, and the considerations here do not presuppose certain answers. They are simply areas to which you should give some thought because they are likely to be the source of unexpected obstruction later if ignored in the beginning. See Exhibit 7.1 for schematic drawings relating to preplanning models.

EXHIBIT 7.1

Pregroup Planning Models

Pregroup Planning Model
(for use when group composition *is not* predetermined)

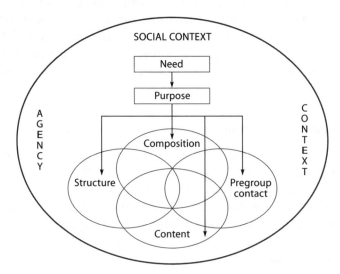

Pregroup Planning Model
(for use when group composition *is* predetermined)

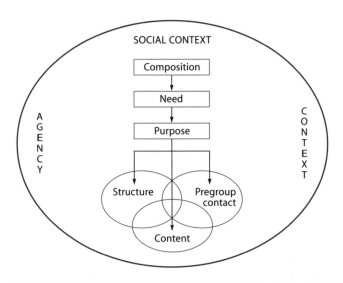

Source: Kurland & Salmon, 1998, p. 209

Need   You will want to identify the major and relevant issues that confront the population from which you will draw members. This means you want to know your clients well and what potential members see as their needs. You will not likely be successful in constructing a vital, functioning group if you don't have a good understanding of members' lives and struggles and if you don't focus on some aspect that is important to them. For example, if you work with several young mothers who live in poverty, you will probably want to consider some direct dimension of that battle (for example, managing a meager household budget, taking an assertive stand with landlords, meeting children's needs) rather than offering a group whose activity is based on, say, sharing needlework skills. On the other hand, needlework skills may be very appealing to women who have little outlet for creativity or companionship and seldom feel as if they accomplish much through the day. The point is to know your clients' needs and respond to them in a way that is consistent with your agency's purpose.

Purpose   You will want to consider both collective and individual objectives: What hopes will the group as a whole have? What expectations will individuals have? Ask yourself, what is the function of the group, and what will your role be? You may focus on, for example, counseling, teaching, or facilitating social action. Consider how member interaction will contribute to the purpose of the group.

Composition   This concerns the number of members and workers and their characteristics, such as gender, age, experience, skill, beliefs, and values. The major area of consideration is the degree of homogeneity or heterogeneity that will be preferable. In general, scholars agree that some common characteristic or situation should provide a unifying focus, but there should also be some difference to sustain interest and the potential for growth through exposure to different ideas. Frequently a particular condition, such as living with cancer, can bridge many differences on other dimensions, such as age or ethnic background, but these aspects should be evaluated carefully in each situation.

Behavioral characteristics, in addition to descriptive variables, are also important. For example, you will want members to have a compatible (among each other) interpersonal style, level of verbal development, and understanding of the potential for groups. This doesn't mean the same level, but ideally the variation should not be so great as to present overwhelming obstacles. Different kinds of groups will vary on the balance of these components—for example, similar ages in children's groups would probably be more important than in most adult groups.

Structure   You will need to decide whether the group will be open or closed and what the trade-offs are for your particular group. What is the agency's position on this question? What are the challenges to you with either form?

Structure also refers to the logistical arrangements of the group: where it will meet, how often, and at what time. Other practical questions to be answered include: What size room will be optimal? Will members require transportation? Will a fee be charged? How will confidentiality be maintained? How much coordination within the agency will be required?

Content   The activities or other means used to accomplish the group's purpose may require special equipment or educational or art materials. Consider how the meetings will actually go. Who will do what, when, how, and why? If the group will use discussion, will the content facilitate interaction among members?

Pregroup Contact   You will need to do some work before the group meets for the first time. Accordingly, you should think about these issues: How will members be recruited? Will you conduct pregroup individual interviews? How will members be prepared for the group experience? How will they be oriented to ensure maximum participation?

Agency Context   Consider both how the agency will affect the group and how the group will affect the agency. Do agency personnel support group work for the population served, and is group work consistent with the agency's mission and emphasis? Do not assume support without confirming it. Your group is likely to have repercussions for others—for example, a children's group is often rather noisy, the clerical staff may inherit increased administrative responsibilities, and individual workers sometimes feel possessive of their clients. It is to your advantage to get any concerns like these out on the table and to address them as directly as possible.

Social Context   Finally, consider surrounding influences that could affect the group. Will the group compete with other community services? Are there appropriate resources for members after the group? Social context includes cultural context. Do the cultural contexts of the members support group participation? If you want to facilitate a group for adolescent girls, you will want to consider whether their families will approve of that kind of activity.

Worker Perspectives: Getting Started

After considering the aspects of preparation, you will want to turn your attention to the processes of getting the group planning under way. Several activities that will help you focus your efforts are discussed next.

Contacting Prospective Group Members   There are many ways to build up the membership of a prospective group and to connect with potential group work clients. We'll look at two here: outreach and on-site service referral. **Outreach** is a method for contacting people who are reluctant to come on their own to the agency, and it applies especially to those who perceive barriers to their acceptance there (Brown, 1991). It is an increasingly important strategy in the contemporary climate. It also takes some savvy to be successful and is probably best taken up with your supervisor or other experienced workers in the agency who will know more about likely avenues for this kind of recruitment. Sometimes this can be accomplished quite directly, such as through connections with a school guidance counselor, and other times it requires more legwork and concerted coordination.

Contacting prospective group members directly through **on-site service referral** is another frequently useful way to connect with potential members. You might, for example, recruit members from your caseload of individual clients, or you might ask your peers for referrals after you have established their support of your effort. Postings and announcements are helpful, but they usually need some personal context, such as another staff member's enthusiastic recommendation, to be effective.

In nearly all scenarios, a pregroup interview is ideal. First, it allows you to get an in-depth sense of how this person will fit in the group and whether she or he is an appropriate member. It also offers you a chance to get a perspective on the dynamic components in relation to other members of the group. At least as important, it provides the opportunity for the prospective group member to air any anxieties and get a sense of what this new experience will be like, to ask questions, and to make a more empowered choice about joining. This is also the time to raise any issues about fees or associated costs of joining the group. Finally, you should recognize this kind of contact with group members as a form of engagement, assessment, and planning that carries with it all of the requirements in the way of knowledge and skills that engagement and assessment and planning with individuals entails.

Remembering the Logistics   Surprisingly, many workers fail to attend thoroughly to the logistics, or the nitty-gritty detailed mechanics, of preparation. While you consider many heady and philosophical dimensions of what it means to be a person in a group, you must also make sure there are enough chairs, that one of the meetings isn't scheduled on a religious holiday for some members, and that all members have transportation to get to the group. You will want to be sure that the domestic violence group for men does not meet at the same time and place as the group for their survivors. You will want to consider competition with other known schedules, so that the parenting group doesn't conflict with the mothers' and children's group. It is impossible to avoid all conflicts or awkwardness, but giving thought to as many of these aspects as you can is worth the effort.

Planning with Group Members   A number of aspects of the group are best planned with the members as their first order of business. Both you, as the worker, and members share their expectations of the group. You will want to be transparent about what you (you alone or with a co-facilitator) are trying to accomplish. Likewise, members are encouraged to talk about their perceptions of their roles. Confidentiality is often one of the first dimensions discussed, and, as you can imagine, unless all members feel safe in revealing their struggles and feelings, it is not likely that many will participate fully.

Other concerns often include a set of **norms**, or expected rules of conduct, for how the group will conduct its business. These establish a productive group climate and require active participation from members so the worker is not in the position of dictating regulations for the group. What the norms are will depend on the type of group. For example, I once facilitated a socialization group for seven-year-old boys in residential treatment for whom "no hitting" was the major expectation. "No shouting" might be applicable to an anger management group, or "celebrating holidays" to a single parents' group. Some groups also discourage contact between members outside of the group, because it may dilute the group process, and others encourage it, because it fosters translation of group benefits into the "real world." This again will depend on the type of group and perspectives of the worker and members. The major issue here is to facilitate group members' involvement through a relatively clear set of behavioral expectations that in turn will increase their comfort in being in the group and will encourage their maximum participation.

New workers may want to consult with other more seasoned group workers about the less obvious concerns that members in a particular context are likely to bring with them. These can then be raised and discussed among the membership. For example, if your group members come from differing cultural backgrounds, and one subgroup tends to interpret tardiness as disrespectful while another sees it as simple flexibility, you might want to raise the idea of "coming on time" as one to be negotiated. In other groups this may never be a problem; so this is another situation in which knowing the membership can help you anticipate particular issues that may affect group process. All of these early negotiations with group members serve, like the interview, as important opportunities for both engagement and ongoing assessment.

Locating Resources to Benefit Group Members   Depending on the focus of the group, you will most likely engage in the mutual identification of resources for group members and accentuate the inclusion of their natural assets, such as friends, family, or neighbors, into the helping network that may also include services. This emphasizes the connections between the group and the outside world. By making this a joint discussion with and among members early in the process, you are demonstrating your expectation that the group has both the ability and the responsibility to deal constructively with its own issues. As resources outside the group are identified, the potential network expands for all members and supports the interdependence between people, groups, and the environment.

Knowing How Active and Directive to Be   This is one of the more challenging aspects of group facilitation and intervention for most new workers. Workers often sense that if they don't keep a strong hand in the control of the group and its agenda that it will explode or become chaotic. On the other hand, if the worker sits back and just lets the group evolve without close attention to process, it *can* become chaotic, and members can be hurt or the group can become fragmented and thereby lose its meaning to members. How active the worker's facilitation needs to be depends on many factors: how connected the group is at any given time, the functioning of its members, and the presence of internal, or **indigenous leadership**, that is, leadership that evolves within the membership.

Generally, the worker will be more directive in the early stages of groups, in groups with lower-functioning members, in groups with little indigenous leadership, and in task-oriented groups. As the group progresses, the worker will want to back off and encourage a growing group ownership of the activity. The key here for any worker is to recognize what is needed and to be flexible with respect to the degree of direct leadership used. Usually, the overall goal for group workers is to reduce their activity to as little as possible while maintaining a safe environment and encouraging members to be in charge of their own group.

Making Use of Group Process and Problem Solving   The tension between the needs of individual group members and those of the group as a whole reflects the major substance of group work practice. The negotiation of differences and the creative enrichment that is possible from the process are the greatest values of the effort. The goal then will be the reconciliation of difference through a genuine compromise that benefits both the individual and the group. One of the group's clearest responsibilities is to establish an acceptable expression and appreciation for difference. Let's look at a simple example, described in a worker's notes of the eighth meeting of a socialization group of 12-year old girls, who were referred by the school as having a "rocky time" both at home and in adjusting to middle school life.

The girls were bustling around preparing crepe paper streamers and searching for birthday candles, giggling, joking about how old Lila was really going to be. Some said she was probably going to be 60 or so, judging by how glum she had seemed last week about the party they were planning. Lila was late, and when she finally showed up, she looked more miserable than ever. Finally, she blurted out "I HATE BIRTHDAYS!!" in a voice very unlike her usual somber tones. The other girls were horrified and silent for a moment—almost unheard of in this group. Lila started to cry. Finally, she choked out the story: Her mother had died the night before her birthday two years ago, and she didn't know how to tell anybody in the group that before. The very word "birthday" was a terrible reminder. She didn't want to celebrate.

The girls seemed to feel sorry, they liked Lila, but they also really wanted to celebrate birthdays in this group. It was an important ritual for them. I confess I didn't have a clue what to do, as their facilitator. After a moment, Betsy, whose grandmother came from France, cheerfully volunteered, "Well, let's be treès Français in this group and say we're celebrating our Anniversaries! That's what the French call them, the anniversary of birth!" The others responded loudly, hoping their ritual was rescued from certain demise. Lila was silent. She looked up. Finally she almost smiled and said, "I think that would work." And that was that. The group took on a "French theme" ever after and was the only group of 12-year-olds I ever knew that celebrated their anniversaries!

This example not only demonstrates that differences, both simple and serious, can often be resolved with some good will and ingenuity, but also that it was not the worker who came up with the solution here, but the group itself.

The dimensions of planning and getting started have been covered in some depth because of their widespread applicability. They should assist you in making the leap into facilitating your own group. We will look now at some representative theoretical constructions relating to social group work that will give you some conceptual ideas about how groups function and develop.

TRADITIONAL THEORETICAL PERSPECTIVES AND IMPLICATIONS FOR PRACTICE

Just as there are many theoretical models for social work practice with individuals, there is also a full legacy of theory related to groups, their purposes, processes, skills, and end points. In this section we will consider several classic and developmental models. Later on we will focus on group work skills, examples of current groups, and finally, we'll consider some contemporary innovations in group work.

The Social Work Library

To learn more about the origins of the mutual aid model, read Schwartz's early work.

Three of the classic models—the **social goals model**, the **remedial model**, and the **reciprocal model**—are reviewed briefly because of their contributions to current group work. These models were developed in the late 1950s through the1970s. They reflect, however, much of the work that came before them, as well as after, since theory is nearly always embedded in the context of previous theory. You will find that these particular perspectives are still useful in social work practice with groups in various current contexts. You will probably recognize their purposes, if not their names. See Table 7.1 for a description of these three classic models.

MODEL TYPE	MAJOR FOCUS	WORKER ROLE	EXAMPLE	AUTHOR
Social goals	Democratic values, social conscience, social responsibility, and social action; uses strengths of members.	Fosters social consciousness and serves as model for democratic values.	School groups that promote student affiliation and contributions to student governance.	Pappel & Rothman, 1962
Remedial	Prevention and rehabilitation aimed at "deviant" populations; changes and reinforces individual behaviors.	Works both in the group and outside of it to ameliorate conditions in environment; acts as motivator.	Discharge group in psychiatric hospital for patients who want to increase capacity to negotiate the community.	Vinter, 1974
Reciprocal	Interaction in an attempt to fulfill mutual affiliation goals; mutual aid.	Serves as mediator between each member and the group as a whole; finds common ground.	Adolescent survivors of substance abuse who assist each other in maintaining sobriety.	Schwartz, 1961

TABLE 7.1

Classic Models for Social Group Work, 1950s to 1970s

Developmental Models

Another classic theoretical perspective on group work, the **developmental model**, is defined by the apparent nature of group evolution. The assumption in developmental models is that the group changes and grows in somewhat predictable ways during its course. This doesn't mean the group goes through a rigid progression but rather a series of ripening relationships in which members are perhaps ambivalent about joining at the beginning, then jockey for position within the membership, grow closer together through the work of the group, establish differences from one another, and finally separate at the group's ending. This perspective reflects the idea of stages or phases and has been extremely influential in contemporary group work. Developmental models are still the norm in many practice contexts and are frequently very useful in alerting the worker to possible dynamics, gauging what is happening, and thinking about how to intervene. Here we will look at two different models—the Boston Model and the relational model.

Boston Model First developed at Boston University's School of Social Work, the **Boston Model** (Garland, Jones & Kolodny, 1965) has remained a prominent feature in social work education and particularly in practice.

The Boston Model outlines five stages of group development: preaffiliation, power and control, intimacy, differentiation, and separation.

- During **preaffiliations** members may feel some ambivalence or reservations about joining the group as well as excitement and eagerness.

- In the **power and control** stage, members vie with each other and with the worker for influence and status within the group.

- **Intimacy** occurs when the members become closely connected, having worked through their power issues; they may seem more homogeneous than at any other time in the group.

- During **differentiation** members are safe enough to express and value the differences among each other and the worker; the homogeneity of the former phase matures into a respect for difference.

- In the final stage, **separation**, members begin to withdraw from the group in anticipation of its ending.

Although the authors propose a general progression through these stages, they do not claim a rigidly linear sequence. There are likely to be points in the life of a group in which one or more members seem to loop back to the behavior common to a previous stage or tend to jump ahead to another one. The model has served as the basis for a number of more recent studies related to worker tasks and skills according to stage (Berman-Rossi, 1993), worker responsibility in mixed groups (Mistry & Brown, 1997), worker response to diversity (Cox & Ephross, 1998), and worker establishment of commonality in the first stage (Northern & Kurland, 2001), to name just a few. See Table 7.2 to learn how the developmental stages have been applied to three different group populations.

There are also several take-offs on this stage scheme in the current literature in which the stages divide slightly differently, and some have additional substages. The group population also influences the degree to which members progress through the phases and the way they do it. For example, in an adaptation applied to older institutionalized persons in a group, Kelly and Berman-Rossi (1999) found that separate stages emerged in which the members first challenged the institution and then challenged the worker. In an empowerment-oriented group (Lee & Berman-Rossi, 1999), adolescent girls in foster care demonstrated an impulse to take flight rather then enter the intimacy stage (not surprising, given their family history of chaos and separation).

This very well known and well-used model for stage development in groups is not, of course, universally accepted. It has its critics as well as variants. One of the more useful variants is the relational model.

	BOSTON PROTOTYPE	FEMINIST	FEMALE ADOLESCENT FOSTER CARE GROUP	OLDER INSTITUTIONALIZED PERSONS: FLOOR GROUP	
	Garland, Jones & Kolodny, 1965	*Schiller, 1995, 1997*	*Lee & Berman-Rossi, 1999*	*Berman-Rossi & Kelly, 1997*	**TABLE 7.2** *Three Models for Stages of Group Development Based on the Boston Model Prototype*
Stage 1	Preaffiliation	Preaffiliation	Preaffiliation: • Approach-Avoidance • Power and Control	Approach-Avoidance	
Stage 2	Power and Control	Establishment of a Relational Base	Intimacy and Flight	Intimacy	
Stage 3	Intimacy	Mutuality and Interpersonal Empathy	Differentiation	Power and Control 1: Challenging the Institution	
Stage 4	Differentiation	Challenge and Change	Termination	Power and Control 2: Challenging the Worker	
Stage 5	Termination	Termination		Differentiation & Empowerment	

Source: Adapted from Berman-Rossi, Kelly, 2003

Relational Model   This model derives from feminist theorists and practitioners who have objected to the exclusion of women in developmental theory building. For example, many feminists challenge Erik Erikson's famous male-normed psychosocial sequence of life stages on grounds that he has stereotyped girls as being concerned with "inner space" and boys with "outer space." Furthermore, some feminists believe the intimacy stage, a clearly relational dimension, actually precedes the identity stage in girls, which reverses Erikson's order. Carol Gilligan believes that the identity and intimacy stages are intertwined in girls (1982).

The feminist orientation to the importance of relational aspects of development offers a different emphasis for women and girls and appears in group work models as well. Although the **relational model** incorporates stage development, it proposes that women go through stages that are different from those of the Boston Model. The second and third stages reflect the emphasis on relationship that is established before the conflict, or challenge, stage. The model is posed as follows (Schiller 1995; 1997):

- *Preaffiliation:* Members experience ambivalence about joining.

- *Establishment of a relational base:* Members build strong, affective connections with others.

- *Mutuality and interpersonal empathy:* The connections deepen into a commitment to mutual aid.

- *Challenge and change:* Differences are recognized, and the connections may change in nature.

- *Termination:* Members conclude their work and separate.

This model has solid utility in feminist groups or in groups working with women because it supports one of the more carefully considered gender constructions relating to women's development and theory (Lesser, O'Neill, Burke, Scanlon, Hollis & Miller, 2004); that is, the importance of established relationship and relational patterns as a precursor to engagement in challenge.

Group Work Skills

All of these theoretical models require skills. Even though group work is sometimes seen as different from one-to-one models in social work settings today, many of the same generalist practice roles and skills of individual work are not only applicable but vital to group work. When interviewing potential members or maintaining a group-centered focus, you will find that looking with planned emptiness, looking at the old as if new, jigsaw puzzling, listening, supporting, empathizing, and more—all of these have as important a place in group work as they do in work with individuals. These can be expanded, fine-tuned, and customized for some specifics of the group, as follows.

General Facilitating Skills   Some additional skills that encourage a focus on the group as its own entity are "thinking group," scanning, and fostering cohesiveness or unity (Middleman & Wood, 1990, pp. 96–102). **Thinking group** assumes an orientation in which you, as the worker, think of the group as a whole first and individual members second. This concentration on the whole can take some time to get used to. For example, you will want to avoid a prolonged exchange with a single group member because that focus hinders the group's communication.

Scanning is a way of taking in visually all members—the "group version of the attending skill" (p. 99). **Fostering cohesiveness,** or connectedness, means building a sense of "we" through language, encouragement of rituals (for example, marking the beginning and end of each meeting in a specific way), and recording the group's progress. These skills build the spirit of group membership and facilitates a sense of belonging to something significant. Development and recording (through a chart on the wall, for example) of group agreed-upon norms or customs contributes to a sense of connection, as well.

Group Communication Skills   The patterns of communication that you use in a group should be chosen carefully. If you just respond to the members who speak up, there is likely to be a subset of members who are marginalized and excluded. On the other hand, if you always go around the group, member by member, some members will feel pressed to contribute, and all will feel a certain amount of routinization. You will want to encourage a respectful balance in which all members can have their say without any that dominate.

In another twist on communication, you may want to invite participation by all members (especially quiet ones) and ask if others in the group think or feel the way this (currently speaking) member does. You will want to remind members periodically of the group's commitment by verbalizing the norms that the membership agreed upon, and you will want to emphasize the group's accomplishments and history when appropriate.

One of the more challenging group work skills in communication is **redirection,** or redirecting questions and concerns away from you back to the group or to individual members. For example, some members will continue to address you over time as the source of authority for the group. This is not surprising, given the power dynamic that many group members may have experienced as clients in other services. By the same token, some members will complain about other members through a third party (often you!). In both these situations, you will want to redirect the message. In the first scenario, you can turn the question back to the group. For example, a member asks you whether visitors can attend a group meeting. That issue hasn't been addressed before, so you turn it back to the full membership: "How do others see this question?" or "How do you as a group want to handle this?" Within this response you may also want to invite quieter members to participate while softening the messages of the louder voices. In the second scenario, you could simply say, "Why don't you tell Bernice that?" or "I don't think you need my help in talking to Kate about that." The goal is to facilitate direct, constructive, nonhurtful communication within the group and the environment that supports it.

Another useful group skill involves the establishment of both consensus and difference. You will want to invite agreement on various issues (for example, on the visitor issue), and you will also particularly want to invite disagreement. It can be very difficult to register dissent in a group of folks who approve some-thing heartily, particularly for a person who is not highly vocal to begin with (re-member Lila). Early and strong feelings of connectedness and strong group bonds can make that dissent even harder. Later, as the group matures, that ex-pression of difference should be less troublesome to members. You will want to support difference and encourage others' capacities to deal with it also.

Finally, for the worker, probably one of the most challenging skills for ef-fective group work is exercising silence. If the facilitator is talking, the members are not. The group should engage in most of the interchange and frequently can be supported in doing that by the worker's well-placed silence, which al-lows the communication patterns of members to develop.

INTERFACE: SOCIAL JUSTICE, DIVERSITY, AND HUMAN RIGHTS

Social work with groups is a natural setting for practitioners who are particularly committed to social justice, diversity, and/or human rights concerns. As dis-cussed elsewhere in this book, much of social injustice is rooted in exclusion—from resources, opportunities, respect, supports, and so on. This kind of exclu-sion is especially evident in the experiences of those considered "other," or different. In this culture, that tends to mean people with disabilities, people of color, in poverty, elderly people, people with alternative sexual orientations; un-fortunately the list is very long (see Greif & Ephross, 2005).

Group work, then, precisely because it brings people together in meaning-ful connection, can serve as a forum for increasing understanding, apprecia-tion, and respect for others. In short, group membership can reduce the effects of exclusion and the injustices associated with it. There is potential in social work practice with groups to identify, establish, articulate, and mediate the rights, as well as needs, of group members within the microcosm of the group. This can be an important and empowering experience for many people who may have rarely (or never) understood their own social contexts in terms that affirmed their rights as human beings (Kurland, Salmon, Bitel, Goodman, Ludwig, Newmann & Sullivan, 2004). This arena—human rights and social work with groups—is currently understudied and, I believe, holds great promise for the integration of human rights practice into the profession.

Common Social Work Groups

As you know, social work has a long history of using the group as a means to carry out the profession's values and concerns. Here I will describe three com-mon types of groups that social work students and practitioners often facilitate: psychoeducational groups, support groups, and empowerment groups.

You will no doubt notice that these three types of social work groups overlap in outcomes. The support group educates, the psychoeducational group empowers, the empowerment group supports, and all deal with some aspect of social justice, diversity, or human rights, as each issue and population represents some dimension of exclusion, which in turn leads to unmet needs and violation of rights (see Goodman, 2004).

Psychoeducational Groups   This model for group work has wide applicability, particularly among adults who face a new or unanticipated struggle and can benefit from education as well as group support. **Psychoeducational groups** focus on the education of group members regarding a psychological condition. One approach has been especially helpful to parents of young adult children stricken with mental illness. Frequently, the young people are in their early 20s and their parents may never have been touched by mental illness before. Local community mental health agencies often offer group sessions to the families to help them learn more about mental illnesses, what to expect in terms of their children's behavior and symptoms, how they can best provide support, and how they can cope with their own grief. These groups have been particularly effective and were started in the mental health arena by the National Alliance for the Mentally Ill (NAMI).

 Web Links

Go to the NAMI site for more about education and support in groups for families of people with mental illness.

Psychoeducational groups usually incorporate a large amount of factual information, but also rely on a supportive and accepting attitude both by worker/facilitators and other group members. Some groups are quite structured, with a curriculum and lessons in sequence, and others are freer in form. In some locations, parents who originally attended these groups have become group facilitators themselves, generally with training and technical support from the local agency.

Support Groups   A good example of a **support group** in contemporary life is the HIV support group. The proliferation of HIV in the past 25 years has engendered strong feelings in nearly everyone. No matter how social workers feel about it, they are frequently in the position of working with people who either have HIV, live with someone who has HIV, or love someone who has HIV. The associated stigma and isolation for some of the men and women living with HIV is as devastating as the disease. This makes support a critical component, and the support group can offer a chance to share feelings, combat loneliness, gain information, exchange resources, and normalize the overall experience. Similar issues arise for families and other loved ones of someone with HIV and social workers may facilitate groups for them as well.

 Web Links

Explore 17 different support groups for cancer patients found on the University of Michigan Cancer Center Web site.

 The Social Work Library

To hear the client voices of TANF recipients, read the research article on support groups by Anderson-Butcher, Khairallah & Race-Bigelow.

Workers need to understand the effects, symptoms, and issues that people with or touched by HIV experience. Because HIV can invoke such volatile emotions, it is particularly important for facilitators to acknowledge and understand their own reactions and biases regarding the disease and those living with it.

Empowerment Groups   Empowerment as a principle generally incorporates three major areas of concern: (1) the personal, including attitudes, values, and beliefs; (2) the interpersonal, including knowledge, skills, and networks; and (3) the sociopolitical, including individual and collective action (East, Manning & Parsons, 2002). These components are well suited to illumination in **empowerment groups** because membership itself can support the personal and interpersonal dimensions of empowerment as well as the critical analysis of the political environment and participation in change efforts. This means that group members are empowered from the earliest planning and participate in such processes as the identification of needs, as discussed earlier (Breton, 2004).

Recall the situation in Chapter 2 of Georgia, who experienced intimate partner violence and joined an empowerment group with other women who had been in violent relationships. This group supported Georgia's personal needs for esteem and dignity, offered her the opportunity to expand her interpersonal skills and connections, and opened the door to analyze and take action in the wider context of societal institutions that both sustain and challenge the status quo (see Donaldson, 2004). You get a glimpse of a similar experience in the personal and interpersonal realms with Marcy's revelations at the beginning of this chapter.

Contemporary Innovative Social Work Groups

At the same time that group work has many traditional approaches in full use today, it also reflects, as does the profession as a whole, the sociocultural context of the times. Accordingly, several innovations in working with groups reflect current theoretical, political, and social issues. Two contemporary issues that the profession has addressed through group work models are battering against women, with constructionist groups, and new approaches to crime, through restorative justice groups.

Each of the efforts described here represents a vital, responsive attempt to counter the negative effects of a contemporary societal issue, and each demonstrates creativity and courage. Note that these are living works in progress and as such may not be proven effective, and many conclude with recommendations to improve the experience. Although they are based on recognized social work perspectives and guided by research inquiries, they will no doubt evolve and be fine-tuned as they undergo evaluation procedures to gauge effectiveness and pinpoint the need for change. They take risks in forging new territory and, I believe, reflect group work's solid potential in groundbreaking efforts.

Constructionist Groups for Battered Women   A **constructionist group** is a social work group that is facilitated from a social constructionist perspective. This means the facilitator recognizes that reality is created through shared meanings and usually wants to offer members the opportunity to develop new understandings of themselves through the group process. We will look at a constructionist group that embodies feminist and narrative theories as well as the postmodern notion of how a person develops a new and preferred **representation of the self**, or a new view of her or his own worth and identity. In this feminist group the members accomplish their new representations of the self by resisting and protesting the male violence they have experienced. The work of the group includes three processes: (1) revealing and undermining the oppressive discourse relating to battered women, which is a *political* process; (2) identifying and detailing the protest that women actually use in response to violence, the recognition of which reflects *change;* and (3) reconstructing the identities of participants based on the protest. This last process is celebrated in an empowering "**definitional ceremony**" (Wood & Roche, 2001a, p. 17), which allows the women to present to an audience of people important to them their new understandings of self.

To illustrate, the worker in this group helps to point out the common themes of the women's conversation relating to the violence they have experienced. For example, some women adopt a socially imposed understanding, which incorporates shame and guilt when male partners batter them. They believe that their own shortcomings cause violence against them and that they are responsible for changing their behaviors in exchange for safety. The worker helps to counter that thinking by asking perspectival questions that help to break the logic of self-deprecation (for example, "What would your sister say about the way Mike treats you?" "What did the court say about this?"). Such questioning over time encourages a focus on multiple realities by helping women see that others would not think they "deserved" violence or "had it coming," or should "just put up with it."

At this point the worker seeks descriptions of how the women in the group actually have responded, that is, in what ways they have resisted and protested. Protest may be in the form of simply not accepting the negative statements made by the batterer, or it may be considerably more confrontational, such as getting a restraining order. Some protest is as earthy as giving older bread and milk to an abusive partner while saving fresher food for a child. These incidences of protest, however they are expressed, begin to form the basis for a new understanding of the self as a person of agency who can make real and meaningful life changes.

Group members ask where a woman got her ideas for the protest or the courage to carry it out, and they also consider what the protest says about her. These explorations challenge her identity as helpless and worthless as they lead to a new view. The worker and other group members then anchor this new more positive representation through reinforcement. They do this by seeking to enrich the story through the woman's further detailed description, and finally they celebrate her new identity as she sees it through a definitional ceremony. Through an emphasis on process rather than group stages, this group is committed to helping the women in its membership discover the other side of their survivorship and become who they want to be.

Web Links

Narrative Approaches is a comprehensive site devoted to narrative theory and offers papers on many topics, as well as books and other resources.

New models like this one, based on narrative ideas of the story and constructionist ideas of self, are highly useful in political contexts in which contemporary views on gender and power relationships are highlighted. They are especially applicable in domestic or sexual violence centers as well as in some community mental health centers.

Restorative Justice Groups for Combating Crime   In another response to a contemporary phenomenon, in this case, the climate of punishment and hard-line approaches to criminal offenders, social workers have been among those advocating for a different strategy. Seeing the criminal justice system as bogged down in practices that neither heal nor rehabilitate, scholars and practitioners have developed an approach thought to be both more relevant and responsive to the issues of offenders as well as survivors (see Van Wormer, 2004). A loosely associated collection of strategies called **restorative justice groups** focus on crime as an interpersonal conflict that has repercussions on the victim, offender, and community at large. The emphasis is more on the harm done to the relationships of those hurt, and their restoration (see, for example, Boyes-Watson, 2004), than on the violation of the law (Lovell, Helfgott, & Lawrence, 2002). The involvement of the community as an invested party in the occurrence of crime represents an important focus. It is the community that loses when its members are caught up in crime and the community that gains when they return with relationships restored.

The particular series of groups described here took place at the Washington State Reformatory. The purpose of the groups was to address (1) offender accountability, (2) the rights of victims, and (3) citizen involvement in the justice process in a way that balanced all three. The major work of the three groups was accomplished through the story of each participant's personal crime experience. Each week one victim, one offender, and one community member shared their personal accounts. Such storytelling increases understanding, validates experience, reduces isolation, and increases the vision for change. Group participants then determined how offenders could respond to the needs of individual victims and what needed to be done to restore the harm done.

The group progress and process variables of these groups were seen as largely consistent with classic models of developmental group work theory (that is, there was initial anxiety and a stage of conflict, followed by greater connectedness) but were also influenced heavily by individual members so that each of the three group meetings reflected different development. The authors noted a number of additional obstacles to the development of group unity, as well, such as the emphasis on crime, the large number of participants, the fragility of participants, problematic group dynamics at times, safety concerns, confidentiality issues, and the implications of diversity, among others.

This emphasis on an alternative strategy to deal with crime that heals and helps people reconnect with each other holds encouraging promise in a society struggling with the alienation of both victims and perpetrators. We will look at another example of this kind of alternative justice that addresses a wider community issue—child abuse—in Chapter 10.

STRAIGHT TALK ABOUT GROUPNESS, POWER, AND ONGOING EVALUATION

One of the more difficult aspects of facilitating groups for many students and new workers involves learning to trust the group process and to maintain a stance of **facilitator** (not necessarily "leader" and certainly not "runner of"). You will need to learn to share the control of the relationship(s), to share the helping role with group members, and to allow the group its own unique path in developing what it will come to be. This can put you in a challenging place by definition. A tolerance for letting go of control will stand you in good stead. Fortunately, most workers agree that those early anxieties regarding control and its management abate substantially with experience.

The worker's overall role and purpose in social work with groups is to encourage and release the strengths of the group. The concern for individual well-being and growth is augmented by the social factors of the group, one member to another. Consistent with trusting the group process, you will need to avoid overinvestment in the centrality or power you may attribute to your role. The goal, after all, is for the group to gain its voice and develop its strength, even as individual members continue to grow. You will not be able to take credit, even in your own mind, for all of the potential successes in your group. In exchange, you will have the privilege of experiencing and respecting the power of group connection and the autonomy it ultimately can exercise as it liberates the power of its members.

The emphasis on the group does not mean that your own role in how the group goes is any less important. You are responsible for the safety of each member in the group and for making sure the group processes its own activity. Accordingly, you will want to evaluate what's going on in the group on an ongoing basis, just as you do in other forms of practice. This will vary according to the nature of your group. For example, if you are working in a task group, you will want to monitor progress in completing the group's project. If you facilitate a group for school-aged children, you will want to make sure that an appropriate developmental level is used. Other forms of evaluation that are especially useful come from members: Is the group meeting their social and affiliation needs? Do they continue to feel safe in it? Is it a helpful forum to address the issues they want to deal with? We will look at more formal evaluation measures in Chapter 12, but, as always, considering the work is an ongoing process.

CONCLUSION

In emphasizing the importance of relational components in our lives, first as people and then as social work practitioners, I have attempted to make the case for social work practice to mediate the culturally imposed isolation of many citizens through the use of purposeful groups. Currently there are many exciting adventures into group work in the service of contemporary theoretical perspectives, social justice, and diversity that could not be reported here. Scenarios relating to cultural inclusion, gender and disability, collaboration, and spirituality in models that emphasize process over stages and story over problem all point to the empowering direction that social group work is taking as it retakes its place in the history of the profession. Group work has renewed and significant potential for the future and particular relevance for the social justice, diversity, and human rights connections that give social work its meaning.

In order for this potential to be fulfilled, the Council for Social Work Education and other academic and professional organizations will need to renew their commitments to the power of human connection through greater support for group work instruction in schools of social work. This will be increasingly important, I believe, in the globalism of the unfolding 21st century in which our individual paradigms are likely to be more vigorously challenged.

MAIN POINTS

- We are all part of groups; they give us meaning and provide critical human connections. Western independent achievers tend to underestimate the gifts and power of group connection even as they seek them.

- Group work in the profession has been a controversial topic but remains a vital part of practice that lends itself especially to social justice, diversity, and human rights perspectives.

- Organizing a group requires careful planning and continuous consideration for the value of the group as a whole.

- Traditional theoretical models for group work include the social goals model, the remedial model, and the reciprocal model.

- Developmental models, such as the Boston Model and others based on it, have provided a widely used theoretical perspective on group development. Many applications of, and departures from, this model can be found in the contemporary practice environment.

- Group workers need to hone their skills for working with individuals and develop some new skills for group work, such as thinking group, scanning, fostering cohesion, facilitating redirection, and establishing both agreement and disagreement.

- Contemporary examples of innovative group practice, such as construction-ist groups and restorative justice groups, help to provide vision and possibility for responding to current cultural and social issues as they unfold.

EXERCISES: PRACTICING SOCIAL WORK

In preparation for this exercise, review the Town Map on the interactive case study with the Sanchez family in order to familiarize yourself with the community's institutions and resources.

Getting Started

You are a social worker recently hired at the center that works with the Sanchez family and their community. You are aware from your own observation even before starting there that many area youth have been involved in fatal alcohol-related car accidents. There is a general level of concern in the agency for those young people who have lost friends, and in some cases siblings, in this series of accidents. The concern is both for their grieving process and also for what is thought to be an increased likelihood that they, too, will use alcohol more frequently in an effort to deal with their feelings of loss. You and your supervisor believe the center should offer a group with these youth in order to deal with this situation more effectively.

1. Breaking out into small groups of four or five, respond to each of Kurland and Salmon's eight areas to consider. Which do you consider most important here? Why? Choose a scribe for your group to keep a record of your discussion.

2. Review the material on getting started and develop a strategy that you think would be the most workable for this particular group. What particular aspects of this group influence your thinking? Where are the sticking points?

3. Notice whether there is any disagreement or conflict within your own group on any of these issues. How did you resolve it?

4. Consider the diversity within your own group—what issues would impact on the facilitation of the center's group? Must the worker be of the same population group? What are the advantages? The disadvantages?

5. Imagine that you have to defend your choice of this group format to the center's board of directors. Develop a rationale for offering this group that

is based on the available resources, social justice, diversity, and human rights considerations. Be as specific and convincing as possible.

EXERCISES: THE SOCIAL WORK LIBRARY

Read the classic paper by Schwartz on how the social worker functions in a group. Consider Schwartz's ideas of mutual aid and "lending a vision." Then consider the situation below and identify how the worker could make the most of mutual aid in each of the choices for intervention.

Choosing Priorities

As a skilled individual and group work social worker at a local community health center, you have several young clients who have been diagnosed with attention deficit hyperactivity disorder (ADHD). They are Hispanic children that range in age from six to eight. Although you usually meet with the children individually, you also notice their parents when they pick them up from appointments. Some of them seem very sad about their children and a few of them appear frustrated or angry. The children themselves seem somewhat isolated and all are experiencing social problems in school.

Assume that you have both the time, interest, and agency support to offer a group. Choose from the list below what you think the most appropriate intervention might be.

1. Consider offering a play/social skills group for the children.

2. Consider offering a support group for the parents.

3. Consider offering a psychoeducational group for the parents.

4. Consider offering an empowerment group for the children.

Be prepared to make a case for your choice in class. How might one choice intersect with another? Compare with peers.

OTHER EXERCISES

What Do You Make of This One?

You're facilitating a support group for adolescent women who have recently given birth to babies and are preparing to return to their high schools. Some of the babies are being partially cared for by their grandparents, and some have been adopted through the agency. Some of the group members have fairly significant issues with returning to school and others are eager to get back into a "normal" social life again. Most members are participating quite well, although one, Janine, has said almost nothing in the three meetings that have already occurred. All the members of the group are African American. You are a white, female student, 23 years old.

At the beginning of the fourth meeting, the mood of the entire group seems contentious. After some brief preliminary pleasantries and a restatement of what you thought the group agreed upon for this week's session (hoping that would bring everyone on board), you realize that Janine is very quietly crying in the corner. At the same time, two of the other members start calling your name angrily, competing for your attention. They tell you they are annoyed at the group, at the plan for today, at the agency, and at Janine who is sitting there acting like a "baby."

Skills

1. Identify two skills from the chapter that you would use here and give an example of what you say.

2. Why would you choose these particular skills? (What do you hope results from your use of them?

Theory

Which of the model types do you think offers the best explanation for what is going on here?

CHAPTER 8

Exploring the Family Story

> The social work profession and the family have traveled a long distance together, sometimes in close companionship and sometimes on divergent paths, only to meet once again on the same road. Our profession began in the company of the family and has returned to it once again.
>
> Ann Hartman and Joan Laird, 1983

> . . . to think larger than one   to think larger than two or three or four
> this is me   this is my partner   these are my children   if we say,
> *these are my people* who do we mean?   how to declare our bond   how
> to keep each of us warm   we are in danger   how to face it and
> not crack

Melanie Kaye/Kantrowitz, in *We Speak in Code: Poems & Other Writings*, 1980

FAMILY IS THE EARLIEST, MOST BASIC, AND SOME SAY MOST CHALLENGING small group we experience. It is also probably the most powerful in shaping who we come to be. For some of us, family means home, safety, and acceptance that seem to thrive in the air. For others, family means violence and danger. We may feel important and cherished with family or never quite good enough or even useless. We may feel swallowed up in its dysfunction, or we may long for, and bask in, the wholeness of unconditional support. Most of us probably experience a mix of feelings in between these. Family is a complicated enterprise, and many of us harbor some of its tensions on occasion that make us both joyful and troubled. Yet we all have experience of some kind or another in a family, and most of us have ideas (or dreams) of what our families could or should be.

This chapter explores the concept of family—what it is, what it means to people, and how it fits into the contemporary social context. It also examines several theoretical perspectives for thinking about families and some alternatives, structures, and types of families, as well as dynamics, skills, and tools for working with them. Finally, it describes the challenge and necessity for coming to a balanced position regarding the impact of families on clients and on yourself.

FAMILIAR PERSPECTIVES AND SOME ALTERNATIVES

Because of the enormous and rapid changes in social rules in the United States and much of the West, it has become fashionable in recent years to mourn the demise of the family. A traditional vision of the ideal U.S. family portrays a nuclear group consisting of two heterosexual adults and two or perhaps three children. The father supports the family economically, and the mother supports it emotionally. There are clear roles, rules, and jobs that each member undertakes. If the mother also works outside the home, she is still free to participate in the kindergarten car pool, do the laundry, entertain friends, and "be there" for her husband and children. A more contemporary version of the father makes him increasingly sensitive to his wife's and children's feelings and needs, but his work still takes priority.

Those nostalgic for the visions of family in prior eras are appalled at what they see today as a lack of morality in many young families. There is distress about young adults who live together with no permanent commitment. Single women often choose to become parents and don't suffer the social stigma so prevalent only a few generations back. People of nontraditional orientations, especially gays and lesbians, who worked very hard in earlier times to conceal their sexual identities, are joyfully parenting children, and many are serving as foster and adoptive parents in conjunction with state child protection agencies. What a change! Although these developments in our cultural norms are devastating to some, the devastation probably reveals fear about change itself more than the actual state of the family.

Nonetheless, there are some very real issues in the surrounding context of the family that create concerns. The overwhelming divorce rate seems closely related to the ever-growing number of children living in poverty. Commitment to the stability and endurance of the most caring sense of family values in some settings seems to have vanished, as children are routinely dropped off and picked up at whoever's place will provide a bed. The number of unmarried teen parents is unprecedented, and the percentage of black teen parents confounds an already terrible statistic.

The associated legacies of perpetuated poverty, increased family violence, widening health and mental health problems, and a sense that two generations—child and the child's child—have sacrificed much of their potential are difficult phenomena to be hopeful about. There are, in some respects, good reasons to mourn the family. These are serious issues, and many people, often women and children, are hurt badly by their proliferation.

But there are other ways to look at family. In keeping with this book's focus on multiple realities, we can explore the experiences of others that help to expose fantasies about the family and present more balanced views. Consider Exhibit 8.1, which describes the experience of family for countless people who have been **marginalized,** that is, who have lived in the margins of our culture and others.

EXHIBIT 8.1

Family: Views from the Margins

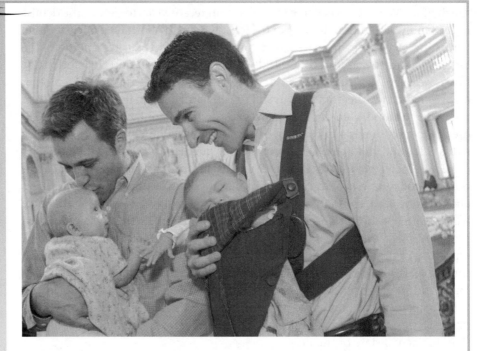

Family is a joining of hearts.

- What we may consider now to be the ideal family has never actually flourished in any culture for any length of time: Children have historically been considered commodities that enhanced the economic status of their fathers, who owned them, and their value was often equated to the amount of work they did; childhood as a time to be nourished and cherished is a relatively new and narrowly prescribed phenomenon of the West and some of the wealthier nations in the East. The United Nations' instrument "The Rights of the Child" reflects the need for considering children as genuine people and not possessions. In contrast, in many parts of the United States children are prostitutes, drug dealers, and hired thieves. In much of the world they are all these and also warriors.

- Ideal conceptions of the family have served to restrict and diminish the role of women; as categorical caretakers, many women throughout history have been required to abandon their dreams and have also been seen as property to be exploited. Men, too, are assumed to fit into tightly proscribed roles that may not be compatible with their identities or goals.

- In many families of the past, some children died in infancy or early childhood and some parents died by their early 40s, which produced a crisis for remaining family members, resulting in placements with distant relatives, community members, or in orphanage care. The idealistic notion of earlier times puts blinders on the realities of disease, early death, and other forms of danger that surely shaped the overall experience of family.

- It is still the family, even in contemporary U.S. society, that is the primary force for socialization and nurturing of children and support of the community. As an example, the families of children with major mental illnesses still provide most of the care and nurturing of their adult children, in spite of federal and state programs designed to assist them.

- The definition of family as rigidly restricted to blood ties and heterosexual partners or adoption has always marginalized and scapegoated significant numbers of people who have meaningful and productive relationships and who make significant contributions to the community, the socialization of children, and the general economic and social order.

- More contemporary notions of family have liberated both men and women to develop and carry out the roles of child caretaking, economic provision, management, personal development, and health care in a way that doesn't deny their individual aspirations and talents; the same principles hold for lesbian and gay families with biological or adopted children.

- Contemporary families have a great deal more biological control over the number and timing of pregnancies and can plan family composition in a way that is consistent with their finances and other internal demands (for example, one partner is in school or another is committed to the care of a parent). Women are no longer biological baby-making machines with no control over their bodies or their futures.

EXHIBIT 8.1

continued

HISTORICAL ANTECEDENTS FOR FAMILY WORK

The profession has a long and somewhat disparate history of work with families, shaped by the context of the times and by shifts in its own allegiances. Yet the importance of family is probably greater today than it has ever been before. In community mental health centers and youth agencies, hospitals and schools, welfare and child protection efforts, social workers time and again are drawn into explorations of the family and how to strengthen it.

Why is there such a concern for the maintenance of the family? What do we as a culture expect the family to do, and how do we think the family should work? Although there are many possible responses to these questions, we will look here at two particular perspectives that seem to have special relevance for social workers today—the family as a functioning unit and the family as a system.

The Social Work Library

For a classic paper on the centrality of family to social work practice, read Hartman's article.

Family as a Functioning Unit

A relatively concrete way to think about why the family is so important is to explore what the family is actually expected to do. The following functions are among those that are usually seen as critical to the contemporary maintenance of families:

- Create an environment in which children can be nurtured and socialized.

- Provide the material and economic necessities for sustenance and growth.

- Offer members emotional security, respect, safety, and a place for appropriate sexual expression.

- Provide a haven for privacy and rest.

- Assist, protect, and advocate for members who are vulnerable or who have special needs.

- Provide support for members' meaningful connection and contribution to community life.

- Facilitate the transmission of cultural heritage.

- Provide a socially and legally recognized identity.

The responsibilities reflected here emphasize not only the functional roles of individual family members and their needs and identities but also the connection to their communities and the overall societal environment. This compilation is not prescriptive; that is, it does not specify *how* children should be nurtured but allows for individual and cultural interpretation. Rather than seeking individual or family dysfunction, the exploration of these tasks in various areas of family life tends to highlight strengths as well as areas for improvement. In that respect, this set of functions serves as a useful guide for assessing the degree to which societal expectations are met in any particular family.

Family as a System

You have probably read about systems theory as a conceptual way to assess and view the world. Because social work involves itself in interactions among people and between people and the environment, it adopted systems theory in the 1970s with great enthusiasm. In general, **systems theory** posits that a system involves a series of components that are highly organized and dependent upon each other in an orderly way. In the profession, this idea is applied to several different levels of practice (individual, group, family, community) and is still influential in social work theory in spite of a growing number of critiques that suggest it is too rigid and tends to place the worker outside of the work. Nevertheless, systems theory holds continuing authority in many views of structural arrangements, particularly the family. Three elements of systems theory are particularly important:

- Change in one component
- Subsystems and boundaries
- Family norms

Change in One Component   Probably the most powerful idea in the systems theory for social workers is the proposition that change in one part of the system will affect all other components. Therefore, it is useful information that a child's father has just been sent to prison when you are exploring why that child has taken to angry outbursts or sullen withdrawal in school. Or you believe that a mother's being beaten by her partner is likely to have repercussions on her daughter's fragile health. Social workers often find this kind of connection, of one part to another, intuitive and also useful. Still, you will want to guard against seeing such a situation as producing an automatic response. For example, the child whose father goes to prison might respond by being more attentive to his mother or by working harder in school or in another way that isn't at all obvious outside the family.

Subsystems and Boundaries   Another dimension of systems theory that is relevant to social work is the idea of **subsystems,** which are a way of organizing various relationships and planning how to engage with them. For example, the individual can be thought of as a subsystem of the family and the family as a subsystem of the community and also of the culture. A family may also be a subsystem of more than one larger system, or of differing systems, so you must be thoughtful about making unqualified judgments regarding where someone or some group fits into the scheme.

In thinking about family, social workers often distinguish between, say, the subsystem of the parents and the subsystem of the children. The relationship between these subsystems is reflected in the kinds of **boundaries,** or limits, that separate the systems that the family constructs. If the children are included in all decisions the family makes, the boundaries are **permeable,** meaning that information and interchange goes easily across them. Taking a different view of parental authority, these could also be termed **diffuse boundaries,** meaning that they are too loose and that parents should take on more of the decision making than their children do.

You can see that what is considered an appropriate boundary between the subsystems of parents and children may vary considerably depending on culture, the times, background, or simply the boundaries that parents themselves were raised with. You can probably cite examples in your own family in which these boundaries seem quite different from those in, perhaps, your roommate's or your best friend's.

Family Norms   Most families seem to establish **family norms,** or rules of conduct, that are related to boundaries and subsystems. These are similar to the norms described in Chapter 7, in application to groups, but have an additional complication in families in that they are often held as sacrosanct and not up for negotiation. They may also never be articulated, even though everyone in the family is very clear about them. This aspect can make them difficult to address and challenge. Sometimes it doesn't even occur to family members that there *is* a rule. It's just clear what a member does or does not do. For example, everyone in the family may understand that no one will enter into a dispute with Dad at the dinner table, or that everyone will say grace, or that all of the children will go out of state to college. Some of these rules apply to everyday boundaries and may simply make some mundane things a lot easier (for example, if the bathroom door is closed, don't go in). Other such rules may signal secrets that are taboo or too hard to talk about or that perpetuate unjust or oppressive situations, such as all the girl children know not to find themselves in the same room alone with Grandpa, or no one asks Mom how she got that bruise on her face.

In applying a systems analysis to family norms, a worker might recognize that it would be feasible to interrupt the family's patterns of behavior or relationship by breaking a rule. For example, if one of the children spoke out one day about the bruises on Mom's face, it might lead to her breaking the silence about her partner or empower her to make changes. Yet, it might also result in violence directed at the child who raised the issue in the first place; so the worker would not likely encourage a child to take such an action, unsupported. Family norms in such cases are often very powerful and need to be carefully evaluated before any family member is put at risk.

Implications of Family Systems Theory for Generalist Practice

Along with the notion of function, two specific dimensions reflected in family systems theories have greatly influenced generalist social work practice with families. The first is family structure, and the second is intergenerational patterns. In many respects these represent a classic approach to Western notions of the family and have influenced the responses of many social service policies and agencies. Many of you may discover that these ideas have shaped part of your thinking also.

Family Structure   The relationship among the generations of a family, especially between the subsystems of children and parents, constitutes the

family structure. The idea here is that the boundaries between children and parents should be clear and that parents should be in charge of major decisions as they also carry out appropriate caretaking functions (Minuchin, 1974). The difficulties that families experience are usually thought to be a result of blurring the boundaries between these two subsystems.

Some family boundaries may be so diffuse that the result is **enmeshment,** which suggests that family members are too close, have few distinctions in role or authority, and enjoy very little autonomy or independence (Nichols & Schwartz, 2001). In its worst scenario, enmeshment may result in incest. On the other hand, if the boundaries between family members are too rigid, the family is thought to be **disengaged.** This means the subsystems are so separated that there is very little sense of family identity, and parents are apt to relinquish much of their caretaking role as they pursue their own interests and children pursue theirs.

When you read about or work with young people who seem to have little or no effective connections with their families, and get into trouble, you may wonder how their parents set (or did not set) boundaries and how they have seen their roles. In some respects, you are using this theory when you cite the misplacement or laxness of parental boundaries when children go astray. The work in such cases is to restore clear and appropriate boundaries between children and parents that support parent caretaking and authority. This particular position is reflected in court decisions regarding delinquent young people and a judge's requirement, for example, that parents receive training on managing their children or that they supervise a child's curfew restriction.

Intergenerational Patterns   The identification of **intergenerational patterns** has likewise played an important role in social work practice with families. The term refers to the assertion that families transmit their patterns of relationship from one generation to the next (Kerr & Bowen, 1988). For example, if your adult client, Jane, is so closely connected to her mother that she experiences great anxiety when they are separated and therefore cannot work outside the home, Jane is likely to establish that kind of relationship with her daughter as well. The anxiety generated by any effort to be separate from her mother is contagious and makes it difficult for Jane to think clearly because her feelings are so intense. In this way she becomes dysfunctional, tends to be dominated by feelings, and passes that pattern on to the next generation. This emphasis on feeling in a family sometimes results in constant emotional uproar, frequent violence, major feuds, difficulties with the law, and generalized struggle in accomplishing the basic family functions considered earlier.

Although the whole of intergenerational theory is quite complex, it has influenced attitudes about families. People may not recognize it, but they are using these ideas when they talk of "welfare families" and "incestuous families." These terms reflect the assumption that problematic, emotional patterns and the resulting behavioral consequences (such as violence, inability to focus on work, and substance abuse) appear to be transmitted from generation to generation. Social work then involves breaking cycles, bolstering the strengths, and supporting an appropriate level of autonomy in individual family members. These principles are reflected in many social and educational programs, in which social workers often participate, that are designed to break patterns of economic dependence, substance addiction, lack of educational focus, and the like.

You can see here that people incorporate a systems orientation whenever they look at crime or drug addiction or school violence among youth and expect in some way for most of these to be related to the families involved, whether or not that is a fair assumption. Yet many of us may have known a child who behaved illegally or violently whose parents are caring, hardworking, and doing the best they can. This is a reminder that the applicability of family systems theory, like any other theory, can be questioned, and that it doesn't automatically fit in all situations. The desire to find a rational cause for human behavior sometimes sets people in motion to use only the methods they have used before. It is also interesting to note that in such child-related problems, many people are eager to jump to blaming the family's behavioral shortcomings or background while not addressing the broader (also systems) aspects of poverty, disenfranchisement, or racism.

Systems perspectives can be helpful and seem to support logical approaches in assessment, especially of complex arrangements, like the family. They have a general cultural appeal, and they do not constitute a magic, one-stop answer for thinking about, assessing, or working with families. You should recognize that systems views have strong currency in today's analyses of social issues while you remain open to the possibility of other ways of thinking about them and are careful not to blame or scapegoat any particular person simply because it seems logical or fits with a possible systemic interpretation of a family situation.

THE CONTEMPORARY CONTEXT FOR FAMILY WORK

The real-world, real live family of today is only rarely the idealized TV version with a stay-at-home Mom, fully employed Dad, and two bright, talented (and usually white) children. Social workers often work with families who might be seen as "other"; that is, they don't fit dominant fantasies of what family life is or should be. In addition to their being different, these families also lend richness and diversity to our culture. The following sections briefly identify several types of family constellations that are not usually considered mainstream—grandparents raising grandchildren, gay and lesbian parents, single-parent families, mixed-race families, and families that include people with disabilities—and suggest some specific implications for working with them.

Keep in mind, however, that there are many more forms of families now, and more will develop in the future. Other current configurations appearing in the literature (and in practice) include adoptive families, foster families, step families, blended families, dual wage earning families, and, of course, many combinations. In the coming generations the profession will need to expect and remain open to ever-evolving forms of the family. This kind of sociocultural change provides social workers with the opportunity to contribute to a sustained and meaningful impact that will benefit clients across all levels of society.

Grandparents Raising Grandchildren

In many cultures of the past, grandparents had a significant and ongoing role in the nurturing and socialization of children. Some groups today, typically those who are less mobile, such as inner-city populations, or those of strong ethnic identification(s), have maintained those patterns, as consistent with their cultural and instrumental needs. The extended family is an age-old pattern of organization that has been obscured by the mainstream societal changes of the industrialized and "informationalized" 20th and 21st centuries. These changes reflect a break with the traditional cultural patterns of their parents and their parents' parents.

In contemporary society there has been a reemergence of grandparents assuming primary (rather than supportive) parenting roles (Hayslip & Kaminski, 2005), many as a result of family violence, drug addiction, and/or incarceration of their adult children. Further, the growing pressures on many child protection agencies have contributed to the increase in parenting grandparents because child protection workers often see blood relatives as preferable to, and more available than, unrelated foster parents. Many grandparents are healthy, active, and potentially able to take on the responsibility of raising their children's children.

Much more is involved, however, than simply being "able." Many grandparents have reached a place in their lives when they can pursue some of their own interests and dreams that have been put on hold while they worked and raised families. Others may find it exhausting to keep up with young children, who have come from troubled situations and have multiple needs, demands, and activities. As you would imagine, some grandparents take on the unexpected role joyfully and fully, and others are enormously burdened, sometimes guilt ridden because of their own children's inabilities to parent. They may also be struggling with aging, illness, and their own continued need to work. In any event, many parenting grandparents, even if eager to care for grandchildren, are likely to want and need significant support from social agencies.

Social workers working with grandparents need to use the major skills and perspectives of generalist practice. They also need to recognize the need for and offer several types of support as they sensitize themselves to the complexities of the emotional and instrumental stresses that grandparents experience. Grandparents

Web Links

For more on grandparents raising grandchildren, go to the North Dakota University Extension Web site.

may need financial support (Fuller-Thomson & Minkler, 2005), counseling, resource coordination, advocacy, policy development (Cox, 2003), and frequent reassurance that they can and do offer their grandchildren a good home (Bullock, 2005). In some situations, recovering birth parents have visiting privileges or partial child caretaking responsibilities on a preliminary or trial basis. In such cases there may be a great deal of tension between grandparents and parents. These and other conflicts may indicate the need for additional assistance from social workers on an ongoing basis.

Gay and Lesbian Parents

The Social Work Library

For more on the perspective of lesbian parents, read Laird's paper.

Gays and lesbians may become parents through several different means. One partner may be the custodial parent of children from an earlier heterosexual relationship. Some lesbian couples seek artificial insemination and give birth to children. Also, many informal arrangements for parenting still exist, particularly in ethnic communities in which the custom affirms the community's responsibility to raise the child.

A more recent development has supported the adoption or foster care placement of children in state's custody with gay and lesbian parents. The ever increasing pool of children needing a home and the decreasing pool of prospective adoptive parents (Brooks & Goldberg, 2001) has led, just as with grandparents, to less traditional, more creative efforts in placement planning. As you might expect, this has been a highly controversial strategy for dealing with child welfare, as it strikes at the core of the fantasy version of the family. Concerns about identity issues for the child, parental adequacy, and the overall mental health of both parents and children have been raised and researched. In general, growing evidence demonstrates little or no lasting, pejorative effect of parental sexual orientation on the mental health of either parents or children (Green, Mandel, Hotvedt, Gray & Smith, 1986). Research has also shown no relationship to the adequacy of parenting skills or orientation (Bigner & Jacobsen, 1992) and no impact on the future adjustment of children in adulthood (Tasker & Golombok, 1995).

 Web Links

The links to lesbian Web sites found in the Web Links Section of the online learning center offer some helpful connections focusing on lesbian mothers.

As prospective parents, gays and lesbians still face obstacles in their pursuit of foster care or adoption and experience institutionalized stigma even at the hands of social workers. Lacking any evidence to the contrary, social workers in both the practice and policy components of the profession should support the efforts of sexually nontraditional people seeking parenthood. Social workers entering into practice scenarios with such parents will benefit from using a "'cultural' metaphor rather than a 'systems' metaphor" (Laird, 1996, p. 565). This means they should listen for the value of difference and suspend judgments made on the basis of a heterosexual view of normality. Workers will also want to rely on their clients' narratives in order to explore how lesbians and gays create family culture. Here the practitioner will want to take up the constructionist stance of the ethnographer, "not knowing," exploring, rather than applying a "machine-like" (in other words, systems, p. 566) theory to a family's experience of parenting. These emphases discourage the search for dysfunction and pathology as they invite the worker to give expression to the strengths and resilience of the parents (see Van Den Bergh & Crisp, 2004). Workers also need to recognize the effects of lingering cultural discrimination directed against non-heterosexuals and especially to draw upon a critical awareness of their own biases regarding the strengths and viability of such people as parents.

Single Parent Families

Focusing on language, consider how the words used to describe families are not only telling of overall attitudes and beliefs, but also shape how social workers choose to work with them (Kissman, 1995). A term like "single parent," without the corresponding "double parent," families implies that one is normal and doesn't require description, while the other is "other." As you notice the implications of such terms as "broken family" or "split family," consider how deprecating labels influence initial perceptions and then may affect the work that follows. It is easy to lose sight of the strengths and commitment of women or men managing families on their own if the work is prefaced with a sense of deficiency or deviance.

Accordingly, one study found no difference between children of color from single parent families and two-parent families regarding their social skills when socioeconomic status is controlled (Kesner & McKenry, 1995). Another discovered that single fathers, while rarely studied, are viable caretakers for their children, even though they may experience role ambiguity in carrying out a nurturing function while trying to work (Greif, 1995). The issue here relates to the tendency on the part of some social service providers in particular to see single parenthood as a blight that necessarily leads to insecure, delinquent, and otherwise unhappy and dysfunctional households.

On the other hand, there is some support in both the literature and practice worlds for recognizing the unique challenges of single parenting as they impact both the social work relationship and the parenting functions. Four major issues that frequently arise from divorce or separation are (1) a lack of resources to cope with stress, finances, or other responsibility; (2) unresolved family-of-origin issues often brought on by the single parent's need for assistance from his or her parents, at least temporarily; (3) unresolved divorce issues, such as anger, grief, loneliness; and (4) an overburdened older child. Known as a **parentified child**, an older child may be pressed into providing excessive household chores or child care for a younger one, thereby becoming more like a parent than a child. This in turn makes it hard for the child to seek age-appropriate nurturance and attention (Jung, 1996).

Some useful practice skill/interventions that are especially helpful in working with single parent families have been proposed by Jung (1996, p. 589):

- *Joining* reflects the worker's effort to show clients that they are cared about and that the worker understands them and their struggles. This is similar to engagement.

- *Empowering clients* supports their agency and capacity to address their own issues; values their uniqueness and skills.

- *Involving significant family members* emphasizes collaboration, reduction of stress, and pooled resources.

- *Allocating resources* may indicate agency planning, outreach, and networking.

- *Highlighting small changes* emphasizes the strategy of making little shifts that ease overextended schedules and increase energy; such changes can also highlight success and autonomy.

- *Articulating self-efficacy* emphasizes competence, accomplishments, and empowerment for greater control over management of family issues.

These principles are consistent with a strengths-based, empowering approach that recognizes both internal and external factors and supports single parents in their ongoing efforts to provide security and nurturance for their children.

Mixed Race Families

One of the gifts of an increasingly diverse society, the growth of families with mixed racial and ethnic backgrounds, is notable in most U.S. cities, midsized towns, and even in many rural villages. Interracial marriage and partnership appears to be gaining in acceptability since 1967 and is certainly increasing in real numbers (Oriti, Bibb & Mahboubi, 1996). Shifting immigration patterns in the United States, globalization, and the breakdown of ethnic barriers in Europe all appear to have an effect on the incidence of racially and ethnically mixed families.

Perhaps few other developments in the everyday life of our communities offer a greater opportunity to think about people differently. While some will persist in grieving for the purity of "race" (a social and cultural construction by most accounts), others will learn to value the contributions of other cultures and to challenge the notions associated with racial privilege. It is important, however, not to minimize the negative power of the persistent oppression met by many ethnically diverse families in our culture. In this arena, professionals also need to be educated in this multicultural society regarding our national and cultural history. In this way workers might find joy in the richness of our diversity and also confront the legacy of oppression and hatred as client families (and perhaps our own families) experience it (Schmitz, Stakeman & Sisneros, 2001). Flexibility, shared goals, and a willingness to explore and address challenges are critical in working across culturally and ethnically diverse communities.

Two special educators have proposed a model, called the "**posture of cultural reciprocity**," for working with diverse families in their field (Kalyanpur & Harry, 1999). This process holds promise for social work as well and requires that workers not only recognize the cultural aspect of their own personal values but also those of the profession. This posture is achieved in four steps, as shown in Table 8.1.

TABLE 8.1

Working with Diverse Families: Racial and Ethnic Diversity

The steps to achieving Kalyanpur and Harry's posture of cultural reciprocity are listed here, with an example application in social work.

STEP	EXAMPLE
"Step 1: Identify the cultural values that are embedded in the professional interpretation of a student's [or client's] difficulties or in the recommendation for service."	This would lead to asking why, for example, a culturally different client's behavior is bothersome to you. (Is she late for appointments? Does she interrupt you? Does she respond to you indirectly? How do you interpret her behavior?)
"Step 2: Find out whether the family being served recognizes and values these assumptions and, if not, how their view differs from that of the professional."	For example, you may discover that your client has a different sense of time from yours and that punctuality has little meaning for her. Here you would want to explore how she approaches time, what it means to her, and whether she recognizes your approach to it.
"Step 3: Acknowledge and give explicit respect to any cultural differences identified, and fully explain the cultural basis of the professional assumptions."	This requires you to enter into a dialogue regarding your assumptions and beliefs and how they are different from your client's. For example, you might recognize and appreciate the less frantic approach to time and deadlines while you explain the need in your agency to abide by a schedule.
"Step 4: Through discussion and collaboration, set about determining the most effective way of adapting professional interpretations or recommendations to the value system of this family."	Work out a solution that respects the nature of the family's values. You might settle on a more flexible appointment time at the end of the day, or agree on a time range, or make outreach visits if that is possible.

Source: Kalyanpur & Harry, 1999, pp. 118–119

These principles imply a constructionist understanding of cultural difference and value the distinctions without denying you, as the worker, your own orientation. These principles also provide a useful framework for working with people of other cultures and are consistent with social justice and human rights as they enhance inclusion and reflect a basic assumption of cultural strengths.

Families Including People with Disabilities

Social work has not always maintained a consistent, professional commitment to disability work in spite of its general dedication to the reduction of oppression and discrimination. Partly because of their focus on the medical model, many social workers have set their sights on cure and have not approached disability work with the same sense of urgency they direct toward fixing things. Evidence suggests that this is changing with the advent of family-centered models of care, which have recently gained prominence in some medical and many educational settings.

The Social Work Library

Read Mackelprang & Salsgiver's contemporary perspective on how social work might partner with the disability movement.

Family-centered care is an approach that prioritizes the family's goals (over professional goals) and recognizes family members as experts on their own experience (Shelton & Stepanek, 1994). It is a promising method for working with families in many arenas, especially with those who have disabilities. When children have comprehensive and severe health challenges, such as neurodevelopmental delays, interdisciplinary teaming is an appropriate response. Social workers can play an important role on such teams that, by their nature, address an array of the many needs of children growing up with serious disabilities. Workers can also support families in ways that go beyond medical or educational requirements.

When a child with profound disabilities is born, family members usually have to reorganize their everyday lives as well as their long-term dreams. Often one parent has to stop working to orchestrate all the services and treatments the child needs. The time requirements for involvement with school teams, medical teams, and interdisciplinary teams, as well as the individual services of a speech pathologist, audiologist, occupational specialist, pediatrician, psychologist—the list is sometimes quite long—can turn a family upside down. Siblings are affected, family interactions are affected, and parents often struggle with the emotional ramifications as well as the physical consequences of exhaustion. Social workers can offer support, time management ideas, and help with expanding parents' ability to identify resources. In addition, many families struggle with gaining access to services they are entitled to receive and therefore may need social work advocacy in their negotiation of a complex system.

Social workers and disability scholars have proposed (among other things) the following (Mackelprang & Salsgiver, 1999):

- People with disabilities are capable, or potentially so.

- Disabilities are not equivalent to pathologies and do not require fixing.

- "Disability" is a social construct to which social workers must respond politically.

- People with disabilities have the absolute right to control their own lives.

These ideas imply a social work presence based on advocacy, structural principles, and the skills to work for social justice.

Disability work with families is a ripe arena for social work practice and offers practitioners many opportunities. They may engage in significant relationships that use ethnographic methods of exploring the meaning of the disability to the family (Cook, 2000), and they can assume a strengths-based, resilience stance (Russo, 1999) consistent with the profession's commitment to social justice, diversity, and human rights.

 Web Links

Parents with Disabilities Online is a "one-stop" site for parents with disabilities. Features include personal narratives, practical information (such as accessible recreation sites and toys depicting people with disabilities), and links to empowerment networks.

CONTEMPORARY TRENDS AND SKILLS

Theoretical perspectives are a reflection of the sociocultural context. Looking at some of the perspectives in Chapter 1 that have contributed to social work's stance, you saw that theories don't just pop up out of nowhere. They are usually some sort of response to the theoretical climate that precedes them. The same seems to occur in theories of family work. We'll look here at three different perspectives that have some components in common and others born in reaction to each other. All correspond in some ways to traditional perspectives and offer an evolving focus.

Narrative Theory in Family Work

You will recognize narrative theory from earlier discussions. It is based on a postmodern, constructionist perspective that breaks with systems models, charging that they are mechanistic and don't adequately reflect the worker's inevitable inclusion in the work. Narrative proponents suggest that people make sense of their lives through stories. Family interpretations of ongoing events either tend to support the ongoing narrative or refute it. Those stories that are included in the sense making serve to organize subsequent experience. When there are exceptions, they are often dismissed or forgotten as not representative of the real family. The language used to interpret and describe various family stories is significant and fits into the context of the ongoing experience. Let us explore how this works.

The family story about Liza, six years old, the last child, and only girl in a family from an upscale neighborhood, casts her in the role of the Black Sheep. She is naughty, clumsy, sassy, and disruptive. Any tiny scrape that Liza gets into (forgetting her pencil, or knocking over her milk) becomes just another piece of evidence. Her family members shake their heads. What to do with someone so naughty, clumsy, sassy, and disruptive? When Liza's first-grade teacher reports to her mother that Liza is exceptionally well liked by both her peers and teachers and that she is bright and fun, Liza's mother is incredulous. She suspects the teacher has her confused with another student. Or Liza must be faking. The *real* Liza, as everyone knows, is naughty, clumsy, sassy, and disruptive, as Black Sheep are inclined to be.

Here you get a glimpse of what might be a preferred reality, the story Liza's teacher tells, that is added to the family's account. Each story carries the power of the context to perpetuate and expand it, which in turn will influence the way Liza, as the major character, plays her role. If her family persists in maintaining the original home story, she is likely to respond over time by becoming increasingly rude, failing, or developing truly disruptive conduct. On the other hand, if her family at any point re-authors the story by recognizing the exceptions to their ideas about Liza, her story may unfold quite differently. We all have multiple stories, but some have more power, relevance, and a wider audience than others. Liza's alternative story (told by her teacher) has the potential to influence her future in positive and significant ways.

Thickening the Story   Although narrative theory has many components, we will look at some of the most relevant concepts for generalist work with families. You may recall from Chapter 5, **thickening the story** refers to the worker's effort to expand thin (Morgan, 2000) or **problem-saturated stories** that have little depth, sustain problems in a stuck mode, and seem to lead nowhere (Freedman & Combs, 1996). Liza's first story is a good example of a thin account. She has no redeeming virtues and is simply a naughty, clumsy, sassy, disruptive Black Sheep. A thickened version of Liza's story reveals her likable personality, her talents, and her ability to connect with people in spite of, or in addition to, whatever proclivities she has toward being naughty, clumsy, sassy, and disruptive.

Let us look at another example, the Smiths, a family who has experienced a great deal of difficulty in child raising. One child has been taken into the custody of the state, and now child protection workers are investigating to determine whether another also needs to be removed for reasons of safety. The mother disparagingly claims, in defeat and sarcastic resignation, that her family is "just one of those families." Child welfare workers may likewise see the family as "just one of those families" because various children have been in custody for three generations (as was Ms. Smith).

Rather than assessing the narrowly defined dysfunction of this family, the narrative worker would search for the exceptions to this story to enrich it and make it more complex. For example, the worker might ask about Ms. Smith's ability to keep a family together for 10 years in gross poverty, or to overcome a major childhood health challenge, or survive homelessness. The effort is to expand the narrow failure story so that the family can see itself as having potential, which in turn can support re-authoring the story to reflect the way the family would like it to be. The family then can shape its future to fit the new story. You can contrast this approach to the one taken in the section "Intergenerational Patterns," earlier in the chapter. Through a different lens, it offers the potential for hope through development of the family's resilience and positive attributes.

Externalizing Problems   The notion that problems are external, or separate, from people is known as **externalization**. The person is not the problem, "the problem is the problem" (White & Denbourough, 1998). Narrative workers try to identify and help the family to name the issue that is creating difficulties. By objectifying or personifying it, family members can develop a relationship with it, rather than be consumed by it, and ultimately they may control it.

Narrativeapproaches.com has papers that can be downloaded and information on workshops, conferences, and instructional pieces (for example, "Ten Second Introduction to Narrative Therapy"), definition of terms, and special focuses.

For example, if a family feels overwhelmed by the demands of a child with disabilities, the resulting "worry" may be externalized. The worker can then ask about it, help family members label it, and support all those times when the family takes control over "the Worry." By separating it from the family's identity, the worker can explore with the family ways to defeat it or at least keep it at bay.

Unearthing the Broader Context   One of narrative theory's most relevant contributions to generalist social work practice is a consistent emphasis on the political context of the family. The worker will be highly sensitized to the danger of reinforcing the oppressive dimensions of a dominant pattern (such as racism) in society.

Therefore, if a six-year-old child, Damion, is exhibiting what seems like inordinate fear in going to school, the worker will not want to externalize this prematurely as "the school creeps" or "school scares" if in fact Damion is being taunted and bullied because of his color. The politics of the family's experience is always in the forefront, as in the Just Therapy work developed in New Zealand and described in Chapter 2.

The Dulwich Centre Publications site lists all of their books and articles and describes workshops and conferences. This is the prototype narrative group from Adelaide, Australia.

Solution-Focused Family Work

Like many contemporary family models, **solution-focused practice** defines the family broadly and does not limit its conception to traditional or legal forms (Christiensen, Todahl & Barrett, 1999). Solution-based models deemphasize history or underlying pathology (Nichols & Schwartz, 2001), focus on brief interventions, and narrowly define the arena of specific problems within the context of particular environmental variables. Solution-focused workers usually emphasize a cognitive approach, support a collaborative stance with clients, and tend to reject notions that problems serve any unconscious or ulterior motive. Accordingly, solution-focused workers believe firmly that people want to change and assert that any attribution of resistant behavior to families is more about the interpretation of the practitioner than it is about families. One proponent (deShazer, 1984), early in his work declared resistance "dead" and in turn redefined clients' balking at practitioner directives as their way of educating the worker about what is needed to help them.

Solution-focused workers emphasize the future, in which solutions can be used within the specification of clear, concrete, and achievable goals. Because of the self-proclaimed simplicity of the approach, along with its time-limited, highly specific emphasis, solution-focused work has become an important contemporary model covered by health insurance, as it generally aspires to quick, specific, and direct results, thus avoiding costly protracted professional relationships.

Environmental Focus   Because of its ecological orientation, solution-based work looks to the community as a resource and always seeks to understand the problem in terms of how it is played out in the surrounding context. Accordingly, the worker assumes that a woman who has abandoned her children, for example, may be embedded within a culture in which she experiences gender discrimination, poverty, or perhaps racism, and these will be considered as contributing to her current inability to care for children.

All of these considerations are part of the assessment, and a single diagnostic or strictly pathology-oriented label as a unitary explanation is not seen as adequate. The overall understanding of the family's difficulty is rooted in their everyday, unique living experience to which they bring their own personalities and idiosyncrasies within the larger context, which also shapes that experience.

Search for Exceptions   Like narrative proponents, solution-focused workers concentrate especially on identifying and bolstering the attempts made by families that have been successful. The goal for solution-focused work is to increase the talk about solutions and decrease the talk about problems. Client families are asked to remember when their efforts worked, even when they seem like very small incidents occurring very rarely. Solution-focused workers direct their attention to those exceptions and explore the contextual factors that made the exception possible. In this way workers give families the message that they have the strengths to cope, that they have in fact done it successfully before, and that they can do it again (DeJong & Berg, 2002).

Saleebey (2002) credits solution-focused therapists with promoting a greater emphasis on strengths through their "exception" question that encourages the identification of, and focus on, those situations and times in which the client was successful. See Exhibit 8.2 for more on discovering strengths through similar questions.

Client Competence   Solution-focused work emphasizes the skills, strengths, and competence of clients in a way that is consistent with many postmodern

Survival questions:
- How have you managed to survive this far, given all the challenges you have had to contend with? What have you learned about yourself and your world during your struggles?

Support questions:
- Who are the special people on whom you can depend? What did they respond to in you?

Exception questions:
- When things were going well in life, what was different? What parts of your world and your being would you like to recapture?

Possibility questions:
- What are your hopes, visions, and aspirations? How can I help you achieve those goals?

Esteem questions:
- When people say good things about you, what are they likely to say? When was it that you began to believe that you might achieve some of the things you wanted in life?

Source: Adapted from Saleebey, 2002, p. 89

EXHIBIT 8.2

Types of Questions for Discovering Strengths

approaches. This focal point serves to heighten the collaborative stance workers take with clients and assists the partnership in maintaining a positive direction in the work (Berg & DeJong, 1996). The assumptions inherent in their ecological orientation encourage workers to look to environmental, structural supports for solutions rather than to internal dynamics for pathology. Workers do not disregard individual responsibility for behaviors such as those that occur in child abuse or domestic violence, but these are viewed as evidence that the client's actual resources and skills are underused (Christiensen, Todahl & Barrett, 1999). Thus, the assumption that people can grow and change and ultimately be responsible is sustained.

Constructionist and Social Justice Approaches to Family Work

The contemporary approaches described here are complementary and share some constructionist notions that are represented in the client-defined meanings of family, the lack of rigid ideas of so-called normal family development, and the collaborative partnerships built with clients. Narrative and solution-focused ideas also take up social justice issues in their concerns for the contextual locations that clients experience everyday. In that respect, they are more alike than they are different, and each has a positive contribution to make to contemporary social work practice.

Constructionist theories call for using a critical perspective that reaffirms social work's long-standing tradition in working with families. Some family therapy models have diverted social workers away from the profession's commitment to social justice and nonpathologizing concepts. As a response to these phenomena, critical social construction suggests the development of a perspective that focuses more directly on constructionist ideas and social justice principles.

Critical Constructionist Emphasis   Critical constructionist social workers explore the meaning of family within a broad contextual framework. Models describing the family present the worker with multiple perspectives that can be viewed critically, especially because such models have implications for practice. For example, if you assume a theoretical model in which the family is considered basic for human survival and absolutely sacrosanct, you might view the family, as many did for centuries, as immune from outsider interference in its internal dynamics, including family violence. If you take up another model that asserts that family is important but has some limitations in its power and autonomy, you are likely to respond differently (Witkin, 1995). Therefore, the worker will want to question such models and consider what they mean for clients.

The constructionist worker will go beyond the critique of any particular model and policy, however, and will question the role of theory in general when it has implications for the politics of practice. She or he will explore how theories are embedded in institutions and policies that affect families and their abilities to meet their needs. This will likely include some analysis about who benefits from the model, whose voices are included in it, and who may be harmed by it. For example, who profits from recent notions of welfare reform? How do different approaches impact people who are poor or of color? You saw another example of this questioning earlier in the discussion of gays and lesbians as parents and the critique of the use of systems theory in such scenarios. This kind of inquiry will be in the forefront of the constructionist worker's considerations.

 Web Links

For another perspective, see the site of the National Black Child Development Institute, a nonprofit organization providing support and offering programs, workshops, and resources for African American children, their parents, and the communities in which they live. Geared largely toward educational opportunities for black youth, the site takes up a social justice stance in its statements regarding the rights of black youth and their families.

Social Justice Emphasis   Constructionist theorists call for consideration of both external and internal dimensions of social justice. By external, they mean that social workers will direct their attention to ensuring that all families are granted the rights and privileges of society, not just the idealized families of dominant groups. Diverse families, by ethnicity, sexual orientation, class, or any other difference, should be guaranteed the same access to the benefits of the culture; when they are not, the social worker is called upon to intervene in whatever ways are applicable, including legal advocacy, legislative advocacy, public education, or other forms of social action.

The internal focus requires the worker to look within the family itself for reflection of justice for all family members. Clearly the worker needs to challenge overt and specific oppressive behaviors such as intimate partner violence and child abuse but also is encouraged to look at family structure, gender relations, and roles, which by many accounts of today's society, need considerable work. Critical constructionist social workers will take up these concerns through such activities as education and advocacy for more just family and employment practices and policies.

As with the innovative groups discussed in Chapter 7, this particular focus on family by practitioners is a work in progress. It does not have a widely developed research base or a traditionally recognized theoretical base. It does, however, reflect social work's continuous and energetic effort to develop practice models that both confront and support various dimensions of contemporary society.

FLEXIBLE SKILLS AND TOOLS FOR DEVELOPING DIALOGUE

Families are a special breed of groups and as such benefit from the careful use of the same skills that assist individuals and groups to engage in their work together with you. Your work with families is likely to vary according to your practice setting and the constraints of your agency. For example, if you are on the intake unit of a child protection team, your early engagement with the family will probably differ from your colleague's who works in a community mental health agency. The theoretical lens through which you are working will also influence the way you interact with family members. You may want to do a fairly formal assessment of the family's functional patterns from a systems focus, or you may ask family members how they think you might help them, as in solution-focused work. In any situation, you will want to invite the family to tell their story; your agency mission and purpose and your own theoretical biases will influence the approaches you take in doing that.

General Skills Guidelines

Here are a few specifically family-oriented guidelines that are useful in most family work models:

- Make the family as comfortable as possible.

- Assume responsibility for the tone and nature of the meeting.

- Transmit some form of positive regard or warmth, support, and respect.

- Engage with and hear from each member of the family.

- Fully explore the family's purpose and goals in coming to see you.

- Agree upon what the focus of the work will be.

- Recognize your own biases around family forms and norms.

- Attend to communication and interrelationship patterns.

Written homework assignments, task designation, role-playing, rehearsals, and teaching are sometimes helpful depending on the family's situation, their investment in the process, and the framework you are using in the work. In addition to the individual and group skills, reframing and perspectival, or circular, questions are two techniques with good applicability in many family situations when carefully used.

Reframing   An approach used frequently in family work, although not limited to it, **reframing** is a practice skill in which the worker conceives of and describes a situation in different terms. It can be especially helpful in family conversations in which one member says something incendiary to or about another, which sometimes occurs in conversations with the social worker. Carefully used, reframing can assist both recipient and "sender" to view the situation with diminished uproar so they can begin to listen to each other.

For example, a 15-year-old boy, who sees his mother as an autocratic barrier to his enjoyment because she won't let him go out with friends who drive, says, "There is no person on the face of this earth who is more controlling and overprotective than my mother. She is just like Hitler! She keeps me locked up in the prisoners' camp." You may suggest that the boy's mother cares so much for him that she fears he will be hurt in an automobile accident or in some other way if he goes out with his friends.

When reframing, offer a plausible alternative that does not resonate as a gimmicky or Pollyanna effort to diffuse strong feeling and, accordingly, will be heard by the parties involved. The danger lies in interpreting what someone else is thinking or feeling without directly having been told. In the example, it is quite likely that the mother is really not out to torture her son (and that she truly worries about his going out with friends who drive), but he may or may not be able to "hear" her sentiment as reframed. Another reframe might be more effective depending on the nature of the relationship and the people involved. Developing the content of such interpretations requires judgment and skill; use reframing cautiously and only when conditions are relatively straightforward.

Perspectival Questions   Mentioned in connection with individuals in Chapter 4 and with group work practice in Chapter 7, perspectival questions can be especially useful in family work. By seeking the perspective of another family member, you can help clarify the feelings and meanings of one member's view of another. If the family is experiencing stress because the eldest son is leaving home, you might ask the teenage daughter, "What do you think your mother will do to prepare for Johnny's leaving?" Or you may ask the mother, "What will your daughter miss most about Johnny?"

The responses to these questions may communicate ideas and feelings that no one in the family has openly recognized before. This kind of assistance in communication is particularly relevant when family members assume they know all they need to about the responses of other family members because of long-term, stuck patterns of argument or difference or saving face. Like reframing, this is a technique to be used carefully and only when you are confident that you can handle any response. The daughter in the example may say something in response like, "Mother will sew name tags in Johnny's underwear so he won't lose it in the dorm laundry room at college," or, alternatively, she may say, "Mother will no doubt start to drink again." The same element of the unexpected that can open up new ways of thinking for families can also throw a curve ball to the unwary or unprepared worker!

Tools and Mapping

Chapter 5 discussed genograms and ecomaps as helpful mapping tools for assessment. These two tools are widely used with families and offer many uses for workers. They are compatible with most models of family work, although some narrative theorists believe they are potentially mechanistic, privilege only one interpretation, and may be seen as deterministic. These are potentially valid objections, but the tools can be used in a way so as not to foster the unwanted rigidity. For example, everyone in the family may be asked to participate in the genogram, or each member could make her or his own map of the family relational patterns (see Exhibit 8.3). Ecomaps and other variations that demonstrate relationship patterns can liberate some families from what seems like endless talking, and they usually enjoy developing them and examining the final product.

Sometimes ecomaps are used in a visual service evaluation when the goal has been to expand community connections in general or specifically (for example, engaging in more recreational pursuits) or to alter them (such as improving the relationship between the school and the family of a child with disabilities).

The culturagram, which you also saw in Chapter 5, was developed and refined to explore and facilitate empowerment of families from other cultures. The resulting map illustrates content from inquiries relating to the specifics of the family's experience from immigration to their celebration of values in a new land. A culturagram is shown in Exhibit 8.4. This tool not only helps workers avoid stereotyping their diverse clients, understand the internal experiences of families, and recognize differences among families, but also helps demonstrate to families the ways in which they have been successful (Congress, 1994; 2000).

Ongoing Evaluation

The ongoing evaluation of the family work that social workers do is often largely contingent on, and defined by, the context and goals of the original

EXHIBIT 8.3

Graphic Representation of Different Views of the Family within the Family

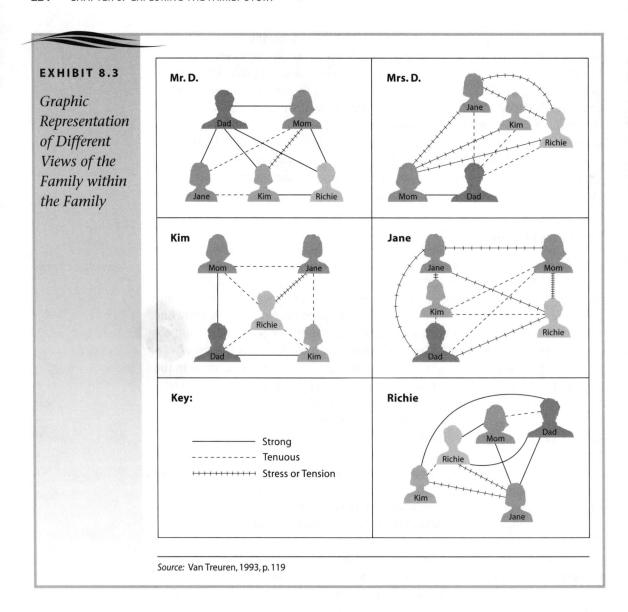

Key:

——————— Strong

- - - - - - - Tenuous

++++++++++ Stress or Tension

Source: Van Treuren, 1993, p. 119

contact. If you are working with a family in child protective services, the first goal will likely be imposed externally as the continued safety of a child or children. There may be other goals, such as the parents' improved skills in managing a large family or meeting the health needs of a particular child. These in most cases are documented in written goals, and you will want to pay attention to them along the way, just as you do in other forms of practice.

You will also want to consider your own role with the family and whether or not your relationship seems to be working. This is usually a more reflective

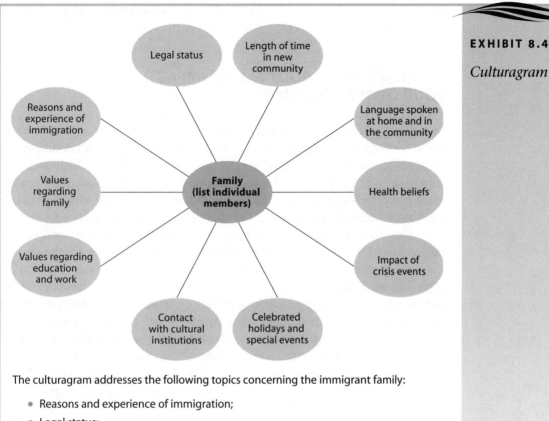

EXHIBIT 8.4

Culturagram

The culturagram addresses the following topics concerning the immigrant family:

- Reasons and experience of immigration;
- Legal status;
- Length of time in new community;
- Language spoken at home and in the community;
- Health beliefs;
- Impact of crisis events;
- Celebrated holidays and special events;
- Contact with cultural institutions;
- Values regarding education and work; and
- Values regarding family.

Source: Congress, E., 2001

and interactive process. Some questions you can ask yourself and members of the family are. Does every member feel valued as if she or he can contribute to the work? Are there issues regarding the family's culture? Does the family still agree with the direction of the work? How is the work changing their experience? Checking in with families, through a dialogic process, to make sure they feel heard, understood, and are invested in the work you are doing with them is just as important as it is with other levels of practice.

STRAIGHT TALK ABOUT FAMILY IMPACT: YOUR OWN AND OTHERS'

Families are a powerful ingredient in our lives. They have inspired fierce loyalties, lethal conflicts, abject miseries, and quiet pleasures throughout all of history and continue to do so today. Whether you view your own family as supportive or toxic or any of the many positions in between, you will want to have reached some sort of peace with it. It is difficult to deal with the family situations of others if they trigger feelings by their similarity to (or even difference from) your own. This doesn't mean that everything in your family has to be perfect or even fully resolved. It does mean that you should have enough of a handle on your own family situation so that it does not intrude into or influence your work in ways you don't recognize. This issue falls into the arena of supervision, and you will benefit from sharing with your supervisor any current raw struggles you are engaged in with your own family, especially if you are also seeing families.

Even granting a reasonable sense of comfort with your own family, you will likely experience situations, at some point or another, in which your feelings are difficult to manage. Egregious abuse exists in some families, and although contemporary theoretical perspectives can help you temper your responses and recognize that people do the best they can, the litany of injuries or aggressions emerging in court reports or police accounts or living room conversations can bring on powerful emotions in the most seasoned and balanced worker. Fortunately, you can use supervision, agency supports, peer connections, and personal strategies for coping with them. The most encouraging dimension for social workers today is, I believe, that the vast majority of families inspire the greatest admiration for their resiliency, spirit, resourcefulness, and agency in the midst of potentially demoralizing circumstances.

CONCLUSION

The contemporary family both supports and challenges the social worker everyday. Because workers engage with the family and its struggles in our culture, a goal for the profession will be to develop additional and relevant models for working with them that recognize their strengths, agency, and resilience. Education and advocacy for shifts in the structural and political arrangements that exist for them will also be required. As a culture we still value the importance of the family, and social workers will need to be a part of the solution for creating environments in which families of all kinds are validated and supported.

As the structure and meaning of family itself continue to change, you will want to keep alert for your own capacities to honor those notions of others. As a form of "group," the family has particular resonance and serves as a grounding point for understanding human collectives. With that dimension in mind, we are ready to explore another group variant, the world of organizations, in Chapter 9.

MAIN POINTS

- Historical antecedents for social work's involvement with families, including family function and systems theories, shape much of how workers think about them today.

- An idealized, or fantasy, notion of the American family still exists today, but social workers recognize and work with many forms, including grandparents raising grandchildren, gay and lesbian families, and mixed race families.

- Several contemporary theoretical perspectives have emerged that are consistent with critical social construction, the strengths perspective, and social justice orientations. These include narrative theory, solution-focused work, and constructionist approaches.

- Your practice setting will govern much of your work with families, but you will need the same skills that assist individuals and groups, along with some family-oriented skills such as engaging the whole family, reframing, and recognizing your own biases around family forms.

- Mapping tools can be helpful in assessing and evaluating the work with families; they can also help to empower families to change.

- Both your own and your clients' families can have a major impact on your work. Ongoing evaluation includes not only documenting achievement of externally imposed goals but also determining whether your role and relationship with the family are working.

EXERCISES: PRACTICING SOCIAL WORK

For this exercise, read Carmen's case file. Address her Critical Thinking Questions #1, 2, and 3. (For #2 read at least one article in each of the two areas that concern Carmen: the impact on families of children with special health needs and outcomes of children in different types of families.)

Break into groups of four or five and develop a potential work plan for the family, based on your answers to the Critical Thinking Questions.

1. Identify the areas in which you think the major challenges will fall.

2. Strategize how you might work with the whole Sanchez family around these challenges.

3. Develop a plan to insure Carmen's maximum participation in the process.

EXERCISES: THE SOCIAL WORK LIBRARY

Read Hartman's paper on family focus, then study the following family situation, and finally answer the questions. Review the sample interview on the CD of the Sanchez family to recall Hector's feelings about his family.

All in the Family #1

As the undocumented nephew of Hector and Celia Sanchez, Roberto Salazar has experienced a lot of health challenges in addition to earning a living. He is currently living with the Sanchez family because of an injury that keeps him from working. He has many skills but has hit some hard times and seems defeated right now.

You are the worker who is charged with monitoring the status of Hector and Celia's Section 8 housing voucher. While Hector and Celia generally do very well at managing their rent payments, they are having particular difficulties in meeting the schedule because of extra expenditures in support of Roberto. There is a particular emphasis in the agency currently on keeping expenses down and on tightening up on maintaining Federal regulations which haven't been observed very stringently. Your supervisor is especially concerned with this aspect of the program.

You go to visit Hector one day and he assures you that—even though he knows the landlord can evict him and his family for violating regulations regarding who lives in the house—Roberto is family and, of course, he and Celia will house and feed him. He remembers how lonely he was at Roberto's age and how an uncle had helped him out; he has no doubt that he can assist Roberto by having him stay with them temporarily. He tells you how important it is for immigrants to stick together and support one another, especially family. You are feeling some pressure from the agency to report and help resolve the issue of Roberto's unacceptable presence in the Sanchez home.

You tell yourself your supervisor is never going to understand this.

1. What do you think Hartman would think about Hector's values?

2. How might a family focus differ from an individual focus in this situation?

3. How will you respond to your supervisor?

Compare your responses to those of your peers. Identify and team up with another student whose approach seems similar to yours and develop a unified approach. Brainstorm in class regarding different or creative ways to approach this situation.

OTHER EXERCISES

Not in My House

You are a social worker on an interdisciplinary team that works with children who have autism and their families. The child referred to the team is Jenny, who is three years old. Jenny is the light of her father's life—she is lively, energetic, and bright-eyed. In the last year, though, she has become rather quiet, preferring to play by herself, and less interested in the special outings her father loves to share with her.

After a series of anxious appointments with the pediatrician, Jenny was referred to a specialist in developmental pediatrics. Many observations and checklists later, Jenny was diagnosed with autism. Her parents, Catherine and Jason, were devastated. Her two and a half-year-old brother, Sammy, was oblivious.

Over a period of a month, Catherine began to adjust to the diagnosis. She connected with a supportive group of parents dealing with autism in children and did a lot of reading, both in the library and on the Internet. She also spent a lot of time with Jenny, playing and coaxing her to interact with her. Jason, however, was notably uninterested in Catherine's activities. He began to refuse to go to Jenny's doctor's appointments. During one very argumentative dinner with Catherine, he stated that he did not believe the diagnosis; he thought Jenny was fine, just going through a stage, and accused Catherine of "selling out" her own daughter.

Jenny is referred to the interdisciplinary team by her pediatrician. Catherine engaged in the process enthusiastically, if painfully. Jason attended the assessment and seemed sullen, participating very little. The team concurs that the family would benefit from your "support work" around the diagnosis. Catherine and Jason agree to meet with you. You have the feeling that this might be your only chance to engage Jason.

Respond to the following questions to compare with your peers.

1. What do think is going on in this family? (Identify a theoretical perspective you think most applicable.) How does your choice of perspective influence your approach to this family? (Be specific.)

2. Generate a list of three questions or issues that you think would be very important to address in your first meeting.

3. Review the "general skills guidelines" section and identify which would seem the most useful and which the greatest challenge to you. Explain.

As you compare with your peers, what different (from your own) perspective was most useful to you? Describe it in a paragraph.

All in the Family #2

As a practitioner at a community mental health center, you generally see individuals and families. You have recently been called by a family and will conduct an intake appointment later on today. The following is all the information you currently have about the family:

- The father, self identified as African American, made the appointment.

- The family consists of mother, father, and two adolescent sons.

- The eldest son is of most concern to the family, having expressed some suicidal thoughts and fairly recent but increasing withdrawal from school, family, and community life. Last year this son was a well-known school athlete and this year is not active in any school or athletic activities.

- There was a hint that alcohol or other drug use is involved in the family; it wasn't clear how or by whom.

- Both sons are reluctant to come in but will because their father has indicated they will.

- Mother will "go along."

In your preparation for this appointment you are considering several dimensions of the work that appear below. In small groups, discuss these and explore the questions. Report back to the full group.

- You are not African American but are of Jewish heritage, which is relatively rare in the town. You know there are many cultural differences between you and this family but believe you can bridge those to some extent because you consider yourself different culturally as well. What might you need to watch for in your own assumptions?

- What model of family work (of those in the chapter) do you think will provide the most useful base?

- What specifics of information will be important to clarify first?

- What specific approaches do you think will be most important here with this particular family?

- How would you begin with this family? What particular skills would you use? What might you actually say? (Give an example.)

Working in and with the Organization

"Why study organizations?" There are two answers to this question. The first answer is obvious. Organizations surround us. We are born in them and usually die in them. Our life space in between is filled with them. They are just about impossible to escape. They are as inevitable as death and taxes . . . the second answer to the question . . . is . . . organizations have outcomes.

Richard Hall, 1991

Minds, my mind and yours, are run by the same principles. We are not unique. We mirror what is around us. If we walk into a red room, we become red. If we are always in a group of angry people, it is hard not to become angry. If we are with someone who is clear, our mind reflects that back and we become clearer.

Natalie Goldberg, 1994

THERE ARE PROBABLY FEW THOUGHTS THAT ENGENDER MORE ambivalence among practicing social workers than the idea of the organization. Workers may think of organizations as huge, frustrating bureaucracies, as small supportive neighborhood havens, or as complicated collectives that both give them direction and swallow them up. You will profit greatly from studying them. Organizations are everywhere!

On a more personal level, the associations that individual social workers make with organizations are undoubtedly influenced by their own specific experiences. Whether they have felt nurtured, thwarted, or even deceived by them, organizations play an immense role in the work lives of most social work practitioners. Although there has been considerable growth in the number of social workers choosing independent practice settings (Gibelman, 1999), the majority today still work in agency settings.

This chapter focuses on the general nature of organizations and social work agencies in particular as it influences the experience of practitioners. We will explore a number of dimensions concerning purpose, structure, and internal relations, and the impact of these on the work. The discussion emphasizes the practitioner's interface and how the context of agency function shapes professional practice. Later in the chapter we will look at several ideas for effecting change within agencies and explore some exemplary strategies, through partnerships and alliances that cross agencies, alter the ways they do business, and help them become more responsive to the worker's primary priority—the people she or he serves.

GENERAL PERSPECTIVES ON ORGANIZATIONS

The Social Work Library

Jane Addams' autobiographical work offers a comprehensive look at the early issues in social work organizations.

Distinctions between organizations are generally based on social constructions of meaningful difference. For example, the difference between profit and nonprofit organizations is useful in many instances and perhaps not in others. In looking at these distinctions, then, it is helpful to consider the meaning they have within their particular settings.

For this discussion, we will look at three variables through the lenses that are typical to social or human service-oriented organizations, although they often have a broader applicability as well. There is a large amount of highly theoretical literature relating to the sociology of organizations, but the relatively concrete dimensions of the agency's (1) purpose, (2) structure of governance, and (3) internal power relations provide standpoints that are important to most practitioners because they shape their practice experience (see, for example, Freund, 2005). Let us start here with purpose.

Purpose

The stated purpose of an organization reflects its reason for being and in that way reveals its general goals and activities, if not the finer points. This, of course, says nothing about the means it uses to reach its goals or its faithfulness to its original guiding principles, but it describes in broad terms what the organization sees itself to be concerned with. A brief review of three types of purposes follows, with an example in the human services realm. These purposes are to fill a public mandate, to provide a particular service, and to foster social change in regard to an ideological concern.

Organizations Sanctioned by Law   Organizations mandated by law include some of the social services that are most widely recognized by the public. Child protection, usually housed within a very large and visible state organization, is one example. Workers are expected to act in the best interests of children, their safety, and to support healthful, effective family life. The law explicitly requires child protection workers in most states to carry out some clearly specified activities in service of the organization's legal mandates. Workers are typically subject to public scrutiny and may feel the weight, and perhaps occasional rewards, of what sometimes seems like an impossible task.

Organizations with Service Goals   These organizations usually develop as a result of some kind of socially agreed upon need or concern. For example, youth who have already dropped out of school, or who are at risk for it, are often quite visible in local communities. As a culture, we voice our support for the education of all citizens and generally agree that large numbers of school dropouts are not a good thing for our communities or for the individuals involved, who are then likely to become dependent on state resources, may violate the law, or in some other way become less than ideal citizens. Youth services organizations generally try to prevent or repair situations in which youth leave school prematurely, get into legal trouble, get into substance abuse trouble, and so on. Workers frequently have to convince the general public of the importance of their work, which is usually not as well known or well funded as those services mandated by law.

Organizations Arising from Social Movements   Some **grassroots organizations**, which are organizations started by ordinary citizens rather than bureaucrats, arise in response to ideological positions regarding particular social problems. The early development of shelters for women who are battered by partners or spouses is an example of the influence of workers whose commitments and energies were channeled into a **social movement,** which is a political effort designed to change some aspect of society. Frequently the founders and workers of such organizations are indigenous workers, meaning they have themselves experienced the social oppression or physical aggression that the organization works against. Workers often have extraordinary commitments to their mission and frequently have to legitimize their activity to a public that is ambivalent about making significant social change.

Structures of Governance

How an organization governs itself is another variable in functioning that most social workers want to know about, especially if they are considering practicing in it. Organizational structure, much like family structure, refers to the way in which various members and tasks relate to one another. There are usually accompanying rules, or norms, which are communicated to some degree (not always clearly) to all.

   We will explore three kinds of organizational structures here as representative of those found in many contemporary agencies: bureaucracies, project-teams, and functional structures.

Bureaucracies   We will look at bureaucratic structure because it has so many repercussions for workers and how they practice. The bureaucracy may not seem to be as good a match as other structures for human service organizations; nevertheless, it is a common pattern in many state and some local agencies in which social workers are likely to be employed.

German sociologist Max Weber invented the term **bureaucracy** as a conceptual type, rather than a reality, of structure. The following 10 points describe the characteristics of a bureaucracy as Weber described it (Netting, Kettner & McMurtry, 1993):

- Each position in the organization has a limited area of authority and responsibility.

- Control and responsibility are concentrated at the top of a clear hierarchy.

- The activities of the organization are documented in a central system of records.

- The organization employs highly specialized workers based on expert training.

- Staff demands require full-time commitment, and each position represents a career.

- Activities are coordinated through clearly outlined rules.

- The relationships among workers are characterized by impersonality.

- Recruitment is based on ability and relevant, technical knowledge.

- The private and public lives of the organization's members are distinct.

- Promotions in the organization are made by seniority.

You can probably identify aspects of the bureaucracy that you find difficult. These might include the top-down hierarchical authority or the impersonality of relationships among members. Yet, notice also how many of these ideas have been incorporated into notions of what is fair or right in how things are run. For example, the idea that recruitment is based on ability (rather than, say, the fact that the boss is your uncle) seems intuitive to most of us, as well as reflecting some moral dimension that seems right.

Agencies that seem the most oriented toward bureaucracy are often those embedded in larger systems, such as state or federal government. Therefore, child protection, public mental health, and corrections are fields in which bureaucratic approaches have tended to be most common and sometimes seem to be most rigid. Interestingly, and probably because of this phenomenon, these are also arenas in which some of the most creative and innovative alternative responses have been proposed.

Project-Teams   This model contrasts sharply with the bureaucracy. **Project-teams** consist of a group of people who work through internal committees or task forces that take on an individual issue that arises. They tend to be, by definition, more flexible since internal committees may be able to choose their focal points for activity and interpret their purposes as they match members' concerns. They also tend to have a very open sense of authority and minimal hierarchy. Often such groups can maintain this structure for a limited time only, as they sometimes get either too large or their resources become subject to more careful accountability.

For example, a feminist collective responding to the needs of women who are battered by their partners may designate a project-team to develop, locate, and run a shelter. Team members may organize as shelter staff in such a way that everyone shares the tasks of managing the agency's physical space and everyone is paid the same salary. This structure appeals to some, but may be challenged by concerns relating to, for example, the appropriateness of a person with a master's degree answering phones or vacuuming the shelter office. Such alternative structures sometimes become more mainstream as they hire new workers who demand a competitive salary, or get more funding from outside sources that require hierarchal reimbursement for workers.

Functional Structures   Often when an agency becomes too large for a single head to cover all the details of all the programs, a layer of administration will be added. These administrative additions are usually divided literally by function, that is, by who does what, thus the name **functional structures**. In a youth services agency, for example, the executive director may appoint an experienced counselor to head the counseling unit. Likewise, the same executive might appoint a long-term youth worker to head the program for runaway youth and another worker to head the agency's work with youth in state's custody. In this relatively simple scheme, the three midlevel administrative leaders would probably be seen as equal, or at the same level, and might form a management team, which works directly with the executive director. Frequently, these administrative roles are added to already existing direct service roles, so that the head of the counseling unit, for instance, would still retain a smaller than usual number of counseling clients. As the agency grows larger, the unit heads might stop doing direct service altogether in order to keep up with their expanded supervisory and administrative activities. Such workers may happily step into this role or may regret the loss of direct service, client relationships.

Internal Power Relations

Most workers quickly discover the unique power arrangements in organizations that may be obvious or rather subtle, but clearly exist. In Chapter 4 we looked at some sources of the worker's power, including agency, expert knowledge, interpersonal, and legitimate power. The following discussion considers the view of authority as "consensual power" (Netting, Kettner & McMurty, 1993, p. 126), which implies that it is noncoercive and agreed upon. We look here at authority based on tradition, charisma, and rational/legal principles.

Traditional Authority   Authority attributed by title or ancestry, such as a king or a pope might claim, is **traditional authority.** Because it seems counter to many of the core philosophical foundations of the United States, this kind of authority on its face seems mismatched to our culture. Yet, in many ways Americans respond to some less-flamboyant claims made courtesy of inheritance or family history. The number of presidents of large corporations, for example, who were sons of former presidents suggests something other than chance operating. Corporate heads and business tycoons are frequently members of the original family starting the enterprise. This is a subtle but still-present notion in our culture. It is probably less operant in human service agencies but is still discernible on occasion.

Charismatic Authority   This type of authority tends to be unstable, as charisma is a fickle entity, but it is highly present in U.S. organizations. In fact some may claim that it's the "American way!" As contrasted to traditional authority, the **charismatic authority** model suggests that a captivating personality (rather than heritage, ideas, skills, or commitments) is the variable required to gain consensual power. You see this kind of authority operating in state and national elections, for example, when movie stars and celebrities run for and win public office without experience or a clear-cut platform.

Rational/Legal Authority   This is based on ability to achieve and is persuasive rather than coercive. An example of **rational/legal authority** is Joyce, an agency employee who received solid training in program development, conducted extensive research in the local community, and is well known for her work with youth. She is likely to be persuasive in her appeal to initiate a new community youth program. This is the sort of authority you would expect to find in a bureaucracy. It is probably fair to say that even alternatives to bureaucracies usually hold up this kind of authority as ideal. We as a culture tend to value what seems rational and well founded. However, it would be a mistake, in my view, to dismiss the influence of traditional and charismatic authority as obsolete. Not all decisions or patterns of power are logical or fair. Furthermore, there are probably times when people really don't want to act out of logic alone, when other matters of value may be more important.

Interfaces among Dimensions of Organizations

You have learned several dimensions of organizations in this chapter that influence both the way practice is carried out and the worker's experience. The discussion focused more on defining some of the variables, such as structure, and made only a few of the many connections between them. You have probably noticed that some variables are more likely than others to be associated with certain other dimensions. For example, an agency whose purpose reflects a social movement and ideological position, such as a battered women's shelter, is more likely to adopt a team structure rather than an intricately bureaucratic one. The "flatter" hierarchy of this kind of organization, arising from feminist organizational roots, is also more likely to be subject to charismatic or rational authority, as workers with interpersonal strengths may tend to take on leadership even without formal endorsement.

These are not iron-clad associations and should not be looked at as standard or prescriptive in any way, but rather as likely or consistent. The connections are meant to help you understand the nature of organizations and develop a framework for examining their distinctions and impact on workers. Ultimately, that understanding should assist you in discerning what combination of dimensions (for example, a flexible team and a flat hierarchy) best fits your talents and work style. Finally, this understanding should contribute to your knowledge of how agencies in various environments help clients reach their goals.

SOCIAL WORK PRACTICE IN SOCIAL AGENCIES

Much of the previous discussion applies to social work agencies as well as organizational dimensions in general. Let us turn now to the specific culture of social work agencies and roles and how you might make sense of them.

Understanding the Culture

Organizational culture consists of history, philosophy, styles of communication, patterns of decision making, stories, expectations, collected preferred personal styles of workers, and myths, along with behaviors and rules, which are widely understood and may or may not be reflected in the agency's mission statement. Answers to relatively mundane questions, such as whether workers should expect to put in overtime without compensation or whether student interns should carry beepers while on call, represent the types of issues that are shaped by sometimes less than obvious cultural assumptions. The other organizational variables we've explored, such as purpose, structure, and power relations are all likely to have an impact on the culture. See Exhibit 9.1 to review some of the facets of your own organizational style.

EXHIBIT 9.1

Rate Your Organizational Style

Using the key, rate yourself on the items listed here to review your organizational style. Add other items you think are important. Be prepared to discuss this survey in class and to apply it to your field placement. What obstacles do you encounter in fulfilling these points?

☐ I offer positive feedback to my colleagues for behaviors that contribute to effective services.

☐ I involve my colleagues in seeking changes in policies and programs that affect service quality.

☐ I value learning about my colleagues' points of view.

☐ I seek feedback that will help me to enhance my skills and knowledge.

☐ When I have a complaint, I discuss it with the person involved rather than talk about it behind her or his back.

☐ I involve others in arranging opportunities to discuss practice/policy issues/topics.

☐ I write notes of congratulations to others regarding professional or personal events/accomplishments.

☐ I come prepared for team meetings and case conferences.

☐ _____

☐ _____

Key: **0** (not at all)   **1** (a little)   **2** (a fair amount)   **3** (a great deal)   **4** (best that could be)

Source: Gambrill, E., 1997, p. 594

 Web Links

Explore the demand for human rights for women and families internationally at the Madre Web site. Go to the history and mission for an example of a broad mission statement with specific goals.

The idea of "organizational culture" is very broad and somewhat imprecise. It is a useful concept but not always distinctly focused. Here we will explore some additional variables, identifying a few of the more formal concrete artifacts representing culture and then some of the more informal subtleties.

Mission Statement   Nearly all social work agencies have **mission statements,** which can be exceedingly useful in that they are usually concise and cut to the quick of what the agency is setting about to do and with whom it works. Most agencies spend considerable effort crafting a statement that clearly provides the reader with the reasons the agency exists. One disadvantage of overrelying on a mission statement is that its very brevity necessarily restricts particular details you might find useful (how clients, as well as workers, are treated; whether the agency is hierarchical or more collegial, for example). Still, the mission statement can tell you a lot about an organization.

Physical, Material Surroundings   What does the agency look like? Few social work agencies find themselves housed in luxurious surroundings (and you might be suspicious if they did), but the physical atmosphere of an agency can reflect a great deal about its culture (Weeks, 2004). If client areas are dark, messy, or lacking in privacy, there may be some reason to question how clients are viewed. Are there places for staff to gather to do business? To socialize? Are offices decorated with posters or plants or personal effects? Although it is a mistake to overinterpret such signs, they can suggest areas for further exploration.

Statements Made about Itself   Many agencies have occasion to describe themselves in unofficial ways that may reflect a more day-to-day reality than the formal statements do. Newspaper articles about particular programs, clips on staff members, or introductory pieces for tentative partnerships or community forums provide clues about the flavor of the work and the way the agency supports its workers to do the work.

Language   The language used in agency settings not only reflects how the workers view each other, their work, and their clients, but also constitutes those views. That is, language shapes the thoughts and feelings put into words as well as reflecting them. This postmodern notion about the role of language and the way people create and sustain meanings based on it is discussed in earlier chapters (particularly in Chapter 2). By *language* here, I mean not only specific words, but also tone, quality of respect, range of sentiment, and degree of empathy.

Staff use of language that is disrespectful of clients is a serious issue in agencies not only because it violates the *Code of Ethics,* but because it violates the core commitment to respect people and treat them with dignity. Further, it creates that disrespect in others. It is not altogether unusual to hear of new workers "settling into" the pejorative language patterns in use and calling it "adjustment." The language used by staff in talking about each other and about other community resources and agencies also reveals this aspect of culture. As you would expect, it is likely to be consistent with the kind of valuing reflected in talk about clients.

Procedures   Simple procedures, such as the manner in which a new client is greeted or called for an appointment while in the waiting room, or given paperwork, can make a great deal of difference to the overall experience of "clienthood." Workers must be respectful and sensitive about fees, confidentiality, expectations regarding appointment times, and negotiations in scheduling. These aspects of working with clients are relevant not only as an individual practitioner's expression of respect but also as clearly understood agency policy. Exhibit 9.2 gives you an opportunity to assess how people are treated in your agency, or one that you are considering. Note that the concern for dignity includes employees as well as clients.

Social Justice/Diversity Factors   As you have probably noticed, aspects of social work practice that affirm social justice and support diversity are not the exclusive property of individual practitioners. We have looked at how justice and dignity can be nurtured and sustained in face-to-face practice with individuals,

 Web Links

The Canadian Centre for Social Justice site evolved from the Jesuit Centre for Social Faith and Justice with the primary goal of strengthening justice initiatives, particularly as they narrow the gap between rich and poor. The centre is committed to working for change in partnership with social movements and offers material in publications, media, and activist action.

EXHIBIT 9.2

Dignity Assessment and Human Services Guide

When you have completed this assessment, be prepared to identify the areas in which your field placement can improve. Be prepared to discuss in your practice class or your field seminar.

1. Persons seeking services from my agency are more likely to experience:

_____a poorly maintained waiting room

_____a place to sign in and be told to take a seat

_____having their name called out and being told to "follow me"

_____nonverbal cues from the staff that they are a bother

_____treatment that says "you are another case"

_____a warm and well-furnished waiting room

_____a courteous and personal greeting

_____being personally met and invited to the office

_____nonverbal cues that suggest we are glad they are here

_____treatment that says "you are a person"

2. Persons seeking services in my agency are more likely to be:

_____treated as problems that need to be solved

_____given treatment based on the medical model

_____seen as problems

_____seen as needing an expert

_____treated as partners in a mutual process of deciding how to proceed

_____provided treatment based on a competency model

_____seen as people with issues and needs

_____seen as the expert

3. Employees within my setting are more likely to experience:

_____getting written memos about new changes

_____being on the firing line alone

_____wishing for another job

_____feeling like their consumers are not important to the agency

_____feeling like they are a drain to the community

_____feeling unimportant to the agency

_____lack of respect for other employees

_____being asked for input about new changes

_____being supported in their roles

_____joy in coming to work

_____feeling their consumers are important to the agency

_____feeling like they are a resource to the community

_____feeling important to the agency

_____respect for other employees

4. My experience with the context tells me that:

_____respect for human diversity is ignored

_____membership in the community is blocked to those who are different

_____social services are at best tolerated

_____respect for human diversity is valued

_____membership in the community is open to all

_____social services are willingly supported

Source: Locke, Garrison & Winship, 1998, pp. 278–279

groups, and families. Organizations must also reflect these concerns in order to avoid the disconnects that clients sometimes register when they find their workers to be "nice people" but feel victimized by agency practices. In these times of increased accountability to clients, workers need to go beyond concerns for the internal administrative practices of agency function so that they also attend to the dimensions that have particular and direct relevance to its constituents—or those who would be constituents if they felt welcome.

Posters, magazines, or signs in the client waiting area that are in the language of the group convey a welcome. Activities and services that clearly take into account cultural values (for example, a neighborhood dinner that respects ethnic food restrictions) send a message. Many ethnically dominant white middle-class practitioners struggle in their individual, professional identity to become competent in working with other cultures, and it is equally critical that agencies do the same kind of soul searching. Exhibit 9.3 addresses some of the assumptions that underlie agency practices and approaches that are critical in establishing a helping center for people within their social locations.

Web Links

Amnesty International (AI) is an independent worldwide movement of people who campaign for internationally recognized human rights. Its mission is to engage in research and action in order to prevent and end abuses of the rights to physical and mental integrity, freedom of conscience and expression, and freedom from discrimination within the context of its work to promote all human rights.

Getting Along in Host Settings

Many social workers practice in **host settings**, such as hospitals, nursing homes, public and private schools, and correctional facilities, which frequently have a social work presence. Various programs maintained by the court system, aimed at diversion or advocacy efforts, often include social workers. Substance abuse treatment centers, housing programs, and many disability projects may hire full-time practitioners or part-time consultants. A number of organizational aspects to this phenomenon may challenge the worker as well as offering her or him many diverse opportunities. We will look at two of these here, that of being a guest in a host setting, and being a member of an interdisciplinary team.

Guest Status   Just as it does in the social world, guest status in host agencies carries both expectations and privilege. The problem is that the metaphor may not seem consistent with the kind of work that most practitioners want to do. Let us look at the experience of Diane to illustrate this.

Diane is a recent graduate of a BSW program in social work and is hired to be the discharge worker in a tightly run residential psychiatric treatment center. A psychiatrist on the center's staff serves as medical director. A public health administrator is the executive director. Diane is the first social worker this center has employed. The nursing staff had generally carried out the discharge work until the growing numbers of patients and their earlier discharges required a more focused approach. Diane is welcomed warmly by staff, who are very glad to see her because they hope she will fill an acute need. Diane will, in the best scenario, learn a lot in this location because she is exposed to very different views on some

EXHIBIT 9.3

Basic Assumptions across Systems or Agencies for Cultural Competence

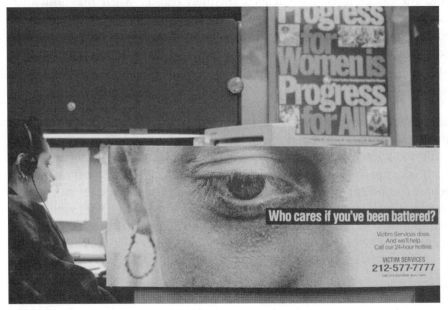

Validating client experience.

Identify any items with which you disagree and be prepared to discuss in class.

- Respects the unique, culturally defined needs of various client populations.
- Acknowledges culture as a predominant force in shaping behaviors, values, and institutions.
- Views natural systems (family, community, church, healers, etc.) as primary mechanism of support for minority populations.
- Starts with the "family" as defined by each culture, as the primary and preferred point of intervention.
- Acknowledges that minority people are served in varying degrees by the natural system.
- Recognizes that the concepts of "family," "community," etc., are different from various cultures and even for subgroups within cultures.
- Believes that diversity within cultures is as important as diversity between cultures.
- Functions with the awareness that the dignity of the person is not guaranteed unless the dignity of his/her people is preserved.
- Understands that minority clients are usually best served by persons who are part of or in tune with their culture.
- Acknowledges and accepts that cultural differences exist and have an impact on service delivery.

- Treats clients in the context of their minority status, which creates unique mental health issues for minority individuals, including issues related to self-esteem, identity formation, isolation, and role assumptions.
- Advocates for effective services on the basis that the absence of cultural competence anywhere is a threat to competent services everywhere.
- Respects the family as indispensable to understanding the individual, because the family provides the context within which the person functions and is the primary support network of its members.
- Recognizes that the thought patterns of non-Western peoples, though different, are equally valid and influence how clients view problems and solutions.
- Respects cultural preferences which value process rather than product and harmony or balance within one's life rather than achievement.
- Acknowledges that when working with minority clients, process is as important as product.
- Recognizes that taking the best of both worlds enhances the capacity of all.
- Recognizes that minority people have to at least be bicultural, which in turn creates its own set of mental health issues such as identity conflicts resulting from assimilation, etc.
- Functions with the knowledge that behaviors exist which are adjustments to being different.
- Understand when values of minority groups are in conflict with dominant society values.

EXHIBIT 9.3

continued

Source: From Cross, Bazron, Dennis & Isaacs, M.R., 1989

of the same issues she has training and experience in (such as ethical commitments and treatment strategies), and she also has the opportunity to observe first-hand how these views differ in real terms, or functionally. These can be enriching experiences that are available because of the diversity in the setting.

However, Diane discovers quickly that she has no role in any of the decision making regarding who gets discharged at what time; she is expected to act as a technician in carrying out the instructions of others. This is not because Diane is disliked or not seen as competent; it is simply because she is seen as extraneous to the discharge (medical) decisions at hand. Further, when Diane notices that some of the staff are not treating patients with dignity, she is ambivalent about whether she has a right, or the nerve, to speak up.

Meanwhile, she begins to feel undervalued—like a guest who has no say in what's for dinner and isn't welcome to criticize the menu. The center is, after all, a medical facility with medical issues to worry about. She knows she has much more to give this institution than mechanical placements of patients into community nursing or care homes. Diane will want to articulate what she can offer in a way that will facilitate the staff's growth rather than engendering their resistance and resentment. Specifically, part of her task will be to engage in an ongoing dialogue with staff about the complexities of discharge planning (for example, the need for day programming, work, training, housing, emotional support, family support, income support). In addition, she may at some point want to take on some of the aspects of the center's practices that are inconsistent with socially just and respectful treatment.

As you can see, this can be a difficult business, and no worker is likely to be successful by barging in on the first day and challenging broad and time-honored practices of another discipline. On the other hand, social workers need not give up their stake in how a facility functions because as guests they feel it belongs to another discipline, which in turn relieves them of responsibility for how clients are treated.

The Social Work Library

For another perspective on interdisciplinary work, see Fast's article.

Interdisciplinary Teams   Projects and programs that include members of several disciplines (such as medicine, public policy, and social work) create **interdisciplinary teams.** These can provide an enriching and exciting atmosphere in which to practice social work. Although social work educators may emphasize regularly that practitioners need to look at the whole person in an integrated conceptualization of the work to be done, the truth is that nearly all service provision, across disciplines, is highly fragmented. It is not unusual to discover that a family you are seeing has as many as seven or eight other service providers—for example, vocational counselors, therapists, psychologists for cognitive skills work, income maintenance specialists, physicians for medication checks, and support workers.

You may be wondering what the difference is between working in a host setting with other disciplines and working in an interdisciplinary context. The key concept here is that in a truly interdisciplinary commitment, no single discipline is privileged over another—the value is in the total contribution of an integrated approach. In order to be effective, each discipline must honestly value each of the others. Workers need especially effective collaborative skills when working with other professionals, as well as skills in tolerating and resolving conflicts. Although this seems consistent with social work values of respect for other views and diverse approaches, it is much more difficult to carry out than you might expect! We are all members of larger cultures and have internalized many biases that exist in them. For example, in many medically oriented interdisciplinary teams, physicians are dominant and appear to have a privileged standpoint. Also, the socialization of most professions can encourage somewhat narrow views among initiates so that there is a tendency to think your own discipline is more humane than others, or at least more "right." Nevertheless, such settings offer vast opportunities to wrestle with the challenges of providing an integrated, highly skilled approach in the best interests of clients, as well as to explore the internal dynamics of teaming through the lens of multiple realities.

ORGANIZATIONAL CHANGE

So far in this chapter we have explored several means to assess or describe attributes of the organization and of social work practices within agency settings. At this point we will look at the implications of this kind of assessment as they suggest ways that you might participate in monitoring your agency and in facilitating active efforts to make changes in it.

The Social Work Library

See Hyde's article on multicultural development to explore an important contemporary issue in organizational change.

Organizations are entities that change in much the same way people do. Entrenched bureaucracies, like rigid personalities, tend to change slowly. More open agencies, like people, tend to make purposeful changes more easily. Regardless of purpose, however, change occurs. This is why an erosion of commitment can occur in some organizations as workers and their visions change and original investments are diluted, reshaped, or are no longer applicable. Most organizations can trace a history of rules that don't seem to have any ongoing purpose beyond "we've always done it that way."

There are at least three phenomena that force or inspire organizations to change:

- *Inertia:* This phenomenon both impedes change and leads to change. For example, when an agency does not respond to the needs inherent in the shifting population patterns of the community, it is likely to find itself without clients and/or lose its funding; at, or most likely well before, that point its survival will require a more effective response to changing conditions.

- *Comprehensive, careful assessment of the totality of the organization's functioning:* This kind of assessment is often instigated by the executive director or the head of the board of directors in response to funding or programmatic issues that suggest a large-scale overhaul is needed. **Strategic plans**, which are comprehensive, formal plans for change, sometimes are developed out of this sense of shifting need and usually involve incremental, highly focused modifications that are estimated to contribute to a preferred result.

- *Concern about some particular aspect of agency functioning:* Workers' concerns for a disrespectful, wrong, ineffective, wasteful, or in some other way troubling aspect of service may be the most accessible route for staff to use to effect change. They may notice first from the front lines when clients experience difficulty with agency practices, and they can voice their ad hoc concerns without undertaking the responsibility for developing a brand-new management plan.

Let us take a closer look at this third process. Both experienced and novice workers will benefit from developing some political savvy about the challenges of making changes in an agency. Careful consideration of several issues regarding the agency's willingness and capacity to change, along with some typical obstacles to change, can equip you in preparing to enter the change arena. The recognition of opportunities and openings through dialogue are also components here.

Considerations Before Fomenting Change

Before confronting colleagues with your proposal for change, you will want to be as specific as possible regarding what your concern is. Use client examples when feasible. Vague statements of "discomfort" about things that are "not right" are not likely to be as convincing as statements put in clear, behavioral, and values-oriented terms. Translate what you see as problems for clients into what the agency needs to do. For example, if you think the problem is that pregnant adolescents in your youth agency have nowhere to go, consider various options related to how your agency should respond. Should it provide shelter? Should it facilitate referral to housing agencies? Should it coordinate with other youth programs? This translation of problem into need will help others understand what they can do to meet the demands of the situation. Here are some additional suggestions:

- If you suggest any kind of tentative approach, be careful that it doesn't implicate additional or more difficult work for a particular employee or category of employees.

- Get some history on the agency's record of making policy or program changes. Did such decisions induce widespread disgruntlement? Were they perceived as coming from the top down, that is, made in an authoritarian way? Long-term co-employees are useful, although not unbiased, sources for this kind of history.

- Get an idea of how well supported your or your group's ideas are across the agency. Can you anticipate resistance in some places? Apathy? Support?

- Make sure you are well acquainted with the agency's mission statement and any statements of vision or values. Is the change you'd like to see compatible with the agency's formal or informal positioning?

- Make sure you understand the structure of the agency, including subgroupings, and divergent goals. How do individuals fit into this scheme? Are there charismatic leaders in one system and not another? Is any subsystem more likely to agree with your position than another?

- Make sure you understand the impact your suggestions may have on all members of the agency.

These are only a few of the possible areas that may be applicable when thinking about changes in your agency. You can probably think of others that speak more specifically to your particular situation. The overall message is that you will want to be careful and comprehensive when you propose changes to agency functioning. There's quite a difference between casual grumbling regarding the fact that the watercooler in the clients' waiting area is out of water (as well founded as that may be) and a serious, thoughtful proposal for doing agency business differently.

Obstacles to Change

After you have assumed the role of advocating change, you will likely be confronted with one or more obstacles. You are probably familiar with some of these; in fact, you might have experienced their effects:

- Environmental constraints, including funding issues, limited resources, and competition over resources, all can act as obstacles to change.

- Personal history and conflicts in an agency can influence attitudes toward suggestions for change, and obstacles may seem to have little to do with the issues directly involved. For example, a senior staff member may seem to automatically reject any suggestion by another staff member, possibly because of prior differences and persistent bad feeling.

- Individual worldview issues, such as ideas about the general potential for change in people, the wisdom of trusting nonexperts, and a fear of conflict (among others), can influence reactions to proposals for change. For example, if three out of four of the agency's supervisors don't believe clients should have input into programming, your suggestions regarding client inclusion in program planning are not likely to be well received initially. You will need to do more work.

- External relationships with other community agencies may affect the climate of change. For example, if a suggested change in substance abuse services is perceived as competition in programming or unnecessary duplication of the services of other agencies, workers may resist it (and perhaps rightfully).

A list of obstacles might go on for many pages. Again, consider as many of the constraining and comprehensive variables as possible. These should be seen not as reasons to give up change efforts, but rather as useful information in preparing for whatever challenge lies ahead.

Strategic Tinkering

"Organizational tinkering" is a time-honored and lower-key substitute for undertaking wide-range or ambitious changes (Pawlak, 1976). Because large-scale changes can be difficult to take on from within, tinkering is a viable alternative in the right circumstances. One of the more strategic time periods in which to tinker is between administrations when there is a lame-duck period during which changes are put on hold until the new administrator arrives. Workers can take advantage of this period by taking the following actions:

- Complete a favorite project earlier than scheduled.

- Slow down a project that has been controversial.

- Organize your peers to suggest changes that were not acceptable to the outgoing administrator.

- Develop and propose criteria for choosing a new administrator.

- Ask to participate on the search committee for the new administrator.

- Write a paper describing your position for the new administrator.

- Suggest changes in the governance rules to increase widespread participation in decision making.

- Suggest that a workgroup facilitate the transition between former and new administrator.

Many of these tinkerings (especially those relating to participation in governance) might be feasible on an ongoing basis or in times other than bureaucratic succession, and they can all be taken up by front-line workers with full caseloads.

Ongoing Dialogue about Change

In a postmodern view of change, the function of dialogue plays an increasingly visible and powerful role. Recognizing the power of language, the process of social meaning making, and the potential for taking part in reshaping their world, social workers can take up and engage with bureaucratic practice components (and people) to influence the development of individual and organizational approaches. There is nothing inevitable about the arrangements that guide institutions or practice—people have made them what they are, and people can make them different. You can make changes by using dialogue to explore the ideas of reality that you and others hold, the assumptions that you and others take for granted, the different perceptions regarding peoples' needs and interests, and the values and ideologies used in making choices (Gil, 1998a). This is not an easy or quick process, but it is an important one.

Likewise, informal channels can constitute one of the more effective ways to address the organizational constraints that get in the way of human rights practice (Ife, 2001). If you take a social constructionist perspective here; that is, if you believe that your view of social reality is shaped by social processes, you can see that the potential for this kind of interchange is great. The practice, then, of continuous, patient, and genuine dialogue, which includes a willingness to be changed as well as to change, may prove to be one of the more effective tools in confronting structural barriers and building more responsive organizations over time. See Exhibit 9.4 for an interesting "code of ethics" for workers involved in organizational development.

EXHIBIT 9.4

Code of Ethics for Social Organization Development: A Proposed Oath of Conduct

Committing to oath of conduct.

I will begin my involvement by developing a grasp of the organization members' unique subjective appreciation of the organization, despite whatever critical stand I may take later toward the organization.

I will determine for myself the degree to which the overall purposes of the agency are compatible with my personal values and the norms of the social work profession.

I will be frank in revealing my values and assumptions, explaining my goals, and describing the techniques and processes I will use to achieve them.

I will not impose my viewpoint on the agency. I will work to create a climate in which moral-ethical issues may be critically evaluated, and I may even play an active part in that criticism.

I will work to bring about shared responsibility, accountability, worker involvement, and mutual engagement in task accomplishment and problem solving.

I will work to bring about an institutional culture compatible with human dignity and self-determination.

I will work to bring about changes in either the organization's ends or means to achieve a healthier setting for the agency's employees and its clientele.

Source: Brueggemann, 2002

Theoretical Perspectives on Organizational Change

How do organizations actually change once they commit themselves to it? Here we will briefly consider three theoretical perspectives that attempt to describe the processes involved and explore what that might mean for you as the worker:

- Self-learning model

- Systems model

- Power-politics model

You can probably recognize some dimensions that you have experienced in all of these models, in spite of their diversity. No agency, composed of people as agencies are, is likely to function completely within the confines of one model. It will be useful for you to notice how your agency reflects these approaches to change.

The **self-learning model** asserts that the contemporary organizational climate, which emphasizes accountability and accessibility to clients, information technology, and a tight resource pool, leads to the wisdom of self-correction in agencies (Gambrill, 1997). This involves ongoing monitoring and solicitation of feedback from clients and other stakeholders who provide information about their experiences with services. This model also assumes a rational process in which all members of an agency agree on the general goals, means, and ultimate vision for the work and will work together to attain them.

Although it is naïve to believe that any agency will inspire universal loyalty to a set of goals without dissent of any kind, the self-learning model has widespread applicability in small, well-focused organizations with clear goals and values because it relies on common ground, the wisdom and creativity of people, and the capacity of groups to develop positive directions. We will explore a critical skill for the actualization of this model, participatory decision making, later in this chapter.

The **systems model** recognizes the agency as a system composed of many individuals, subsystems, rules, roles, and processes operating within the wider environment. This model asserts that efforts involved in agency maintenance and survival need to be balanced with specific achievement goals. Job stress, staff disagreements, and social and emotional needs of employees need to be considered and addressed because they have potential to divert workers from their original commitments. Change efforts in this model are more likely to include attending to such maintenance functions as clarification of goals, improving morale, and emphasizing better communication among employees.

The systems model is represented in such activities as agency retreats, training sessions, and requests for consultation regarding staff relations or in redefining agency direction (Campbell, 2000). In an important respect, this approach recognizes the impact of human service work by acknowledging its stresses and recognizing the necessity to attend to the human side of the professionals who constitute the organization and engage in the work.

Assuming that the agency is essentially a political body, the **power-politics model** emphasizes competition for resources, personal advancement, and inter- and intrapower struggles. It asserts that the primary path to change requires strategic access to the people who have the greatest power and primary influence. A characteristic tactic is to convince any people asked to effect change from within that it will be in their best personal interests as well as the agency's. Instigation of pressure from outside sources, such as the media, is also seen as potentially necessary and instrumental in facilitating change.

This last model may seem to have a ruthless quality to it, but many of its principles are worth remembering, even if you find the assumptions to be cynical. In large bureaucratic environments, the ideas in this model may seem quite visible. The value of them, I believe, is that they point to some of the more challenging human-nature components in organizational functioning that do, in fact, exist on one level or another in almost any setting. They also reflect the realities of conflict and the struggle for resources that are a part of the social location of all agencies.

INNOVATIVE WAYS OF DOING BUSINESS

Although some of the constraints to change may seem daunting, you can take heart in recognizing the many constructive responses that have developed among workers, administrators, clients, and community stakeholders. These relate to approaches that will enhance the way social workers and social work agencies do business. We will look at only two examples here. They focus on an internal process in (1) participatory decision making and (2) an interorganizational coalition in the form of a local partnership.

Participatory Decision Making

In Kaner's *A Facilitator's Guide to Participatory Decision Making* (1996), the foreword introduces two major ideas. The first asserts that people must participate in and "own" the solutions to the problems of their organizations, or those solutions will fail. The second idea holds that an organization's success is due not only to its products and services but to its ability to capture and focus the talents and goodwill that reside in its members. These two reflections provide social workers with some good advice regarding a helpful process of decision making for the self-learning organization. Let us take a look at this model.

The Model Many organizational groups, when left to business-as-usual decision-making techniques, get bogged down in business-cultural values that inhibit what could be a rewarding and creative process. This business orientation encourages an overemphasis on polished arguments, fast thinking, slick presentations, and premature conclusions that tend to stifle diverse ideas in order to facilitate a smooth process for arriving at decisions quickly and easily. The result is that some potentially useful ideas are labeled impractical or impossible or simply stupid. This fosters a climate in which some members are silent or sullen, assuming they have nothing to say that anyone else will consider worthwhile and/or that the decision makers have heard all possible ideas anyway. The group barely tolerates new ideas or different views in this culture and certainly doesn't consider them seriously as members rehash old opinions and positions. Group members don't engage in expanding the vision because they believe such an effort would involve conflict, take too much time, require too much work, or otherwise be too bothersome. They arrive at decisions that are based on the ideas of those holding the most influence in the recent past and that are frequently not owned by other constituents.

The major obstacle to genuine, full participation lies in bypassing a necessary stage of struggle (called the "Groan Zone," Kaner, 1996, p. 19). In this **divergent process**, ideas emerge that are not necessarily smoothly put, popular, or apparently headed toward a decision point, even though they may be new and creative. This groan zone is characterized by confusion and frustration, and many people find it difficult to tolerate the ambiguity or the discomfort inherent in trying to integrate divergent ideas. But the integration is where the richness is, and it is also the vehicle for truly **participatory decision making**, in which all voices are heard and respected. With adequate orientation, a genuine commitment to full participation, and skillful facilitation, the group can undertake, engage in, and negotiate this difficult phase effectively. On the other side of a successful struggle, a **convergent process** (coming together) emerges that incorporates the exploration of diverse and useful principles, creative reframing of the groan zone struggle, and strengthening of useful ideas as the process heads toward an inclusive decision point (p. 185). See Table 9.1 for a sample of the convergent process as it reframes the problems experienced by organization members.

Participatory Values Four core values are critical to participatory decision making: full participation, mutual understanding, inclusive solutions, shared responsibility. These create an underlying framework for the entire process and are consistent with the values inherent to social justice, diversity, and human rights. They also represent postmodern approaches in which the voices of all stakeholders are respected, not just the most eloquent, quick thinking, and fast talking among members.

The convergent process in participatory decision making is reflected in reframing the organization's presenting problems.

TABLE 9.1

Participatory Decision Making

PRESENTING PROBLEM	REFRAMED PROBLEM
It's them.	It's all of us.
It's a problem.	It's an opportunity.
Our goal is unachievable.	We don't have our goal broken into realistic steps.
We don't have enough resources.	We are wasting the resources we do have.
Our employees are incompetent.	Our employees don't have enough time to do a quality job.
We can't get along with each other.	We haven't made the commitment to work through our feelings toward one another.
We don't have any power in this system.	We haven't found our leverage points in this system.

Source: Adapted from Kaner, 1996

Participants need to make a commitment to struggle through the process in order to arrive at a sustainable agreement to which everyone has contributed. The skill of **suspended judgment,** which involves listening to ideas without making immediate and premature decisions on them, is critical here. Finally, in this decision-making model, participants have to tolerate the pressure and learn to trust the process of inclusion as well as trust their fellow decision makers. When decisions are based on inclusive processes, all participants will buy into them, increasing their utility and promise for the future. You might find it useful to consider how your agency made the last important decision in which you were involved. To what degree was it inclusive? Was there a willingness to struggle with divergent ideas in the groan zone? How might the process have been different? With what result?

Local Partnerships: Human Rights in the Real World

Although social workers can take guidance and inspiration from well-known or published efforts, they can also learn from the potential impact that **local partnerships** or **interorganizational coalitions** have on the context of practice. These structures represent cooperative agreements, formal or informal, among local institutions, programs, agencies, or the like, usually for the accomplishment of a specific purpose. I will describe one such partnership.

Arising originally from local commitments to a domestic violence agency, an idea was proposed by a professor in the department of social work at the University of Vermont. She envisioned a community-wide network of agencies that would partner with the university to address the culture of violence across the state. Box 9.3 includes a summary of this collective's vision, purposes, and positions, as well as the working definitions of their core values.

BOX 9.3

The Anti-Violence Partnership

COMMUNITY COLLABORATION AT THE UNIVERSITY OF VERMONT: VISION, MISSION STATEMENT, PHILOSOPHY, GOALS, ACTIVITIES, DEFINITIONS

Vision
We Envision: Vermont as a civil society safe, just, and free from violence.

Mission Statement
The Anti-Violence [Partnership][1] supports and sustains unified approaches within the community to understand and change the existence and acceptance of violence and works toward its prevention and elimination. The [Partnership] promotes, protects, and enhances the quality of life of those victimized by a culture of violence.

[Partnership] Philosophy
The [Partnership] subscribes to the belief that safety is a fundamental human right and that violence is a violation of this right.

Our Values and Ethics
The mission of the [Partnership] rests on the core values of *safety, agency, restoration, accountability,* and *justice.* The core values of the [Partnership] inform broad ethical principles. These principles guide its practices, relationships, and self-assessment, particularly in making decisions regarding ethical issues. These are set forth as follows:

- The [Partnership's] central ethical obligations are to protect and advance the right to safety and to promote the community's responsibility and capacity to ensure it.
- The [Partnership] places the interests of those who are endangered and victimized by violence above its own self-interests.
- The [Partnership] promotes meaningful victim/survivor participation in defining safe and just practices.
- The [Partnership] holds its own practices and relationships to the same standards of accountability that it promotes for others.
- The [Partnership] pursues social and individual change.

The Partnership's activities include discovering and sharing information through research, evaluation, and facilitated dialogue, as well as providing technical assistance in the way of coalition building, policy development, cross trainings, grant writing assistance, and program design.

WORKING DEFINITIONS OF THE VALUES OF THE ANTI-VIOLENCE PARTNERSHIP

Safety
(Victim/Survivor-centered): No violation of one's person, no intrusion into one's home, and a reduction of fear (Hart, 2000, cited in Danis & Harris, 2000).[2]

Agency

(Victim/Survivor-centered): The ability to make and implement decisions free from inter-ference from the perpetrator (Hart).

Restoration

(Victim/Survivor-centered): Returning health, relationships with children and family, and emotional well-being as well as compensation and replacement of all destroyed posses-sions and payment for all incurred medical, counseling, and other damage costs created by the perpetrator (adapted from Hart).

Accountability

(Perpetrator and Community-centered): Perpetrators stopping their violence, giving up the belief that they have direct ownership of the victim, and being accountable to both the victim and the community. Communities holding perpetrators accountable as victims/survivors define this, while simultaneously not holding victims/survivors responsi-ble for perpetrator's actions (adapted from Hart).

Justice

(Victim/Survivor and Community-centered): The legal, judicial, social, economic, and other aspects which constitute the basis of a society upholding the dignity of its members, and ensuring security and integrity of persons ... the pursuit of justice also has wider implica-tions, satisfaction of basic human needs and the equitable sharing of [social and] material resources (United Nations, 1992, p. 16).[3]

---

[1]Originally "Institute."

[2]Danis, F., & Harris, M. (Spring/Summer 2000). CSWE participates in national meeting on domestic violence. *Social Work Education Reporter, 48,* 7 & 23.

[3]United Nations (1992). *Teaching and learning about human rights: A manual for school of social work and the social work profession.* New York: Author.

Source: From Roche, 2001

BOX 9.3

continued

There are several dimensions of this work to notice. First it is explicitly human rights based in its commitments. The language and obligations of the partnership are steeped in the social justice issues of human needs and the human rights perspectives of "ensuring the security and integrity of persons" (Rocher, 2001, p. 4) as well as safety. The partnership also embeds its concerns regarding domestic violence within the social location of cultural violence as a broader phenomenon, yet retains its original sensitivity to its inspirational roots and illustrates its philosophy through the lens of violence against women (see the section on values and ethics). Finally, the infusion of its ethics is made discrete through its refinement and explication of a clear statement regarding each of the guiding values of the collective partnership. It explicitly casts the

 Web Links

The United Nations site was created in 1997 to provide Internet space for discussion of issues of gender equality. Do the Women Watch "gateway" for information and resources on these issues.

Web Links

The Family Violence Prevention Fund (FVPF) has worked to end violence against women and children around the world. It was instrumental in developing the landmark Violence Against Women Act passed by Congress in 1994.

 Web Links

For an interesting view of how young people have responded to violence, see the site developed by teenagers in Massachusetts and geared toward helping them intervene in dating violence or other violent relationships among people they know.

interests of the endangered above those of its own survival (in contrast to some coalitions for whom the primary goal is the coalition). This work is remarkable in that it is a motivational example of what a few people who hold an abiding commitment, possess strong and sophisticated organizational skills, and are willing to engage in an enormous amount of work can accomplish.

Ongoing Evaluation

As a practitioner you are probably not likely to take on large organizational re-structuring projects at this point in your career, but you might certainly partic-ipate in organizational program evaluations and change. When you do, you will want to explore your own role in these and get feedback from peers and su-pervisors on your work. Since there are more layers, involving more people than in direct practice, you will particularly want to check in with peers and staff when you are organizing or participating in change efforts from within. Periodic review of the general considerations discussed earlier in "Considera-tions Before Fomenting Change" (and any others you discover) may help direct your attention to trouble spots. Misunderstanding, omissions, and commis-sions are all highly likely in change efforts. For example, one of your colleagues may perceive you as hostile or unduly critical if you advocate for change in a program in which she or he has a vested interest. You may simply want to make a good program better. Attention to relationships with peers and staff and eth-ical positioning in change efforts is as important in agency business as it is in client services.

STRAIGHT TALK ABOUT ORGANIZATIONAL LIFE

This chapter has highlighted both the most challenging and the most exhila-rating aspects of social work practice in an organizational setting. It is often tempting to see the organization as the "bad cop" in practice contexts because it so often seems to pose confounding or complex barriers to some of the most simple helping tasks. Although this can obviously be frustrating, there are at least two points that are helpful to remember. The first relates to loyalties and collusions, and the second relates to the personal price of making change efforts.

In much the same way that some people seem to like to blame their fami-lies for all that goes awry, some workers point to the organization when the work becomes challenging or proves more difficult than expected. This is partly because there are genuine constraints inherent in organizations that are not al-ways obvious at the beginning and should be addressed, and partly because it is sometimes easier for a worker to adopt a thoroughgoing cynicism that eases her or his sense of responsibility or even failure.

This is an understandable response, but the problem with it comes when practitioners start to collude with clients about the hopelessness of the agency and the fact that it stands in the way of the worker doing anything helpful. The worker may feel temporarily relieved by engaging the client in her or his desperation with the system, but that comfort may come at a cost to the client. This stymied stance conveys a difficult message to people looking for hope. In its most extreme implication, it may promote a generalized, scornful distrust of all such efforts as they seem to be ineptly carried out by do-gooders who are helpless and caught in troubled agency structures that say one thing in their mission statement and do quite another.

This is not to imply that the worker can never identify problematic agency policies or obstacles to clients. In fact, the heart of empowerment practice may lie in just that kind of working alliance with a client: a joint effort designed to promote more effective responses to particular clients and all clients. This is a different message from that sent by workers who are angry, frustrated, and unable to muster the skills or energy to address injustices and are simply negative and give up. In my view, any worker who consistently feels that kind of inability to function in a particular agency owes it to her- or himself, as well as the agency's clientele, to find another setting in which to practice.

On the other side of this issue, some workers will eagerly engage in efforts to uproot the direction of an agency with very little understanding about what makes bureaucracies or semibureaucratic structures so slow in making amendments. You may receive advice or supervision from more seasoned professionals who tell you not to bother trying to change anything, or not to change anything as a new or young worker, until you are so well established that you are not likely to be censured or fired. These positions, like many of this sort, carry a kernel of good sense along with a lot of chaff. As discussed earlier in this chapter, you need to think about many aspects before entering into an effort to change an institution that will most certainly respond by resisting. You need to know what the organizational strong and weak points are, and you need to know your own strengths and areas for growth. You need skills for working with people that apply to colleagues and bureaucrats as well as clients.

A worker who will never address any agency policy or constraint that she or he sees as problematic because of fear of criticism or even job loss is likely to have a difficult time in a social work career and, further, is likely to be ineffective. Social work practice as an occupation requires workers to take principled, well thought out, respectful risks across all settings in order to carry out the work of the profession.

CONCLUSION

Organizations represent an administrative layer that separates you from the client, as well as a structure that facilitates your work. They are many sided and may often seem challenging, with a life of their own that is hard to put your finger on. The structure of social work agencies is always changing, just as the people within them change, and with human service shifts in funding, relational collaboration, and accountability patterns, social workers in the next generation are likely to experience very different arrangements. Whatever their nature, organizations are important to practitioners on all levels because their impact is felt daily and shapes the work. It is worth making some sense of the organization you work in and attempting to reach some kind of peace with it so that you can make the most of your practice. You will not, I hope, sit passively as the opportunities to participate appear, but will take an increasingly active role in shaping the organizational life of the agency or partnership in and through which you work.

With these ideas of participation and shaping as grounding points for generalist social work, we are ready to explore the world of community practice in Chapter 10. As the discussion expands outward, into an ever-broadening circumference, you will find the community and its surrounds a compelling field that is ultimately as wide as the globe.

MAIN POINTS

- General organizational practice can be explored along a variety of dimensions that influence the worker. Among others, these include purposes, structures, and internal power relations.

- Social work in social agencies, as a kind of organization, is facilitated by understanding the culture that is reflected in physical and social arrangements. You will want to be aware of whether language used about the agency and among staff is respectful and the assumptions underlying agency practices are just.

- Social workers frequently work in host settings, such as hospitals and schools, either as a guest or part of an interdisciplinary team.

- Organizational change making can be prefaced and facilitated by analyzing various internal considerations and obstacles. Strategic tinkering, and ongoing dialogue are two methods for influencing change.

- Theoretical perspectives on how agencies actually change are reflected in diverse models that reflect worldviews. Three models are the self-learning model, the systems model, and the poltical power model.

- In spite of resistance to change, many organizations have been influenced positively by workers who have developed internal practices and interorganizational and local partnerships that contribute to new ways of looking at social work practice.

- The relationships you have with your agency will be a part of your practice. You need to know the organizational strong and weak points as well as your own strengths and areas for growth.

EXERCISES: PRACTICING SOCIAL WORK

Getting a Handle on Organizational Tension

Imagine you were hired as a social worker at the center that serves the Sanchez family a little over three months ago. As you've settled in to your job responsibilities, you notice some tensions within the agency. Several of your co-workers are grumbling at "the way things are around here" and your "honeymoon" period is definitely over.

As you consider why you feel so unsettled, you decide to assess the agency more systematically to see if you can pinpoint anything that potentially could be changed. Referring back to the chapter, and using your internship agency as a template for the center, conduct your own mini-assessment, addressing the following points briefly (one paragraph each):

- Purpose

- Structure of government

- Internal power relations

Next:

- Identify which of the theoretical perspectives described in the chapter you think is most relevant to the way the center (your agency) works as an agency. Support your answer.

- Based on what you know about the agency, describe some of the additional aspects of the culture.

- Identify what you think is the most effective strategy for making change at the center.

EXERCISES: THE SOCIAL WORK LIBRARY

Read Jonathan Fast's article on interdisciplinary conflict in a school-based health center. Locate and interview a social worker who works in a similar interdisciplinary context in your local community (from a hospital, school, nursing home, etc.). Using Fast's framework for analysis, identify one or two conflicts that have occurred in this setting and then select the method (from the three that Fast identifies) that most closely resembles the way in which the conflict was actually resolved. What were the lessons learned?

OTHER EXERCISES

Let's Not Fix What Ain't Broke

You're a social worker at the center under Melinda's supervision and work with adolescents on alcohol and drug treatment issues. Not long ago, you suggested in a staff meeting some ideas you have about extending the service hours of the agency so that families might have greater access to support and planning for their children. There was a fair amount of enthusiasm among most of workers and you agreed to the director's request that you put together a written proposal to be taken up in the next staff meeting.

When you go to your weekly supervision meeting, you discover that Melinda, as your supervisor, is quite angry with you. She becomes rather shrill and accuses you of not taking into account how much more work it would be for her to have to work evening hours. She would have to change her whole life around, she says, and make all kinds of other arrangements for child care as well as any social time with her friends.

This takes you by surprise. Your relationship with Melinda has always been cordial if not exceptionally close. How will you respond to her?

Identify two skills you would use and give examples of what you might say.

1) _____

2) _____

How would you then proceed in your proposal for the staff meeting?

a. Go ahead with the proposal and just pretend this never happened.

b. Give up the idea entirely and wait for another time.

c. Attempt to meet with her again when she was calmer, so you could explain your thinking.

d. Go to the head of the agency or someone "above" your supervisor.

e. Seek supervision from outside the agency on this question.

Generate other answers and compare with your peers.

Life at Work

Decide which structural model of agency governance discussed in the chapter is most likely to be the setting in which each of the following statements is made.

What other aspects of agency culture can you identify?

"My supervisor watches every move I make. He is so afraid I'll do something I'm not supposed to."

"In my agency, everyone takes a shift on the beeper, everyone cleans up and everyone takes a turn on cleaning the bathroom."

"I've been here for a year and I've never met the unit on the third floor."

"Everyone knows their own job in my agency; no one is confused about it."

"My supervisor is often here until 8 o'clock; she lives and breathes this place."

"In my agency there's a power cartel that gets to meet with the director."

"Things are never the same at my agency from week to week; I'm never sure what I'll be doing."

"My best friend in this agency suddenly became my supervisor!"

CHAPTER 10

Working in and with the Community

The world is on the move. Billions of people all over the world are yearning to be truly secure—free from fear and free from want and able to live in peace and dignity . . . the choice is not between multilateralism and unilateralism; it is between cooperation and catastrophe.

Kofi A. Annan, Secretary General, United Nations, 2003

WE TEND TO EXPERIENCE COMMUNITY, LIKE MANY CONCEPTS THAT are central to our lives, long before we define or analyze it. In the most basic sense, communities provide the place in which we find identity and meaning for ourselves as people, individuals, parents, children, lovers, friends, and social workers. **Community** is the structure, both tangible and metaphoric, that supports our connectedness to others over time.

This chapter examines community and your relationship to it, both as a practitioner working within it and as a change agent attempting to influence it. We will explore the lenses of type and function through which community is given meaning and then consider two methods of inquiry into its study. The chapter also discusses social work practice that is designed to change the community or to strengthen its responsiveness to its members. Within that topic, we will look briefly at classic and contemporary models and their implications for approaches and skills today. Finally, we will expand our vision to consider the global community as the ultimate collective and the concern of the future.

FROM THE INDIVIDUAL TO THE SOCIAL

Chapter 7 discussed the individualism that characterizes U.S. culture and frequently runs counter to the desire for connection or community. The human service system has reflected this societal preoccupation with individualism in its emphasis on the self and the perpetual pursuit of self-fulfillment. The yearning for community is resilient, however, even as it is threatened. The notion of **interdependence**—the idea that we are all dependent on one another—is a more natural (and accurate) human inclination than independence and has a great deal of resonance in practice models that emphasize health and recovery based on both professional and peer support.

In all its complexity, community is an important concept for social workers because of its ramifications for clients. It represents both connection and alienation. Communities play a critical role in clients' lives, as they shape their experiences and also influence workers' ability to affect outcomes. Even when workers never go outside of the traditional one-to-one social work relationship, the success of their efforts depends in large part on the nature and responsiveness of the community.

For example, if you are working with a young mother who is receiving welfare benefits and you are trying to assist her in finding shelter, the community's overall capacity to provide low-cost housing will influence your work. If your client can't find housing because local landlords won't rent to "welfare mothers," then you have another kind of community issue to face. Knowing how to tackle that problem, who makes the decisions, who has the power, who is working for more socially just responses, and who will work with you, will make a huge difference in your ability to help your client. You need to know your community at the very least, whether or not you envision working directly to change it.

The Social Work Library

See Reynolds' early study of the client/community relationship in social work practice.

Before we explore the many ideas associated with social work practice and the community, we will need to take a closer look at some of the distinctions in its definition and the nature of its functions. Let us begin by exploring community types.

TYPES OF COMMUNITY

Understanding the distinctions in community types will ground you for working within them and for conducting community assessments. This section describes three types that are often cited in the literature: communities of locality, communities of identity, and personal communities (Fellin, 1995).

Communities of Locality

When we talk of community, most of us think first of places, like Los Angeles, California, or Beer Bottle Crossing, Idaho. **Communities of locality** are structures of connectedness based on place. Large communities of locality, like Los Angeles, are likely to have several communities within them. Beer Bottle Crossing, as a much smaller community, is less diverse along some dimensions, such as ethnicity, but should not be thought of as uniform or completely homogenous, either.

Communities of locality may or may not have clear, physical boundaries, like a river, a mountain, or in the case of some planned communities, a gate or wall. Even though communities of locality are defined in relatively concrete terms, these may be experienced differently by their members. The planned community's gate, for example, may send out a forbidding message of exclusion to some and a comforting signal of safety to others. The degree to which people perceive themselves as full-fledged community members will depend on many dimensions, but access to the community's benefits is certainly among the most influential.

Communities of Identity

There are other sorts of communities that are certainly a part of your life. **Communities of identity** relate more to your affiliations than to place. There is a student community, an Asian community, a lesbian community, a veterans community, a black community, a skateboard community, and so it goes. These communities represent a common interest or identification with a group of people who share a similar sense of belonging. In some cases this kind of community may be relatively minor in your life (for example, the skateboard community may lose its fascination over time), and some represent the core of who you are (for some, the Jewish community plays this role; for others, the gay community, for example).

Communities of identity frequently play a significant role in the choices that social workers make about where and how they will commit their efforts. For example, many practitioners who have invested much of their work lives in practice settings such as shelters for battered women, residential care facilities for children with disabilities, or AIDS care agencies have made some sort of identification with the populations they serve. They may be **indigenous workers** (the worker is or was a member of that population), or the attachment may result from an acquired interest. Even in the latter case, such an interest is often sparked by a personal connection: a sibling with a disability, a parent with a degenerative medical disorder, or a gay friend who has died of AIDS. This illustrates the power of the sense of connection and commitment often found in such communities.

Personal Communities

As you consider your own relationships, you will no doubt recognize that you are a member of numerous communities yourself. You may belong, for example, to the Catholic community, the bisexual community, the suburban Detroit community, the midwestern yoga teacher community, and the undergraduate student community. Your **personal community**, then, consists of a collective of both locality and identity.

The significance of your personal community, besides your own socialization, is that it expands the scope of your social interactions as well as your understanding of resources, helping networks (formal and informal), cross-cultural dimensions, and community idiosyncrasies. Because your personal community consists of both locality and identity components, it provides you with a particular context for multiple aspects of your practice, including interpersonal and community change goals. In this way your personal community integrates your personal and professional lives and enriches each.

COMMUNITY FUNCTIONS

From this broad brush discussion of community types, we can go on to explore the actual functions that communities carry out. Although there are several ways to think about this, we will look first at a traditional, familiar scheme for organizing community functions that makes intuitive sense. Then we will look briefly at a more postmodern view that expands the lens and emphasizes the dimension of interaction within it.

Traditional Framework for Community Functions

Five functions that communities serve for their members are often cited in the literature (Warren, 1978). See Table 10.1 for a description of these classic functions:

- Socialization
- Production, distribution, and consumption of goods and services
- Social control
- Mutual support
- Participation of residents

Social Constructionist Ideas about Community Functions

Consistent with the ideas of social construction—that is, that people both shape and are shaped by social processes—we can explore the *relationship* of the self and the community. Through this lens, community functions are seen not as external systems that are applied to community members, but rather as interactive mechanisms or processes that contribute to, and then reflect, the formation and substance of members. This contemporary perspective identifies three functions (Brueggemann, 2002, pp. 115ff.):

- Community as a "source of the Self."
- Community as the "bearer of the Self."
- Community as a "creator of humanity."

TABLE 10.1	FUNCTION	FOCUS	EXAMPLE
Traditional Community Functions	Socialization	Transmission of values, beliefs, culture, and patterns of relationship *from* community residents *to* community residents.	In some rural communities, stoicism is expected regarding personal troubles; residents may be socialized to share them only with family.
	Production, distribution, and consumption of goods and services	Tangible services such as food, housing, clothing, and intangible services such as banking, transportation, and recreation.	The corner grocery store, the dry goods store, the well-baby clinic, and the bus stop.
	Social control	Enforcement of laws and formal codes.	Police protection, zoning ordinances.
	Mutual support	Formal or informal community or religious supports.	Support groups for addictions, shelters for women experiencing domestic violence, social services.
	Participation of residents	Opportunities to exercise preferences in religious activities, political party affiliation, and governance; extends to recreation and education.	Local town meetings, school boards, city commissions, rural granges.

As you read this perspective on the functions of community, you will notice that the same functions are taken up—socialization, production of goods and services, social control, mutual support, and participation—in a contemporary context. This view articulates a more interactive pattern; that is, it explores the interrelationships between individuals and the functions of community rather than a separate listing of functional provisions. It also acknowledges that there is alienation and disempowerment in U.S. communities today and that people in the United States have created problematic structures to live by. This may resonate when you consider your own life, your relationships to the institutions in which you work or study, and on a broader scale, the struggles to balance the needs of work and family, and sense of apathy or disempowerment in governance processes. On the other hand, this is a most hopeful picture of what communities can be at their best because it always emphasizes the capacity of people to gather their inner resources and exercise their agency, the ability to shape their own lives, and change them.

Community as a Source of Self   This idea asserts that none of us is a unitary, indivisible self composed entirely of our own perceptions, feelings, and attitudes. Nor are we passively embedded within a machinelike system that shapes us in whatever way suits its whim while we try valiantly to adapt. Rather, we are always social selves with the capacity to shape who we are and choose who we want to be.

Although each of us is anchored in a biological and genetic organism, we do not become distinctive selves except through our social interchanges with others. This is developed and confirmed through our relationships, first with significant others, or family, and then through the group, and community. Within these constellations, we take on different roles in different situations. We learn, then, that we are leader in this situation and follower in that. We shape ourselves to meet the needs of our community roles. The significance of this message for social work practitioners is in the belief that people have the capacity to influence as well as be influenced. Workers don't encourage clients to give up or adjust because they see any particular course as inevitable; they see clients as people with agency and capacity to work toward making their worlds what they want them to be. Georgia, the woman you first met in Chapter 2, who experienced domestic violence is a good example of the transforming impact of this kind of community (here a community of identity) on ordinary people.

Community as a Bearer of Self   Here the individual is seen as embedded within the public "megastructures" of modern communities that produce the economic goods and services and dominate a large part of our lives with concerns for money or possessions. This creates a situation in which we tend to have separate private lives in addition to our public lives, which requires us to juggle both. This often creates alienation on personal, social, and political levels, as we find ourselves increasingly isolated. On a personal level we may find little connection and no satisfactory meaning in our work, which may seem demeaning or irrelevant and which we try to counteract through a joyless consumption of more and more things. On a social level, we struggle to find the time to support our most meaningful structures, such as family and friendships; and on a community level, we feel estranged from the centers of power and cynically unable to influence the matters that are most important to us—witness the voting rates in U.S. elections.

The implications for practice lie in the critical need for community organizing, which we will take up shortly. Community, as an ideal, has the capacity to mediate these forms of alienation so that individuals can live, work, and participate in affirming, communal ways. Strong communities restore personal connections through opportunities to develop and live out our own commitments; they restore social connections through valuing others as people (rather than as commodities that can be bought and sold); and they restore political connections by developing empowerment through coalitions and organizations that help us, as ordinary people, to reengage in political processes and decision making.

Community as Creator of Humanity   In this function, the community expands social relationships to assume broader arenas of public concern or the public good. As community members recognize that they have shared concerns, they begin to see that these are not just personal issues but rather are socially instituted. For example, child abuse as an issue has evolved from a private concern for how some people beat their children to a public offense against all of us as citizens. From this illumination, we believe that some collective response will lead to social change. Consider, again, Jasmine Johnson, the African American single mother you met in Chapters 4 and 5, as you thought about her experience in terms of social justice and human rights as well as through her own personal lens. This humanity, created by the conviction that bigger things are at stake than our own sensibilities, is part of what inspires people to open their doors to the terminally ill, abused children, or newly arrived refugees. It is also the way in which human rights gives meaning to social work and grounds it. This in turn is what community practice is about in the profession.

DISCOVERING AND UNDERSTANDING THE LIFE OF A COMMUNITY

Having looked at community types and functions from different vantage points, we will now look at some of the methods social workers use to discover and understand the life of a community. These approaches incorporate ideas of engagement and assessment that are quite similar to those in other levels of practice.

No matter what your position, as a social worker you will have to make some sense of your community. There are at least two general ways to approach this task. One way is to look at your community of locality with the purpose of discovering its unique characteristics, including the strengths, skills, stories, problems, and concerns of its members. This allows you to put your clients' experience into context and know what dynamics you are likely to experience in your work. This is a **community inquiry**, which we will explore shortly.

Another way to study a community is to start by narrowing the concern to a particular community of identity or population believed to need specialized or different services and to assess the degree to which the human services system meets those needs (or does not). This process is sharply focused to consider specific social work intervention. Because of its precision, it is sometimes considered more practical than comprehensive studies and is called a **needs assessment.** Ideally, these two methods are integrated rather than constituting an either/or choice.

Community Inquiry

In general you will want to begin your inquiry from the perspective of the whole community (or a subset of a very large community) and then move to smaller and more specific units like neighborhoods or particular populations. Your methods will include examination of records and documents (for example, a city charter), interviews, and observations.

Getting Your Bearings   Getting out and about is one of the best ways to begin this process. You can start by walking around city hall, picking up pamphlets, getting a map, a newspaper, a phone directory, and reading a little local history. You many want to attend popular community events, such as free concerts or political rallies. You will want to notice broad dimensions like ethnic composition, geographical divisions, and apparent patterns of community life. Are the streets deserted by 8:00 p.m.? Are there many elderly people? Are many children playing outside during school hours? Are large numbers of young people hanging out during the day, apparently without work? The idea here is to see it all—the poverty and the prosperity, the empowered and estranged, the "high life" and the "low life" (Hardcastle, Wenocur & Powers, 1997, p. 124).

You will also want to engage in **participant observation**, which means you will join the community, make friends, and be where events are happening. You can eat lunch locally, chat with the mail delivery person, ask questions of the wait staff, notice, listen, and remain faithfully in learning mode. You can inquire about where to go to get a ticket to a hockey game or find low-cost housing or get a driver's license. Although any citizen can be your informant, you will want to cultivate relationships with **key informants** who can act as guides to the inner workings of community life. These may be formal leaders, such as mayors or ward leaders, or informal, such as longtime citizens' advocates, volunteers, or the custodian of a central school. Clergy, educators, and community center staff may also serve in this capacity. In all cases you will want to take the perspective of respectful learner, interacting with and connecting to community members, and avoid presenting as an expert or a change agent. This approach will greatly assist you in becoming familiar with your community. Although it is not scientific, it can orient you and your agency so that you develop a sense of clients' lived community experience. See Box 10.1 for a simple community interview framework.

Digging Deeper   When you have an idea (which remains flexible) of what the community feels like and how it goes about its business, you can take on a more systematic method for analyzing its various dimensions. There is a great advantage in conducting this kind of inquiry before developing new services for a particular population (Hardcastle, Wenocur & Powers, 1997). Such a study provides context for your population of concern and sharpens your understanding of community dynamics.

BOX 10.1

A Community Quality Interview Schedule

Identify yourself as a student performing a community survey. State that the survey will take two minutes. Ask if the respondent is willing to be interviewed. If the respondent agrees, the interviewer asks the following questions:

Are you a resident of the community?

yes _____ no _____

If yes, for how long?

Is this community a good place to live?

yes _____ no _____

If not, what are the undesirable things about this community?

What can be done to improve this community?

Consider the advantages and disadvantages of this approach. The questions are brief, simple, and to the point. You could probably get consent from almost anyone to participate, you would be understood easily, and you could probably survey many people, depending on your available time.

On the other hand, there is a lot of room for interpretation, especially in such questions as "Is this a good place to live?" Your participants may have a lot of different ideas about what makes a community a good place to live, and they might respond negatively if they think only one aspect isn't what it should be or positively if only one aspect seems good to them, making your results fuzzy. You would also want to consider the different experiences your participants have had when you think about what could be done to improve the community. For example, when people live in poverty, their responses may be very different from those who are more affluent.

You might expand the usefulness of this instrument by identifying themes or issues you could follow up in another inquiry. Or you might want to target a particular institution, such as child welfare, for a further look when it is raised in the initial interviews. Try to imagine other ways you could use this tool.

Source: Survey format from Brueggemann, 2002, p. 131

There are many frameworks in the literature for this kind of analysis. Accordingly, in order to gain as comprehensive an understanding as possible, you will want to address most or all of the following dimensions of the community:

- History, geography, and boundaries.

- Demographics, including subgroups.

- Values, beliefs, traditions.

- Evidence of oppression and discrimination.

- Political structure and power arrangements/relations.

- Strengths of the community, resources, talents of members.

- Institutions relating to economics, major employers.

- Institutions relating to religion, education, and social welfare.

- Structures relating to housing, transportation, and recreation.

As you investigate these areas, your key informants will provide their perspectives and direct you to other people you might contact and interview. You might get a list of community organizations and contact some of their leading members. You will also want to use your participatory observation skills by attending school board hearings, political planning meetings open to the public, or state government caucuses. Find out what the role of the local university is in community life, and look for newspaper stories or local television coverage about the areas of your interest. See Box 10.2 for sample questions that will help you find out about various dimensions of these topics.

Assessing Specific Population Needs

In practice agencies, social workers often know there is a population of community members that is vulnerable, at risk, or otherwise in need of particular services. This population, for example, might be composed of runaway or "throwaway" adolescents who are homeless, people with HIV and their families, or formerly hospitalized psychiatric patients. The important areas for examination in these cases are the specific parameters of the population itself and the extent to which the human service system at large is meeting its needs. In the effort to narrow the focus from community analysis to particular social problems, workers will work toward understanding the characteristics of that population, profile their problems, and identify patterns of resource availability (Netting, Kettner & McMurty, 1993) among other things. The tool for conducting this examination is called a needs assessment.

Needs assessments often take the form of surveys, and they are frequently required in order to provide a systematic rationale to funders or organizations.

BOX 10.2

Discovering and Understanding the Life of a Community

The following are representative questions you might ask members of the community. They inquire about a mix of the participants' own views and their sense of significant community facts.

REPRESENTATIVE QUESTIONS FOR A COMMUNITY ANALYSIS

- What are the boundaries of this area or community? What do you call it? Do old-timers call it something else?
- Where do people stop to chat, hang out, or relax around here?
- Have you ever seen anything written up about this area? Should I read it?
- What are the good and bad points about living here?
- What special problems or central issues does your (network, area, neighborhood, community of common interest) have?
- Who are the important civic leaders in your community and why?
- Who are the chronic gripers in the area? What is their complaint?

Source: Hardcastle, Wenocur & Powers, 1997, p. 137

They are often stated in behavioral terms, and they add clarity to an already identified approach to service delivery. There are several methods that involve assessing the general population, target populations, service providers, key informants, secondary data sets, social indicators, record reviews, and information from other agencies (Netting, Kettner & McMurty, 1993). Each focus has advantages and disadvantages regarding efficiency, cost, ease, and the likelihood of bias. Most social workers today believe strongly in including the voices of the client system being targeted for service, even when they are difficult to locate or engage.

The framework for the needs assessment in Box 10.3 reflects a generalist practice approach (Day, Shelly & Macy, 2000, p. 234). It can conceivably be carried out by students within a semester's field placement. This is a brief example of a needs assessment. You might want to be more complete in many places and more specific about what has been tried and what has worked. The example gives you a picture of what such an assessment might look like relative to a client group you may encounter.

Skills for Participatory Action-Research

In order to gain an understanding of your community, and how it might change, you will want to use many of the skills of engagement and assessment that you have learned about in previous chapters. Listening, remaining open, and clarifying, among others, are as useful in working with communities as they are with

Imagine that you are a practitioner in child welfare services in a relatively remote rural area of your state. The community is composed of an entire county characterized by a much higher than average rate of poverty, substance abuse, and criminal justice violations. A substantial number of children in the county, from ages 6 to 13, have endured prolonged childhood sexual abuse. These children were first placed in foster care, but many have been removed and placed in residential facilities because their acute emotional disruptions have been reflected in dangerous or out-of-control behaviors. This, of course, is costly for the state, but more important, it signals a distressing trend in your local child protection agency that has terrible implications for both the current quality of life and for the future community integration of the children involved.

Because of the behaviors and issues displayed by the children in your caseload and those of your peers, providers and foster parents think there is a serious indication for more intensive individual clinical services for the children. You set about to undertake a needs assessment survey in order to demonstrate the urgency of this situation.

PURPOSE

Why: A substantial and growing number of children have experienced childhood sexual abuse and cannot be maintained in the agency's foster care system. They have required costly residential facility placement that could well be avoided with increased individual, clinical community-based services.

What: The survey will assess the parenting experiences of the foster parents in the community who have fostered children with documented sexual abuse.

Who: The client population of concern is all community children in state's custody, ages 6 to 13, who have experienced documented childhood sexual abuse. The client system comprises the foster parents and their children. The parents will fill out the surveys.

Where: The area to be targeted is countywide (name).

When: The survey will be conducted over a period of three months and cover foster care over the last two fiscal years.

ASSESSMENT DIMENSIONS

System composition: The children, their foster parents, remaining family members. Most foster parents maintain meaningful relationships with their foster children and wish to continue to work with them. A few foster parents have workable relationships with members of the child's biological family. Some have withdrawn from the state pool and decline any further contact with the children or their biological families. The families of origin are only minimally involved.

Strengths, resources, and stressors: The children have many strengths, and many have exhibited impressive resilience. Some have done very well in school; others have been well connected with churches or synagogues. Their foster families have provided much in the way of energy, devotion, and effort but cannot cope with and manage dangerous behaviors. The families of origin are highly stressed in most cases, and though they can periodically act as supports for their children, they are frequently in need of services themselves.

BOX 10.3

Sample Needs Assessment Survey

BOX 10.3

continued

Support network: Community schools, recreational facilities, religious organizations, and community clubs have extended a great deal of support to these children. The children give voice to this support as well. However, this network is limited in what it can cope with and is significantly taxed by many of the children's behaviors.

Organizational support: Several community service organizations have provided the children with donations for special needs and recreational pursuits. The local YMCA has organized a swimming course with accompanying volunteers to assist the children. Big Brothers and Big Sisters has been highly involved in providing companionship to the children. The local community mental health agency has been able to offer a very limited number of services on an individual basis.

Service needs: The foster parents overwhelmingly perceive a need for in-depth clinical services for their children. They indicate a very strong willingness to facilitate their children's use of such services. They also perceive a need for increased family support services, case management, psychoeducation, and advocacy training.

individuals or groups. An additional set of skills that are extremely useful in understanding the community can be linked in a process called **participatory action-research,** which is an ethnographic skills-based approach to the work.

The major focus of this approach is the lived experience of community participants as they seek social change. When a group of people with a common commitment explore their situation and make decisions to act in a way that liberates them and "creates justice," they are "transformed—losing fear, gaining confidence, self-esteem, and direction" (Smith, 1997, p. 6). In most cases this is policy practice in the sense that its efforts are directed toward changing the external arrangements, policies, and programs that affect people's lives.

This kind of change cannot effectively derive from the worker's notions about what the community needs, but emerges from within the community. The worker's role in such a process is to facilitate the communal exchange of ideas and experiences that will help community members arrive at common ground. The process is often undertaken through listening to the stories of the people involved, which in turn creates a dialogue about the realities of everyday life (Arratia & de la Maza, 1997). Workers must be *of* the community as well as in it, "must live with the people, walk with them, work with them, be with them" and understand that "what is important is reading the context of peoples' lives" (Debbink & Ornelas, 1997, p. 17).

This means that you as the worker will gain as much entrance to the community as you can in order to understand what living in it is like for people. Extending your role as participatory observer, you deepen your involvement into the realm of identifying and facilitating changes that community members want. This is an empowerment-based approach and consistent with the

 Web Links

The Caledonia site offers 16 tenets of participatory action research, each of which explains aspects of the process and its effectiveness.

strengths perspective. Its particular applicability for communities lies in its recognition of and respect for the centrality of the community experience to people who are experts on their community. In this way it is also consistent with critical social construction, acknowledging the multiple realities that are brought to bear in any community context. Participatory action-research offers community members an opportunity to take their power back and use their needs to drive the transformation of their lives.

CLASSIC THEORETICAL PERSPECTIVES FOR COMMUNITY PRACTICE

We have explored some ways of discovering what makes a community what it is, how it contributes to the development of civic life, and how it interacts with self-development. We have also considered more formal ideas about studying it and two frameworks. From here, let us move more directly into the process of community change.

Community organization is a classic and time-honored social work approach. Social work curricula at one time were organized around casework, group work, and community organization as the three major methods of intervention. Even though the profession has been diverted from this framework, retaining very few MSW programs with concentrations in community organization (Mizrahi, 2001), many ideals of community organization have persisted. In generalist practice they are often integrated with, rather than distinct from, other frameworks for the profession. Although community intervention began in the 1800s, three models of community organization began to emerge in the late 1940s and were described in the literature as locality development, social planning, and social action (Rothman & Tropman, 1987). We will take a brief look at these models to consider the ways they are distinguished from each other, and some of the assumptions and implications they have for contemporary community practice. All of these models are largely directed to communities of locality.

Locality Development

The focus of **locality development** traditionally has been on the expansion of a community's capacity to cope with and resolve issues as they arise. Self-help processes that build indigenous competence serve this goal. In general, this model also perceives existing community power structures as helpful because they have the ability to facilitate change in a collaborative manner. Because all community members participate in the process for determining what changes should be made, the assumption is that all members will benefit.

The social worker's role in this process is one of facilitating and enabling consensus. She or he assumes that any significant existing differences within the community can be reconciled in the best interests of all. Clients are included in the change process as full participants intricately involved both in the development of goals and as participants in the change process.

Social Planning

In this early formulation, **social planning** was conducted by workers who were usually considered experts and who came into the community, often from the outside, to solve particular problems. Their interests in task identification and achievement were far more important than the community's individuality or character. The social planner's primary skills were systematic data collection, analysis, and rational choice making among alternative methods of implementation. Workers made decisions about how problems should be solved through this process and delivered their answers, sometimes quite authoritatively.

This kind of social planning fits the metaphor of the business deal. The power structures within the community basically hired the planners and acted as sponsors for the change. Through the planners' efforts, various manipulations of systems were made and implemented to effect that change. The citizens of the community were viewed as consumers of the effort, and there was little attempt to involve them in the process.

As you probably notice, some of the ideas in this model don't fit especially well with contemporary thoughts about social work practice. Postmodern views might find this approach the most problematic, but even more traditional models today recognize the importance of involving the people who will ultimately live the change in the process at all steps. Although there is a place for careful planning and all the skills that go along with it, most social workers now believe that change cannot generally be successful as a product delivered from outside. Recall the parallel discussion of participatory decision making in Chapter 9.

Web Links

Go to the site for the Institute for the Study of Civic Values for information and ideas on neighborhood organizing and how to create a national network of activists.

Social Action

Web Links

The Kimsoft site offers a public information search engine for politics, policy, and political news. It is geared toward political activism and provides links to information on many of the hot issues of the day, ranging from legalizing marijuana, to promoting a national day for Native Americans, to education on anarchy. It also connects to many global sites concerned with global issues.

As a method of community organization, social action is generally aimed at shifting power structures in order to change institutional responses. These efforts have often been aimed at organizing people who were not organized or participatory before. Conflict is a central notion in this view of practice, as the intervention points up inequitable contrasts in resource allocation, power, and ownership. Client involvement is usually in some kind of direct action, such as a demonstration or picket line, that highlights injustices and difference.

Historically, there has been a certain combative quality to this position that some social workers find difficult. The worker was considered to be a partisan, that is, clearly on the client's "side," against the "enemy" and the oppressive power structure that "victimizes" citizens. The language of this early depiction was fueled by radical activists (for example, Alinsky, 1971) and contrasts with the more collaborative, dialogic approach taken up in much of social work practice today. Yet it is the most clearly political of the three models and is highly invested in social justice.

CONTEMPORARY AND POSTMODERN PERSPECTIVES ON COMMUNITY PRACTICE

Early conceptualizations of community organization practice have served the profession well, but they are no longer sufficient to describe the context of social work's efforts. Just as the times have influenced other aspects of practice, they have also required alternative lenses for viewing policy practice for community work in contemporary settings. For our purposes here, the contemporary term **community development** is used interchangeably with community organization practice.

Given all the pressures on communities and on social workers, there are likely to be many challenges to community organization work in the future. Gutierrez (1999) has identified six key issues:

- *The **devolution,** or decentralization, of control of many federally funded programs and policies to states, which in turn increasingly seek community input:* For example, some federal block grants for child welfare have placed the allocation of funds under state or local control, which offers opportunities for community participation. Social workers are frequently in a position to contribute to these discussions through state and local agencies, public hearings on regulations, and legislative testimony.

- *The increasing inequality in the fabric of our social, racial, and ethnic relations:* Social workers will continue to play a central role in working with and advocating for a more responsive community for all citizens.

- *The increasingly multicultural composition of society:* This feature of contemporary culture enriches us as citizens and also challenges the profession to ensure greater inclusion, participation, and improved social justice responses.

- *The trend in community organization practice to focus on communities of identity rather than locality:* This appears in such efforts as planning groups for HIV prevention funding, or increased supports for children with disabilities.

- *The increasing integration of community organization ideas and strategies into other models of practice:* This factor is currently operating in generalist conceptions of social work practice, as workers intervene across system levels.

- *New problem areas and particularly identity-oriented initiatives relating to gender, ethnic, and race issues:* Current efforts to institutionalize and legalize gay marriage demonstrate one aspect of this focus.

These issues reflect many of the major dimensions of contemporary society that challenge all human service professions, and they also present unique and exciting opportunities for the renewal of vibrant community practice. Some approaches represent an integration of classic models, such as community development with grassroots organization for social action, which is generated from the people living in the community rather than professionals (Arches, 1999). We will look at three contemporary approaches to community work: strengths-based community practice, community development through engaging difference, and community-centered practice.

Strengths-Based Community Practice

Consistent with much of social work's historical approach to practice, community development work has often taken a problem-oriented stance. Frequently the work has started with an investigation to turn up dysfunction and assess the need for services. Further, professionals have been more likely to attain funding when they emphasize liabilities and shortcomings that can be treated. The resources in such situations then go to service providers rather than community citizens. In this way, the story has become driven by experts and focused on problems (Chapelle, 1999) while missing community strengths and creating whole communities that seem to run on—and increasingly depend on—services alone.

Social work as a profession has always recognized a strong connection between the individual and the community. Likewise, the strengths perspective reminds workers of the connection between individual resilience and community support (Saleebey, 2002). This implies that the resiliency demonstrated by so many individuals is possible because the community nourishes strong connections. As an example, many formerly troubled young people have cited caring adult mentors who were involved in their lives and had high expectations for the way they functioned in the community.

Just as social workers support conducting individual assessment through the lens of strengths, they also apply those principles to the community. First, you look to the community's assets, which you will discover through partnering with residents (see Mannes, Roehlkepartain, & Benson, 2005). Then, the question to be asked is "Under what conditions do people in communities experience well-being?" (Chapelle, 1999, p. 42). The particular skills that you need to undertake an assets-based community strengths inventory include (Saleebey, 2002):

- Assessing individual skills and strengths and linking them to those of other residents or groups.

- Combining resources and, in collaboration with residents, developing programs the community truly wants and needs.

- Making sure that participants who make contributions to the community have opportunities to achieve personal or family goals through connection with others.

- Helping residents to strengthen their sense of belonging through activities that bring them together.

- Helping to keep the connection between individual resilience and community activity by creating meaningful work, responsibility, and opportunity.

You can see aspects of the three traditional methods of community practice (locality development, social planning, and social action) integrated in this approach. Strengths-based approaches to community organization activities that work reflect a focus on practical, assets-based community projects that are driven by community goals and inclusive participatory practices. They become increasingly comprehensive and vision based as they grow, and they struggle with and attempt to minimize the barriers of institutional racism and oppression (Saleebey, 2002).

 Web Links

The Community Tool Box site contains several thousand pages of practical information about community health and development. It includes skills, planning, and connecting; from the Work Group on Health Promotion and Community Development at the University of Kansas in Lawrence.

Community Development Through Engaging Difference

In keeping with postmodernism as a perspective that recognizes multiple realities, blueprints for change that are based on any absolute view of truth are not likely to be accepted. Postmodernists tend to speak out against both the injustices of the status quo and the traditional change strategies that are imposed, especially when they don't deal satisfactorily with real challenges (Lane, 1999), such as difference.

 The Social Work Library

Use the case study found in Arches' paper to explore some typical dilemmas arising in grass roots community organizing.

Two stories of community development practice illustrate the importance of using context rather than a one-size-fits-all approach. The first involves a run-down and isolated area outside Sydney, Australia, that was the subject of a land development project to revitalize the area. The government had made active efforts, through the establishment of a new "housing estate," or housing development, to bring in new residents. Offering attractive land prices, the government's Land Commission brought more than 3,000 new residents to the estate, maximized its profits, and had not, within three years, developed any social infrastructure.

Enter three part-time community development workers, funded by the government of Australia to do a project around child care issues, as defined by the authorities. Knowing nothing of the area and having no amenities (not even an office), the workers walked around the community, asked questions, and set about to understand their context. They met with residents in their homes, at schools, and the local pub. Through their commitment to initiating and maintaining dialogue with the residents, the workers learned that the child care issues they had been sent there to investigate were much more complex than they had expected. They also discovered that the needs identified by local bureaucrats and social planners did not match the concerns of the women, who were largely the child caretakers. For example, the women were interested in child care centers and park development, proposals that did not appear in any of the planning reports or needs assessments. It was through these workers' dialogue with the community that the women's voices were raised, heard, and incorporated into a more responsive provision of service that also shifted the power arrangement.

The second story is of the arrival of an experienced social worker into a settled community of public housing. This practitioner discovered that her work was not going to be framed by studying the previous statistics or developing a new community profile, but rather (because she was interrupted constantly with day-to-day business) by meeting people, learning what concerned them, what they wanted for their community, and taking action "on the go." She walked around with several residents to explore the landmarks, housing, neighborhoods, services, meeting place, and areas of crime. She also discovered her own organization in greater depth and developed an understanding of the local power relations and conflicts among community leaders. Rather than offering a set of common skills for practice, this community developer stressed that a way of being was most important for her work: "humble, visible, accessible and credible" (Lane, 1999, p. 140).

The moral of these two brief stories is probably quite clear to you. It rests primarily in the value of recognizing and honoring the differences that exist in communities. It depicts the local voice as a diverse, ever-changing network of people who negotiate common meanings in context. It resists any government or agency imposed top-down agenda (however well studied) and the notion of accountability to funders rather than to citizens affected by the development strategies.

Although it recognizes and honors multiple realities, the community development approach does not promote the "anything goes" stance of which postmodernism is sometimes accused. Rather, it allows you—as do the positions described in the early chapters of this book—to take an ethical and moral position regarding your own values, even while recognizing that these values are not universal. Although you may retain your ideas regarding the positive potential of community, you will certainly encounter values that you oppose. When, for instance, you find yourself in the midst of racist community attitudes, you can value the difference registered and still attempt to counter it. Among many alternatives, you can confront racism directly in everyday conversations or attempt to expand others' horizons. When people join in

 Web Links

Explore the knowledge and interests of indigenous peoples all over the world at the CWIS site. The goal of CWIS is to establish cooperation between nations to democratize international relations between nations and between nations and states.

common concerns, they may discover that they speak a similar language in spite of the legacy of racism. Your values can remain clear and transparent while you engage in seeking community.

Community-Centered Practice

As a final example of an alternative contemporary approach to community work, let us take a look at a process originating in New Zealand, called **family group conferencing** or **family group decision making**, which has been adapted to reflect local contexts. The approach has applicability in a variety of situations, but here we look at its implementation in the context of rethinking child welfare (Burford & Pennell, 2000). In Box 10.4, Minnesota social work practitioner Suzanne Lohrbach describes the process in a case of child maltreatment.

BOX 10.4

Family Group Conferencing

This approach to child welfare is in use today in some locations and is grounded in a commitment to the connections that communities can provide. Its emphasis is on the inclusion, rather than exclusion, of members who exhibit problematic behaviors and is aimed at restoring community integration.

"The philosophy underlying this strategy stresses the community's investment in children (crossing the boundaries of any one profession), supports a collaborative, rather than litigious and adversarial, approach to ensuring child safety, and an empowerment focus for both families and communities to resolve violent situations in a way that reflects the values and needs of each. It is, then, centered in the community.

"In situations of child maltreatment, all involved, interested, and responsible members of the family, extended family, friends, and other support people are brought together in a conference with child protection workers, other professionals as relevant (for example, police, clergy, doctors), and other members of the community as deemed necessary. The purpose is the development of a plan of action in response to the context of the maltreatment concerns. Here's one example of model implementation: A child protection worker is involved with a family where there has been substantiated child maltreatment. The 13-month-old boy had sustained a brain injury, and the family explanation and medical opinions did not match. There was a decision to be made regarding the care and protection of the child and a plan to be made around child safety. The social worker made the referral to the local Family Group Conferencing project. All family members agreed to the referral.

"The conferencing coordinator, in careful preparation for the conference, then works with the family to clarify the purpose of the conference, to identify whom to have in attendance, safety planning with all involved and the details around location and any cultural considerations. It is important that all participants, particularly children, youth and survivors of violence have the option of support people present. These supports help to maintain the safety of all family members during the length of the process because they encourage accountability (Burford & Pennell, 2000). Relevant professionals who can contribute to the meeting are also identified and invited. For example, medical personnel

BOX 10.4

continued

from the local hospital were involved to provide the family with the explanation of the injuries to the child.

"During preparation, the coordinator describes the conference process, and each participant is asked to think through and bring to the conference their concerns, the strengths that they see, and any resources/ideas they have to offer. The coordinator also works with participants on alternative ways to bring forward their information.

"For example, an aunt who could not be in attendance wrote a letter to be read at the conference. The professionals attending the conference are similarly prepared and additionally asked to bring forward, in an objective manner, information they have that is critical to the decision the family is to make.

"The coordinator has also gathered information from the family on their preference for beginning the conference, inclusive of any opening message or ritual that is customary for them. All participants introduce themselves and identify their relationship to the child. To ensure that all present have access to the same information, the social worker presents the formal facts relating to the reason(s) that the agency is involved. The information is presented in the family's primary language through co-facilitation with an interpreter where necessary. Other service providers and community members present additional information. Family members present their views, ask questions and seek clarification.

"When all of the information is provided and the family is satisfied that they understand what has been presented, the coordinator and other service providers leave the room so that the family can deliberate on the information and develop a plan to respond to the needs of the child. When the family completes the plan, the coordinator and other participants return to the room for the presentation of the plan. Any areas of continued concern with the plan are raised, the plan may be enhanced, and consensus is reached that the plan satisfies the agency requirements. The plan may include elements such as alternative supervision, relative respite care, and detailed family support regarding stress management, assistance with transportation, and sometimes more professional services specifically targeting areas of risk.

"There are many considerations in this demonstration project. Child safety, well-being, and permanency are primary. Family plans must include the capacity to resource the plan, the confidence that, if carried out, there will be a positive outcome, and the willingness of both family members and service providers to follow through."

Source: Case study courtesy of Suzanne Lohrbach, LICSW

 Web Links

Go to the Real Justice site for more on restorative justice and family group conferencing. It provides links to conferences, resources, and other related topics.

Although this model requires a sense of commitment to the community, it also supports faith in the inherent competence and capacity of families, even those previously engaged in abuse, to build safety around risk through community involvement and support. The approach requires open and direct dialogue about abuse, it privileges collaboration, and engages community members and families in developing plans that are meaningful and relevant. It highlights family needs and strengths rather than professional power and returns the community to its members. Currently, an additional focus is under way to increase the cultural responsiveness of this model by adapting it to African American, Cherokee, and Latino/Hispanic communities (Waites, Macgowan, Pennell, Carlton-LaNey & Weil, 2004).

THE WORLD AS COMMUNITY

The impact of meaningful connections with others is particularly significant in an era in which we can traverse the globe in a matter of hours. In this section we will consider this and other aspects of the world community as they relate to increasing global interdependence. Ease of travel and widespread interdependence are already making an impact on social work practice in the United States and will certainly influence the work in coming decades.

The recognition that we all live in a global village is at once daunting and exciting. Chapter 2 described some of the dimensions of the global era and highlighted some of the economic aspects of globalization that are relevant for social workers in the United States. In many respects these are alarming in their implications for world poverty. In others they point up opportunities barely even dreamed of a generation ago. Let us look more closely at **global interdependence**, which is the connectedness of all nations, and explore some of the implications it holds for social work practice in the United States.

Global Interdependence: Implications for U.S. Practice

Social work practitioners in Western nations are generally less aware of global interdependence than are our counterparts in less-powerful countries (Healy, 2001). This is partly because so far, Western nations have been largely protected from the negative effects of globalized economics (or at least have become myopic regarding them) and partly because social workers have persistently put their energies into individual models of practice.

There are four ways in which global interdependence influences social work practice at home, no matter where home is. Most of these have to do with political, social, and technological events whose repercussions do not observe national borders. Briefly, the four influences are as follows (Healy, 2001):

- International events and political forces have resulted in the migration of populations all over the world, including the United States. Culturally competent skills and an understanding of the social problems associated with refugee status and transborder issues are important for social workers in nearly every major U.S. community today.

- Homelessness, poverty, violence, street children, HIV, and unemployment are found everywhere in the world, as are the challenges of increasing longevity, runaway contagious disease, and growing divisions between the haves and have-nots. Social workers will want to look for innovations in dealing with these problems from multiple sources, not just Western countries. Mutual inquiries and information sharing will be increasingly relevant as these conditions are addressed on a worldwide basis.

- The actions of one country directly influence the social and economic well-being of others, as well as the world's overall social health. The distinction between what is domestic and what is international is no longer clear. We are all affected by the world arms race, the world economy, and nuclear accidents. What one nation does or does not do has the potential to be felt around the world.

- The opportunities for sharing and communicating internationally are greatly increased by the technological events that bring us e-mail and the Internet, baggy jeans and Coca-Cola, eye-witness accounts of wars, and interviews with weeping villagers from places we've never heard of. The potential for using these resources to share agendas and communicating meaningful experience is almost endless.

Looking through a human rights lens, Ife (2001) cites the fact that the needs of individuals for food, shelter, work, and community life remain local and pressing within this global context. Therefore, he suggests that social work's role should be to bridge the gap between the global and the local, through linking universal rights and local needs. See Exhibit 10.1 for a list of potential priorities for social work practice in this pursuit.

International Social Work

The idea of international social work is somewhat complex, and several definitions of it exist in the literature, ranging from narrow (working in another country) to broad (intergovernmental work). Healy (2001) identifies four dimensions, described here:

- *Internationally related domestic practice and advocacy:* This is the aspect of international work that is mostly likely to occur in your practice. For example, your adolescent client, Joseph, has come to your city from Bosnia as part of the Refugee Resettlement Program and is on your caseload. He is struggling with English, he is trying to adjust to the youth culture in your midwestern city, and his family is impoverished. As Joseph's worker, you will need to know about his home culture, what his experience has been in resettling, and how you can work appropriately with him on the issues he faces now. You might also see it as your responsibility to assess the prevailing policies of your own community with regard to Joseph's experience and others like him and to advocate for improved responsiveness.

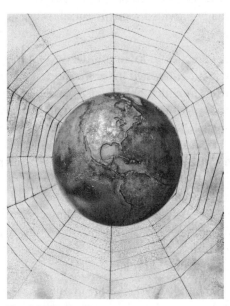

The global local web

- Concentrating on community development as a focus for practice, and the incorporation of community development approaches in all social work practice.

- Extending the practice of policy advocacy to international forums.

- Developing techniques to enable the disadvantaged and oppressed to find a voice not merely in national forums but also globally, in international solidarity.

- Making effective use of the new technologies to link both workers and community groups globally.

- Including global forces as a critical component of problem analysis and consciousness raising.

- social work roles and positions in international nongovernmental organizations (NGOs) and United Nations (UN) agencies.

- Incorporating a strong human rights analysis alongside more traditional social work needs-based practice.

- Seeking opportunities for social workers to develop internationalist understandings through such things as exchange programs and international courses in schools of social work.

- Developing further analysis and research about the link between the global and the local across social work knowledge, values, and skills.

Source: Ife, 2000, pp. 62–63

EXHIBIT 10.1

Priorities for Social Work Practice Linking the Global and the Local

- *Professional exchange:* This involves the exchange of information and experience across borders and the ability to use such content to improve practice and policies at home. As a worker, you might read other countries' professional journals in your particular field of interest, correspond with professionals, go to international meetings, monitor list serves, or host visitors from other countries. You will engage in a learning process in which you might, for example, study and integrate particular ideas and practices from other perspectives into your own work or into the policies that influence it. At a community level, you might borrow and adapt technologies or innovative ideas on behalf of clients. For example, you might consider the Grameen Bank, which designed a loan project that helped poor women of Bangladesh to start small businesses that eventually provided some financial security (Healy, 2001).

- *International practice:* This is direct practice in international development work agencies. For example, if you are interested in international relief and development work in countries in which war is a pervasive backdrop for children growing up, you might become part of a relief organization, such as Oxfam, CARE, or UNICEF. Such agencies generally attempt to help local community structures regain their equilibrium and provide for the specialized needs of children living through war. In such a position, your basic and cross-cultural social work skills, along with a facility in community development, could be critical to the success of the program. In general, the goal for such programs is building community capacity and local ownership and control. This kind of community work across cultures requires a careful, sensitive practice stance combining solid relational skills, respect, and the willingness to learn.

- *International policy development and advocacy:* This effort involves social workers as members of worldwide movements that attempt to influence policy and advocate for particular issues. For example, a colleague of mine was a member of the Non-Governmental Organization (NGO) forum, under the auspices of the International Association of Schools of Social Work (IASSW), that was held at the United Nations Fourth World Conference on Women in Beijing, China, in 1995. The goal of the forum was to influence UN policy decisions regarding women's human rights. This group, which drew participants from 27 nations, focused on domestic violence and the development of action strategies for antiviolence work in home settings. They drafted 10 recommendations to reduce gender-based violence that the IASSW offered to the appropriate UN policy group. The creation of the Anti-Violence Partnership described in Chapter 9 was a response to this effort.

 Web Links

For another specifically nonviolent approach to fighting oppression, see the site of the American Friends Service Committee, a Quaker organization committed to relief and prevention of suffering in immediate aid and long-term development worldwide. It is committed to nonviolence and confronts oppression and injustice through international and national service.

Skills and Approaches for a Global Community

By now, you have seen, or are beginning to see, that social work skills are cumulative. By that I mean that the first skills for hearing the story, discussed in Chapter 4, are expanded by those used in group and family work, and organizations, and then in communities. In spite of the sometimes awe-inspiring breadth of global practice scenarios, these skills remain grounding approaches for your work. The skills required in participatory action-research, as discussed earlier, are invaluable in global social work practice because they work to bridge the gaps in understanding between you and communities of people whose histories, languages, and cultures are different from your own.

You can use the following seven steps from Ramanathan and Link (1999, pp. 225–230) to a global orientation to expand your thinking as a developing global citizen. Because everyone tends to get entangled with the work in front of them, these can provide a helpful, grounding reminder that there is a big world out there. Furthermore, "the globe is us" (p. 230).

1. *Making a personal review of global awareness:* Each of you will want to reflect individually on your own orientation. For example, how often do you think about social conditions in other countries? How aware are you of facts such as where your clothing is made and under what conditions? How well do you know the globe? What kind of language do you use when speaking about other parts of the world?

The Social Work Library

Check out Prighoff's chapter for more on the importance of a global perspective.

2. *Expanding knowledge of practice in a range of countries:* You will want to consider practice in other countries as informing your own and think about how often you consider yourself the expert and other countries' approaches as secondary or inferior. How much do you know about other approaches? Are you willing to import ideas from other places rather than exclusively exporting them?

3. *Understanding "cultural competence" and respect for language:* You will want to consider how well you understand the dynamics of culture and its implications for access to power and resources. You will want to understand culture as a phenomenon common to all, rather than as a specific ethnic variable that requires special techniques. Think about how well you understand the ideas of cultures other than your own and how respectful your language is about and with other cultures. How often do you assume your own culture is the worldwide norm?

4. *Analyzing global policy instruments built upon consensus:* You will want to review the global policy statements that apply to issues of concern to social workers. For example, the UN Convention on the Rights of the Child for children's issues or the UN Beijing Conference for domestic violence are relevant documents of the worldwide concern for human rights (Marsh, 2003).

5. *Becoming historically aware:* You will want to know and understand the historical context of U.S. policies. For example, you need to acknowledge their role in the treatment of Native Americans and the perpetration of violence against women and against people of the Global South. You need to be aware of your technological privilege in this information age. You need to remain attuned to the issues of distributive justice, energy resources, and other dimensions related to the distribution of technology and the ethics associated with it.

6. *Reviewing values and ethics:* You will want to review your basic commitments to the profession and to yourself and consider how well you apply them globally. Do you respect the dignity of all the peoples of the earth? Do you reflect a preoccupation with material goods? How do you reconcile this focus with the fact that global resources are finite? How do you maintain your own well-being when that of others is violated everyday? To explore this perspective, see Exhibit 10.2, an ethical code for social workers in the global world (Brueggemann, 2002).

EXHIBIT 10.2

A Renewed Ethical Code for Global Social Work Practice

- Macro social workers work to create a society that aims toward the truth, seeks justice, and becomes good. As we seek those values, there are a number of principles to which we attend.

- Macro social workers challenge society to be everything that it can potentially become, while living with the reality of conditions as they are.

- Macro social workers must have the courage and the will to challenge those forces that condone, perpetuate, or cause human suffering.

- Macro social workers speak for those who cannot speak for themselves, advocate for those who have no voice, seek empowerment for the powerless and well-being for those whose lives are deprived.

- Where required, macro social workers stand outside the social consensus, shatter norms, and challenge the status quo. We may refuse to participate in social processes or systems that are destructive to the human condition.

- Macro social workers value and seek to rekindle in the life of society a sense of authentic community, a substantive conception of democracy, economic justice, and a way of ethical reason in which individuals realize their potential. We have a vision of and a desire to restore community among people.

- Macro social workers are committed to society's future. We work to bring about the very best that society can become, even when it actively resists becoming that best. We try to bring new creative energies to bear on society, forging a pathway to its future.

- Macro social workers are against death makers, violence, and destruction. We fight against oppression of people and of the human spirit where they occur. We are against greed and avarice, compulsive exploitation, ruthless competition, and mindless individualism. We are against dehumanizing social systems and the divisiveness that undermines others.

- Macro social workers are against deception that saps the human spirit. We fight against denial in any of its forms. We question the conventional wisdom of our age when it promotes injustice, poverty, inequality, powerlessness, and helplessness.

Source: Brueggemann, 2002, p. 438–439

7. *Evaluating local variations and uniqueness.* As a social worker, you will want to continue to balance the tension between upholding universal principles that will strengthen the profession and valuing individual and local expressions of uniqueness. The "goal is not 'sameness,'" but rather a "unified purpose" (Ramanathan & Link, 1999, p. 230).

STRAIGHT TALK ABOUT SOCIAL WORK AND WHY YOU CHOSE IT

This chapter has emphasized a community and global perspective in contemporary and future social work practice. For some whose interest in the profession was born out of community spirit and activism this will be a welcome homecoming, a divergent path from the *DSM* and individual pathology that are such common areas of focus today. For others who entered the profession with an individual direct practice lens, it may seem to stretch the boundaries and require travel into uncharted territory. The world has become at once a smaller and a more complex place. It pulls you in competing directions. I believe it will demand the best of your creativity and your spirit. A classic social work scholar, Bertha Capen Reynolds, says it best with the title of her classic 1964 volume: social work is indeed *An Uncharted Journey.*

Those of you who feel you are a long way from the community and global orientation that this chapter is all about can experiment with applying the thinking in the seven steps and with the implications in the context of your own local practice. I hope the connections that become evident to you will also provide an energizing and exciting glimpse into the potential of the future. The more you experience them, the more your own orientation may expand to include many standpoints you never would have anticipated.

CONCLUSION

Community and global orientations are simultaneously exciting and unsettling (Moxley, Gutierrez, Alvarez & Johnson, 2004). They challenge many assumptions and make demands that you may not have envisioned. Your ability to remain "unknowing," to be flexible, and to look at the world, including your practice, in different ways may be absolutely critical for the profession's future.

This is not a new phenomenon to social work, though. The profession has flirted periodically with international concerns throughout history. Both Mary Richmond and Jane Addams spent time in England to gather ideas and models of practice in the 1800s. An International Conference of Charities, Correction and Philanthropy was held in Chicago in 1893. Social work's interest in international issues and education has been an on-again, off-again affair for as long as the profession has existed (Kendall, 2001). Between the two world wars the profession was diverted in its international interests, but these interests reemerged when the United Nations was founded after World War II. Another period of national preoccupation during the 1960s followed; and so the cycles go. The global orientation is not likely to retreat, however, and social work's legacy in the communal—by neighborhood, county, state, nation, and world—is an integral source of its strength and vision for the future. As a social worker and world citizen, you belong to a profession at a crossroads of taking leadership in issues of social and economic justice and human rights both at home and beyond. You are in good company. You have colleagues all over the earth (see Weiss, 2005).

Having considered the range of system levels, from direct, one-to-one practice to international social work, we will now retrace our steps to consider some of the thornier issues in social work practice that challenge workers as well as clients. These include the preponderance of oppression, involuntary treatment, a culture of violence, managed care, and self-care responses to burnout.

MAIN POINTS

- Communities play a critical role in workers' and clients' lives, even in traditional one-to-one practice. Understanding their type and function, from both traditional and postmodern perspectives, will help you to assess them.

- There are multiple models through which to discover and assess the community. These may be broadly focused, such as the community inquiry, or more narrowly focused, such as the local needs assessment.

- You will use many of the skills of engagement, assessment, and intervention in community work as you do in individual work. In addition, you will find the skills of participatory action-research useful as an ethnographic approach to your work.

- Classic theoretical perspectives regarding community organization practice include locality development, social planning, and social action.

- Contemporary approaches to community change efforts include strengths-based models, strategies for focusing on difference, and community-centered practice.

- Social workers of the 21st century needs to expand their knowledge and orientation to the concerns of global interdependence, whether or not they practice on that level. International social work as a field offers exciting and useful opportunities, from internationally related domestic practice to policy development and advocacy of global issues.

- U.S. social workers will need to become more sophisticated regarding global issues and the ways in which they influence practice by personally assessing their level of global awareness, expanding their knowledge of practice in other countries, reviewing values and ethics of the profession in a global context, and otherwise pursuing education in this area.

EXERCISES: SOCIAL WORK PRACTICE

In preparation for this exercise, review the Town Map on the interactive case study of the Sanchez family. What do you discover about the center's position in the community?

Getting Organized

In your position as social worker at the center, you have observed that there are some strained connections between the center's staff and the Hispanic community it serves. Consider how you might facilitate the organization of community members into an advisory council to the center's Board of Directors. This council would assist the Board in developing practices that are more responsive to and consistent with Hispanic culture and the Hispanic community. Consider the following:

1. Identify the type of community represented by this population and consider the impact on the members.

2. Which of the traditional functions would be addressed by the work of this council?

3. Which of the social constructionist ideas about community function discussed in the chapter do you think fits this population the best?

4. How might you combine the strengths-based community development ideas with the community development to engage difference?

EXERCISES: THE SOCIAL WORK LIBRARY

Read the Arches article on community practice and focus on "The Case" in which she presents five dilemmas that may arise in community development work when there is competition for limited resources. Using your own experience with community as a reference point (the one in which you live, work, or go to school), apply one of the dilemmas Arches addresses to your community and describe the particulars. Then choose at least one of the strategies she identifies that you think could resolve the dilemma by empowering community members and counteracting the alienation that results from inadequate options. Compare with your peers and discuss any differences.

OTHER EXERCISES

It's a Small World

Review the material in the chapter that identifies four ways in which global interdependence influences social work practice. Using the Sanchez family as a focal point, identify and describe the ways in which the Sanchez family context in particular is shaped by each of the four dimensions of global interdependence. Add any other ways you think would make an impact.

Then, still focusing on the Sanchez family, apply the seven steps to a global orientation at the end of the chapter and explicitly relate these steps to your own cultural sensitivity as one of the family's workers. Write out or be prepared to discuss in class how these considerations might impact your own approach to the family.

CHAPTER 11

Negotiating Troubling
Contexts

I have tried to address social work that is both dirty and dangerous. I have examined social work that is contaminated by daily life, with regard to both clients and social workers. Social work cannot be scrubbed clean . . . Real people with dirty shoes track across the order, the wax, and the polish of the organizational floor. Real floors and real social workers get dirty week after week.

Gerald A. J. De Montigny, 1995

IT TAKES COURAGE TO PRACTICE SOCIAL WORK. Centered in the core of human need, social work reflects all of the messiness that human problems can conjure up. It is even thornier to practice social work from the perspectives of social justice, human rights, strengths, and critical social construction because these approaches challenge the status quo of many institutions and, in many cases, our own thinking. The joys of social work practice are not diminished because of these struggles, however. In fact, the connections and privilege gained from entering the lives of clients is enhanced through wrestling with some of the compelling questions that arise. This does not suggest that you will find all the answers through this kind of struggle; you will not, and you will want continuously to remain open to the experiences of others, especially your clients who come to you in challenging situations.

This chapter takes up only a few of the troubling contexts you may experience. It will not solve all the dilemmas they pose, but it may assist you in thinking about ways to manage them that are consistent with your values and the practice perspectives of this book. We will look at marginalized populations and related contemporary funding issues; involuntary or mandated client scenarios; the cultural phenomenon of violence; and the infusion of managed care into the social service system. Although these topics appear to be discrete on one level, you will gain, I believe, a sense of their interrelatedness as we go. Finally, we will look at ways that you can sustain yourself and your commitment to ethical practice in the contemporary context.

MARGINALIZED POPULATIONS

The legacy of social work practice rests in service to those at the margins. In its early days social work focused on people caught in the consequences of poverty, urban turmoil, dangerous working conditions, and the displacement created by industrial life. The profession became diverted from some of these larger social issues by the advent of psychological approaches and a more individualistic, internal focus. Nevertheless, much of social work, complicated as it may be by assumptions about unconscious motivations or psychological intricacy, remains with those who are *also* marginalized—people who are poor, addicted, ill, violent, and subjected to violence and demoralizing environmental circumstances. To illustrate this point, let us explore a far too common component of practice with marginalized populations—reduced funding for social services—and what it might mean to you as a worker.

When the Funding Gets Cut

By definition, people who are marginalized are not valued in a way that confirms their humanity and respects their human rights. That lack of respect plays out in countless ways that are both personal and public. For example, whether social services are adequately funded is a mark of how a society values (or does not value) the populations served by them. Although every society faces absolute constraints on its resources, in the United States those constraints would more accurately be called preferences. For example, the United States has persistently valued the arms race over the social needs of its population(s) and has consequently chosen to fund the former much more fully than the latter. There are, of course, several arguments to defend those decisions, but they do not negate the effects of inadequate and diminishing funding patterns on social programs.

 Web Links

The Institute for Research on Poverty (IRP) is a national, university-based center for research into the causes and consequences of poverty and social inequality in the United States. It covers research, conferences, publications, and has several poverty links.

You will recall from your history of policy that since 1981, when Ronald Reagan became president, funding for public programs that provide much of the supports to marginalized groups has declined. Reagan, and others after him, attempted to increase the contribution to services by individual states and to spur the private sector to take over many social services. The result has been a dismantling of many services once considered essential. This policy climate has significant repercussions for the practice world. You have probably already experienced in your internship or volunteer work a lack or cut in resources that limit what you can do in the way of helping your clients get to where they want to be, even if that place is simple subsistence.

Clients may become enraged at the way their options are limited and their potential is squandered. Some may take out their anger on social workers, who are then likely to feel trapped within a system they joined so they could be of help. Instead, the system seems to discriminate against clients. This reality can create a serious stalemate for workers, who sometimes respond to these conditions in ways that are painfully ineffective in helping either their clients or themselves. Some of the understandable but less than optimal responses, identified by Von Bretzel (1997), include rationalizing, identifying with the rules and regulations, and becoming numb. They are discussed here:

- *Rationalizing:* This describes a way to think about situations that makes them "all right" rather than intolerable. For example, if the cutoff level for income supports is reduced so that many people are turned away who once would have qualified, workers might try to "see the point" and begin to find reasons why the cut is necessary or even beneficial. This may protect them from feeling that they are violating their commitments and principles and can be a common way to respond to large bureaucracies or public services that already seem highly impersonal.

- *Blaming the victim:* Much has been written about this phenomenon. It is a form of rationalizing in which the worker, when welfare is restricted, for example, begins to hold the client responsible, say, for her own poverty or for having three children with no child support. It is predicated on making a negative judgment against clients because they haven't managed as well as the worker, for example. This response, although quite human on one level, does not take into account all of the external variables that may be at play. It may be helpful here to reconsider the dynamics of privilege and how it works in real worker-client situations.

- *Identifying with the rules and regulations:* Another version of rationalizing, this position defends the content of the rules without exploring the fit for the client. For example, a worker tells his client with a substance addiction that she can regain custody of her children when she has established sobriety, has a job, and an apartment. The worker may feel those are reasonable requirements for raising children. However, in many situations there is no support for such a client to receive treatment or to gain job skills, secure employment, or ever save enough to pay all the deposits on an apartment. When the worker no longer recognizes the improbability of the requirements, she or he has lost touch with the client's reality and has joined the spirit of the regulations as punitive deterrents.

- *Becoming numb:* This describes one relatively simple effect of having to withhold services time after time after time. Since most people can't maintain a state of heightened regret indefinitely, especially in the face of intense deprivation, it is self-protective to stop feeling at all. I believe that social workers have to develop some "hardening" of feelings to keep from being swallowed up in others' agony, but becoming numb is dangerous for clients and also for workers.

- *Avoiding client contact:* One of the saddest of responses, avoiding contact usually represents a direct rejection of the reasons most people go into social work in the first place. If workers have to deny services or dictate punitive "deals" (for example, attendance at workfare in exchange for a welfare grant to pay the rent) too many times, they may simply not want to face any clients only to deny their needs again. In such situations workers might experience an overwhelming sense of futility and detachment and sometimes will choose to relate in as aloof a manner as possible.

- *Abandoning the public sector:* This is the final way for coping with the stresses of an inadequately funded public sector. The worker may just opt out of dealing with such contentious situations, frustrating constraints, and feelings of futility. Some practitioners drop out of the profession entirely, others seek private sector positions that seem less troubled, and still others go into private practice. Although these decisions are, of course, a matter of personal choice, remember that much of the need and therefore much of the potential to serve is likely to remain in the public sector. It is not, as De Montigny says, "clean," but it is also where many of the rewards are.

Responses for Survival

The Social Work Library

To explore radical practice in social work, read Gil's work on injustice and oppression.

In spite of how challenging this situation can be, it is not hopeless. The crisis generated for social workers in cases of too little funding is a function of feeling as if they are working against clients. In order to function with integrity, then, workers need to be clear both to their clients and themselves that their commitments are not to the regulations but to the client. The following suggestions for redirecting the alliance between client and worker and reaffirming the relationship can offer hope in some of the most difficult contexts (Von Bretzel, 1997):

- You can make it known that you don't agree with rigid or punitive policies. You can discuss with your clients what you think is unjust, and why, in a way that reflects an empowering focus, rather than defeat (we looked at this in Chapter 9). Agency culture may require sensitivity to covert versus overt messages along these lines.

- You can become highly informed about alternative resources and assist clients in filing relevant appeals and complaints.

- You can make some personal contact with each client in spite of the constraints on your time. Listening and establishing a genuine, even if cursory, relationship will help reduce stress for both you and the client.

- You can put as much effort into working with marginalized clients as possible, even when it seems fruitless or discouraging.

- You can use a strengths perspective with marginalized clients. You can recognize what extraordinary skill and wherewithal it takes to survive in an oppressive system.

- You can expect that in the contemporary context of services many clients will not tell you the truth. This is not because of some fundamental deficiency or lack of honor; it is because they have learned that telling the truth will often yield punitive results, the removal of supports, or other punishments.

- You can know what kinds of local and regionwide social action will accommodate client participation. Both you and clients can engage in efforts to change policies and effect better services. Agency offices should have supplies of fliers, petitions, and other relevant materials to inform you, your peers, and clients about policy initiations or shifts, so that all of you can become active change agents. This is an empowering process for everyone involved.

 Web Links

Explore the National Alliance to End Homelessness Web site. The alliance is a nonprofit organization whose mission is to mobilize the nonprofit, public, and private sectors of society in an alliance to end homelessness. The site includes policy and legislation, practices, and publications and resources along with several links.

- You can remember the power of a single respectful relationship. Even when it is difficult to find a way to help, clients will recognize and on some level respond to you as a person—maybe the first in a long time—who treats them decently, affirming they are real people with real needs. You will also benefit from taking this standpoint in spite of how challenging the work is. The relationship provides sustenance in the most difficult of settings.

- You can remember that the occasional explosive response from an angry, frustrated client is not personal; it is generally in reaction to punitive policies that seem overwhelming. You can develop skills to defuse anger and to keep from interpreting client anger as a personal affront.

The Question of Participation

Finally in this discussion of funding issues, the question of participation arises. Should practitioners work in settings in which inadequate funding, grueling eligibility standards, or psychological emphases on deficits seem to preclude true assistance to clients? This is in many cases an intensely personal dilemma, as well as a political one. Some practitioners have great difficulty negotiating public sector services even after making every effort. Others, paradoxically, seem to thrive on the challenges. Without prescribing an answer to this common situational conundrum, I suggest considering the profession's mission, which has been to improve the lot of oppressed people. As it happens, public sector services have no monopoly on oppression—it exists institutionally on all levels—and it is clear in the beginning of the 21st century that both public and private institutions need as much help and commitment as they can get from social work practitioners, among others, who are willing to challenge injustices and work toward the attainment of basic human rights for everyone.

INVOLUNTARY, MANDATED, AND NONVOLUNTARY CLIENTS

When you first thought about social work practice, you may have assumed that people would come to you because they wanted your services and believed in the possibility, at least, that you would be helpful. The principles of self-determination and working toward the preferred reality seem counter to coercion, and some social workers question the appropriateness of this kind of practice. Yet, because of the constant tension between social work as an agent of social control and an agent of change, a significant proportion of clients (in some settings, *all*) are involuntary.

Involuntary has several different meanings. In some ways all clients are involuntary in the sense that very few are happy to experience the issues that bring them to services. Certainly those people who seek public sector welfare services are likely to be involuntary in that way. So the distinction between voluntary and involuntary is not always clear cut, but three ways of distinguishing this type of client are accepted in the profession.

Rooney and Bibus (2001) define **involuntary clients** as the group of people who receive services but do not seek them out. They divide this category into mandated clients and nonvoluntary clients. **Mandated clients** are legally required to receive services in order, for example, to reclaim children, escape criminal charges, or sometimes avoid institutionalization. Such mandates occur most often in the systems of care that are heavily shaped and sanctioned by the law in the first place, such as child protection, mental health, and criminal justice. **Nonvoluntary clients** are not formally or legally obliged to participate in services but are pressured into getting them. For example, people with substance abuse issues may be "strongly encouraged" by their employers to seek help, or a parent "takes" an adolescent to family counseling. In these situations the client is in some way persuaded that she or he needs to get services in order, for example, to keep the peace or remain married or stay employed.

There are many patterns of engagement within these scenarios, some of which are not predictable. For example, some angry mandated clients become convinced that they can benefit from genuine involvement, whereas others simply wait out their time. Nonvoluntary clients may simply go through the motions to satisfy someone else, or they may work for real change. The whole notion of involuntary clients presents several challenges as well as opportunities for workers, which we'll explore next.

 Web Links

Discover the National Organization for Forensic Social Work Web site. It describes the organization and expands on the application of social work to questions and issues relating to law and legal systems. It addresses many social/legal issues, such as child custody, divorce, spousal abuse, and juvenile justice.

Challenges in Working with Involuntary Clients

For many social workers, both students and more seasoned practitioners, the idea of working with someone who doesn't want to be there is uncomfortable if not daunting. In some cases, the issues have to do with the interface the worker needs to maintain with the mandating agency, which may seem rigid or overly authoritarian. In others, workers might feel a distaste for the behavioral conduct associated with the involuntary client (for example, relating to child abuse, criminal activity, or substance abuse). In still others, workers simply wonder how to build a relationship in such circumstances. These are certainly understandable concerns, but they put many more limits on the situation than are necessary. Let us take a look at the engagement issues in involuntary work and the opportunities that such work presents.

Engagement with Involuntary Clients   Being well prepared for your first visit with an involuntary client is the first step. This doesn't necessarily mean to review theory or read records; you need first to prepare *yourself*. In general, you can expect that your client might be angry, hostile, or fearful. If you are assaulted by spiteful or even hateful remarks at the beginning of a meeting, you can feel surprised and hurt, so it is helpful to know how you are likely to react and to think ahead about how to respond.

Involuntary clients often take on a "visiting relationship" (DeJong & Berg, 2002), which means they usually have some idea about what you might offer, don't agree that they have a problem, and aren't really sure they want anything to do with you. So they just visit for a while. Although this seems challenging, it can actually assist you in refraining from taking any angry remarks personally, because the client is, after all, just visiting.

Another way to prepare yourself for the resentment and negativity of some involuntary clients is to try hard to place yourself in their position. Remember the times you have felt coerced, invisible, unrecognized, or ignored. You can connect with some part of that scenario that can make you more empathic and help you to understand the client's disinclination to trust anyone, let alone you.

Not all clients, of course, will barge in with this level of antagonism. Some will be overly polite or seem very "tight," as if you won't be able to touch them in any way. Some may actually see meeting with you as an opportunity to think about making changes. Since the tendency might be to decide the client is resistant before you start the work, stay as not knowing as you can. In any case, the most helpful approach is to listen, as it is in any client situation, to the story. Find out how the client sees it. Ask about how things could have been different, respect the client's reality without challenging it, and assume the client has both strengths and competence in spite of the current predicament. Find out what is important to the client and how she or he wants things to change. This is often an excellent situation for perspectival questions (see Chapter 4 for a review) because they can reveal that there is more to the client than the involuntary situation and that she or he is not just "bad," or a personified crime—for example, "a B & E" (breaking and entering) or a "shoplifter." If your substance-using adolescent client feels like a "loser" and worthless, you might ask, "What would your best friend say is your greatest strength?" or, "What would your favorite teacher say you're good at?" (DeJong & Berg, 2001, 2002). For more on useful approaches with involuntary clients, see Box 11.1.

In most cases of mandated services, you will have some externally structured pattern for your work. This can be a set number of sessions (such as 12) or a curriculum to follow. You may need to explain this to your client in order to encourage the engagement process. One of the major ways you can assist your client is to give her or him as much control as you can. You can do this by emphasizing any choices that are real (for example, you may be able to meet once or twice a week, on Tuesdays or Fridays) and by being as clear as possible

---

BOX 11.1

Involuntary Clients

Guidelines for Interviewing Involuntary Clients

- Assume you will be interviewing someone who starts out in a visiting relationship to your services.
- Assume the client has good reason to think and act as he or she does.
- Suspend your judgment and agree with the client's perceptions that stand behind his or her cautious, protective posture.
- Listen for who and what are important to the client, including when the client is angry and critical.
- When clients are openly angry or critical, ask what the offending person or agency could have done differently to be more useful to them.
- Be sure to ask for the client's perception of what is in his or her best interest; that is, ask for what the client might want.
- Listen for and reflect the client's use of language.
- Bring the client's context into the interview by asking relationship questions.
- Respectfully provide information about any nonnegotiable requirements and immediately ask for the client's perceptions regarding these.
- Always stay not knowing.

Source: DeJong & Berg, 2002, p. 179

about the requirements handed down to you. If the court requires you to notify authorities if your client misses a single session, inform her or him of that. Consider that mandated clients typically feel as if control and choice have been ripped away from them, and stay attuned to those issues. You will want to provide all the information you can about the contingencies as a respectful gesture of recognition.

Legal Entanglements   In spite of your best efforts to engage your client, mandated or not, you may find yourself in the spot of having to take a position on what is in her or his best interests or in the interests of related children. This situation can become difficult when you have been trying to respect the story and work with what the client wants to have happen. Do not decide prematurely that the single parent in a child protection scenario isn't ready to have her children back or that your elderly client can't live safely in the community. You want to keep working at what the client thinks needs to happen to get to a place where her or his preferred reality can be realized.

Nevertheless, there are times when you may simply have to take a conscience-driven stand that may seem to work against the client. In such cases, inform her or him before any court hearing or the like. Avoid any surprises for your client that would further violate trust. My experience has been that an honest "this is the way I see it" dialogue at least conveys respect even if the client doesn't agree with the assessment. Another way to help the client see how the situation looks to others is to ask perspectival questions, such as "What do you think the judge might think about the times when you left the baby alone?" (DeJong & Berg, 2002).

Opportunities in Working with Involuntary Clients

Although involuntary situations challenge both the worker and the client and few social workers would say these are ideal scenarios, it is equally misleading to describe them as disastrous. They present some golden chances to engage people who might never undertake any change without being pushed into seeking services. They also present workers with an opportunity to practice their most cherished social work skills. By hearing and respecting clients' stories, assuming they can grow, and believing that their situation is workable, you have the chance to engage them in ways that can potentially transform their lives.

Individual Scenarios   I once worked with a man who was adjudicated by the court as a perpetrator of domestic violence, but because he also had a substantial history as a client of mental health services and had just been discharged from a psychiatric hospital, the administrative staff of my agency decided I should meet with him individually. This departure from the agency's standard intervention (which was group work for men) was made on the grounds that the client was fragile and would not do well in the potential confrontation of a group. He was painfully embarrassed at being singled out as inappropriate for a group process, angry that he was treated like a "common criminal," and exceedingly hostile about meeting with me.

Using a basic approach of respect, a willingness to hear him out, and a position of wanting to understand his life, I was able to connect with him after several sessions. He then confided that he had never had the opportunity to talk about the challenging issues in his family and that he felt humiliated and stigmatized in receiving mental health services. By the end of the 12 mandated sessions, he wanted to engage in further work, and he had come to believe that he could change his violent behaviors by responding differently to the stresses he felt. This was not a case of brilliant work; it was simply an example of the way people can respond to an affirming approach that recognizes their strengths.

Group Work   Many scenarios in involuntary treatment employ groups as the method of choice. For example, we looked at innovative practice in the family group decision-making model in Chapter 10, which involved a child protection violation and used a large group of community and extended family members. More traditional models also use groups for working with domestic violence, parenting issues, and substance abuse. Because group work focuses particularly on interrelatedness and extension to the "outside" world, there are many opportunities to engage involuntary clients in a process from which they can benefit long after the treatment period.

Three important areas for group work include process (how people do what they do), linking (making connections with other people and situations), and inclusion (involving everyone present) (Thomas & Caplan, 1999). These areas are especially applicable for mandated groups because they focus on connecting members through the group process and bringing them back into the fold of a community. Some of the skills necessary for successful group work are validating experience, clarifying, paraphrasing, linking one member's response to another's, collaborating, developing group rituals, role-playing, setting tasks, and processing body language (Thomas & Caplan, 1999). These skills draw upon a combination of individual and extended group work skills that can facilitate the work of connection and open up the critical subject of power as it relates to involuntary groups.

Power Issues   You probably have noticed a clear association with power, coercive power at that, in any kind of involuntary and especially mandated service. Even if all you have to do as the worker is fill in the blanks on the form indicating that your client attended 12 mandatory sessions, you have a great deal of power in determining how the client's life goes on from that point. You need not only to recognize that power and to be as comfortable with it as possible, but also to articulate your understanding of it to your client and elicit the same from her or him. This is a place for transparency, as it creates a rich climate in which to talk about power and what that means to your client. It also presents you with an opportunity to struggle with the tension between your role as a person of social control and your role as a person who assists people caught in social control.

Focusing on power provides a context in which you can discuss with your client what needs to happen to get where she or he wants to go. For the client, this might be as simple as getting authorities "off my back," or it may involve much more complex efforts to change a system that she or he experiences as oppressive. The woman trying to regain custody of her children who has to see you, get clean, get a job, and find a home with no instrumental supports might, for example, want to join with others in an empowerment-focused approach to influence the system in helping her meet her mandates.

VIOLENCE

None of us can remain oblivious to the increasing violence in our culture. It looms in almost every newspaper, television news story, and on all too many urban street corners and rural crossroads across the country and beyond. From the wars waged overseas to the high school horrors executed in quiet heartland towns, violence is expressed in ideological as well as interpersonal terms, and it is a common theme everywhere. Social workers are frequently in the position of working with the effects of a violent culture and are not immune from direct exposure to violent threats in the workplace. The escalation of violence in our lives has become an insidious component of contemporary experience and should be addressed on personal, agency, and policy levels.

The Culture of Violence

Although it can be comforting to think of violent acts as discrete, chance occurrences, there is often a difficult-to-deny connection between them and many historical, political, and cultural processes that reflect a cycle of escalation. When there is persistent domination of one group by another for purposes of exploitation, a state of "**societal violence**" results (Gil, 1998a, p. 60). This kind of violence breeds negative, destructive attitudes and relationships that are reinforced by periodic eruptions in social contexts.

Societal violence is characterized by acts and conditions that inhibit people from meeting their basic needs and achieving their dreams or potential (Gil, 1996). Consider, for example, the dynamics of a culture that systematically denies equal opportunities to women (Abramowitz, 1989) or rationalizes attacks against those who are weak or defenseless (Shachter & Seinfeld, 1994). School bullying, interracial taunting, and sexual harassment are just a few pervasive examples that are translated into interpersonal persecution that is informed by societal violence. Occasionally these situations escalate into physical violence on an interpersonal or social level, as witnessed by isolated attacks, school murders, or race riots. Our society is likely to remain violent as long as we condone and perpetuate the barriers that prevent people from meeting their basic needs.

The Social Work Library

For another connection between violence and social work practice, read Danis's paper on domestic violence.

Social workers are committed to minimizing violence (Marsh, 2003). They can observe the growing disparities between rich and poor in the United States, consider the wider political components that seem to spur people to hate one another, and renew their efforts to work for a just society. Workers can address racist and economic policies of welfare reform that punish people of color and keep poor people poor. They can analyze legal approaches to weapons legislation, their commitment to antiviolence principles, and their positions on war. These are all at the heart of people's lives and as such are in the realm of social justice–oriented social work practice from the most local to the most global levels.

Violence in the Social Worker's Own Workplace

This discussion of oppressed people, involuntary clients, and violent cultural conditions has a connecting thread to the context of social work practice. Considering that practitioners are very likely to work with the people who are most affected by the quality of this cultural fabric, it is not surprising that, as reflective symbols, social workers are increasingly the objects of violence themselves (Jayartne, Croxton & Mattison, 2004).

The Nature of Violence against Social Workers   As far back as 1995, Newhill documented that "physical and emotional violence by clients toward social workers is increasing in all settings" (Newhill, 1995, p. 631). Further, in a random survey of NASW members from two states, a majority of the respondents had experienced client violence. Gender and setting appeared to be significant (Newhill, 1996), with women in correctional and child protective services at greater risk.

Unfortunately, the trend toward violence against human service workers has not abated (Spencer & Munch, 2003). In one study some workers were subject to physical assault, and "all workers were routinely subjected to psychological aggression" (Shields & Kiser, 2003, p. 13), such as outbursts of anger, profanity, or intimidation. This conclusion was based only on those workers who responded to the survey (and those who had experienced violence might be more likely to respond); nevertheless, this is a startling finding.

What Social Workers Can Do   As an individual worker in a context of potential violence, you can take some reasonable precautions based on common sense and effective communication. See Box 11.2 to consider these strategies.

Skills for Working with Angry Clients   Probably the single most useful tool for working with clients who are angry or hostile is empathy. Empathic responses to clients demonstrate that you recognize they are upset, would like to understand the reasons for their distress, and want to assist them. In turn, such

---

What Social Workers Can Do in the Context of Violence

BOX 11.2

Violence

- Always inform your client of the time you expect to make a home visit. Keep to that schedule as closely as possible. This is not only respectful, but you are more likely to be safe if you don't surprise anyone with your appearance.

- Consult with others (especially a supervisor) before entering a situation you think may be dangerous. If your client has a history of violence and is highly stressed or is known to have firearms or other weapons, don't make a home visit or an office visit after hours without talking it over with others who may have more experience and can consult with you about your decision.

- When you leave the office to make home visits, always inform someone about your schedule. Check by phone in worrisome (or all) situations.

- Pay attention to your surroundings. If you are on a home visit and you hear fighting or crying from outside the residence, reassess the timing of your visit. If there is activity that seems suspicious and/or is not what you expected, avoid confrontation.

- Don't put yourself physically in a position to be trapped in a potentially violent client's home. Keep a clear path to the door, so you can leave quickly if necessary.

- Make connections with the local police if you work in a dangerous neighborhood, or with local shop owners or residents in rural areas. Alert them of your plans when circumstances warrant and to the extent that confidentiality permits. Know when police should accompany you, and don't hesitate to ask them when appropriate.

- Don't challenge an angry client with rebuttals or consequences. A calm, kind, and reflective presentation can encourage deescalation.

- If you sense clearly that something is wrong and you are at risk, even if you can't tell exactly what it is, leave. There is time for analysis later, and if you overreacted, you can explore that in a safe environment.

- Report incidents of any kind to your supervisor, or use an agency-designated process if there is one. This both helps you work through your own reactions and skills and facilitates the agency's effective response to its workers.

responses can defuse the anger of people who are inclined to strike out at the world for causing them to suffer. In addition to this overall compassionate stance, you will want to observe the following:

- Recognize your own tension. Be alert for feelings of defensiveness, and prepare yourself to avoid returning angry or hostile comments.

- Acknowledge the client's strengths as you listen, and include them in your responses when they can be heard as genuine (rather than patronizing).

- Focus on positive and current alternatives that are realistic and open to the client.

- Avoid moralizing or lecturing, no matter how destructive you think the client's conduct has been.

- When necessary, focus on keeping your own control rather than on the client's anger.

 Web Links

See the British Department of Health site for discussion of several aspects of violence in the workplace of caregivers.

What Agencies Can Do   In situations of potential violence, agencies need to assume some of the responsibility to avert danger. Agencies need to recognize and validate the hazards to which workers are exposed, so that they will report their experiences openly. Policies for handling incidents should be clear and worker focused. Opportunities for processing and group consultation should be frequent and responsive. Preparation for workers entering possibly dangerous situations and debriefing for those who have experienced aggressive or violent clients should be standard practice and should not require that the worker initiate a formal request. Larger agencies should consider establishing a management team to address violence specifically and should offer training on physical safety and verbal deescalation procedures that meet worker needs and interests. No worker should have to endure the double jeopardy of encountering client violence without agency support (Spencer & Munch, 2003).

MANAGED CARE

In the first sections of this chapter, we explored several variables in and of the environment that are frequently seen as external to the prototype of social work practice. That is, the average social worker is unlikely to choose the situational dynamics (although, as noted, some practitioners learn to thrive on them). Here we will look at a proactive, constructed human invention—managed care—as another contextual structure that is externally influenced and is frequently imposed on workers and agencies. Like involuntary services, which shape the work, managed care also often dictates the limits of health and mental health services and sometimes determines whether any service is provided at all.

Although social workers in private practice are still the most likely to encounter the constraints that managed care puts on practitioners directly, agency practice is increasingly influenced by its regulations, as well. The advent of managed Medicare and Medicaid also affects the care of people who are poor, of color, elderly, children, and people with disabilities and makes managed care a critical topic for generalist social workers. In this discussion, we will look at the effects of managed care on agencies and its implications for social work staff.

What Managed Care Is

Although managed care has become a familiar term, you might not have a precise definition for it. Managed care is an enormously complicated system of physical and mental health service delivery. It is an amalgam of insurance programs and differing payment programs that has evolved over several decades. In the simplest terms, **managed care** stresses two major objectives: (1) to retain or increase the quality of care and (2) to control its costs. Even more simply put, its purpose is "effectiveness with efficiency." Some of the other dimensions that apply to nearly all systems today include steering consumers to less-expensive care when possible, requiring preauthorization from primary care providers, and undergoing utilization review.

The Context for Managed Care's Evolution   The ideas behind managed care are not new, but our modern version was generated by the passage of Titles XVIII and XIX of the Social Security Act in 1965. Basically constituting an antipoverty program, these two titles had the effect of increasing access to services and related medical costs to an extent that was both tremendous and unanticipated (Veeder & Peebles-Wilkins, 2001). This was also a time of greatly expanding and expensive technology, products, and pharmaceuticals in a social climate of political protests, space travel, the civil rights movement, women's rights, and an exhilarating sense of affluence. It was a time for everyone, even those in the depths of poverty whose health care (including mental health) had been dismal, to demand better services as a right, and it resulted in gargantuan health care costs. Until this time, employers generally paid the costs of insurance for their employees, while the government paid for people not working.

Efforts to reduce both the extent and the amount of employers' coverage (supplemented with copayments made by the insured) alleviated some of these costs but didn't do enough to make the system workable. A third broad approach was introduced by insurance companies, which involved matching consumer needs to professional services at the lowest possible cost. This required that in-surance companies initiate and maintain a **network of providers** who agreed to accept a fixed rate for services rendered (Wernet, 1999). Case managers frequently facilitate the matching of client to provider and monitor the ensuing costs. Basi-cally, this third solution represents the birth of contemporary managed care.

Managed Care and Agency Practice   In many managed care arrangements, the insuring company contracts with the social service agency in an umbrella agreement. Depending on what services the insurance company actually supports, it approves the credentials of individuals at all levels within the agency to deliver those services it covers. This affects you as a worker in a men-tal health agency because these agreements usually provide for services at a prenegotiated rate in a prenegotiated structure that looks at statistical indices for determining, for example, how many sessions you can offer your client. Assuming you are a practitioner in an agency that has contracted with the managed care company for coverage of services you deliver, your work with clients will be subject to the company's regulations.

The managed care representative, who may be a case manager (review Chapter 6 on case management in and outside of social work), will review and scrutinize your paper documentation as well as decide how long you can see your client and what services you can offer. This is the "gate keeping" function of managed care. It is based on an assumption that in order to contain costs, the managed care company must set strict limits, or you (not personally, but as a representative of a group of providers) would see the client for an excessive length of time or provide extraneous services. These services might include some types of outreach or transportation that are not covered in most cases be-cause they are not seen as professional, even when they are critically needed.

Other implications of managed care for workers involve the referral process. For example, even if you do not provide clinical services yourself, you may want to facilitate referrals, in or outside of your agency, for your clients who may seem in great need of ongoing support. In such situations you may need to assist in arranging for the client's primary physician to make a referral or in locating an in-network provider that is acceptable to your client and agreeable to working with her or him. Further, you are likely to encounter the systemwide limits on service delivery as your client's care is restricted to a par-ticular type of mental health intervention over a particular time period.

Additional Implications for the Climate of Social Work Practice

The managed care environment has had significant repercussions for many practicing social workers at both the bachelor and master levels. Because of the transformation that it has engendered through the requirements imposed on service delivery, and the objections many social workers have voiced regarding those requirements, serious questions arise about the future of the profession in this environment. Let us consider social work's viability in this climate and then look at the ethical dilemmas it poses.

Maintaining Viability in the Managed Care Era   In order for independent social workers to remain viable in the competitive arena of managed care, they will need to recognize and develop acute business skills in negotiating and competing for contracts. They will also have to apply their flexibility in learning and adjusting to technological advances (Sowers & Ellis, 2001). Further, if agency social workers want to survive within this climate, they too will have to come to grips with several issues, even though these issues may be distasteful to them. These issues include (Dziegielewski & Holliman, 2001):

- Placing greater focus on behavioral outcomes that demonstrate a positive cost-benefit relationship—that is, social workers will need to demonstrate that their services are worth their cost.

- Increasing their marketing of social work services to health care providers, which will require social workers to market themselves more.

- Promoting social work as an important component in successful interdisciplinary teams.

- Including such macro activities as lobbying for political recognition.

- Exploring nontraditional, business-oriented roles in which a practitioner might own and manage a private practice.

Not all social workers have been willing to make these adjustments. It is currently possible to practice in settings that do not incorporate managed care directly, but these will be increasingly difficult to locate. Masters-level private practitioners also have the option of not contracting with managed care companies at all, which adds quite a challenge to the work of making a living. There are other ways in which social workers can respond, which I will address shortly. Collectively, these will be significant issues in your future practice, as there is a general forecast that managed care is, in some guise or other, likely to be with us for a long time.

Practicing Ethically in the Managed Care Context   A troubling arena within managed care is that of ethics. Just as the private fee-for-service arrangements seem to represent a conflict of interests (when, for example, the worker or agency who sets the cost of treatment is the same person or agency who determines how long a person requires the treatment), there appears to be a fundamental disconnect between the idea of maximizing access to, and quality of, care while curtailing its costs.

The Social Work Library

To consider another controversial dimension of contemporary managed care, read Kirk & Kutchin's work on deliberate misdiagnosis.

This basic dilemma occurs because of competing **fiduciary relationships**, in which one member (A) has trust and confidence in another member (B) that B will act in A's best interests. Clients are the As in this equation, and social workers are the Bs. Workers have created a professional and both privately and publicly recognized trust that they will act on behalf of clients, and they are ethically committed to that position. In this relationship, their judgments and activities are consistently based on a sense of justice codified in the *Code of Ethics.* If, however, workers have also contracted honorably with a managed care company (C), agreeing to work toward greater efficiency, then they have another fiduciary relationship that can easily conflict with the one with clients (Galambos, 1999). If workers are pressured into working against the client fiduciary relationship in order to honor their agreement with C by restricting services, they have a serious conflict of interests and ethical commitments.

In terms that are more specific to the *Code* and to ethical, social justice–oriented, human rights practice, managed care requirements raise serious questions about access to and cutoff from services, confidentiality, and health care as a market commodity. Let us look at each of these questions individually.

- *Access:* The managed care process can have an enormous impact on the people in private or public programs who need services most—people in poverty, with disabilities, and people of color. Two of several reasons for this are (1) some employers have to cut covered services because their costs are so high, and (2) many social service agencies, to which vulnerable populations are most likely to go for help, will have to curtail their services in light of their reduced income from managed care (Reamer, 2001b). This tends to leave the people to whom social workers are most committed out in the cold, which is not only in opposition to the *Code*, but in violation of the grounding principles of social justice and human rights. Another aspect of access that is particularly troubling to social workers is the termination of services when a client's benefits have run out. In some situations, managed care seems to mandate the abandonment of clients. Here it is clearly the responsibility of the worker and/or the agency to create an alternative to deserting the client who still needs services. This might mean referral to another agency, reduced rates or a **pro bono** arrangement (without cost—literally "for the good"), or assistance in appealing an unfavorable decision by the managed care company.

- *Confidentiality:* Because the representative from managed care, as a third party, sees client records, reviews them, and makes regulatory decisions about services, the client experiences severe limits on her or his confidentiality and privacy. In some systems, clients have to enter themselves into the managed care system by personally phoning a representative who asks very personal questions. This process may alienate someone who is struggling to get help with a problem and has finally worked up the courage to see a practitioner. If the company is far away, this can seem like a bad dream in which the client has to tell a total stranger the details of her or his most painful experiences. If the company is close, there is a chance that the client could be talking to a neighbor, or the wife of her daughter's teacher, or the baker's son. Further, the advent of technologically transmitted records and the ease of access to them are major concerns for confidentiality, particularly because the practitioner cannot control access of records once they are shared (Reamer, 2001b).

- *Health care as a commodity:* On a more philosophical, but nevertheless compelling level, this shift of health care into a dominion of for-profit ventures has transformed it from a human right (see Article 12, Universal Declaration of Human Rights) or a "social good" (Veeder & Peebles-Wilkins, 2001) to a market-driven commodity, like automobiles or television sets. Decisions regarding access, method of treatment, and length of care are made by businesspeople rather than providers. Unfortunately for many clients, there are substantial constrictions on the care they receive as they seek services from beleaguered agencies that suffer cutbacks, program elimination, and downsizing. This is an exceptionally troubling idea for many social workers because making health care a product represents a devaluation of one of their most cherished values and commitments.

 Web Links

See the United Nations site for the human rights position on standards of health and accessibility to health care services.

Benefits of Managed Care

In this brief discussion of a highly complex topic, you can tell that the values and commitments represented in this book are in conflict with much of the consequences of managed care. I am admittedly opinionated on the topic. I do, however, want to point out some of the potential benefits generated in the shift away from fee-for-service systems.

- Some enlightened models of managed care actually meet or go beyond what traditional health insurance has provided in the past by covering such items as family services, prevention, and substance abuse treatment (see Daley, 2005).

- Managed care may have rescued a crashing system of costs and insurance. In fact, it might have prevented the total demise of health care coverage in this country (Browning & Browning, 1996), particularly for mental health issues, and most particularly, for people in poverty.

- Managed care's emphasis on short-term treatment may benefit clients by encouraging practitioners to help them build support networks in their communities rather than depending on long-term professional services (Browning & Browning, 1996).

- The precision required in managed care processes encourages practitioners to be focused, sophisticated, and knowledgeable.

Most of these possibilities relate to doing things differently from the fee-for-service arrangements that created astronomical, escalating costs and failed so many people so acutely.

Principled Responses to Managed Care

No matter how you respond privately to managed care, it appears to be a growing phenomenon. If social workers choose not to participate, the cost is likely to be increasing neglect of the people who need them most. Just as ethical, responsive social workers are needed in public sector work, they are also needed in agency work, and both sectors are increasingly governed by managed care principles. While recognizing the ethical dilemmas that managed care can create, social workers have an opportunity (and obligation) to respond in ways that can effect social change.

Social workers can take up a wide range of alternative responses to get around some of the issues. For example, establishing collaborative partnerships with primary care physicians is often received favorably by managed care companies (Lesser, 2000). Workers can also use strengths-based instruments to document service effectiveness (Early, 2001), and they can view the assessment process through a postmodern lens by remembering that mechanisms used in managed care, such as the *DSM,* represent social constructions of illness that reflect a political agenda, rather than "reality" (McQuaide, 1999). In order to revisit the more disturbing ethical issues identified in managed care, however, let us look at some more direct, alternative approaches to them.

Access   Workers negotiating directly with managed care companies or influencing agency administrators can enter into negotiations around the following aspects of access (Galambos, 1999):

- Giving the provider discretion over resources.
- Developing a peer review committee that oversees service delivery.
- Requiring informed consent (eliminating nondisclosure clauses that keep the worker from discussing other options with the client).
- Developing administrative teams for interdisciplinary dialogue, identification, and evaluation of needed changes.

With respect to work with clients, workers can respond by (Galambos, 1999):

- Developing service guidelines that set out the terms honestly.
- Measuring outcomes so that client progress can be established.
- Explaining the grievance procedure.

Confidentiality   On the assumption that more-attuned workers and agency procedures are critical in a managed care environment, workers can take some specific actions related to confidentiality. Rock & Congress (1999) suggest the following:

- Become familiar with federal and state laws concerning confidentiality and court decisions related to it.
- Learn the *Code of Ethics* thoroughly and share the limits of confidentiality with your clients.
- Assess the level of confidentiality needed in your agency.
- Explore how well your agency observes procedures to maintain confidentiality.
- Inform your clients how your agency keeps records and observes confidentiality.
- Advocate on all levels for improved procedures.
- Engage in collaborative partnerships with interested others on all levels.
- Educate providers about the significance and mechanics of confidentiality.

Overall Responses   Workers in general will need to keep advocating for changes in policies and confronting the ethics violations they see in managed care procedures. Here are some ways to do that effectively (Reamer, 2001b):

- Documenting how many clients have been refused services, have had services limited unduly, or terminated prematurely.
- Documenting how many practitioners have left social work practice because of the frustrations of managed care.
- Documenting the experience of both practitioners and clients regarding confidentiality breaches.
- Documenting fraudulent billing practices. How many practitioners provide inaccurate diagnoses to get access to services?
- Documenting the overall impact of managed care on client outcomes.

Managed care is a significant component in service delivery in the contemporary and future practice context. Although it poses many challenges for social workers, it needn't lead them to give up or drop out of the system. Social workers have always been creative and resourceful about changing from within and pressuring for changes from outside. Through careful monitoring of how the dominant trends in managed care influence ideas of what is ethical practice, practitioners can work *within* the system but not be completely *of* it (Keenan, 2001). The managed care environment provides another useful challenge for the profession's growth and identity in the 21st century.

SUSTAINING ETHICAL PRACTICE IN THE FACE OF CHALLENGES

So far in this chapter you have learned about some formidable aspects of contemporary practice. In my view they are the same liabilities we all face in living everyday, so you won't be able to escape them by becoming an accountant! In fact, as a social worker, you have the opportunity to challenge them and influence more satisfactory responses. Social workers are asked to confront these issues in a way that distinguishes the profession from most others and even from many of the helping disciplines.

This part of the chapter focuses on both the sustaining and ethical dimensions of the challenge in social work practice. By sustaining, I mean the ability to keep going in spite of setbacks and situations that don't go as you had hoped; to keep growing in response to new ideas, perceptions, and client-informed experience; and to keep a vision of what social work practice can be and how you can contribute to it. The ethical aspects of practice sometimes become obscured by the struggles workers experience. Just as practitioners need to guard against rationalizing funding cuts or avoiding client contact, they need to keep the ethical considerations of omission as much in mind as those of commission. For example, not working for active reform of harmful systems (omission) is as neglectful as committing an outright violation of the *Code*. If workers increasingly withdraw, defending themselves against the challenges of dehumanizing contexts, they can slowly lose the spirit of ethical practice without even realizing it. Let us look at ways to preserve it.

Supervision

One of the most effective ways to negotiate troubling practice contexts is to engage fully in a positive, supportive supervisory relationship (Smith, 2005), in which both the supervisor and the worker can grow. As the worker, you need to contribute to that relationship by bringing something to the process; supervision is not a commodity that is given to you (or done to you), but rather it is an interactive relationship. The term *supervision* conjures up images of a hierarchy. Literally interpreted as "watching from above," it suggests an authoritarian relationship in which one member judges and corrects the other. Fortunately, social work supervision is not limited to that configuration, in spite of the inevitable evaluative nature of the term. "Co-vision" (Roche, Dewees, Trailweaver, Alexander, Cuddy & Handy, 1999) is another much less used term to suggest a collaborative process in which two or more people consider the practice issues and work together to achieve an approach that recognizes the knowledge and experience that each contributes. My use of the word *supervision* here includes that more collaborative understanding.

Supervision, then, in all its forms—individual, group, ad hoc, formal case, and peer—has the potential to contribute a great deal to sustaining ethical practice in challenging contexts. Hearing others' beliefs about the issues involved in a sticky practice situation, for example, can expand your thinking and help you work through the places in which you are stuck or perplexed. This is the dialogic process discussed in Chapter 3 in which there is a genuine interchange regarding the values and ethics of a case situation. Effective, collaborative supervision can provide technical support, in that it has the potential to increase and improve your practice responses, and emotional support, in that it reduces isolation and increases hopefulness. See Box 11.3 for tips on how you can use supervision effectively.

Tips for Using Supervision Effectively

- Be prepared for each session by reviewing your work and identifying the issues you want to discuss.
- Demonstrate a genuine eagerness about learning more and expanding your knowledge and experience base in practice.
- Take responsibility for your work, your thinking, and your reactions.
- Trust in so far as possible in the supervisory relationship so that you don't need to cover mistakes or deny any struggles you have with the work.
- Assume a willingness to take thoughtful risks.
- Understand the parameters of your work and the expectations your agency/supervisor has of you.
- Respect the difference between the focus of supervision (how an issue affects your work) and the focus of psychotherapy (how an issue affects your emotional life).
- Remain open and nondefensive if/when your supervisor suggests you do things differently.
- Demonstrate a respectful and professional approach to relationships with all colleagues, including your supervisor.

BOX 11.3

Sustaining Ethical Practice

Burnout

As you have seen, several areas of challenge in social work practice might lead to increasing discouragement and ultimately to the emotional and physical exhaustion associated with burnout (Nissly, Barak & Levin, 2005). Working with people who experience oppression and trying to help with inadequate resources, engaging involuntary clients who may challenge your capacities, confronting a violent culture and avoiding its direct expression against you, coping with the bureaucratic tensions of managed care—all of these may seem to confound and certainly challenge your best intentions in the practice of social work. These can be added to the organizational pressures discussed in Chapter 9 that can emerge and contribute to frustration and alienation day after day. Here, we briefly take up two more phenomena that are difficult to manage: the incidence of painful events and the occurrence of personal triggers. Then we will look at some general strategies for dealing with the stresses that lead to burnout.

Painful Events   Although most of social work practice deals with people's struggles, and does so as a routine dimension of the territory, many (probably most) practitioners at one time or another experience a particularly jolting event that shakes their confidence and makes them question their capacity or commitment. This event often takes on the character of crisis—for example, a client suicide, a murder, an unspeakable case of child abuse, or an annihilating fire, to name a few. Sometimes these are experienced as trauma that splits the worker's world wide open, taking a generally well-balanced human being off guard. Because such events reflect a departure from the worker's usual ability to cope, she or he may be reluctant to recognize or acknowledge it. This can be dangerous for the worker's own stability and ability to bounce back; so it should be addressed. Workers need to allow themselves to be human in this profession, and the experience of overload, contrary to negative connotations, can reflect the traits of a caring, human person.

When isolated situations such as these occur, the worker should seek and receive as much support as possible. Some time off, debriefing sessions, or a shift in responsibility may be indicated. The worker's response should be normalized, and she or he should be encouraged to direct the agency's or supervisor's response so as to maintain some degree of control when it feels as if there is none. With appropriate supports and adequate time, most workers will work through such situations and return to their practice as committed as they were before.

Personal Triggers   In a related but distinctive scenario, the worker may have some unresolved or not-quite-resolved personal issues that affect her or his capacity to carry out the work of the agency. For example, a worker who experienced an abusive father in childhood may harbor a great deal of rage. This may be understandable and normal, but is a serious problem if, for example, the worker verbally or physically attacks a client who may be suspected of child abuse. In such cases the agency response is likely to be different from that for a painful event. The event is much more likely to become a supervisory issue that is addressed in an administrative or corrective way. The worker here will need to engage in some process (such as therapy or education) that will effectively change her or his behavior. These incidents can make for a very tough experience for someone who is committed to the profession and has the capacity to make a solid contribution to it. The intensity of the trigger situation can lead a worker to assess herself or himself as inadequate and not suited to the profession.

Because everyone has areas that can be triggered, this phenomenon should be normalized to the extent possible. That doesn't mean that the worker's behavior is acceptable—it is not in this scenario, and will need to change. But none of us can claim perfect balance, and if you begin to slip into negative judgments, you can remind yourself that if your own triggers are less obvious or extreme, you are very fortunate.

 Web Links

The Successful Academic site is geared toward career academics that may be like your instructor. Ask her or him to go there and take a look.

Self-Care

Beware of the fate of Don Quixote:

> *In short, he so busied himself in his books*
> *that he spent the nights reading from twilight till daybreak*
> *and the days from dawn till dark;*
> *and so from little sleep and much reading his brain dried up*
> *and he lost his wits.*
> — CERVANTES

In carrying out this work, social workers need to learn to care for themselves, even as they care for clients. Although this process will take on different dimensions in different people, there are some relatively general categories that are useful across the board:

- *Learning to use yourself as a resource:* Several chapters covered the importance of knowing your own responses, biases, and limits in various processes of the work. Self-awareness is critical not only in ethical, culturally sensitive practice but also in taking care of yourself. Appreciating your strengths and accepting your vulnerabilities will help you make good practice connections with clients as well as avoid expecting too much of yourself, which frequently leads to feeling disheartened. In the face of so much need, you may expect to save the world and inspire clients to love you while you do it. When you know that about yourself, you can laugh at your own grandiosity, let go of the need for all clients to like you, and continue to do the best job you can do.

- *Coming to grips with shared power:* This is another issue we have looked at in the context of engaging, assessing, and intervening in client situations. The strengths perspective is a particularly good fit with this idea because it assumes that clients have their own abilities to control their lives and don't need you to do it for them. This carries an unexpected benefit of reducing the pressure to be all-knowing and all-delivering, which can be terribly burdensome in addition to harmful to clients. You do not have to assume responsibility for clients' behaviors; you cannot be responsible for any behavior other than your own.

- *Focusing on practical goals:* This is related to the impulse to rid the world of all evil. With such a goal, you will always be disappointed and will continue to fail. When you concentrate on the strengths clients have to achieve their own goals and when you stress social justice and human rights in ways the client can relate to, you are more likely to see joint successes more frequently. This in turn will bolster your commitment.

- *Finding your own systems for support:* Social workers understand the importance of support for clients but sometimes forget its value to themselves. Support, both in the workplace and outside of it, is critical for the connectedness discussed throughout this book. Developing a group of peers at work can be helpful and enjoyable. Such a collective can function as a peer supervisory/support network or a strictly social group. Friends outside of work and family are also critical. Spiritual support in the way of religious affiliation or a more informal connection with the dimensions that seem most important in life help put the occasional but inevitable disappointments and frustrations of the work into a perspective that helps keep you from feeling overwhelmed and dropping out in despair.

Although social work will never be an easy job, it needn't be overwhelming. Recalling the joys and connections of working with people can fill out the compensation side of the balance sheet. Taking control of your own reactions and caring for yourself will enhance your capacities to stay committed.

STRAIGHT TALK ABOUT THE SOCIAL WORKER AS A WHOLE PERSON

Just as social workers emphasize the whole client person in context, they need to think of themselves as whole people, too. This means that they aren't just workers. Like clients, they are children, partners, bicycle racers, amateur politicians, musicians, parents, belly dancers, and artists. They are good in some roles and need work in others. They may connect well with involuntary clients and yet steer away from children or elders. They may be stimulated by institutional settings or find them hopelessly oppressive. They may need to work on how to change urban agency policies effectively or thrive in rural hills where the sole agency has no walls and policy is an on-the-go venture.

Workers may also be subject to restrictions related to social justice themselves. Their human rights may be violated daily, and it is likely that they—although inadvertently—violate those of others daily. Their identities are privileged in some contexts and devalued in others. When you see yourself as a whole human, belonging in a context, you will be more likely to engage in your human work with enthusiasm and vigor.

CONCLUSION

This chapter has dealt with some of the most difficult and challenging aspects of social work practice today in an effort to help you experience the contemporary climate (rather than to discourage you). The areas covered here are limited to a selection of what I think are likely to influence your practice the most, but many other areas exist. These include the increasingly litigious climate in which ethical complaints are made against workers and supervisors, the effects of partisan politics on the practice environment, the impact of professional licensing, and the potential resurgence of local grassroots efforts in the states.

As we near completion of this book, the next chapter will address ending the work with clients and groups, and disengaging from people you will most likely have become attached to. We will also consider strategies and complications for evaluating practice and for critiquing professional efforts.

MAIN POINTS

- Practice with marginalized populations in the public sector is associated with challenging funding cuts to which social workers can respond in a variety of ways. They may become discouraged, blame the victim, or abandon the public sector; they may also become highly informed about alternative resources and engage in social action.

- The phenomenon of involuntary/mandated/nonvoluntary clients creates challenges for social workers that can be met effectively if framed adequately and met with a basic approach of respect and willingness to hear the client's story.

- Violence is a pervasive quality in U.S. culture and influences both the work of the social work practitioner and the potential for her or his personal safety. Workers can engage in social justice–oriented practice to try and minimize societal violence, and they and their agencies can develop skills and policies to deal with situations of potential violence associated with clients.

- Managed care—the complex, bureaucratic environment in which social workers are increasingly involved—presents ethical challenges of access, confidentiality, and commitment to clients. Managed care is not likely to go away, and workers must look for ways to maintain high professional standards.

- Effective supervision is a useful interactive relationship for negotiating difficult practice contexts.

- Burnout reflects physical and emotional exhaustion in a complex practice context; it may arise out of painful events and personal triggers and can be mitigated through appropriate agency response.

- Several aspects of holistic self-care can carry you through difficult moments and are consistent with ethical practice. As in your work with clients, you will want to think of yourself as a whole person, with strengths and vulnerabilities and a need for your own systems of support.

EXERCISES: PRACTICING SOCIAL WORK

Review the case file and Interactional Matrix on Roberto Sanchez and consider the following:

Coming to Grips with Trouble as Roberto's Worker

Imagine that immigration authorities have finally identified Roberto as an undocumented worker. In addition to legal counsel, he needs the services of a social worker, and you have been assigned to work with him.

In exploration of your own biases, beliefs, and judgments, identify which of the challenges in working with involuntary clients will be the most applicable to you. In addition, respond to each of the following topics:

- How will you prepare to meet and engage with Roberto? What are the major issues for you in this scenario?

- How will you approach the legal entanglements inherent in Roberto's story?

- How will this discovery of Roberto's illegal status affect Celia? Joey? Hector?

- Identify your own attitudes regarding undocumented workers. How will these attitudes impact your work? Are you comfortable with your position?

- What do you see as the most important opportunities in this assignment with Roberto? Who will they benefit?

EXERCISES: THE SOCIAL WORK LIBRARY

Read the Danis article on the criminalization of domestic violence. Locate a domestic violence shelter or program in your community and identify yourself as social work student taking a practice course. Ask if you might meet with an intake or hotline worker. Take a local inventory of the tools (protective orders, victim advocacy, court responses and the like) that Danis identifies and ask how the worker sees their relevance and use in that particular community. Which are most used? Which are seen as most effective? Which are problematic? Compare with students from a different community if possible.

OTHER EXERCISES

When the Scam Goes Bad

You are a new student intern in an agency that serves adolescents and their families in a variety of situations. Your first case assignment is that of a young woman of 16 who has been mandated by the court to get "counseling" because of her involvement in a small shop lifting scam that is orchestrated by a group of six young women of similar age and circumstances. She is now face to face with you in your office (or whoever's office you had to borrow).

Respond to each of the following scenarios by identifying one of the perceptual skills that Middleman and Wood delineate (review Chapter 4). What do you know about yourself that influences your thinking about this scenario? List two attributes.

Next identify how you would respond to your client in each of the following scenarios. Identify other skills as specifically as you can. Give examples.

1. You extend a cordial greeting to which she responds with a sullen stare, and no answer.

2. You extend a cordial greeting and she tells you, with considerable hostility that she is only in your office because she has to be. She has no intention of changing and she knows you will just try to tell her to be a different person from who she is.

3. You extend a cordial greeting and she complains bitterly that her parents are a pain, that her teachers are boors, and that other people have messed

up her life from the beginning. As she finishes, she begins to swallow hard on her words and starts to cry.

4. You extend a cordial greeting and she responds with a long and enthusiastic account of how well she gets along in school, what an awesome boyfriend she has, and how cool her life in general is, except for this "little trouble" she's in.

Compare with your peers and discuss in class.

Ms. Sara Jane: Another Kind of Involuntary Client

Sarah Jane is a southern woman, 82 years old. She used to think of herself as a Southern belle. She moved north from Alabama with her husband when they were still in their 20s. They had five children and worked very hard throughout their lives, and finally, after their children were grown and on their own, were able to afford a small but comfortable house. But then Sarah Jane's husband developed lung cancer in his early 80s and died within a matter of a few months. Sarah Jane was heartbroken, having lost her husband of so many years, her workmate, and her partner. Their oldest son, Fred, was very helpful during the first two years, calling a lot, making sure she had groceries, and trying to cheer her up.

Sarah Jane didn't cheer up very well. She didn't think it was very important to keep the house so spotless anymore and didn't worry about her appearance as much either. She ate Cheerios for dinner. But she thought she was doing pretty well as things go. So she was very surprised when Fred started pushing for her to move into supervised living at a senior residential center. Sarah Jane wanted to stay right where she was. Fred was a pretty strong person, very determined, and a bit intimidating. It was clear he felt in charge of his mother, that his motives were pure, and that he was going to call the shots.

You're the worker in the senior center. Fred has asked you to meet with him and Sarah Jane with the idea that you would convince her to make the move. You think Fred seems well intentioned, but you also feel some tension about his insistence in this matter. As the social worker in this scenario, how will you prepare for this interview? Think about Sara Jane's "involuntary" status here, about son Fred's commitment to his mother, and about ethics in social work practice.

1. List three ideas or principles you think are the most important to keep in mind at this point in your work with this family.

2. List the most challenging aspect for you under each of the three headings: (a) Sara Jane's position; (b) Fred's position; (c) ethical practice.

Ending the Work, Consolidating the Gains, and Evaluating Practice

I said by the middle of next month I wouldn't be able to meet with the group anymore as I am leaving the hospital. There were nods. Everyone looked at me blankly. I said we talked last week about having things we like break away or taken away. I asked if they remembered. No one responded . . . I said this is hard to talk about, or at least I find it hard . . .

Germain & Gitterman, (1996), p. 318

ENDING IMPORTANT THINGS IS ALMOST NEVER EASY. Even when all participants in a relationship agree that it is time to move on, ending can be a wrenching process, often punctuated with doubts about whether you have given or done enough, or wishing, in some vague way, to start over. This is a common experience that you have probably had yourself, perhaps when you left home or broke off with a boyfriend or girlfriend. Endings tend to raise ambivalence: On the one hand they may be sad, while on the other hand they represent a kind of freedom to be on your own, make a new start, and be who you want to be.

The endings between social workers and clients often reflect these tensions. Some workers, as well as clients, will be tempted to minimize any significance in saying good-bye and simply "slip out the back." Others will not even want to talk about it, finding it more comfortable just to be gone. Yet others tend to make scrupulous notes with phone numbers and schedules and agree to call each other often. Some clients will feel exuberant, as if they have just graduated from an exacting program in which they have excelled, and others may see ending as invalidating (Cox & Ephross, 1998). People tend to develop patterns about endings, and usually these serve to mitigate the loss that inevitably occurs in all significant relationships.

This chapter will address the processes of ending a professional relationship with your clients. Because you both experience endings, it will concern both you and your clients' responses. We will then look at ways to evaluate the work more formally on a number of different levels, both as practitioners and as human beings.

ENDINGS

There are great variations in the way endings occur in social work practice. The age, gender, ethnicity, class, working style, and personality of both the client and the worker certainly play a role. The social location of the work, its purpose, the agency, the perspective used, and the organizational pressures surrounding the work also have an impact. Even within this enormous range, however, general planning is necessary.

Planning the Process: Overview

We begin by considering several tasks that relate to endings. These do not necessarily apply to every social work relationship, and their order does not need to be rigid. The specifics of the practice situation will guide much of the timing and ordering, but these tasks are common to a wide range of relationships and are consistent with ethical practice. They are

- Negotiating the timing.
- Reviewing the agreement for work.
- Processing successes and shortcomings.
- Making and clarifying plans.
- Sharing responses to ending.
- Respecting cultural consistency.

Negotiating the Timing   In some circumstances you and your client specify the number of sessions at the beginning of the relationship. Task-centered approaches, for example, often set the closing date during the first meeting. Frequently the same is true of mandated arrangements or managed care situations in which the agency is bound by prearranged guidelines. All of these are, of course, artificial proclamations that the work is done, and they are all externally imposed. In some cases, clients may request an additional number of sessions (as in task-centered models), and workers may petition for an extended number of sessions (as in managed care).

These boundaries tend to distract from the ideal timing for ending, which is when the worker and client have reached the mutually formulated goals. As simple as that is to say, it is not always that clear, particularly if goals have not been clearly established. Even when goals are put in precise behavioral terms (for example, "I will not eat more than two 100-calorie snacks a day"), which should make them easy to measure, there is some risk that they may still miss the mark. (Your client may still crave six 100-calorie snacks a day and therefore fears that meeting the goal technically does not meet the spirit of the issue.)

Nevertheless, you will need to make a reasoned judgment that the client no longer needs your services. Because you and the client may not necessarily agree on the exact moment when that occurs, in many cases you will need to negotiate the timing and criteria, remembering that you are each subject to your own foibles relating to ending relationships.

There are at least three areas for you to think about in your negotiations. The first has to do with your responsibility to do as much as possible to prevent an unanticipated ending. In many circumstances you won't have control over the timing, but in others you can anticipate, if not change, the conditions. Managed care restrictions may determine an ending date that you think is not appropriate. In such a situation you can at least prepare the client for the possibility that your appeal for more sessions may be denied. If your agency is about to cut services, or your position is threatened, or you know you are leaving your job or internship on a particular date, you need to be straightforward about these circumstances and make the smoothest transition arrangements you can.

The second issue has to do with maintaining an ongoing dialogue with your client about how things are going, whether the work is helping, and what needs to happen for the client to know she or he has met the goals. Earlier chapters have touched on this; it means that the negotiation of the preferred time to end the work should not pop out of nowhere two weeks before you think you should close. It should in some sense be the goal from the beginning of the relationship and always be before you as you go along in purposeful work.

The final issue involves predetermined endings. Knowing that you will have 12 sessions doesn't mean you can ignore the issues involved in ending or you can take for granted that your client shares your understanding of when the work will be completed. Some clients may assume you can or will extend the number of sessions as you prefer, and others might expect if they behave well (especially in mandated sessions) that they will be "dismissed" early. You will always want to be as clear as possible about whatever limits are imposed on you for the work and as open as possible as to what those mean to your client. Even when both sides clearly understand the ending date, either the client or you may still experience difficult ending dynamics.

Reviewing the Agreement for Work   In the process of finishing your work together, you and your client should review the agreement you made for work.

This agreement may have taken the form of a written contract, or it may have been much less formal, but it still should have been clear. You will want again to negotiate the understanding each of you has about the agreement, as it may have changed in view of the actual work you did together or because of other circumstances in the client's life or yours or in the agency's ability to offer services.

Processing Successes and Shortcomings   As you have gone along in the work that you and your client have undertaken, you will have processed some of the things that went well, the things that just missed the mark, and any approaches that clearly headed in the wrong direction. This type of assessment should not appear mysteriously at the last meeting. Nevertheless, processing a summary of successes at the end is a good way to gain some perspective on the whole experience and to see how the client's view of the work has developed. Sometimes, for example, an experience that seemed difficult at the time, in retrospect is associated with growth. Recall from Chapter 6 the client with mental illness who had always struggled in finding housing. You may have suggested that she was ready to meet with the landlord on her own, which at the time seemed very challenging to her. As your work together has progressed, however, she may see that it was a useful push that helped her to recognize her strengths. Further, looking through an empowerment lens, this success might be seen as a "power gain" (Lee, 2001, p. 254) in that it suggests your client's ability to take up her own needs, no longer as a victim, but as a survivor of the power imbalance experienced by people with labels, such as those given to people with mental illness. It is useful for clients and workers to process successes based on power and human rights definitions.

It is not unusual at this point in the relationship, however, for some clients to indicate that they haven't really made as much progress as it seems. They may point to various criteria to demonstrate their own shortcomings or to register some verbal sense of being abandoned. This behavior can be tricky to deal with because it raises the possibility that ending would be premature and possibly harmful. It is also possible, however, that clients choose this means to make known their lack of self-confidence in making their way independently, or their reluctance to leave the relationship. In my experience, the most effective way to deal with such dynamics is to be transparent about the process and discuss it with the client. Whether or not you offer to continue to work with a client for a longer time is a matter of your judgment, your supervisor's judgment, and all the other constraints in the agency or managed care environments.

On the other hand, it is also not unusual for clients to threaten to leave the relationship early in anticipation of ending. This often seems like an "I'll fire you before you fire me" response and is sometimes called **flight**. In this case, you will want to make every effort to engage the client in the process for at least one more session in which you can take up the issue of ending and try to accomplish some closure. Clients who pointedly (and physically) avoid the ending steps in the work, in some cases are the ones to benefit most by a positive process.

The identification of shortcomings in your own work is another area in which you may get an unexpected challenge. When you ask for ideas about what didn't work or what the client would have wanted to be different, you must be truly open to the answer. Sometimes an account of your shortcomings or those of the process itself can come as a surprise to you, especially if you haven't heard such expressions of dissatisfaction along the way. Although hearing critical comments can be difficult, you need to learn what you can from them and remain open to the meanings your client has in making them.

Making and Clarifying Plans   Although there are times when the work is clearly finished and the client is ready to move ahead without your assistance, these are certainly not universal. You will sometimes want to make a referral to a different type of service, or you will need to transfer your client to another worker in your agency or a different one. For example, you have worked with Sam throughout the school year in which you had your internship. As May nears, you realize that it isn't likely that he will complete the work he wanted to do before you leave your position. In negotiation with him you will need to go back and reassess, much as in the earlier phases, where he is, where he wants to go from here, and where it is mostly likely he can continue his work effectively. You will want to help clarify what the options are and assist him in assessing his own needs as they look near the end of your work together. Be aware that this stage represents a potential ending to services, which may either set him back or promote a continuation in his growth.

This is also an area in which you will need to know and understand your referral network well. You saw this in Chapter 6 in the discussion of the broker's responsibilities for building up a body of resources. No matter how skilled your work has been, you have the potential to disrupt the benefits seriously if you make a bad referral.

In those cases when the client is ready with some certainty to end professional services, you will want to encourage a plan for maintaining the gains and/or continuing further growth in the community. Some clients who no longer have the protective atmosphere of the client-worker relationship may find it difficult to stay on track with the changes they made without some clear way to reinforce them. You will want to identify and explore the situations that are likely to challenge the client's gains and consider how they might be addressed if there are future stresses. You can also help by encouraging the identification of a natural network of support before ending the work, or identifying other community resources that will be available. Most clients will have to return to the context in which their struggles arose, so a strategy to cope with that environment can be critical to maintaining the gains.

Sharing Responses to Endings   This may be the most sensitive of the dimensions of ending the work. You will need to anticipate how your client will respond and what issues will require your particular attention. Remember that many clients have endured some very difficult endings in their lives. They may have experienced relationships that abruptly fell apart without their having any control or understanding of them. They may have been removed from abusive homes or witnessed violence that resulted in death or separation. The devastation of poverty and social exclusion frequently creates the chaotic climate that leads to turbulence and disconnection. If ending well with your client turns out to be the most positive aspect of your work together, it will be work well done.

Workers themselves may have experienced the same kinds of chaotic, sometimes traumatic, disruptions as clients. It is crucial that workers know and understand their own history with regard to disengaging from relationships. Many workers have found themselves struggling as much as or more than clients in this process, and they need to gain the insights that will allow them to facilitate a process that is both professional and beneficial to the client. Many new workers will be surprised to realize how attached they become to a client, and they may not know how to deal with these feelings appropriately. This understandable reaction is an issue for supervision. In general, the worker needs to recall, as always, that the relationship is for the client and the client's well-being.

In the process of discussing feelings about ending, let clients know that you feel sad at ending the relationship, that you have enjoyed knowing them, and that you have confidence that they will meet their needs effectively in the future. It is generally not appropriate to express acute feelings of loss so that clients then feel they must help you, and it is not appropriate to continue the relationship beyond whatever follow-up arrangements you might make.

Over the course of a career, many client situations challenge these glib rules. We have explored some of the difficulties in rural practice that involve the potential for dual relationships and less than clear boundaries. In these cases, the worker needs to seek out dialogue with supervisors and peers and needs to be willing to work through the issues for which no simple rule is adequate. The following describes another situation that may challenge these guidelines.

Respecting Cultural Consistency   Just as you honor the cultural dimensions that your client brings to your work together, you will want to anticipate and attend to the meanings she or he makes of endings. Some clients who identify as ethnically different from the dominant culture may resist endings more than others and experience them as a kind of dismissal (Cox & Ephross, 1998). This may be because some cultures establish fewer specialized boundaries among community members with various functions. For example, it is not uncommon in some cultural groups for a child's schoolteacher to be invited to a family birthday party. Living in a culture with tightly woven informal ties, a client may view the formal aspects of ending the work and cutting off the relationship as a reflection of your annoyance or rejection.

On the other hand, some clients may find it difficult to share their emotions verbally about ending because their cultural orientation encourages a restrained and private approach to sentiment. It may be more productive to emphasize the return of the client to her or his ethnic community, whose support and nurturance will help to consolidate the gains. This rejoining of the community is viewed as especially critical to communities of color (Lum, 1986). In some situations a client may bring you a gift, a gesture that represents a more comfortable way to express feelings, reflect celebration, and offer a suitable token of closure. In others you may want to maintain a more formal, business-like relationship similar to the tone maintained throughout the work. Avoid objectifying or stereotyping any client by focusing solely on cultural difference (Diller, 2004). You will need to be mindful of your client as a whole person who brings idiosyncrasies as well as cultural traditions to the social work relationship. The dynamics of endings probably engender more commonalities than differences, and the person sitting across from you saying good-bye is, after all, the same person you have shared the work with all along.

Finally, your own cultural sensibilities about endings will influence the scenario as well. Anticipating your own patterns is helpful, particularly if they are likely to vary from your clients' in any significant way. As mentioned earlier, endings can evoke difficult feelings for all people, and some of us have developed more sophisticated ways than others to get around them. Even in the social work literature, there is much more attention to beginnings than endings. Endings can represent a metaphorical death, and by recognizing your responses to that, you will be able to say good-bye to clients in an effective, positive, and professional way.

Ending Group Work

Although all of the concepts we have explored in ending work with individuals can be applied to most clients in any constellation, there are some additional considerations and dynamics that often occur in groups. As in individual work, the intensity of ending a group is related to the type and function of its purpose. Members of an educational group are likely to experience fewer highly emotional responses than those of a treatment group. A group that has met only six times will probably not feel as invested in the group process as a group that has met for three years. In any event, ending with groups is often a complex endeavor. This is because you will be dealing with endings on three different levels:

- The relationship between group members and the worker.
- The relationships among the members.
- The structure of the group itself.

The worker should recognize and attend to all the meanings that evolve (Kurland & Salmon, 1998). Let us look at each of these levels.

Ending the Relationship between Group Members and Worker   We will look more extensively at this ending than the other two because of the implications for the worker. In this final phase of the group, the worker has several specific responsibilities with respect to the whole group, including (Kurland & Salmon, 1998):

- Prepare members for ending.

- Assess progress toward achievement of group goals.

- Help stabilize members' gains.

- Anticipate individuals' responses to ending.

- Plan timing and content to maximize the sessions left.

- Help members express their ambivalence about the group's ending.

- Share observations of progress and confidence in members' abilities to get along without the group.

- Support members' efforts to move away from the group in preparation.

- Help members connect their experiences in the group to life experiences in the future.

- Develop awareness of your own feelings regarding ending.

You can see that the worker's task is to help the group end positively and help its achievements translate into the "real world" outside the group. The worker also has to monitor her or his own responses; after all, she or he has invested a great deal of effort in facilitating an effective experience, and the more successful it is, the more difficult it might be to end it. Recalling the overall purpose of the group and focusing on the specifics of the process can help balance the response between task and emotion.

There are also a number of typical group behaviors at ending that may be directed either at the worker or the group as a whole. These include (1) denial (or simply "forgetting" that the group is ending; (2) **clustering** (Reid, 1997), which means moving toward more connection rather than less; (3) **regression**—either claiming verbally, or acting out in behavioral terms, that the group is not ready to end; and (4) flight—leaving the group before it ends.

The responses to ending are similar to those that occur in individual work. The fact that they may be multiplied by the number of people in the group can make them feel quite momentous to you as the worker. For example, when an entire collective of 13-year-old girls makes it clear, through sudden and orchestrated hostility to you, that they don't want the experience to end, you can certainly feel the power of the group! In this case, just as in individual work, you will want to see the group's reaction as a function of the process (and perhaps of the success of the group), rather than focused personal assault.

Worker skills that are particularly useful in ending work with groups are as follows (Middleman & Wood, 1990):

- *Thinking group:* As always, in group work, this skill keeps the worker focused on the processes of the group and the priority of its development as an entity rather than on individual members.

- *Summarizing:* This refers to restating what the group has decided or done or acted upon. It is useful in ending work of all kinds.

- *Voicing group achievements:* This refers to acknowledging the group's successes and validating the members own hard work.

- *Preserving group history and continuity:* This involves emphasizing the entity of the group in its social location and linking its history to the members' futures. In the process of ending, the worker will want to focus on the group's continuity as translation to the world outside of the group.

Ending the Relationships among Group Members   In this aspect of ending, members may exhibit individualized versions of denial or flight as well as variations of these. Some members may not attend meetings that are specifically dedicated to ending activities. Others may attend but refuse to enter any group interactivity about endings, or they may simply resign themselves to rejection. Individuals may become increasingly short-tempered and impatient with specific other members, as if to negate the importance of their relationship and to render ending insignificant or even a relief. Sometimes this behavior occurs among members who have worked the hardest at making connections with each other.

In other situations, individual members will question their ability to maintain the changes they have made without the assistance of the group and the worker. These members will sometimes lobby for individual sessions with the worker or a reconstituted "mini group" in which only a few members of the original group would attend. In addition, some individuals may initiate more intense relationships with other group members outside the confines of the group meetings, as if to negate the need for the group. The most helpful thing you can do is articulate what you think is happening in the group. Staying focused on thinking group, rather than on the individuals, can be challenging, but it is part of negotiating a successful ending.

Ending the Group Itself   This ending is at once philosophical and technical. On the philosophical level, you will need to reflect on what it means to you to end this unit of work, this group of unique characters. How will it contribute to your professional growth? What could you have done differently? How will members benefit from it? If the group has been difficult, you may struggle with feelings of inadequacy or a sense of work left undone. When there is an overall sense of the group's having gone well, you may feel exhilarated by a sense of accomplishment, of having crossed a particular hurdle, or of entering into the realm of the skilled. When you consider a metaphor for your experience, would it be death? Divorce? Disengagement? A required course? Graduation?

On a much more practical side, you will need to close out the records of participation, complete the evaluation process (addressed shortly), and terminate the logistical arrangements such as space and place. Finally, you will need to honor follow-up commitments and ensure that any referrals or transfers are made successfully.

Ending Work with Other Constellations

The general principles presented here for ending the work with individuals and groups apply to most other constellations as well. Just as the need for culturally sensitive practice plays out in individual work, so it does for groups. Just as you need to explore the meaning of endings in groups, so you do for families, organizations, and communities. This discussion assumes a cumulative recognition of the important areas for ending the work, based on considerations covered so far, and a flexible application with greater emphasis on some principles than others according to context. With those principles in mind, we will look to some specific variations as additional perspectives.

Endings with Families   In voluntary family work, endings tend to occur when the family is satisfied that they achieved what they came for (unless managed care restrictions mandate an earlier end point). Because there is usually not as much focus on the relationship with the worker as there is in individual work, the emphasis often falls on looking at the ways the family wanted the dynamics of their relationship to be different, and the extent to which they have been successful. There is also likely to be some focus on translating the gains into future situations that the family can predict. For example, if a family is struggling with how to allow an adolescent son freedom to develop a unique identity when he has a history of getting into legal troubles, it will be useful for the family to consider how they will manage that issue when he leaves home for college or when the next sibling reaches an age to declare herself a separate person. These positions are all consistent with the principles of review and exploration discussed earlier.

To take a different perspective, let us identify briefly two postmodern responses to the idea of ending the work with families reflected in solution-focused approaches and narrative approaches. Both of these approaches minimize the difficulty of endings, describing them as an artificial or structural definition of the work. In general, they propose a naturalized and comfortable process that is flexible and controlled by clients whenever possible.

Solution-focused work emphasizes ending almost from the beginning. As a short-term intervention approach, it always stresses the view that the clients have abilities to manage their lives competently. Therefore this model never encourages a long-term relationship in which the family might become attached. One of the very early questions asked is, "What [number] do you need to be in order not to come and talk to me anymore?" (DeJong & Berg, 2002). This refers to the number from 1 to 10, on a scaling question, that reflects the degree of well-being that the client reports experiencing. In this approach, a family's concerns about needing further work are honored, and they determine the number and content of further sessions. There is very little emphasis on the relationship between the worker and the family because "not coming to talk to me anymore" is seen as the preferred reality and a natural and comfortable conclusion to a problem for which the family is already likely to have the solution. In this sense, then, ending is seen as success almost by definition.

In narrative work, there is a similar emphasis on normalizing the point at which the family decides to end. As they develop and begin to live their preferred, alternative stories, families decide they can "do just fine without therapy" (Freedman & Combs, 1996, p. 142). Narrative workers, however, often punctuate the ending of their work by working with families to develop rituals or ceremonies in which the family invites an audience to witness the changes they have made and to rejoice in their achievements. Public acknowledgment of the family's successes not only celebrates them but also provides a structure for their supportive maintenance when the work is over (Morgan, 2000). This focus, like solution-focused work, represents a departure from traditional views of endings while acknowledging the same concerns regarding the maintenance of gains. The reduced emphasis on stages with specific boundaries in both these approaches marks a shifting pattern in which the view of the client as expert is primary.

Endings with Organizations   Because social workers' commitments to organizations are generally more contractual, reflecting terms of employment or internship, than those they make to clients, endings often seem impersonal and mechanical. Although you may be scheduled to leave at the end of a school year, or have agreed to give two weeks' notice before leaving, there is a lot more to think about when you actually begin to make the move from an organizational setting.

On the professional end of the relationship, you will want to minimize the number of loose ends for someone else to tie up. This means reviewing all of your clients' records to make sure they are up-to-date, transitioning any program development activities to the right people, and leaving your work in an orderly way. In some situations, you will want to inform your referral sources, or others forming a network outside the agency, that you are leaving and to introduce your replacement if possible.

On a personal level, consider how your departure affects others in the agency. Obviously this will depend on the context of your work, but some of your fellow employees may have strong reactions. If you have worked consistently with a particular unit of people, or if you have worked closely with support staff or aides, you will want to be respectful of their potential sense of loss, in much the same way you would with clients. Supervisors and administrative staff may also see your leaving as a significant event, and you will want to meet with them and demonstrate your consideration for their responses.

Finally, for your own professional development, reflect on what your time with the agency has meant for you in terms of growth and learning. If you are leaving because of some basic disagreement with agency policies or procedures (and if you have felt some anger toward the organization), it will be important to acknowledge and process that with the appropriate people and come to some understanding of it so you can move on. If you are completing an internship, you will want to reconsider your learning goals, the degree to which you have met them, and explore the reasons for any disappointments or incomplete objectives. Reviewing successes and shortcomings, just as with clients, is a useful activity in the context of your own agreements and commitments. Presumably you will be a different worker, and probably a different person as well, from when you began your work. Ending "right" will serve your ethical and professional responsibilities and leave you well poised for the next chapter of your work life.

Endings with Communities Some community work involves little emotional investment, dependency, or self-disclosure. In such situations, you may not focus so much on the emotional aspects of ending your involvement, but as a departing social worker you will still want to make sure the appropriate people know you are leaving. If you have helped to establish task forces or other community-centered groups, you will want to provide them with feedback, thank them for their collaborative activity, and leave them in good shape and with a strategy for dealing with any issues that they might have turned to you for. It will also be useful, as always, to process any struggles or areas of tension in formulating a community response.

If you have participated in a community as a participant in action-research or as a participant observer, you are likely to have much closer bonds with community members and may feel some grief at leaving. In such cases it is important to acknowledge the privilege you have been granted in joining the community and participating in their decision making. Just as in organizations, you will want to respect the sensibilities of those who have acted as your partners and have allowed you entrance into their world. Be aware of the potential for community members feeling abandoned, as they may feel that theirs is just another project in a long line of your activities. Social workers do not always remember that community members are left to continue their lives while workers may bound off for new and exciting destinations.

Finally, you may be somewhat startled at how hard it is to leave the community context of your work. While you are engaged in all the logistic and process issues of community organization and planning, your affective attachments may go unnoticed, and they can emerge more intensely at the end than you would have predicted. This all goes back to how hard it is to leave almost any situation in which you have made an investment. Whether the experience has been largely positive or conflicted, we as human beings tend to place ourselves in the confines of the context.

Negotiating the Unexpected

All of the ending processes discussed so far have assumed conditions in which ending is planned. However, endings often are not planned and are not under your control. Earlier we looked at several different types of scenarios in which the client leaves the relationship before you expect. In addition to life-changing events, reasons for clients to drop out include shortfalls in the establishment of the relationship. For example, when the client isn't clear about expectations or doesn't share the worker's understanding of the purpose, the meetings may seem unfocused and without direction. Sometimes workers identify outcome goals that the client may not find relevant (even when clients "agree" to them). Sometimes there isn't sufficient clarity about an ending point in the work. In such cases the work seems to go along forever as the client grows discouraged.

A group member may leave because she feels her fellow group members are making fun of her. Another finds it too difficult to tolerate the intensity of feeling generated in the group. A family is so relieved with a small gain that it loses motivation to continue. Sometimes there are agency matters as well: Funding is delayed, program priorities are shifted, student interns graduate. In hospital settings, people get transferred to other units in the middle of the night to make room for a new client. An unexpected legal loophole may change the course of the work with involuntary clients. Scheduling doesn't work. Money runs out.

In sum, there are countless reasons for the work to end prematurely, all of which present the worker with dilemmas about how to respond and what to make of it. The question in many of these situations is what the worker should do. Without pressuring the client unduly, the most useful strategy is to make contact, if possible, and encourage the client to return to the work, if only to end it in a more purposeful way. This approach conveys respect for the integrity of the work while leaving the client in control. If in your view there has been some kind of disconnect in the relationship, you have the opportunity to explore those dynamics and learn something to inform your future work.

In institutional settings in which the client has been transferred to another unit or service, you may want to petition your supervisor for a single meeting so that you can reconnect with your client, if only briefly, to review the work and acknowledge the shift in care. Although institutions tend to organize themselves in terms that meet the staff's, rather than clients', needs, make an effort to prioritize the latter whenever you can.

When you have made every effort, either to continue the work with a client or simply to have one session to end your work together, and your client does not respond, you will need to respect the manner of ending she or he has chosen. It is the client's choice at that point, and you, representing the ideal of self-determination, will humbly understand the limits of your influence. You will most likely hope that your client has made a new plan.

FORMAL EVALUATIONS

The term *evaluation* raises anxiety in many practitioners, but along with tangled visions of charts and graphs and numbers, most social workers can appreciate the importance of evaluating practice. Evaluation can provide feedback about whether the goals of the work are being achieved, about the utility of a particular approach or method, and about the experience of the client in the work (among many other things). Evaluation can be globally focused, behaviorally directed, and process oriented. It can reflect on individual progress, group development, and changes in power structures as it recognizes success. In short, evaluation can be exceedingly useful for practitioners when it is seen as a tool for development rather than a threat.

We will explore some of the issues in evaluation as they increasingly occur in everyday practice. First, we will look at some preliminary guidelines for the generalist social work practitioner who engages in evaluation procedures.

Priorities in Evaluation

There is an ongoing debate about the types and relevance of various evaluative strategies that make sense for social work. In addition, many experts maintain that social workers need to change their ways if they want to survive in this empirical, evidenced-based practice world. Nevertheless, social workers must keep their priorities straight and their commitments clear through recollection of practice principles. This requirement doesn't necessarily undermine your efforts to evaluate, but it does influence the way you undertake this evaluation.

Some client-focused principles regarding evaluation follow (Sheafor & Horejsi, 2002):

The Social Work Library

To read more about differential methods of intervention and their outcomes, see Reid's article.

- *Practice need:* Practice requirements should take precedence over data collection. Workers are ethically bound to act in clients' best interests, which means their services should not be compromised by concerns for collecting data. Some of the scientific evaluation strategies use control groups or staggered treatment designs that may involve withholding services. The client's need for services and service availability should be the sole guiding factors for their timing.

- *Informed consent:* Both legally and ethically, informed consent of the client is more important than the data. Clients need to be actively involved in the evaluation process, and they should be carefully informed of what data is going to be collected and how it will be used. They must consent to the evaluative procedure according to the *Code* (NASW, 1999), Section 5.02.e.

- *Flexible design:* The questions to be answered through a practice evaluation should be viewed as flexible, and the service plan for the client takes precedence over the research design to evaluate it. Questions may be directed at the client's experience (Was she or he helped? Were the goals reached?); the intervention itself (Was it effective? Is it more effective when used in combination with another intervention?); or the worker (Do you as the worker provide some services more effectively than others?). Because some of these questions are apt to emerge as the working relationship with the client proceeds, they may shift from one realm to another. This process of unfolding research questions is consistent with some qualitative types of research, but is not usually supported in traditional quantitative models in which the design is relatively rigid once the process has started.

Having established that as ethical practitioners, the provision of service obligations will take precedence over data collection and evaluation efforts, we can turn now to explore some of the processes available. These processes can provide the kinds of feedback that are consistent with social work's practice requirements, values, and commitment to informed practice.

In the following two sections we will consider two major, very different, methods of evaluation: empirical design processes and reflective assessment. These two evaluation methods serve quite different purposes, and they can help to balance the overall activity. First, they recognize the contemporary requirement for **evidence-based practice**, that is, practice guided by empirical, scientific evidence that the intervention has been successful. In addition, they can validate the contemplative, postmodern social worker's inclination to critique the traditional processes of practice and evaluation through focused critical reflection.

Quantitative and Empirical Processes: Evidence-Based Practice

Because there is substantial overlap with research methods in the quantitative processes for evaluating practice, we will look briefly here at only two tools for gathering such evaluative data: single-subject design and Goal Attainment Scaling (GAS).

Single-Subject Design   An intuitive framework for looking at changes in one client over time is provided by the **single-subject design** (SSD). Usually, this means that the worker takes repeated measurements from one client over the course of their work together (conversely, a worker could follow one intervention over a series of clients).

In order to use this design effectively, you will need to choose a client situation in which you will see the client over a reasonable period of time so that you can take several measurements. Then you and your client will agree on the behavior (or attitude or belief) to be measured and how to measure it. This behavior obviously needs to reflect the goals of the work. It will not be useful to measure a peripheral concern, like whether the client arrives on time (unless greater punctuality is the goal of the intervention). You and your client can select as many of these attributes as you can handle, but in general you will want to limit them to a few after considering a wider range (Bloom, Fischer & Orme, 1999). Measurement can be attained by frequency (how often something happens) or through a standardized scale that yields a numerical result. You will also want to establish a relatively consistent interval for taking measurements throughout your work with the client. For example, if you want to follow how many new social contacts your client initiates over time, you might consider their accumulated frequency over a standard period of time, say, every two weeks.

In most cases you will want to identify the phases of your evaluation as **baseline** (the rate at which or number of times the behavior occurred before the client came to you), intervention, **maintenance** (the period of stabilizing client gains), and follow-up. You can then chart the measures to see a visual pattern. If you can't establish a baseline because your client needs intervention right away, you can still plot improvements as they occur during the intervention (for example, after one month, then two months of working together).

If you can establish a baseline without withholding the intervention for your client, you can see the differences between no intervention and intervention. This provides a bit more evidence that the improvement is a result of your work because it assumes that the baseline measure would continue without your intervention (this is, of course, a big assumption). Further, if the intervention is interrupted (say you go on vacation and no one fills in for you) and the frequency of your client's social initiations is reduced, you can see if restarting your work results in renewed improvement. If it does, the connection between your work and your client's improvement is strengthened, and the possibility that some other event brought on the improvement is reduced. However, such interruptions may not be in the client's best interests, and you won't want to disrupt the course of the work simply to demonstrate its success. The single-subject design is highly flexible and generally easy to use. See Exhibit 12.1 for an example of an SSD graph.

Goal Attainment Scaling   Used in a variety of settings, **Goal Attainment Scaling** (GAS) represents a standardized framework that is customized by inserting individual goals. The basic procedure involves several steps. The first step is to identify from two to five client goals and then develop a scale for each of them based on the quality of the outcome. This scale goes like this (Bloom, Fischer & Orme, 1999):

0 = Most unfavorable outcome thought likely.

1 = Less than expected success.

2 = Expected level of success.

3 = More than expected success.

4 = Most favorable outcome thought likely.

In this example of the single-subject design model, you can see that during the baseline period, before the work began, the client initiated three, then two, then no new social contacts at intervals of two weeks. During the weeks of service, the numbers increased from two to seven, with a setback at week 8. After the work was over, the client initiated seven, then five, then six, and seven new contacts. This indicates improvement from the baseline period and extends over a four-week period following the work.

EXHIBIT 12.1

Simple Single-Subject Design

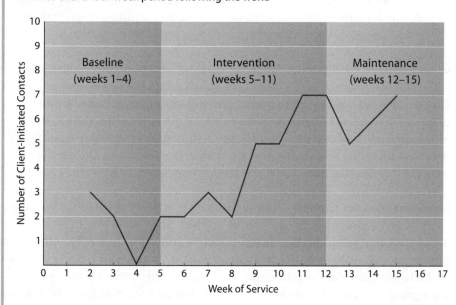

The Social Work Library

For another look at the issues in evaluation of practice, read Rosen, Proctor & Staudt's article.

In this model, the worker and client describe the client's condition before the intervention on each goal in a few words, reflecting position 1 on the scale. Next they indicate how deterioration might look at the lowest point (0). Finally, they describe the best scenario (4), and they distinguish between levels 2 and 3. For example, if one of your client's goals is to attend parenting classes as part of a plan to regain custody of her children, you might agree on the statements shown in Table 12.1. Let us say that you have also agreed on two additional goals: attending GED classes and keeping her apartment clean.

Following this process, you and your client might add further precision to measuring goal achievement by assigning a relative weight to each goal reflecting its importance in the individual case situation. As you can see in Table 12.1, the individual weights might be 75 for attending parenting classes, 15 for keeping her apartment clean, and 10 for attending GED classes, for a total weight of 100. You track your client's progress by putting a check mark in the cell that best describes the client's status at the point of entry into the social work relationship (acting as a baseline) and an X indicating the best description at the point of ending. You then calculate the weighted change score by subtracting the beginning score from the ending score and multiplying the difference by the weight.

The next step involves computing the percentage of possible change for each scaled goal. To find this percentage, you determine the highest possible mark on the scale and then divide it into the actual weighted change score. Finally, you calculate an overall score by adding up all the possible scores for all the goals and dividing that number into the sum of the actual weighted change scores.

Although this procedure may seem daunting to the mathematically challenged, it is actually quite doable; in fact, it becomes intuitive when you do it a few times. Like most such exercises, it becomes easier with practice.

Web Links

Go to the M & D Research and Evaluation site and take the tutorial-style review of Goal Attainment Scaling that demonstrates the traditional means for graphing results.

Other Forms of Evaluation   There are many other quantitative measurement scales and other methods of attaining evaluative data that are not always quantitative. This latter group includes such instruments as client satisfaction scales or reports that clients fill out to evaluate either the agency, the worker, or both. Although these tools are often considered highly subjective and not necessarily rigorous, they can frequently provide both the worker and the agency with valuable information about how the service was experienced by the client.

Considerations for Groups   Although many models of evaluation, including most of those discussed so far, can be applied to group work, there are four broad areas that might be examined for specific indicators that reflect the group process as well as final outcome goals. A worker or an agency might want to evaluate any one of these dimensions particularly: planning a group, monitoring a group, developing a group, and testing the effectiveness and efficiency of a group method (Toseland & Rivas, 2002).

TABLE 12.1

Quantitative and Empirical Processes

Client: _Ima Parent_

Key: ✔ = Beginning level   ✗ = Ending level

Attainment Grade	Task 1: Attend parenting classes	Task 2: Attend GED classes	Task 3: Keep apartment clean
0 **Most unfavorable outcome likely**	✔ No attendance at parenting classes	No attendance at GED classes	✔ No satisfactory ratings for cleanliness
1 **Less than expected success**	Attend less than 50% of the time	✔ Attend less than 40% of the time	Receive satisfactory ratings less than 60% of the time
2 **Expected level of success**	Attend 50–75% of the time	Attend 40–60% of the time	Receive satisfactory ratings 60–80% of the time
3 **More than expected success**	✗ Attend 76–95% of the time	Attend 61–85% of the time	Receive satisfactory ratings 81–95% of the time
4 **Best anticipated success**	Attend 96–100% of the time	✗ Attend 86–100% of the time	✗ Receive satisfactory ratings 96–100% of the time

Summary	Task 1	Task 2	Task 3	Total
Percent of goal	75	10	15	100
Change in score	3	3	4	
Total score	225	30	60	315
Possible total score	300	40	60	400
Percent of goal attained	75%	75%	100%	79%

To evaluate planning, you may need to engage in exploratory activities such as conducting literature reviews, analyzing needs assessments, and assessing previous records of similar groups. One strategy for evaluating group monitoring is to conduct a survey of group members' responses to a single session. Evaluating group development involves a more complex process of identifying a need, gathering and analyzing relevant data, developing a new program, evaluating the program, and modifying it based on the evaluations. Such evaluations require that the worker or the agency facilitate many groups so they have a successive order that can be studied. Within this model, single-system designs and case studies (discussed later in the chapter) can also be used. The fourth area, evaluation for effectiveness and efficiency, is well suited to the GAS method.

Other kinds of group evaluation may be useful; for example, you may want to look at the cost efficiency of facilitating a certain program against an estimated cost (to society, individuals, or employers) of not offering it. You may want to seek more self-report measures in some cases to look at attitudes and beliefs, or you may want to look at the quality of the product of a task group. As with all evaluation methods, the most important initial step in looking at group work is to determine very clearly what you want to evaluate and what kind of data you will need to gather in order to do that.

Strengths-Based Measures for Families   Several instruments are designed to be used in strengths-based practice with families and also to allow social workers to document their service effectiveness (Early, 2001). Because practitioners are increasingly involved in accountability demands, these instruments can be helpful in maintaining the workers' focus. Some of these emerged as strengths-based emphases were introduced in the 1980s and remain useful tools today because they measure family perceptions and assets. The following is a representative list:

- *The Family Support Scale* (Dunst, Jenkins & Trivette, 1988): Measures what is helpful to families. See Exhibit 12.2 for an example.

- *The Family Resource Scale* (Dunst & Leete, 1987): Measures the adequacy of resources in households with young children and emphasizes success in meeting needs, while it also identifies needs.

- *The Family Functioning Style Scale* (Deal, Trivette & Dunst, 1988): Measures family values, coping strategies, family commitments, and resource mobilization. Families indicate to what degree various statements are "like my family."

- *The Family Empowerment Scale* (Koren, DeChillo & Friesen, 1992): Measures family empowerment on three levels: family, service system, and community/political.

EXHIBIT 12.2

Strengths-Based Measures for Families

Family Support Scale

Name _____ Date _____

Listed below are people and groups that oftentimes are helpful to members of a family raising a young child. This questionnaire asks you to indicate how helpful each source is to *your family*.

Please circle the response that best describes how helpful the sources have been to your family during the past *3 to 6 months*. If a source of help has not been available to your family during this period of time, circle the NA (Not Available) response.

How helpful has each of the following been to you in terms of raising your child(ren):	Not Available	Not at All Helpful	Sometimes Helpful	Generally Helpful	Very Helpful	Extremely Helpful
1. My Parents	NA	1	2	3	4	5
2. My spouse or partner's parents	NA	1	2	3	4	5
3. My relatives/kin	NA	1	2	3	4	5
4. My spouse or partner's relatives/kin	NA	1	2	3	4	5
5. Spouse or partner	NA	1	2	3	4	5
6. My friends	NA	1	2	3	4	5
7. My spouse or partner's friends	NA	1	2	3	4	5
8. My own children	NA	1	2	3	4	5
9. Other parents	NA	1	2	3	4	5
10. Co-workers	NA	1	2	3	4	5
11. Parent groups	NA	1	2	3	4	5
12. Social groups/clubs	NA	1	2	3	4	5
13. Church members/minister	NA	1	2	3	4	5
14. My family or child's physician	NA	1	2	3	4	5
15. Early childhood intervention program	NA	1	2	3	4	5
16. School/day-care center	NA	1	2	3	4	5
17. Professional helpers (social workers, therapists, teachers, etc.)	NA	1	2	3	4	5
18. Professional agencies (public health, social services, mental health, etc.)	NA	1	2	3	4	5
19. _____	NA	1	2	3	4	5
20. _____	NA	1	2	3	4	5

Source: Dunst, Jenkins & Trivette, 1988, pp. 175–184

- *The Behavioral and Emotional Rating Scale: A Strengths-Based Approach to Assessment* (Epstein & Sharma, 1998). This scale focuses on children and asks if a particular condition is present or absent.

In strengths-oriented scales, the phenomenon of self-report is seen as an asset. This is a departure from many traditionally oriented, scientific measurements in which the goal of objectivity is thought to conflict with the biases inherent in self-report. Because the strengths perspective supports the expertise of individuals and families about their own lives, experience, and aspiration, self-report is a natural and theoretically consistent method of data collection.

The Social Work Library

For an introduction to postmodern research approaches to "ways of knowing," see Rodwell's chapter on constructionist methods.

The empirical procedures in these scales are just a few among many. Some of these are flexible and with worker creativity, they can meet a wide variety of situations, result in a creditable judgment as to effectiveness, and serve as inspiring affirmation for clients. Within this context, there continues to be a general assumption that quantitative measures are more authentic or convincing indicators than qualitative ones. This seems to be a reflection of the profession's somewhat tenuous relationship to science and science's emphasis on numbers as legitimate indicators of success.

Postmodern Views of Evaluation   In this world of managed care and increasing calls for evidence-based accountability, practical social workers need to be knowledgeable about documenting, evaluating, and accounting for the usefulness of their efforts. Nevertheless, challenges to and criticisms of these methods, based on very different perspectives, do exist and are worth considering. For example, some critics have questioned the contemporary focus on scientific research models yielding quantitative and behaviorally oriented data as a reflection of oppressive male model thinking (Lee, 2001) or as a minimization of the profession's social justice orientation (Tyson, 1995). They further charge that these models exclude the richer and nuanced contributions of qualitative research and overshadow the ethnographic forms of evaluation that question the assumptions of the everyday world.

Critics also point out that some scientific approaches have a legacy of supposedly "proving" that some racial groups are inferior to others from a so-called objective stance (Lee, 2001). These approaches have been based on expectation, researcher bias, and a political agenda that most social workers will not accept. My point here is not to discredit scientific attempts at evaluation, but to emphasize that biases and distortions are ever present. Even when workers find themselves in a place in which they accommodate the system by demonstrating the value of their work through empirical evaluations, they cannot afford to close their eyes smugly to the possibilities of vulnerabilities and opportunities for error in the evaluations themselves. This is a place for a form of bilingualism—that is, you will need to speak the language of contemporary demands, and at the same time keep alert to and keep up with the readings of their critiques.

In addition, many social workers find these empirical methods somewhat mechanical or lacking in substance and want to examine their work on additional levels. Although the push for evidenced-based practice in quantitative terms is not likely to disappear soon, social workers are not restricted to these evaluative strategies. Workers can also use the processes of reflection about their practice (see Lawler & Bilson, 2004).

Qualitative and Reflective Processes

Here, we will consider some additional ways to view the work: case studies and explorations of compatibility with theoretical perspectives and quality of relationship. Although these processes will rarely satisfy the requirements of managed care, they have the power to expand your thinking and create a different kind of consciousness about social work practice. These are not meant to compete with empirical processes but to balance the experience of self-evaluation.

With any of these methods, there are hundreds of questions that could be asked; some are suggested in the discussion. The most useful perspective in my view is to focus your inquiry purposefully on a relatively specific set of dimensions, so that you are not just engaging in random musings. If you want to take your inquiry further, you might engage your supervisor as a second reader in a case study or your peers in a conversational group to look at particular issues. This kind of focus can constitute a useful framework for ongoing staff meetings and professional development activities, as well.

Case Studies   Like single-system designs, **case studies** involve intensive analysis of one individual, group, or family and depend on accurate, careful, and richly detailed record keeping. They usually begin with the engagement of the client and worker and continue throughout the course of the work. Because they don't generate numbers and are really an account of the client's story-in-the-work, they don't yield data that is readily compared to other methods or cases. For that reason, they are not usually recognized as research tools in contemporary practice (Royse, 1995), even when they document client improvement.

Nevertheless, a full case study, though certainly not a new method, can provide you with a rich history for postmodern reflection. For example, in reviewing the initial contact, you might wonder if your sensitivity matched the client's need for validation, you might consider other ways you could have articulated your purpose, or you might reflect on the course of your work if you had taken another tack. Or perhaps you thought you were clear about the agency requirements, but looking back on the records, you can see where there might have been some confusion reflected in the language. How might the work have gone if those requirements were truly clear to the client? There are literally hundreds of ways you can reflect on the work that may be helpful, both in supervision and on your own. A record of what you saw, what you thought about it, and what the client said—all of these can provide material for analysis later. Case studies are particularly useful in noting your own growth as you learn from the experiences that your clients have in working with you and in turn explore your responses to them.

Explorations of Compatibility with Theoretical Perspectives   Another way to evaluate your work is to explore its consistency with the perspectives you want to guide your work. This approach is especially helpful when those perspectives present challenges to you and stretch your thinking.

This book is committed to the four perspectives stressed from the beginning: social justice, human rights, the strengths perspective, and critical social construction. Because these standpoints introduce several different ways of thinking, they can be translated into broad criteria for evaluating the work you want to do. For example, are you consistently recognizing the strengths of your clients, or do you tend to be pulled into the pathology orientation that dominates much of social work practice? Are you alert to social justice concerns when you meet with clients who seem unable to make their way in this culture? Can you truly remain open to the multiple realities that critical social construction emphasizes? Do you rationalize human rights violations because they are so common in our culture?

These considerations can also apply to more specific practice perspectives, such as feminist or narrative lenses. If, for example, you adopt a feminist theory that stresses the importance of power analysis, is your work consistent with that type of analysis? Do you slip into more traditional ways of looking at the issues that your client brings by emphasizing her reluctance to leave an abusive relationship or her lack of self-esteem? Can you keep an analytical structure of gender relations in the forefront rather than falling back into our society's tendency to blame women for occupying a power-down position? Which aspects of feminist theory do you carry out well, and which seem to call for continued growth?

If your framework is narrative, are you completely open to the complexity of the story? Do you wish you had been more transparent in your responses to it? Do you recognize your client as expert, or is there a temptation to believe you know better? Which aspects of the perspective are troubling to you? Which seem to come naturally?

These considerations, of course, don't yield numerical data either. Rather, they can help you decide to what degree you can work within the constraints of particular perspectives, and they can help you identify the ways in which you want to grow intellectually and skillfully.

Explorations of Quality of Relationship   The nature of the relationship you develop with your client offers another opportunity for exploration. Is the relationship consistent with your purpose in the work? Was openness a characteristic of the connection early on? Was openness difficult for either you or your client to establish? What can you learn from the client's struggle? What can you learn from your own? What cultural dimensions influenced the development of the relationship, and what was successful in working through those issues (see Maramaldi, Berkman & Barusch, 2005)?

This might be a situation in which to look at your own idiosyncrasies. For example, do you respond more easily to people most like you? Do you wonder if you encouraged the client's dependence on you? Do you struggle with keeping useful boundaries between you and your client? Are you comfortable with the amount of self-disclosure you engaged in? Are there some kinds of clients that are hard for you to be positive about?

Some other questions that can arise out of this kind of self-examination lead to more generic issues: What is the ideal relationship between client and worker? How does it look? Is it different in one setting from another? Is it likely that all your client relationships will fall into this range of ideal? How does the ideal relationship interface with the client's goal attainment?

STRAIGHT TALK ABOUT RECLAIMING OUR KNOWLEDGE

Finally, as we are nearing the conclusion of this book, I want to consider the distinctiveness of social work as a profession and to consider its greater purposes as they are informed by social justice, human rights, strengths, and the value of multiple realities. This is a profession that lives through a combination of practical orientation and a strong sense of caring. As you struggle to account for yourself and the ways in which you know things, you need to remember social work's legacy of context and care. These are always difficult to measure, and as long as you are pressured to assign numerical indicators, some of your most important contributions will be missed. Social work's distinctive knowledge, based on a practice wisdom of person-in-environment, strength and struggle, and heart and grit is the "humble stuff of lived experience and values and flies in the face of most current views about how social workers know what they know" (Weick, 1999, p. 327).

As an empowering practice, then, with real people and real misery as well as real joys, social work will ask other questions about its effectiveness, including

- Who benefits from this work? If the goals of social work relate to helping clients find empowerment, how are they realized? If a client demonstrates improved capacity to manage a household budget, for example, is there a link to her experience of poverty? Is it identified and challenged? Will she quietly and skillfully manage on close to nothing (and is this progress?), or will the benefit go beyond, to others like her, and to challenge the structure that supports poverty?

- Whose values are most salient? Social work's values are at the heart of the work. Do they dominate the client relationship? How do social workers negotiate differing values among people who don't share theirs? This is one of social work's most challenging dilemmas.

- What changes have occurred in the power structure? Have social workers helped to raise consciousness about oppression and the internalization of it? Have clients joined with others to respond to oppressive imbalances in the structural arrangements of our culture? As work with clients ends, is some move toward empowerment visibly in progress? (Lee, 2001).

These questions lead us back to the beginning of our exploration of social work practice. As a social worker in the 21st century, you will find satisfaction in connecting with clients. You will struggle to meet the demands of their preferred realities and document them for those who require an accounting. You will experience frustrations and successes, answer many questions, and come up with many more than have been raised here. The world will change dramatically and will challenge you with its excitement and danger as well as its incredible potential. You will figure out how to respond to it in ways that are consistent with your basic values, your social work ethics, your sense of social justice and human rights, and your respect for different views and experience.

Your own story as a social work practitioner will be embedded in the hundreds of stories of your individual clients, groups, and families, the organizations and communities you serve, and in the story of global change. Your choices are legion and your opportunities enormous. In the end, these will return to the story of the profession. You as a member of the next generation of citizen/social workers will author the next chapter.

CONCLUSION

In the paradoxical way that some things constantly change while they remain the same, so endings and evaluations continue and evolve. All the same, we will all experience new ways to do things in the future of social work practice. Some of you will work in much more complex settings that integrate public and private sectors through partnerships and alliances that will represent a departure from the agency practice context often discussed here. Some of you will choose more radical forms of practice in which you will challenge the historical and professional legacies you see as unjust or obsolete. Others of you will continue to practice with only incremental changes from the models under which you trained. All of these dimensions of practice will have implications for beginning and ending the social work relationship, for executing and evaluating the work, and for grappling with the obstacles that get in the way of the vision. There are no magic formulas for anticipating all of the implications of change for social work. Your flexibility, integrity, and penchant for the experiential context of your work, as well as your caring for people who struggle, will be your own best guides for the coming age.

MAIN POINTS

- The planned ending process with clients consists of several components that can benefit clients by consolidating the gains of the work and the relationship. You and your client will both want to be clear on the timing, talk over the original agreement and successes and failures, and share your responses to ending.

- The same basic process for ending work, when flexibly used with different emphases, can be applied to groups, families, organizations, and communities. However, some additional and specific components to consider with groups are the different levels of relationships and the structure of the group itself.

- Endings with families, organizations, and communities require thoughtful considerations regarding the relationships formed in the work, the theoretical perspectives used, and the practical, contextual dimensions of the work.

- Unplanned endings pose a special challenge to both workers and clients. Workers can make an effort to reconnect and end the work, but sometimes they must acknowledge the limits of their influence.

- Quantitative and empirical evaluation processes are increasingly required in managed care and other contemporary settings with competitive funding. Two of the many schemes for evaluation of this kind are the single-subject design and the goal attainment scaling.

- The evaluation of groups, families, organizations, and communities may emphasize an empirical process and/or a qualitative one. In some family models the emphasis is entirely on the family's qualitative satisfaction with the outcome of the work; postmodern views of evaluation question the emphasis on standardized, scientific, and quantitative measures and remind workers of their susceptibility to bias even when their work is supported by numbers.

- Qualitative and reflective practices also constitute an important method for evaluation and professional growth as they relate to philosophical commitments, theoretical perspectives, and relationship building.

EXERCISES: PRACTICING SOCIAL WORK

Endings and Beginnings

You initiated and developed the center's group work experience for teens that had lost a close friend or extended family member to alcohol-related traffic accidents (see Chapter 7). The group has been operating through the second semester of a school year and is scheduled to end within a few weeks. Your own sense of its impact is that many of the members (but not all) have found a significant source of solace and strength in each other and you want to facilitate other outlets for that dynamic to the greatest extent possible.

Reviewing the general material on ending the work and the specific aspects of ending a group, identify the dimensions of planning that you think are likely to be most important in this particular group and anticipate how some members might respond. Review the skills for group work, both in this chapter and in Chapter 7. Which do you think might be most critical in this group?

Finally, reflect on what you think you might gain from facilitating such a group. What gaps in your own development as a social worker might be filled? How might you use such experience to enhance your future work?

EXERCISES: THE SOCIAL WORK LIBRARY

Click on the Evaluate Tab on the CD of the interactive case study of the Sanchez family. Review the Introduction, the tasks associated with the process of evaluation, and read the sections on process and outcome evaluation. Is one type of evaluation more common than the other in your agency?

Read the chapter by Mary K. Rodwell on social work constructivist research. Focus particularly on the section that describes the epistemological debate in social work and the positivist and interpretive positions. How would these positions influence the way an agency conducts evaluation? Where do you place your own position on this continuum? Which position do you think offers the most useful framework for evaluating the work that your agency does? Ask your field instructor how evaluation is conceptualized and carried out in your agency and be prepared to discuss with your peers.

REFERENCES

Abels, P., & Abels, S.L. (2002). Narrative social work with groups: Just in time. In S. Henry, J. East, & C. Schmitz (Eds.), *Social work with groups: Mining the gold*. New York: Haworth Press.

Abramowitz, M. (1989). *Regulating the lives of women*. Boston: South End.

Abramowitz, M. (1998). Social work and social reform: An arena of struggle. *Social Work, 43*(6), 512–526.

Abramowitz, M. (2005). The largely untold story of welfare reform and the human services. *Social Work, 50,* 2, 175–186.

Alinsky, S.D. (1971). *Rules for radicals: A pragmatic primer for realistic radicals*. New York: Vintage Books.

American Psychiatric Association. (2002). *Diagnostic and statistical manual of mental disorders IV-TR*. Washington, D.C.: Author.

Anderson, H., & Goolishian, H. (1992). The client is the expert: A not knowing approach to therapy. In S. McNamee & K. J. Gergen (Eds.), *Therapy as social construction*. Newbury Park, CA: Sage.

Annan, K. A. (2003). Quoted in "From the President," *NASW News,* November.

Arches, J.L. (1999). Challenges and dilemmas in community development. *Journal of Community Practice, 6*(4), 37–55.

Arratia, M-I., & de la Maza, I. (1997). Grounding a long-term ideal: Working with the Aymara for community development. In S. E. Smith & D.G. Willms, with N.A. Johnson (Eds.), *Nurtured by knowledge: Learning to do participatory action-research* (pp. 111–136). New York: Apex Press.

Asamoah, Y., Healy, L.M., & Mayadas, N. (1997). Ending the international-domestic dichotomy: New approaches to a global curriculum for the millennium. *Journal of Social Work Education, 33*(2), 387–401.

Beck, J. (1995). *Cognitive therapy: Basics and beyond*. New York: Guilford Press.

Berg, I.K., & DeJong, P. (1996). Solution-building conversations: Co-constructing a sense of competence with clients. *Families in Society,* 376–391.

Berman-Rossi, T. (1993). The tasks and skills of the social worker across stages of group development. *Social Work with Groups, 16*(1/2), 69–82.

Berman-Rossi, T., and Kelly, T.B. (2003). Group composition, diversity, the skills of the social worker, and group development. Presented at the Council for Social Work Education, Annual Meeting, Atlanta, February.

Bigner, J.J. & Jacobsen, R.B. (1992). Adult responses to child behavior and attitudes toward fathering: Gay and nongay fathers. *Journal of Homosexuality, 23,* 99–112.

Bishop, A. (1994). *Becoming an ally: Breaking the cycle of oppression*. Halifax, NS: Fernwood Publishing.

Bloom, M., Fischer, J., & Orme, J.G. (1999). *Evaluating practice: Guidelines for the accountable professional* (3rd ed.). Boston: Allyn & Bacon.

Bohmer, C. (2000). *The wages of seeking help: Sexual exploitation by professionals*. Westport, CT: Praeger.

Bowen, M. (1966). The use of family theory in clinical practice. *Comprehensive Psychiatry, 7,* 345–374.

Bowlby, J. (1969). *Attachment and loss: Vol. 1, Attachment*. New York: Basic Books.

Boyes-Watson, C. (2005). Seeds of change: Using peacemaking circles to build a village for every child. *Child Welfare, 84*(2), 191–208.

Breton, M. (2004). An empowerment perspective. In C.D. Garvin, L.M. Gutierrez, & M.J. Galinsky, *Handbook of social work with groups* (pp. 58–75). New York: Guilford Press.

Briskman, L., & Noble, C. (1999). Social work ethics: Embracing diversity? In J. Fook & B. Pease (Eds.), *Transforming social work practice: Postmodern critical perspectives* (pp. 57–69). London: Routledge.

Brooks, D., & Goldberg, S. (2001). Gay and lesbian adoptive and foster care placements: Can they meet the needs of waiting children? *Social Work, 46*(2), 147–157.

Brown, L.N. (1991). *Groups for growth and change.* New York: Longman.

Browning, C.H., & Browning, B.J. (1996). *How to partner with managed care.* Los Alamitos, CA: Duncliff's International.

Brueggemann, W.G. (2002). *The practice of macro social work* (2nd ed.). Belmont, CA: Brooks/Cole.

Bullock, K. (2005). Grandfathers and the impact of raising grandchildren. *Journal of Sociology & Social Welfare 32*(1), 43–59.

Burford, G., & Pennell, J. (2000). Family group decision making: Protecting children and women. *Child Welfare, 79*(2), 131–138.

Campbell, D. (2000). *The socially constructed organization.* London: Karnac Books.

Chapelle, J.K. (1999). A strengths-focused approach to community development. In C.W. LeCroy, *Case studies in social work practice* (2nd ed.), Pacific Grove, CA: Brooks/Cole.

Christiensen, D.N., Todahl, J., & Barrett, W.C. (1999). Solution-based casework: An introduction to clinical & case management skills in casework practice. New York: De Gruyter.

Clowes, L. (2005). *Crossing cultures in systems of care.* Presented at the 1st New England LEND Conference, Burlington, VT.

Cohen, E. (1999). Noah. In N.A. Robinson (Ed.), Touched by adoption. Santa Barbara: Green River Press.

Congress, E. (1994). The use of culturagrams to assess and empower culturally diverse families. *Families in Society, 75,* 531–540.

Congress, E. (2004). Cultural and ethical issues in working with culturally diverse patients and their families: The use of the culturagram to promote cultural competent practice in health care settings. In A. Metteri, T. Kröger, A. Pohjola, & P. Rauhala. (Eds.). *Social Work Visions from around the Globe* (pp. 249–262). Binghampton, NY: Haworth.

Cook, D.S. (2000). The role of social work with families that have young children with developmental disabilities. In M. Guralnick, *Interdisciplinary assessment of young children with developmental disabilities* (pp. 201–218). Baltimore: Paul H. Brookes.

Cowger, D., & Snively, C.A. (2002). Assessing client strengths: Individual, family, and community empowerment. In D. Saleebey (Ed.), *The strengths perspective in social work practice* (3rd ed., pp. 106–123). Boston: Allyn & Bacon.

Cox, C.B. (2003). Designing interventions for grandparent caregivers: The need for an ecological perspective for practice. *Families in Society, 84*(1), 127–134.

Cox, C.B., & Ephross, P.H. (1998). *Ethnicity and social work practice.* New York: Oxford University Press.

Crosby, J., & Van Soest, D. (1997). *Challenges of violence worldwide: An educational resource.* Washington, DC: NASW Press.

Cross, T.L., Bazron, B.J., Dennis, K.W., & Isaacs, M.R. (1989). *Toward a culturally competent system of care.* Washington, DC: Georgetown University Development Center.

Davis, L. (1996). Role theory and social work treatment. In F.J. Turner (Ed.), *Social work treatment: Interlocking theoretical approaches* (pp. 581–600). New York: Free Press.

Day, P.J., Shelly, S.M., and Macy, H.J. (2000). *Social working* (2nd ed.). Boston: Allyn & Bacon.

Dayley, M.C. (2005). Race, managed care, and the quality of substance abuse treatment. *Administration and Policy in Mental Health, 32*(4), 457–476.

Deal, A.G., Trivette, C.M., & Dunst, C.J. (1988). The family functioning style scale. In C.J. Dunst, C.M. Trivette, & A.G. Deal (Eds.), *Enabling and empowering families: Principles & guidelines for practice* (pp. 175–184). Cambridge: Brookline.

Debbink, G., & Ornelas, A. (1997). Cows for *campesinos.* In S.E. Smith, & D.G. Willms, with N.A. Johnson (Eds.). *Nurtured by knowledge: Learning to do participatory action-research* (pp. 13–31). New York: Apex Press.

DeJong, P., & Berg, I.K. (2001). Co-constructing cooperation with mandated clients. *Social Work, 46*(4), 361–374.

DeJong, P., & Berg, I.K. (2002). *Interviewing for solutions* (2nd ed.). Pacific Grove, CA: Brooks/Cole.

DeJong, P., & Miller, S.D. (1995). How to interview for client strengths. *Social Work, 40,* 729–736.

De Montigny, G.A.J. (1995). *Social working: Ethnography of front-line practice.* Toronto: University of Toronto Press.

deShazer, S. (1984). The death of resistance. *Family Process, 23,* 11–21.

Dewees, M.P. (2002). Contested landscape: The role of critical dialogue for social workers in mental health practice. *Journal of Progressive Human Services,* 73–81.

Dewees, M.P., & Roche, S.E. (2001). Teaching human rights in social work. *Journal of Teaching in Social Work, 21*(1/2), 137–155.

Dickson, D.T. (1998). *Confidentiality and privacy in social work.* New York: Free Press.

Dietz, C.A. (2000), Responding to oppression and abuse: A feminist challenge to clinical social work. *Affilia, 15,* 369–386.

Diller, J. (2004). *Cultural diversity: A primer for the human services* (2nd ed.). Belmont, CA: Brooks/Cole.

Dombo, E.A. (2005). Rape: When professional values place vulnerable clients at risk. In J.C. Rothman, *From the front lines: Student cases in social work ethics* (2nd ed. pp. 177–187). Boston: Allyn & Bacon.

Donaldson, L.P. (2004). Toward validating the therapeutic benefits of empowerment-oriented social action groups. *Social Work with Groups, 27*(2), 159–175.

Doyle, M. (1996). Foreword. In S. Kaner, *Facilitator's guide to participatory decision making.* Gabriola Island, BC: New Society Publishers.

Dunst, C. J., Jenkins, V., & Trivette, C.M. (1988). The Family Support Scale. In C.J. Dunst, C.M. Trivette, & A.G. Deal (Eds.), *Enabling and empowering families: Principles & guidelines for practice* (pp. 175–184). Cambridge, MA: Brookline.

Dunst, C.J., & Leete, H.E. (1987). Measuring the adequacy of resources in households with young children. *Child: Care, Health, and Development, 13,* 111–125.

Dziegielewski, S.F., & Holliman, D.C. (2001). Managed care and social work: Practice implications in an era of change. *Journal of Sociology and Social Welfare, 28*(2), 125–139.

Early, T.J. (2001). Measures for practice with families from a strengths perspective. *Families in Society, 82*(3), 225–232.

East, J.F., Manning, S.F., & Parsons, R.J. (2002). Social work empowerment agenda and group work: A workshop. In S. Henry, J. East, & C. Schmitz (Eds.), *Social work with groups: Mining the gold* (pp. 41–53). New York: Haworth Press.

Ellis, K. Promoting *rights* or avoiding litigation? The introduction of the Human Rights Act 1998 into adult social care in England. *European Journal of Social Work, 7,* 3, 321–40.

Epstein, M.H., & Sharma, J. (1998). Behavioral and emotional rating scale: A strengths-based approach to assessment. Austin, TX: PRO-ED.

Fellin, P. (1995). *The community and the social worker* (2nd ed.). Itasca, IL: F.E. Peacock.

Finn, J.L., & Jacobson, M. (2003). Just practice: Steps toward a new social work paradigm. *Journal of Social Work Education, 39*(1), 57–78.

Fisher, R., & Karger, H.J. (1997). *Social work and community in a private world.* New York: Longman.

Freedman, J., & Combs, G. (1996). *Narrative therapy: The social construction of preferred realities.* New York: W.W. Norton.

Freund, A. (2005). Work attitudes of social workers across three sectors of welfare organizations: Public, for profit, and third sector. *Journal of Social Service Review, 31*(3), 69–92.

Fuller-Thomson, E., & Minkler, M. (2005). American Indian/Alaskan Native grandparents raising grandchildren: Findings from the Census 2000 Supplementary Survey. *Social work, 50*(2), 131–139.

Galambos, C. (1999). Resolving ethical conflicts in a managed health care environment. *Health & Social Work, 24*(3), 191–197.

Galper, J. (1980). *Social work practice: A radical perspective.* Englewood Cliffs, NJ: Prentice-Hall.

Gambrill, E. (1997). *Social work practice: A critical thinker's guide.* New York: Oxford University Press.

Garland, J., Jones, H., & Kolodny, R. (1965). A model for stages of development in social work groups. In S. Bernstein (Ed.), *Explorations in group work: Essays in theory and practice* (pp. 12–53). Boston: Boston University School of Social Work.

Gee, J.P. (1999). *An introduction to discourse analysis: Theory and method.* London: Routledge.

Germain, C.B., & Gitterman, A. (1980). *The Life Model of social work practice.* New York: Columbia University Press.

Germain, C.B., & Gitterman, A. (1996). *The Life Model of social work practice: Advances in theory and practice.* New York: Columbia University Press.

Gibelman, M. (1999). The search for identity: Defining social work—past, present, future. *Social Work, 44*(4), 298–310.

Gil, D.G. (1996). Preventing violence in a structurally violent society: Mission impossible. *American Journal of Orthopsychiatry, 66*(1), 77–84.

Gil, D. (1998a). *Confronting injustice and oppression.* New York: Columbia University Press.

Gil, D. (1998b). Foreword to J.Wronka, *Human rights and social policy in the 21st century* (Rev. ed.). Lanhan, MD: University Press of America.

Gilligan, C. (1982). *In a different voice.* Cambridge, MA: Harvard University Press.

Gitterman, A. (1996). Life Model theory and social work treatment. In F. Turner (Ed.), *Social work treatment* (4th ed., pp. 389–408). New York: Free Press.

Goldberg, N. (1994). *Long quiet highway.* New York: Bantam.

Goldstein, H. (1992). Essay: If social work hasn't made progress as a science, might it be an art? *Families in Society, 73*(1), 48–55.

Goodman, H. (2004). Elderly parents of adults with severe mental illness: Group work interventions. *Journal of Gerontological Social Work, 44*(1/2), 173–188.

Gould, K.H. (1987). Life model versus conflict model: A feminist perspective. *Social Work, 32*(4), 46–51.

Green, J.W. (1995). *Cultural awareness in the human services* (2nd ed.). Boston: Allyn & Bacon.

Green, J.W. (1999). *Cultural awareness in the human services: A multi-ethnic approach* (3rd ed.). Boston: Allyn & Bacon.

Green, R., Mandel, J.B., Hotvedt, M.E., Gray, J., & Smith, L. (1986). Lesbian mothers and their children: A comparison with solo parent heterosexual mothers and their children. *Archives of Sexual Behavior, 15*, 167–184.

Greif, G. (1995). Single fathers with custody following separation and divorce. *Marriage & Family Review, 20*(1/2), 213–231.

Greif, G., & Ephross, P.H. (Ed.). (2005). *Group work with populations at risk* (2nd ed.). New York: Oxford University Press.

Gutierrez, L. (1999). Current, emerging, and future trends for community organization practice. In J. Rothman (Ed.), *Reflections on community organization: Enduring themes and critical issues* (pp. 367–380). Itasca, IL: F.E. Peacock.

Hall, R.H. (1991). *Organization: Structures, processes, and outcomes* (5th ed.). Englewood Cliffs, NJ: Prentice-Hall.

Hardcastle, D.A., Wenocur, S., & Powers, P. (1997). *Community practice: Theories and skills for social workers.* New York: Oxford University Press.

Hartman, A. (Ed.). (1994). *Reflection & controversy: Essays on social work.* Washington, DC: NASW Press.

Hartman, A., & Laird, J. (1983). *Family-centered social work practice.* New York: Free Press.

Haynes, K.S. (1998). The one-hundred year debate: Social reform versus individual treatment. *Social Work, 43*(6), 501–511.

Haynes, K.S., & Mickelson, J.S. (2000). *Effecting change* (3rd ed.). New York: Longman.

Hayslip, J.R., B., & Kaminski, P.L. (2005). Grandparents raising their grandchildren. A Review of the literature and suggestions for practice. *The Gerontologist, 45*(2), 262–269.

Healy, L.M. (2001). *International social work: Professional action in an interdependent world.* New York: Oxford University Press.

Hodge, D.R. (2005a). Social work and the House of Islam: Orienting practitioners to the beliefs and values of Muslims in the United States. *Social Work, 50*, 2, 162–173.

Hodge, D.R. (2005b). Spiritual life maps: A client-centered pictorial instrument for spiritual assessment, planning, and intervention. *Social Work, 50*(1), 77–87.

Holland, T.P. (1995). Organizations. Context for social services delivery. In R. Edwards (Ed.), *Encyclopedia of social work, 19th Edition,* 1787–1794. Washington, DC: NASW Press.

Ife, J. (2000). Localized needs and a globalized economy. Social work and Globalization (Special Issue), *Canadian Social Work, 2*(1), 50–64.

Ife, J. (2001). *Human rights and social work: Towards rights-based practice.* Cambridge: Cambridge University Press.

International Federation of Social Workers (2002). www.ifsw.org.

Jayartne, S., Croxton, T.A., & Mattison, D. (2004). A national survey of violence in the practice of social work. *Families in Society, 85*(4), 445–453.

Johnson, Y.M. (1998). Indirect work: Social work's uncelebrated strength. *Social Work, 44*(4), 323–334.

Jung, M. (1996). Family-centered practice with single-parent families. *Families in society, 77*(9), 583–590.

Kalyanpur, M., & Harry, B. (1999). *Culture in special education.* Baltimore: Paul H. Brookes.

Kane, R. (1992). Case management: Ethical pitfalls on the road to high-quality managed care. In S.M. Rose (Ed.), *Case management and social work practice* (pp. 219–228). New York: Longman.

Kaner, S. (1996). *Facilitator's guide to participatory decision making.* Gabriola Island, BC: New Society Publishers.

Keenan, E.K. (2001). Using Foucault's "disciplinary power" and "resistance" in cross-cultural psychotherapy. *Clinical Social Work Journal, 29*(3), 211–227.

Kelly, T.B., & Berman-Rossi, T. (1999). Advancing stages of group development theory: The case of institutionalized older persons. *Social Work with Groups, 22*(2/3), 119–138.

Kendall, K. (2001). Foreword to L.M. Healy, *International social work.* New York: Oxford University Press.

Kerr, M.E., & Bowen, M. (1988). *Family evaluation.* New York: Norton.

Kesner, J.E., & McKenry, P.C. (1995) Single parenthood and social competence in children of color. *Families in Society, 82*(3), 136–144.

Kissman, K. (1995). Divisive dichotomies and mother-headed families: The power of naming. *Social Work, 40,* 151–153.

Kisthardt, W.E. (2002). The strengths perspective in interpersonal helping: Purpose, principles, and function. In D. Saleebey (Ed.), *The strengths perspective in social work practice* (3rd ed.). Boston: Allyn & Bacon.

Kondrat, M.E. (2002). Actor-centered social work: Revisioning "person-in-environment" through a critical theory lens. *Social Work, 47*(4), 435–448.

Koren, P.E., DeChillo, N., & Friesen, B.J. (1992). Measuring empowerment in families whose children have emotional disabilities: A brief questionnaire. *Rehabilitation Psychology, 37,* 305–310.

Kurland, R., & Salmon, R. (1998). *Teaching a methods course in social work with groups.* Alexandria, VA: Council on Social Work Education.

Kurland, R., Salmon, R., Bitel, M., Goodman, H., Ludwig, K., Newmann, E.W., & Sullivan, N. (2004). The survival of social group work: A call to action. *Social Work with Groups, 27*(1), 3–16.

Krumer-Nevo, M. (2005). Reading a poor woman's life: Issues and dilemmas. *Affilia Journal of Women & Social Work, 20*(1), 87–102.

Laird, J. (1995). Family-centered practice in the postmodern era. *Families in Society, 76,* 150–162.

Laird, J. (1996). Family-centered practice with lesbian and gay families. *Families in Society, 77,* 559–579.

Lane, M. (1999). Community development and a postmodernism of resistance. In B. Pease & J. Fook (Eds.), *Transforming Social Work Practice: Postmodern critical perspectives* (pp. 135–149). New York: Routledge.

Lawler, J., & Bilson, A. (2004). Towards a more reflexive research aware practice: The influence and potential of professional and team culture. *Social Work & Social Sciences Review, 11*(1), 52–69.

Lee, J.A.B. (1996). The empowerment approach to social work practice. In F. Turner (Ed.), *Social work treatment: Interlocking theoretical approaches* (4th ed., pp. 218–249). New York: Free Press.

Lee, J.A.B. (2001). *The empowerment approach to social work practice* (2nd ed.). New York: Columbia University Press.

Lee, J.A.B., & Berman-Rossi, T. (1999). Empowering adolescent girls in foster care: A short-term group record. In C. W. LeCroy (Ed.), *Case studies in social work practice* (2nd ed.). Pacific Grove, CA: Brooks/Cole.

Leigh, J.W. (1998). *Communicating for cultural competence.* Boston: Allyn & Bacon.

Lesser, J.G. (2000). Clinical social work and family medicine: A partnership in community service. *Health & Social Work, 25*(2), 119–126.

Lesser, J.G., O'Neill, M.R., Burke, K.W., Scanlon, P., Hollis, K., & Miller, R. (2004). Women supporting women: A mutual aid group fosters new connections among women in midlife. *Social Work with Groups, 27*(1), 75–88.

Lieberman, A. (1998). *The social workout book.* Thousand Oaks, CA: Pine Forge Press.

Link, R.J., & Ramanathan, C.S. (1999). Introduction. In C.S. Ramanathan & R.J. Link (Eds.), *All our futures: Principles and resources for social work practice in a global era* (pp. 1–13). Belmont, CA: Brooks/Cole.

Locke, B., Garrison, R., & Winship, J. (1998). *Generalist social work practice: Context, story, and partnerships.* Pacific Grove, CA: Brooks/Cole.

Loewenberg, F.M., Dolgoff, R., & Harrington, D. (2000). *Ethical decisions for social work practice* (6th ed.). Itasca, IL: F.E. Peacock.

Lovell, M.L., Helfgott, J.B., & Lawrence, C. (2002). Citizens, victims, and offenders restoring justice: A prison-based group work program bridging the divide. In S. Henry, J. East, & C. Schmitz (Eds.), *Social work with groups: Mining the gold* (pp.75–88). New York: Haworth Press.

Lowery, C.T., & Mattaini, M. (2001). Shared power in social work: A Native American perspective of change. In H.E. Briggs & K. Corcoran (Eds.), *Social work practice: Treating common client problems* (pp. 109–124). Chicago: Lyceum Books.

Lum, D. (1986). *Social work practice and people of color: A process stage approach.* Pacific Grove, CA: Brooks/Cole.

Mackelprang R., & Salsgiver, R. (1999). *Disability: A diversity model approach in human service practice.* Pacific Grove, CA: Brooks/Cole.

Mannes, M., Roehl Kepartain, E.C., & Benson, P.I. (2005). Unleashing the power of community to strengthen the well-being of children, youth, and families: An asset-building approach. *Child Welfare, 84*(2), 233–250.

Maramaldi, P., Berkman, B., & Barusch, A. (2005). Assessment and the ubiquity of culture: Threats to validity in measures of health-related quality of life. *Health & Social Work, 30*(1), 27–36.

Marsh, J.C. (2003). The social work response to violence. *Social Work, 48*(4), 437–438.

Mattaini, M. (1993). *More than a thousand words: Graphic visualization for clinical practice.* Silver Spring, MD: National Association of Social Workers.

Mattaini, M. (2001). The foundation of social work practice. In H.E. Briggs & K. Corcoran (Eds.), *Social work practice: Treating common client problems* (pp. 15–35). Chicago: Lyceum Books.

Mattison, M. (2000). Ethical decision making: The person in the process. *Social Work, 45*(3), 201–212.

McCullough-Chavis, A., & Waites, C. (2005). Genograms with African American families: Considering cultural context. *Journal of Family Social Work, 8*(2), 1–19.

McIntosh, P. (1988). White privilege: Unpacking the invisible knapsack. Excerpt from Working Paper 189. Wellesley College Center for Research on Women. www.utoronto.ca/acc/events.

McQuaide, S. (1999). A social worker's use of the Diagnostic and Statistical Manual. *Families in society, 80*(4), 410–416.

Meyer, C. (1993). *Assessment in social work practice.* New York: Columbia University Press.

Middleman, R.R., & Wood, G.G. (1990). *Skills for direct practice in social work.* New York: Columbia University Press.

Midgeley, J. (1995). *Social development: The developmental perspective in social welfare.* Thousand Oaks, CA: Sage Publications.

Midgley, J. (1999). Social development in social work: Learning from global dialogue. In C.S. Ramanathan & R.J. Link (Eds.), *All our futures: Principles and resources for social work practice in a global era* (pp. 193–205). Belmont, CA: Brooks/Cole.

Miley, K.K., O'Melia, M., & DuBois, B.L. (1998) *Generalist social work practice: An empowering approach* (2nd ed.). Boston: Allyn & Bacon.

Minuchin, S. (1974). *Families & family therapy.* Cambridge, MA: Harvard University Press.

Mistry, T., & Brown, A. (1997). Groupwork with 'mixed membership' groups. In T. Mistry and A. Brown (Eds.), *Race and groupwork* (pp. 12–25). London: Whiting and Birch.

Mizrahi, T. (2001). The status of community organizing in 2001: Community practice context, complexities, contradictions, and contributions. *Research on Social Work Practice, 11*(2), 176–189.

Morgan, A. (2000). *What is narrative therapy?* Adelaide, South Australia: Dulwich Centre Publications.

Moxley, D.P. (1997). Case management by design. Chicago: Nelson-Hall.

Moxley, D.P., Gutievrez, L.M., Alvarez, A.R., & Johnson, A.K. (Eds.). (2004). The quickening of community practice. *Journal of Community Practice, 12*(1/2), 1–6.

National Association of Social Workers. (1999). *Code of ethics of the National Association of Social Workers.* Washington, DC: Author.

Netting, F.E., Kettner, P.M., & McMurty, S.L. (1993). *Social work macro practice.* New York: Longman.

Newhill, C.E. (1995). Client violence toward social workers: A practice and policy concern. *Social Work, 40,* 631–636.

Newhill, C.E. (1996). Prevalence and risk factors for client violence toward social workers. *Families in Society, 77,* 488–495.

Nichols, M.P., & Schwartz, R.C. (2001). *Family therapy: Concepts and models* (5th ed.). Boston: Allyn & Bacon.

Nissly, J.A., Barak, M.E.M., & Levin, A. (2005). Stress, social support, and worker's intentions to leave their jobs in public child welfare. *Administration in Social Work, 29*(1), 79–100.

Northern, H., & Kurland, R. (2001). *Social work with groups* (3rd ed.). New York: Columbia University Press.

Noyoo, N. (2004). Human rights and social work in a transforming society: South Africa. *International Social Work, 47*(3), 359–369.

Oriti, B., Bibb, A., & Mahboubi, J. (1996). Family-centered practice with racially/ethnically mixed families. *Families in Society, 77*(9), 573–582.

Pappel, C., & Rothman, B. (1962). Social group work models: Possession and heritage. *Journal of Education for Social Work, 2*(2), 66–77.

Parker, L. (2003). A social justice model for clinical social work practice. *Affilia, 18,* 272–288.

Pawlak, E.J. (1976), Organizational tinkering. *Social Work, 21,* 376–380.

Perlman, H.H. (1957). *Social casework: A problem solving process.* Chicago: University of Chicago Press.

Perlman, H.H. (1983). *Relationship: The heart of helping.* Chicago: University of Chicago Press.

Pheterson, G. (1990). Alliances between women: Overcoming internalized oppression and internalized domination. In L. Albrecht & R.M. Brewer, *Bridges of power: Women's multicultural alliances.* Philadelphia: New Society Publishers.

Polack, R.L. (2004). Social justice and the global economy: New challenges for social work in the 21st century. *Social Work, 49*(2), 281–290.

Prighoff, A. (1999). Global social and economic justice issues. In C.S. Ramanathan & R.J. Link (Eds.), *All our futures: Principles and resources for social work practice in a global era* (pp. 156–173). Belmont, CA: Brooks/Cole.

Ramanathan, C.S., & Link, R.J. (1999). *All our futures: Principles and resources for social work practice in a global era.* Belmont, CA: Brooks/Cole.

Rapp, C.A. (1998). *The strengths model.* New York: Oxford University Press.

Rappaport, J., Reischl, T., & Zimmerman, M. (1992). Mutual help mechanisms in the empowerment of former mental patients. In D. Saleebey (Ed.), *The strengths perspective in social work practice* (pp. 84–97). New York: Longman.

Rawls, J. (1971). *A theory of justice.* Cambridge, MA: Harvard University Press.

Reamer, F.G. (1983). The concept of paternalism in social work. *Social Service Review, 57*(2), 254–271.

Reamer, F.G. (1998). The evolution of social work ethics. *Social Work, 43*(6), 488–500.

Reamer, F.G. (1999). *Social work values and ethics.* New York: Columbia University Press.

Reamer, F.G. (2001a). *Ethics education in social work.* Alexandria, VA: Council on Social Work Education.

Reamer, F.G. (2001b). Ethics and managed care policy. In N.W. Veeder & W. Peebles-Wilkins (Eds.), *Managed care services: Policy, programs, and research* (pp. 74–96). New York: Oxford University Press.

Reamer, F.G. (2003). Boundary issues in social work: Managing dual relationships. *Social Work, 48*(1), 121–133.

Reichert, E. (2003). *Social work and human rights: A foundation for policy and practice.* New York: Columbia University Press.

Reid, K. E. (1997). *Social work practice with groups: A clinical perspective* (2nd ed.). Pacific Grove, CA: Brooks/Cole.

Reynolds, B.C. (1963). *An uncharted journey: Fifty years of growth in social work.* Silver Spring, MD: NASW Press.

Roche, S. (2001). The anti-violence partnership: Community collaboration at the University of Vermont. Unpublished program materials.

Roche, S., Dewees, M., Trailweaver, R., Alexander, S., Cuddy, C., & Handy, M. (1999). *Contesting boundaries in social work education: A liberatory approach to cooperative learning and teaching.* Alexandria, VA: Council on Social Work Education.

Rock, B., & Congress, E. (1999). The new confidentiality for the 21st century in a managed care environment. *Social Work, 44*(3), 253–262.

Rogers, R.E. (1975). *Organizational theory.* Boston: Allyn & Bacon.

Rooney, R.H., & Bibus, A.A. (2001). Clinical practice with involuntary clients in community settings. In H.E. Briggs & K. Corcoran (Eds.), *Social work practice: Treating common client problems* (pp. 391–406). Chicago: Lyceum Books.

Roosevelt, E. (1958). Presentation of *In your hands: A guide for community action for the tenth anniversary of the Universal Declaration of Human Rights* [online]. Available: www.udhr.org/history/inyour.htm

Rose, S.M. (Ed.). (1992). *Case management & social work practice.* New York: Longman.

Rothman, J., & Tropman, J. (1987). Models of community organization and macro practice.: Their mixing and phasing. In F.M. Cox., J.L. Erlich, J. Rothman, & J.E. Tropman (Eds.), *Strategies of community organization: Macro practice* (pp. 3–25). Itasca, IL: F.E. Peacock.

Royse, D. (1995). *Research methods in social work* (2nd ed.). Chicago: Nelson-Hall.

Rubin, A. (1992). Case management. In S.M. Rose (Ed.), *Case management & social work practice* (pp. 5–20). New York: Longman.

Russo, R.J. (1999). Applying a strengths-based practice approach in working with people with developmental disabilities and their families. *Families in society, 80*, 25–33.

Saleebey, D. (1990). Philosophical disputes in social work: Social justice denied. *Journal of Sociology and Social Welfare, 17*(2), 29–40.

Saleebey, D. (1996). The strengths perspective in social work practice: Extensions and cautions. *Social Work, 41*(3), 296–305.

Saleebey, D. (Ed.). (2002). *The strengths perspective in social work practice* (3rd ed.). Boston: Allyn & Bacon.

Sands, R.G. (2001). *Clinical social work practice in behavioral mental health: A postmodern approach to practice with adults.* Boston: Allyn & Bacon.

Schiller, L.Y. (1995). Stages of development in women's groups: A relational model. In R. Kurland & R. Salmon (Eds.), *Group work practice in a troubled society: Problems and opportunities* (pp. 117–138).

Schiller, L.Y. (1997). Rethinking stages of group development in women's groups: Implications for practice. *Social Work with Groups, 20*(3), 3–19.

Schmitz, C., Stakeman, C., and Sisneros, J. (2001). Educating professionals for practice in a multicultural society: Understanding oppression and valuing diversity. *Families in Society, 82*(6), 612–622.

Schultz, D. (2004). Cultural competence in psychosocial and psychiatric care: A critical perspective with reference to research and clinical experiences in California, US and in Germany. In A. Metteri, T. Kröger, A. Pohjola, & P. Rauhala (Eds.), *Social Work Visions from around the Globe* (pp. 231–247). Binghamton, NY: Haworth.

Schwartz, W. (1961). The social worker in the group. In National Conference of Social Work (Eds.), *The social welfare forum* (pp. 149–171). New York: Columbia University Press.

Shachter, B., & Seinfeld, J. (1994). Personal violence and the culture of violence. *Social Work, 39*, 347–350.

Sheafor, B.W., & Horejsi, C.R. (2003). *Techniques and guidelines for social work practice* (6th ed.). Boston: Allyn & Bacon.

Shelton, T.L., & Stepanek, J.S. (1994). *Family-centered care for children needing specialized health and developmental services.* Bethesda, MD: Association for the Care of Children's Health.

Shields, G., & Kiser, J. (2003). Violence and aggression directed toward human service workers: An exploratory study. *Families in Society, 84*(1), 13–20.

Simon, B. (1990). Re-thinking empowerment. *Journal of Progressive Human Services. 1*(1), 29.

Simon, B. (1994). *The empowerment tradition in American social work.* New York: Columbia University Press.

Smith, B.D. (2005). Job retention in child welfare: Effects of perceived organizational support, supervisor support, and intrinsic job value. *Children and Youth Services Review, 27*(2), 153–169.

Smith, D.E. (1987). *The everyday world as problematic: A feminist sociology.* Boston: Northeastern University Press.

Smith, S.E. (1997). Introduction: Participatory action-research within the global context. In S.E. Smith & D.G. Willms, with N.A. Johnson (Eds.), *Nurtured by knowledge: Learning to do participatory action-research* (pp. 1–6). New York: Apex Press.

Sowers, K.M., & Ellis, R.A. (2001). Steering currents for the future of social work. *Research on Social Work Practice, 11*(2), 245–253.

Specht, H. (1990). Social work and the popular psychotherapies. *Social Service Review, 64,* 345–357.

Specht, H., & Courtney, M.E. (1995). *Unfaithful angels: How social work has abandoned its mission.* New York: Free Press.

Spencer, P.C., & Munch, S. (2003). Client violence toward social workers: The role of management in community mental health programs. *Social Work, 48*(4), 532–544.

Strean, H.S. (1996). Psychoanalytic theory and social work treatment. In F.Turner (Ed.), *Social work treatment: Interlocking theoretical perspectives* (4th ed., pp. 523–554). New York: Free Press.

Strom-Gottfried, K.J. (2000). Ensuring ethical practice: An examination of NASW Code violations, 1986–97. *Social Work, 45*(3), 251–261.

Strom-Gottfried, K.J. (2003). Managing risk through ethical practice: Ethical dilemmas in rural social work. Presentation at the National Association of Social Workers Vermont chapter, Essex, VT.

Swenson, C.R. (1998). Clinical social work's contribution to a social justice perspective. *Social Work, 43*(6), 527–537.

Swigonski, M.E. (1996). Challenging privilege through Africentric social work practice. *Social Work, 4*(2), 153–161.

Tang, K. Internationalizing women's struggle against discrimination: The UN women's convention and the optimal protocol. *The British Journal of Social Work, 34*(8), 1173–1188.

Tang, K., Lam, C., & Lam, M. (2003). International response to racial discrimination: Potentials and Imitations of the United Nations Race Convention. *European Journal of Social Work, 6*(3), 283–296.

Tasker, R., & Golombok, S. (1995). Adults raised as children in lesbian families. *American Journal of Orthopsychiatry, 65,* 203–215.

Thomas, H., & Caplan T. (1999). Spinning the group process wheel: Effective facilitation techniques for motivating involuntary client groups. *Social Work with Groups, 21*(4), 3–21.

Toseland, R.W., & Rivas, R.F. (2002). *An introduction to group work practice* (4th ed.). Boston: Pearson Allyn & Bacon.

Tracy, E.M., & Whittaker, J.J. (1990). The social network map: Assessing social support in clinical practice. *Families in Society, 71,* 461–470.

Turner, F. J. (Ed.). (1996). *Social work treatment: Interlocking theoretical approaches* (4th ed.). New York: Free Press.

Turner, J., & Jaco, R.M. (1996). Problem-solving theory and social work treatment. In F. J. Turner (Ed.), *Social work treatment* (4th ed., pp. 503–522). New York: Free Press.

Tyson, K. (1995). *New foundations for scientific social and behavioral research: The heuristic paradigm.* Boston: Allyn & Bacon.

Ungan, M., Manuel, S., Mealy, S., Thomas, G., & Campbell, C. (2004). A study of community guides: Lessons for professionals practicing with and in communities. *Social Work, 49*(4), 550–561.

United Nations. (1946). *Universal declaration of human rights.* New York: UN.

United Nations. (1987). *Human rights—Questions and answers.* United Nations Department of Public Information, New York: Author.

United Nations. (1994). *Teaching and learning about human rights: A manual for schools of social work and the social work profession.* New York: Author.

Van Den Bergh, N., & Crisp, C. (2004). Defining culturally competent practice with sexual minorities: Implications for social work education and practice. *Journal of Social Work Education, 40*(2), 221–238.

Van Treuren, R.R. (1993). Self-perception in family systems: A diagrammatic technique. In C. Meyer, *Assessment in social work practice* (p. 119). New York: Columbia University Press.

Van Wormer, K. (2004). Restorative justice: A model for personal and social empowerment. *Journal of Religion & Spirituality in Social Work, 23*(4), 103–120.

Vassallo, T. (2002). Narrative group therapy with the seriously mentally ill: A case study. Available at www.narrativeapproaches.com.

Veeder, N.W., & Peebles-Wilkins, W. (Eds.). (2001). *Managed care services: Policy, programs, and research.* New York: Oxford University Press.

Vinter, R. (1974). The essential components of social group work practice. In. P. Glasser, R. Sarri, & R. Vinter (Eds.), *Individual change through small groups* (pp. 9–33). New York: Free Press.

Vodde, R., & Gallant, J.P. (2002). Bridging the gap between micro and macro practice: Large-scale change and a unified model of narrative-deconstructive practice. *Journal of Teaching in Social Work, 38*(3), 439–458.

Vodde, R., and Giddings, M.M. (1997). The propriety of affiliation with clients beyond the professional role: Nonsexual dual relationships. *Arete, 22*(1), 58–70.

Von Bretzel, N.C. (1997). Social work practice with marginalized populations. In M. Reisch & E. Gambrill (Eds.), *Social work in the 21st century* (pp. 239–248). Thousand Oaks, CA: Pine Forge Press.

Waites, C., Macgowan, M.H., Pennell, J., Carlton-LaNey, I., & Weil, M. (2004). Increasing the cultural responsiveness of family group conferencing. *Social Work, 49*(2), 291–298.

Waldegrave, C. (1990). Social justice and family therapy. *Dulwich Centre Newsletter, 1*, 1–46.

Waldegrave, C. (2005). "Just therapy" with families on low incomes. *Child Welfare, 84*(2), 265–276.

Walz, T., & Ritchie, H. (2000). Gandhian principles in social work practice: Ethics revisited. *Social Work, 45*(3), 213–222.

Warren, R. (1978). *The community America* (3rd ed.). Chicago: Rand McNally.

Weber, M. (1947). *The theory of social and economic organization* (A.M. Henderson and T. Parsons, trans.). New York: Macmillan.

Weeks, W. (2004). Creating attractive services which citizens want to attend. *Australian Social Work, 57*(4), 319–330.

Weick, A. (1999). Guilty knowledge. *Families in Society, 80*(4), 327–332.

Weingarten, K. (1995). Radical listening: Challenging cultural beliefs for and about mothers. In K. Weingarten (Ed.), *Cultural resistance: Challenging beliefs about men, women and therapy* (pp. 7–22), New York: Harrington Park Press.

Weiss, I. (2005). Is there a global common care to social work? A cross national comparative study of BSW graduate students. *Social Work, 50*(2), 101–110.

Wernet, S.P. (1999). *Managed care in human services.* Chicago: Lyceum Books.

White, C., & Denborough, D. (1998). *Introducing narrative therapy: A collection of practice-based writings.* Adelaide, South Australia: Dulwich Centre Publications.

Witkin, S.L. (1995). Family social work: A critical constructionist perspective. *Journal of Family Social Work, 1*, 33–45.

Witkin, S.L. (1999). Noticing. *Social Work, 45*(2), 101–104.

Witkin, S.L. (2000). Ethics-R-Us. *Social Work, 45*(3), 197–212.

Wood, G.G., & Middleman, R.R. (1989). *The structural approach to direct practice in social work.* New York: Columbia University Press.

Wood, G.G., & Roche, S.E. (2001a). Representing selves, reconstructing lives: Feminist group work with women survivors of male violence. *Social Work with Groups, 23*(4), 5–23.

Wood, G.G., & Roche, S.E. (2001b). Situations and representations: Feminist practice with survivors of male violence. *Families in Society, 82*(6), 583–590.

Wronka, J. (1998). *Human rights and social policy in the 21st century* (Rev. ed.). Lanham: University Press of America.

CREDITS

Table 1.1: From "The strengths perspective in social work practice: Extensions and cautions," by D. Saleebey. *Social Work, 41,* 3, p. 298. Copyright © 1996 National Association of Social Workers, Inc., Social Work.

Exhibit 2.1: From C. S. Ramanathan and R. L. Link, *All Our Futures: Social Work Practice in a Global Era,* p. 13. Wadsworth, Inc., a company of Thomson Learning, Inc. Copyright © 1999 Thomson Learning, Inc. www.thomsonrights.com, 800-730-2214.

Box 3.1: Second draft of the *Ethics in Social Work: Statement of Principles.* Copyright © 2002 International Federation of Social Workers.

Box 3.2: From F. M. Loewenberg, R. Dolgoff, and D. Harrington, *Ethical Decisions for Social Work Practices,* 6th ed. F. E. Peacock Publishers, Inc., a company of Thomson Learning, Inc. Copyright © 2000 Thomson Learning, Inc. www.thomson-rights.com, 800-730-2214.

Exhibit 3.2: From "The propriety of affiliation with clients beyond the professional role: Nonsexual dual relationships," by R. Vodde and M. M. Giddings. *Arete, 22,* 1, p. 64. Copyright © 1997 University of South Carolina. Reprinted with permission.

Exhibit 5.2: From D. Cowger and C. A. Snively, "Assessing Client Strengths: Individual, Family, and Community Empowerment," In D. Saleebey (Ed.), *The Strengths Perspective in Social Work Practice,* 3rd ed., pp. 115–121. Published by Allyn & Bacon, Boston, MA. Copyright © 2002 by Pearson Education, Inc.

Table 6.1: From *The Structural Approach to Direct Practice in Social Work,* by G. G. Wood and R. R. Middleman, p. 20. Copyright © 1989 Columbia University Press.

Exhibit 7.1: From *Teaching a Methods Course in Social Work with Groups,* by R. Kurland and R. Salmon, p. 209. Copyright © 1998 Council on Social Work Education. Used with permission.

Table 7.2: Adapted from the "Three Models of Stages of Group Development Based on the Boston Model Prototype," by T. Berman-Rossi and T. B. Kelly. Presentation: "Group composition, diversity, the skills of the social worker, and group development." Presented at the Council for Social Work Education, Annual Meeting, Atlanta, February. 2003.

Chapter 8 opening poem: From "Journal: To Crack the Fat Clock Face," in Melanie Kaye (aka Melanie Kaye/Kantrowitz), in *We Speak in Code: Poems & Other Writings.* Copyright © 1980 Motheroot Press. Used with permission of the author.

Table 8.1: From *Culture in Special Education,* by M. Kalyanpur and B. Harry, pp. 118–119. Copyright © 1999 Paul H. Brookes Publishing Co., Inc.

Exhibit 8.2: From D. Saleebey (Ed.), *The Strengths Perspective in Social Work Practice,* 3rd ed., p. 89. Published by Allyn & Bacon, Boston, MA. Copyright © 2002 by Pearson Education.

Exhibit 8.3: From "Self-perception in family systems: A diagrammatic technique," by R. R. Van Treuren. *Social Casework 67,* pp. 299–305. Copyright © 1986 Alliance for Children and Families.

Exhibit 8.4: From "The use of culturagrams to assess and empower culturally diverse families," by Elaine Congress. Presented at the 3rd International Conference on Health and Mental Health, Tampere, Finland, 2001. Used with permission of Elaine Congress.

Exhibit 9.1: From *Social Work Practice: A Critical Thinker's Guide,* by E. Gambrill, p. 594. Copyright © 1997 Oxford University Press, Inc.

Exhibit 9.2: From *Generalist Social Work Practice: Context, Story, and Partnership,* by B. Locke, R. Garrison, and J. Winship, p. 278–279. Wadsworth, Inc., a company of Thomson Learning, Inc. Copyright © 1998 Thomson Learning, Inc. www.thomsonrights.com, 800-730-2214.

Exhibit 9.3: From *Toward a Culturally Competent System of Care,* by T. L. Cross, B. J. Bazron, K. W. Dennis, and M. R. Isaacs, Copyright © 1989 Georgetown University Center for Child and Human Development. Used with permission.

Exhibit 9.4: From *The Practice of Macro Social Work,* 2nd ed., by W. G. Brueggemann, p. 339. Wadsworth, Inc., a company of Thomson Learning, Inc. Copyright © 2002 Thomson Learning, Inc. www.thomsonrights.com, 800-730-2214.

Table 9.1: From *Facilitator's Guide to Participatory Decision Making,* by S. Kaner. Copyright © 1996 New Society Publishers. Used with permission.

Box 9.3: From "The anti-violence partnership: Community collaboration at the University of Vermont," by S. Roche. Unpublished program materials, 2001. Used courtesy of S. Roche.

Box 10.1: Survey format from *The Practice of Macro Social Work,* 2nd ed., by W. G. Brueggemann, p. 131. Wadsworth, Inc., a company of Thomson Learning, Inc. Copyright © 2002 Thomson Learning, Inc. www.thomsonrights.com, 800-730-2214.

Box 10.3: Survey format from *Social Working: Exercises in Generalist Practice,* 2nd ed. Published by Allyn & Bacon, Boston, MA. Copyright © 2000 by Pearson Education.

Box 10.4: Case study courtesy of Suzanne Lohrbach, LICSW.

Exhibit 10.2: From *The Practice of Macro Social Work,* 2nd ed., by W. G. Brueggemann, pp. 438–439. Wadsworth, Inc., a company of Thomson Learning, Inc. Copyright © 2002 Thomson Learning, Inc. www.thomsonrights.com, 800-730-2214.

Table 12.1: Adapted from B. W. Sheafor and C. R. Horejsi, *Techniques and Guidelines for Social Work Practice,* 6th ed., p. 485. Published by Allyn & Bacon, Boston, MA. Copyright © 2003 by Pearson Education.

Exhibit 12.2: From the "Family Support Scale," by C. J. Dunst, V. Jenkins, and C. M. Trivette. In *Enabling and Empowering Families: Principles and Guidelines for Practice,* by C. J. Dunst, C. M. Trivette, and A. G. Deal, (Eds.), pp. 175–184. Copyright © 1998 Brookline Books.

Photo Credits   **Page 65:** © David Hurn/Magnum Photos; **93:** © Spencer Grant/PhotoEdit; **105:** © Bob Daemmrich/PhotoEdit; **202:** © Kim Kulish/Corbis; **242:** © Viviane Moos/Corbis; **249:** © Jim West/The Image Works; **285:** © The Studio Dog/Getty Images

GLOSSARY/INDEX

Abramowitz, M., 35

acceptance, 35–37

accompaniment is both a literal and metaphoric practice in which the worker goes with the client in pursuit of client goals, 99

accountability, 148–149, 255

adaptation, 31–32

Addams, Jane, 35, 289–290

advocacy
    case scenario for, 169–170
    cautions and strategies for, 162
    international, 284
    types of, 160–161
    Web sites, 150, 160, 161

advocate in social work practice is a practitioner who works toward securing the rights and well-being of clients, 160–162

African Americans
    assumptions about, pre–Civil War era, 23
    family support for, 220
    power case scenario of, 102–105

agencies. *See* organizations

agency is the capacity of human beings to affect, rather than simply react to, social and environmental structures, 40

AIDS, 53–54, 264. *See also* **HIV support group**

Amnesty International, 251

Anderson, Walter Truett, 115

Annan, Kofi A., 262

assessment in social work practice is the process of determining the parameters of the practice situation, how they affect the participant(s), and how these factors might be ordered and prioritized for appropriate action, 12. *See also* **needs assessment**
    agency requirements for, 139–140
    client goals, 9, 117–118, 126–133
    diversity and, 124–126
    history of, 116–117
    internalized oppression and, 138

    mapping skills for, 131–133
    narrative theory for, 121–124
    organizational dignity, 240
    planning components of, 137–138
    resource, 133–136
    strengths-based, 120–121, 122, 123
    theoretical perspectives of, 118–124

assumptions, 8, 11–12, 22, 23, 120, 150, 242

attachment theory, developed by John Bowlby, asserts that very early bonding occurs between a mother and infant and subsequently plays a critical role in the child's future capacity to provide and sustain opportunities for his or her own children, 119–120

attentive listening is a skill in which the worker listens for and hears the client's story, not for symptoms or insight, but rather to understand the experience and what it has meant to the client, 94

authority. *See specific types of authority*

autonomy and freedom, 72

baseline is the measurement of the client's behavior taken prior to the initiation of the intervention, and thus it establishes the difference between no intervention and intervention related to a selected goal or goals, 338, 339*f*

Berg, I. K., 218–219, 300, 301, 333

Berman-Rossi, T., 186, 187*t*

biases, 50–51. *See also* **values**

Bibus, A. A., 298

bicultural code of practice is a codification of professional standards of conduct that differentiates between and reflects the diversity of two cultures, 64, 65

Boston Model is the name given to a particular theoretical developmental model for social group work originated by researchers at Boston University, 186, 187*t*

boundaries are the limits or dividers that separate subsystems within a system or a system from the outside world, 205–206

Bowlby, John, 119